Retail Marketing

Retail Marketing

Malcolm Sullivan
Dennis Adcock

Australia • Canada • Mexico • Singapore • Spain • United Kingdom • United States

Retail Marketing

For more information, contact Thomson, High Holborn House, 50-51 Bedford Row, London, WC1R 4LR or visit us on the World Wide Web at: http://www.thomson-learning.co.uk

---

British Library Cataloguing-in-Publication Data
A catalogue record for this book is available from the British Library

---

ISBN 1–86152–602–4

First edition 2002

Typeset by Saxon Graphics Ltd, Derby

Printed in Great Britain by TJ International, Padstow, Cornwall

Table of Contents

Preface

The student needs to look far back in history to find the origins of retailing and hence retail marketing. When our distant ancestors moved from producing all their own goods to trading surplus items for their necessities, they were taking the first small step towards the modern retail system that we see today. As the practice developed so the barter business become concentrated in given areas, or simple markets, as people sought out a more efficient system. Bring all traders together so that everybody can get everything they want in one place. Students today would recognize this as the 'one stop shop' concept. From this it is a short step to primitive retailing as traders begin to see the value of just selling the produce of other traders at a profit.

In these early times few would have seen the need for retail marketing although providing the products required by traders in the right place in the right way was certainly important. The need for retail marketing has, however, increased over time with every turn of the wheel or flex of the accordion. The last decades of the twentieth century saw increasingly sophisticated shoppers and a more competitive and concentrated retail environment that placed a greater burden on retailers and made shopper need satisfaction a more demanding task. In response to these pressures retailers have increasingly turned to the marketing discipline for answers.

The marketing profession's early response to retailers was to apply the techniques and theories developed for the goods producer. McCarthy's 4Ps and other similar models were adapted to the retail environment and for a time provided a limited set of solutions. The development of services marketing allowed marketers to augment this initial approach with allowances made for intangible elements and store personnel. This hybrid certainly provided some of the answers but failed to recognize that while retail marketing contained some elements of goods and services marketing, it was actually a discipline in its own right and should be treated as such.

This book sets out to develop a framework for *retail* marketing by considering retailing and thus retail marketing from first principles. This framework is then expanded to produce a comprehensive body of retail marketing theory and practice. The early chapters set the context for retail marketing by exploring the nature of retailing, the retail environment and shopper behaviour in particular. This foundation is then used to develop a contemporary framework for retail marketing that forms the basis of the bulk of the book's remaining chapters. Online retail marketing is considered throughout the text as well as having one chapter (Chapter 16) dedicated to it. This is essential as the Internet represents the next turn of the wheel or flex of the accordion.

This book has been written for all students of retailing and retail marketing in particular, be they practitioners, undergraduates or post-graduates. Prior knowledge of marketing is not a pre-requisite, indeed being free of the consumer goods marketing mindset could be seen as being something of an advantage. Students and practitioners in related areas such as trade marketing, account management, consultancy, advertising and promotion will also find the subject matter to be both interesting and relevant. The detailed reading lists given at the end of each chapter in addition to the support material allow the student to study each area in greater depth and apply each theoretical concept. It is our intention that readers should be able to use retail marketing in real-life situations and be as fascinated by the subject as we are.

Acknowledgements

The authors would like to thank all the people who have proved invaluable in the production of this book. Competent and patient librarians have been indispensable, as have the many academics and practitioners who have helped shape the book's content and style. Particular thanks must go to the editorial team at Thomson for their constant support and encouragement.

Thanks also go to Stef and Beth, for allowing their husband and father to devote so much time to research and writing, and to Marion who patiently supported and tolerated her husband as the writing progressed and the demands of the book increased. This book is dedicated to you all with love.

List of Figures

List of Tables

An Introduction to Retail Marketing

CHAPTER 1

This chapter:

- Defines retailing
- Defines the retailers' role
- Provides an overview of the purchase experience

An Introduction to Retail Marketing

Introduction

The origins of retailing are as old as trading itself. The traders in a town market, or the hawkers who come to people's door are retail operators in the same way as a major chain of department stores or a home-shopping catalogue company or a web site where goods are offered for sale such as amazon.com.

The initial question that must be considered is: *What is retailing?* When this has been established it will be possible to discuss which forms of retailing are likely to be the most relevant today and acceptable into the future, and to ask how retailers can ensure they compete successfully in a dynamic and ever-changing market.

The dictionary definition of a retailer is '*a dealer or trader who sells goods in small quantities*' or more pedantically '*one who repeats or relates*'. Retailers *interact* with the final customer in a supply network, but they are both buyers and sellers of goods and services in that they also need to acquire the products they offer and in this will negotiate with suppliers of such items. Although retailers might have links to manufacturers and other suppliers, the main purpose of retail is to meet the needs, wants and desires of a specific group of customers. This is achieved through a combination of *goods (in small quantities)* and *services (giving the appropriate level of support)* which meets the particular *wants or desires*.

From an economic standpoint the role of a retailer is to provide real added value, or utility to their customer. This comes from four different perspectives:

- *First* is utility regarding the *form* of a product that is acceptable to the customer. That is the retailer does not supply raw materials, but rather offers finished goods and services in a form that customers want.
- *Second* comes the critical aspect of *place*. Offerings are available at a place appropriate to where a customer wants to purchase.

- *Third* is the *time* utility. In this respect retailers provide a benefit by making offerings available at a time suitable to their customers.
- *Finally* there is utility from *possession* in that retailers facilitate the transfer of ownership to the customer.

All these are real benefits which retailers can offer by getting close to potential customers. It is necessary, therefore, for retailers to fully understand the *motivations* that drive their customers and the different types of utility that a particular retailer can offer.

Retailing will, typically, involve the transfer of ownership of a tangible object, although there is a large service component in every retail operation. The relevance of small quantities differentiates retailers from bulk wholesaling. Retailers usually offer a *repeatable mix* to customers; they are not one-off traders at a car boot sale trying to dispose of surplus items for whatever they can get. But retailers are not benevolent organizations, they are in business in order to make a profit and retail marketing must be considered within this context.

To produce a tight definition of retailing it is necessary to consider the *moment of consumption* and the control of the *purchase experience* (see Figure 1.1). The moment of consumption refers to the point at which the purchased item is first used and this may be immediate or delayed. Immediate consumption involves 'simultaneous' purchase and use, while delayed consumption incorporates a time lag between the purchase and the use.

Control of the purchase experience relates to the ability to *manipulate the environment* in which the customer makes a purchase decision. When a company cedes control (willingly or unwillingly) to another company, usually one towards the consumer end of the supply chain, purchase experience control is remote. In a situation where a company has a much higher level of control, purchase experience control is managed.

Companies that have a very limited amount of purchase experience control (remote) are those that are removed from the consumer end of the supply chain. Such companies are primarily involved in business to business transactions and are known as *manufacturers* or *suppliers*. Manufacturers or suppliers that offer products for immediate consumption are known as *direct manufacturers* or *suppliers*, while the

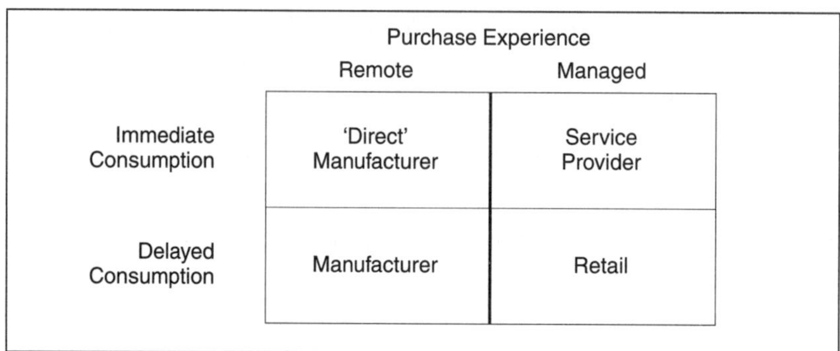

Figure 1.1 Retail classification matrix

more traditional manufacturer or supplier is associated with delayed consumption. Examples of such companies would be a door-to-door salesperson (direct manufacturer or supplier) and an electrical goods producer (manufacturer or supplier).

Companies with a higher level of purchase experience control (managed) are those that are much closer to the consumer end of the supply chain. Companies of this type that deal with primarily immediate consumption are known as *service providers*, while those that deal with delayed consumption are *retailers*. An example of a service provider under this definition would be a cinema, while a retailer in the same sector would be a video shop (sales, more so than rentals).

Now that a working definition of retailing has been considered, it is useful to identify different types of retailer. For this purpose, the *level* of purchase experience control and the number of different product categories will be considered (see Figure 1.2). The level of purchase experience control refers to the degree of control in a relative sense. It has already been noted that retailers manage the purchase experience hence the degree of control relates to how tightly the experience can be controlled. A high level of control would indicate a retailer that has a selling environment with few unmanageable factors while a moderate level of control would indicate a significant number of unmanageable factors. The number of different product categories refers to the number of different product lines (a category is a group of related products). A large number of categories would represent a retailer with a more broad appeal, while a small number would represent a retailer of a more specialist nature.

Retailers with a high level of purchase control are normally those that adopt a store-based approach. The high level of control comes from the retailer's ability to design a *self-contained selling environment* that gives the shopper a quite definite store shopping experience. Retailers with a more moderate level of purchase control typically have a distance-based approach where physical contact between the shopper and the retailer is limited. Examples of these types of retailer would be a clothing store (high level of control) and, in the same sector, a clothing catalogue or online retailer (moderate level of control). Retailers offering a large number of different categories are referred to as 'mass retailers',

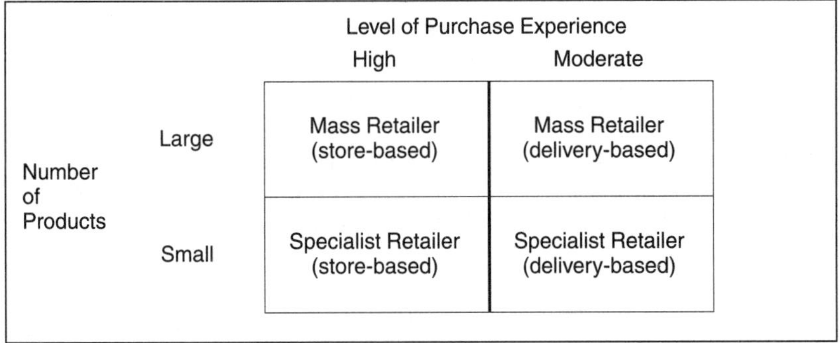

Level of Purchase Experience
High
Moderate
Number of Products
Large
Small
Mass Retailer (store-based)
Mass Retailer (delivery-based)
Specialist Retailer (store-based)
Specialist Retailer (delivery-based)

Figure 1.2 Classifications of Retailers

while those offering a small number of different categories are 'specialists'. Using the same example, a department store would represent a mass retailer (store-based), a broad-appeal clothing catalogue or online retailer would be a mass retailer (delivery-based), a high-fashion clothing store a specialist retailer (store-based) and a catalogue or online retailer selling only specific clothing a specialist retailer (delivery-based).

The Marketing Role of the Retailer

Marketing is not just selling and promoting but it is everything undertaken by a supplier in order to satisfy the needs and wants of customers. To achieve this the supplier must make an *acceptable* and *affordable* combination of goods and services *available* to customers at the *right* time and in the *right* place. Marketing is simply managing the exchange with customers in the best possible way. It also requires attention to the competitive environment since it is no good having a satisfactory offering if another organization is making a superior offer and thereby is achieving all the sales. However the basic principles of marketing are no different for a retailer than for any other supply organization. What is different is the immediacy of many retail marketing exchanges, and the range of activities that can be undertaken by the retail marketer in order to achieve a profitable exchange with a customer.

Since retailing is the bringing together of customers with the final link in the distributive chain, this usually involves some form of direct contact with the actual consumer, which is an important distinguishing feature of retail. In the traditional 'bricks and mortar' store seen on every high street and retail park there is face-to-face contact between the shopper and the employees of the retailer. Similarly in the open-air markets that have been an arena for retail selling for centuries there is direct customer contact and that brings with it both advantages and disadvantages to the retailer in the marketing of merchandise. Such contacts, termed the 'moments of truth', can be crucial to the achievement of, or failure to achieve a sale (exchange transaction). In these 'store-based' outlets there can be a very high dependence on *interactive* marketing because of the direct, personal contact at the point of sale. However there are also many self-selection stores such as the major grocery supermarkets. While these are 'store-based' they rely less on direct personal contact and more on the merchandising skills which are aimed at providing an inviting environment in which to shop.

In any market where direct human contact occurs there is a premium on the interactive skills of the people involved, and a close relationship between marketing and selling. However retailing is not simply selling, as even when there is face-to-face contact there are also many marketing activities necessary before, during and after a sale in order to ensure that the customer is fully satisfied. This is a feature of many retail situations.

There are many ways that a retailer can make merchandise *available* to customers, for instance an automatic vending machine can be used to dispense chocolate or other items. But this is still an extension of, and is related to a 'store-based' operation. Catalogue shops, such as Index and Argos, utilize a different method of self-selection and of course that requires some differences in marketing emphasis. Other styles of retailing such as mail-order catalogues are well established, and now the recent explosion in the use of the Internet is causing a revolution in many consumer markets. In these more remote contacts where the emphasis is often 'delivery-based', it is more often the process, and the perceived credibility of that process, which is critical to achieving a successful exchange. But although remote encounters take place with little direct human contact there are still many marketing activities necessary apart from providing the basic merchandise in order to attract customers and persuade them to make a purchase.

Retail organizations of the past are very different from those known today; although some of the current companies have been in business for much of the last century they have evolved into their present form. While the overall purpose of retailing is substantially the same, the service is continually changing. For instance some decades ago the introduction of self-service in grocery stores shifted the responsibility for selecting and collecting onto the customer, the retailer service becoming more involved with display and merchandising and less on personal customer contact. This has increased the emphasis on wider marketing activities as opposed to sales. More recently the growth of e-commerce has challenged the myth that the key to successful retailing is *Place; Place; Place;* and *Place.*

'Physical' proximity between a potential customer and a supplier is still important in many categories of product. The ability of retailers to increase the *availability* of merchandise is fundamental to success, although increasing the *acceptability* or the *affordability* of an offering to the customer could offset it. This is why interactions can be achieved in other ways, such as mail order, which has already been mentioned, and the Internet. This has taken shopping opportunities a long way forward, allowing an interactive, yet remote contact between the parties. In fact technology has dramatically changed consumer involvement in, and expectations from, some of their shopping experiences. Nevertheless, in many UK towns and cities, outdoor market traders still operate with some success. For certain categories of produce and for some segments of consumers, such markets are still of major importance. However the growth of shopping as a major leisure pursuit has also taken other shopping experiences in another different direction. All of these developments have meant that retailers have had to continually reassess their marketing activities, sometimes changing the emphasis but also learning new skills. However the objective of marketing in retailing industries remains the same, it is to ensure that the *best possible exchange actually takes place between a supplier and a customer while making a profit for the retailer.*

In the classic theory of retail evolution – the *wheel of retailing* (Hollander 1960) – it can be seen that the wheel is now turning at an ever-increasing rate. New forms of retailing are developing in line with changes in customer needs, new customer activities and the acceptance of these new forms by shoppers. New styles of retailing grow and mature, and they can also lose popularity and decline to be replaced by alternatives more in tune with current customer lifestyles. The turns of the wheel of retailing are dictated by both the creative thinking of innovative traders and by changing customer expectations that specific merchandise should be available when and where they want it in a crowded marketplace.

In this environment every retailer has to consider the marketing of their particular service in order to attract and satisfy customers instead of being ignored by them. The statistics regarding the failure of new small retailing ventures are stark, and there is clear evidence of a concentration taking place in the high street with an increase in the numbers of businesses with greater turnover. *Keynote/Business Monitor* PA1003 has published a size analysis of UK VAT registered retail business in 1990–7 (Table 1.1).

Table 1.1 UK Retail Business, 1990–7

Turnover	Number of businesses 1990	1997	% change
Up to £100 000 p.a.	135 241	78 900	– 42
£100 000 – £500 000 p.a.	101 531	106 740	+ 5
Over £500 000 p.a.	15 628	24 165	+ 55

Not only are the larger retail groups growing, they are also becoming ever more powerful in their dealings with their suppliers. The bargaining power has, in many cases, shifted completely away from manufacturers so retailers cannot be considered as a conduit for a manufacturer to distribute goods to customers, rather they are channel leaders dictating the competitive policy of a vertical marketing grouping that that retailer has constructed.

Retail businesses are major employers with over 4 million people working in the sector, but retail has always employed a high proportion of part-time staff and latest figures show over 40 per cent of all UK employees are in this category. The use of part-time employees is a reaction to the perishable nature of retail services; seasonal peaks and troughs are accommodated in this way, as well as the significant direct operating cost that results from a service business.

The employees in retail are the front-line customer contact points. If they are low paid, with a feeling of being in a dead-end job, it can be difficult to achieve the real enthusiasm and customer orientation necessary to achieve retail success in an interactive environment. This is one of the great challenges for the retail marketer, as all the attention to the other aspects of the retail marketing mix can be nullified by a poor experience at the point of sale. Obviously the utilization of self-selection retailing, and other initiatives aimed at reducing the dependence on staff, illustrates that marketing thinking rather than selling techniques are crucial.

It would be a mistake to forget that *marketing* developed from traditional marketplaces and the efforts of suppliers to sell their produce in these locations. Although the early emphasis was on selling activities it soon became necessary to incorporate other specific marketing activities such as research, communications, planning, product development, packaging and merchandising in order to succeed. While modern marketing theory may have stemmed from producers such as the post war fast moving consumer goods (FMCG) manufacturers, more recent developments such as relationship marketing and interactive marketing have evolved from the needs of service providers. These 'new' marketing activities focus on the dyadic link between a specific supplier and their immediate customer. It is here that the needs of retailing coincide with the domain of marketing.

There are two specific dimensions to retail marketing, *first* how to attract customers into the retail environs – shop, restaurant, pub, or the 'virtual' Internet store for instance – and *second* how to persuade those customers to make a purchase from that store. Both are necessary to achieve success.

The History of Retailing

It is, perhaps, presumptuous to suggest that retailing was the earliest form of trading. However, early histories record itinerant traders travelling around the country selling a variety of goods in Saxon times. Trading Fairs became an important part of life in Norman England, and the Domesday Book records markets in many places, often with no known urban features such as Royal estates or attached to churches. There is, for example, a reference to the 'ten traders outside the monastery gates' on record in Abingdon, Berkshire.

In the early Middle Ages the structure of society changed further. Towns were founded by local landowners; these were usually planned around a central area where weekly markets and annual fairs were held. These 'new' towns were often at a convenient location on a major distribution route and the prosperity of these towns was, in many cases, dependent on the success of the market. It is recorded that in Thame, Oxon, the Bishop of Lincoln rented out the central market space for permanent stalls 'because of the high rents he was offered': a sure sign of a successful town. In the early days many of these 'rents' were paid in goods and services rather than money. In pre-Saxon times there had been a thriving barter trade in the markets, where one type of product was exchanged for another. However, the complications of such business, and the wider use and acceptability of coinage caused a steady decline in such trade.

The *Anglo-Saxon Chronicle* shows the main street in Winchester was called *Ceap Street* (Market Street) by the early tenth century, its location determined by the need to serve both the Roman and the mediaeval town. Other names survive in many older towns with streets such as *Cornmarket Street* indicating the concentration of a particular trade in a single location. While there is no record of the marketing activities undertaken by individual traders, it is obvious that in an area of concentration of, say, corn dealers, something over and above the basic commodity was necessary for one dealer to thrive when compared to his neighbours.

Trade was certainly seen in competitive terms, with the growth of one location often achieved at the expense of another. Apparently rival markets were supposed to be 'six and two thirds miles apart' to avoid clashes, but people did not necessarily go to their local market. In 1416 it is recorded that villagers from Cuxham travelled to Abingdon market rather than the closer one at Wallingford. The nearest market was not, therefore, the limit of a customers' horizon. It is interesting to speculate on the reasons for this.

Mediaeval markets were dependent on local sources for supplies of perishable foods because journeys were far too slow to allow for long distance transportation. However customers did travel considerable distances for speciality items. For instance journeying right across England to buy horses and sheep, and going to a convenient location to purchase mill stones, maybe travelling to a port such as Southampton to acquire glassware imported from Italy before it was manufactured in the UK from the fourteenth century. The development of trading can be seen as intimately associated with social developments over the ages.

Retailing has continued to develop throughout the last thousand years. Whenever more goods have become available, there have always been new traders discovering ways to sell (market) them. As new international trade routes opened up, the range of available goods grew, and more specialist retail establishments opened to trade in highly prized imports such as tea, spices and silks. At the same time more local production of key items also developed and the role of the retailer as the critical link between manufacturer and consumer became more apparent.

Further dramatic shifts in retailing have occurred in the last 150 years. The industrial revolution fuelled two major pressures. First increasing urbanization has meant more consumers gathered together in smaller geographic areas. This meant that town-based shops became necessary to serve the local populations. Dawson (1999) suggests that 'city centres became the major foci of *comparison* retailing as middle income consumers grew in number and mass transport focused on city centres'.

Second the dramatic increases in manufacturing output not only drew people away from the rural agriculture; it also made available large quantities of goods from the manufacturing plants. This often required that longer distribution channels were necessary to reach customers. In addition dramatic changes in transportation increased the speed and convenience of trading links for every sort of product. Jefferys (1954) describes 'the beginnings of national marketing direct to retailers by large-scale producers, and of bulk purchasing by large-scale retailing organisations direct from the manufacturers'. Lancaster (1995) and Ferry (1961) studied the development of department stores and commented that early in the twentieth century international sourcing of products was taking place, although it was quite limited. Meanwhile continuing developments in the preservation of perishable items has enabled the distribution channels for foodstuffs to lengthen while still operating effectively.

Dawson (1999) states that 'whilst the independent family owned retailer dominated the market, there were already, by 1900, larger organisations appearing both in the consumer co-operative sector and in the capitalist sector'. Jefferys (1954) estimates that by that time there were 94 firms in the UK with more than 25 branches. These were mainly in footwear, newspaper retailing and grocery. The locations were also changing with the development of central 'city arcade-style' shopping centres (Geist 1983) and shopping parades at suburban railway stations (MacKeith 1986). In fact anywhere that there was an opportunity to get close to substantial numbers of potential customers.

Retail evolved in many ways over the twentieth century. One major change was the introduction of self-service retailing in the mid-1950s. This started in grocery stores but has since spread to other sectors. The move led to major changes in operations, but also enabled the rapid growth of low-margin retailing ('pile it high and sell it cheap!'). The implications for the display and merchandising tasks, both part of marketing, were huge as it became essential that products were presented in a more attractive way to ensure they were selected from the shelves. Successful retailers never forget the importance of meeting consumer needs, but Levy and Zaltman (1975) suggest that 'marketing is the instrument of much social change'. Further application of marketing principles has led to the development of new retail formats such as large hypermarkets and small niche retailers who realize the importance of a focused position as opposed to an attempt to meet the needs of a standard undifferentiated market.

More recently the need to locate physically near to customers has become less important. The growth in car ownership and usage has meant that it is no longer necessary for retail to closely follow customer migration. Retailers have been able attract customers away from the urban centres into out-of-town locations thus providing a new emphasis for retailing and retail marketing. Substantial numbers of consumers are prepared to visit retail parks, and to include such activities in their portfolio of leisure activities. This has been complemented by more effective communications that helped ensure that customers are far better informed as to the location and availability of an immense range of goods. Retail marketing has also developed, especially exploiting the benefits of retailer brands and the opportunities to extend the brand equity into other areas, e.g. Sainsbury's Bank or Boots' Opticians.

By utilizing new technology retailers have able to learn more about the products actually being bought by their customers, as well as improving efficiency – in particular, the introduction of barcodes and scanning produces a great deal of valuable data. More recently retailers have applied more advanced information and communications technologies to drive their business. Data base management, utilizing store loyalty cards and other inputs, can lead to a greater level of *personalization* in offers, and this can be complemented by advances in the area of direct marketing.

Other changes mean that both retailers, and now customers are both able and willing to seek out suppliers from anywhere in the world. There are implications for the range stocked by grocery supermarkets where once seasonal fresh fruit and vegetables are now available throughout the year. Also many exotic products are now appearing in UK retail outlets. But with the growth of the World Wide Web (<www.anyretail.org> – there are really too many to give any single reference here) consumers are increasingly able to explore thousands of additional locations and to benefit from offers that were previously inaccessible. It is therefore appropriate to look anew at the role of marketing within retail industries as we enter the twenty-first century.

The Shifting Balance of Power in Marketing Channels

While retailing has always been a vital final link in a distribution chain, it is only comparatively recently that retailers have taken on a larger role. In many markets today, it is the retailers who define, direct and control many of the activities throughout the entire supply network. They are, in effect, *channel leaders*.

Traditionally manufacturing companies were larger than their distributors, they also had a greater scope of operations. In many markets it used to be the manufacturers that decided the appropriate distribution strategy for their products – intensive, selective, or exclusive. Such decisions were seen as critical to the marketing success of manufacturers, but were possible only because of the power that could be exerted over other channel members. Retailers were often considered as a 'transparent conduit' between producer and final consumer. Also retailers were usually smaller and more localised than many manufacturers as shown in Table 1.2.

Table 1.2 Retailers and Manufacturers, 1988 and 1998

		Turnover and geographical scope, 1988 (million)	Turnover and geographical scope, 1998 (million)
Major retailer	Tesco	£4.119 UK business	£16.069 UK, W. and E. Europe
Major manufacturer	United Biscuits	£2.380 UK, USA, W. Europe	£1.685 UK, Europe, Far East

Source: Company accounts.

Manufacturer power in the third quarter of the twentieth century was both economic, as a result of the disparity in company size, and non-economic, as a result of other factors in the relationship. The up-stream manufacturers were able to dictate products, determine prices, establish strong brand communications with consumers, and manage demand by producing or restricting supplies. Often the marketing research carried out by manufacturers was the major source of consumer intelligence and selective facts were revealed to distributors to support marketing efforts.

Example

In one dispute between a major food producer and a grocery retailer in the early 1970s, the manufacturer was able to threaten to discontinue supplies knowing that the particular retailer would not be prepared to risk the consequences caused by the absence of several brand leaders from the shelves. Today, with the increasing size and importance of that same supermarket, and the growth of the retailer's '*own-label*' products, the leading brands are not so critical. It is doubtful if the manufacturer would even contemplate such action now.

In 1970, all the major advertisers in the UK were manufacturing companies, today the list is as likely to contain many of the top retail companies, such as Currys and Comet in the electrical sector, Asda supermarkets and many of the high street banks. This is indicative that the situation has now changed forever. There should not be any surprise that the retailers, who are after all closest to the final customer, have now become powerful players in most distribution networks. The critical, marketing mix, variables are now controlled by the retailers, and they decide their own policy and determine how to gain influence over 'shoppers'.

This shift of power has developed in three ways:

- *First* major retail groups have grown to match or surpass manufacturing organizations in both size and scope. For instance Tesco and Asda (Wal-Mart) in grocery; Currys/Dixon in electrical goods; Arcadia/Debenhams in clothing; and Toys 'Я' Us in children's toys.
- *Second* the development and increased quality of store's 'own-label' merchandise. The reality has now changed from cheap/low-quality goods to strong brands offering high quality and excellent value. Indeed many store groups are now perceived as respected 'umbrella' brands in their own right.
- *Third* market information is now, more firmly, in the hands of retailers. New technology, such as scanning article numbers (barcodes), gives a wealth of data going well beyond simple restocking issues and allow the retailer to accurately plan ranges, layouts, and promotional deals. Also store cards have enabled the retailers to know more about their customers, and to use this information to offer a more appropriate range of goods.

These dramatic changes have taken place in the UK during the last quarter of the twentieth century. Perhaps the real catalyst was the ending of Resale Price Maintenance (RPM) in the 1960s. Prior to that time manufacturers could dictate fixed retail prices across a wide range of goods. Following a classic legal battle retailers won the right to determine their own selling prices. This increased competition as it brought a key marketing variable under the direct control of individual retail operators.

The power of retailers also means that they are no longer dependent upon a manufacturer regarding what is *available* to sell. Today any good retailer will determine what is *acceptable* to a chosen, target group of customers and set out to secure the relevant supplies for their store. This might involve rejecting a brand leader product, or changing suppliers to obtain a more suitable item, or commissioning production for an exclusive offering. In a recent exercise of retailer power the Tesco supermarket group sourced Levi © Jeans from the USA because the UK supplier refused to make the product available.

Of course retailers can make poor decisions, and they can fail to appreciate changes in the buying behaviour of their customers. Recent examples are easy to find, just look at the performance of the Storehouse Group (Mothercare and Bhs) in the 1990s, or the much publicized trouble at Marks & Spencer and J Sainsbury. While a retailer might be best placed to be close to the customers, each retailer is competing directly against other retailers for a shopper's limited 'disposable income'. Power might have shifted to retailers, but success is still dependent on good 'market-driven' actions. Also retailers seldom undertake production for themselves so they still require good partnerships with suppliers if they are to offer the *right* products, at the *right* price, and at the *right* time to customers.

The Wheel of Retailing

Markets are dynamic, but many of the trends in retailing at the start of the twenty-first century are the result of an evolution that can be traced back over many decades. There has been a steady growth in the size of the largest retail corporations, for instance Wal-Mart had a turnover of £138 billion in 1999. As Dawson (1999) states 'Retailers continue to pursue the benefits of large scale', but over 50 years ago Levy (1948) suggested that 'The large retail business is imbued with a natural and almost unlimited ambition for expansion'.

With growth has come an increase in power with respect to suppliers. But growth has had negative results as well. There is a 'sameness' about many of the high streets in the regional towns of the UK. The variety that once existed has now been subsumed into the standard offerings of Next, Boots, Mothercare, JJB sports, Burton's, Dixon's, Woolworth's, H. Samuel, Body Shop, Virgin/Our Price and the rest. Retail parks often seem to cluster the same electrical superstore, DIY shed, carpet specialist together. The top three grocers, Tesco, Sainsbury and Asda seem to be everywhere and saturation is close with respect to the sites available for major new hypermarkets. But among all the standardization there are independent shops or regional operators with only a few outlets that prove it is possible to compete with the large chains. To do so a retailer must be creative and prepared to differentiate their store from the competition. It is not possible to compete in all areas of standardized merchandise but focusing on appropriate niches can offer rewards. That is what Anita Roddick did when she started Body Shop, and while it is now one of the ever-present high street stores it had to start somewhere. The same applies to all of the other giants of today.

Part of the growth strategy for successful stores is the widening of their ranges, and the exploitation of their brand equity. Moves by Tesco into banking, Boots into optical tests and supplies, Marks & Spencer into mail-order furniture, Sainsbury (Homebase) into DIY show that few retailers see themselves as constrained by traditional areas of merchandise. But there is no guarantee that today's successful retailers will continue to thrive in the future. The problems faced by Marks & Spencer show how rapidly a store can lose out in the dynamic retail marketplace, especially when it forgets the core business or loses touch with the needs of its traditional customers. When it comes to expanding into diverse product categories it might be instructive to take note of the failed links between Asda, Allied Carpets and MFI in the 1980s, or the problems faced by the UK Co-operative movement (which offers many things from funerals to holidays) as it strives to compete with more focused rivals. A major challenge facing all large groups is how to remain in touch with the evolving needs of all their customers.

In many product categories the small supplier finds it difficult to establish and harder still to survive. Yet variety does still exist. There are Asian shops in Southall and Leicester, Afro-Caribbean shops in Brixton and other areas which reflect the ethnic origins of the local residents. In a few towns, groups of small shops have been encouraged such as in the Lanes in Brighton, and the Shambles in York. There are, also, many examples of groups of directly competing retailers offering similar products clustered together. This obviously attracts potential customers to the location and leaves it open to the individual stores to compete for the business. Notable examples of the 'same' stores clustering together are Portobello Road and Camden Passage in London (antiques), China Towns in Manchester, London and Birmingham, Balti restaurants in the Sparkbrook area of Birmingham, and electronic retailers in London's Tottenham Court Road. In the UK there is also the development of US-style factory outlets and malls. These offer heavily discounted or 'seconds' items in a convenient out-of-town location. While the products are not all the same the motivation for customers as regards getting a bargain provides the similarity in such a cluster.

Retailers are not entirely free agents when it comes to setting up new outlets, especially in new geographic locations. Of course it is always possible to find vacant retail premises somewhere but, as the discussion on location shows, there is no point in trading from poorly sited premises. When it comes to new physical sites, the development has to be authorized by local planning departments. They understand that retail has a fourfold impact within a local area.

- *First* is the *physical* role in respect to its siting, for instance if the development is in a derelict area or on greenfield land.
- *Second* comes the *economic* effect that retail has on a locality, both as an employer and generator of ratable income.
- *Third* is the fact that it becomes a focus for *consumer spending* in the area.
- *Fourth* and last, but critical to any community, is the *social role* that shopping and shop visiting have, affecting many patterns of local interaction.

Of course these effects are not present when shopping takes place from remote locations such as over the Internet. The role of shopping as a 'leisure' activity that can stimulate all the senses of sight, sound, smell, and touch fails in such a 'virtual' location. However, these sensory stimuli are not always necessary for satisfactory shopping to occur. Shoppers have many objectives when they visit a retail site, physical or virtual, and it is the *totality of the offering* when matched with the requirements of each specific customer that leads to a satisfactory outcome. It is, therefore, important that retailers are continually checking the relevance of their offerings, and the ways such offerings are made, in order that they do not lose touch with their customers.

The 'wheel of retailing' is a well-tested theory (Hollander 1960) about the evolution of retail operators. It suggests they start small but offering some real advantages, such as specific merchandise or even low price, and this enables them to take customers away from more established competitors. Then, as they prosper they develop their business, offering a greater range or acquiring more expensive facilities, but this can mean they lose the focus that was so important when they entered the market. Such 'trading up' occurs as the retailer becomes established in its own right. It can also increase the asset base, making the retailer more vulnerable should profits stop growing. This in turn leaves room for others to enter and repeat the process.

Hollander was a key observer of retail evolution and he also used the analogy of an orchestra comprised exclusively of accordion players to describe the dynamically shifting retail structure. This so called 'accordion' effect describes how general stores moved to specialize but then widened their range of merchandise again as new classes of products were added. Hollander (1966) suggests that the players either have 'open accordions', representing general retailers with broad product ranges, or 'closing accordions', thus indicating a narrowing of the range, focusing on specific merchandise. He suggested that at any point in time one type of retailer would outnumber the other, but that the situation would continually change through the arrival and departure of different stores. This analogy illustrates the complexity of the retail scene, and the way different attitudes to successful retailing will come in and out of fashion at different times. There is plenty of evidence regarding the swings in types of retailers, but the key objective of every retailer is to achieve some form of *competitive advantage* for their offerings in a very crowded, yet vibrant retail marketplace.

The development of the Arcadia/Burton's group shows some of these 'accordian' features. In the 1980s their success was based on good segmentation and targeting. Individual brands such as Dorothy Perkins, Top Shop, Principles, Burton's for Men and Evans (Outsize) all had a strong identity. After the takeover of Debenhams many of these specialist labels were included as 'shops within' a Debenhams department store. They also retained individual outlets on many High Streets. In 1999 the group demerged, with Arcadia floated off from Debenhams. Subsequently a review of the individual stores within Arcadia has led to a decision to close Principals for Men and Richards. It will be interesting to see how the focus of the remaining stores might change in the future.

Changes in retail structure are not new. Alexander (1988) reported from an article in *The Times* in the nineteenth century: 'In every part of London gigantic businesses are taking the place of a multitude of smaller ones, and their owners entirely disregard the old divisions of trade. They will have cheese in one window, champagne in a second, cigars in a third, and ribands in a fourth.' So even in the Victorian period there was a movement towards the 'one-stop-shopping' concept!

As Dawson (1999) suggests 'the challenge of "bigness" does not lie with managing large shops but with managing, in ever more concentrated markets, the large retail organization of perhaps 2000 or more shops spread across several countries and operating in several sections of retailing'. But as retail groups with high levels of assets invested in retail premises consider the multinational expansion of their operations there is a significant change taking place in the shape of e-commerce.

In the past retailers have found ways of competing without local stores. Mail-order catalogues, telephone shopping, direct response newspaper offers have all become established offering certain advantages to specific groups of customers. As far back as 1986 Ian MacLaurin (now Lord MacLaurin, Chairman of Tesco) suggested to the CIES international conference in Vienna that:

> the upper income group will do an increasing amount of their convenience shopping via T.V., not only freeing their time for comparison shopping but also their 'discretionary time' – time for travel and sport, theatre going, entertaining and the like ... If this proves to be the case, it will have a significant bearing on the entire character of retailing, not least, on store design.

While this prediction did not fully materialize, electronic shopping (e-business) now has a higher profile than any of the previously mentioned developments. At the moment there is still a lot of uncertainty as to the impact of the Internet, and many mistakes will be made as retailers attempt to profit from the new ways of interacting. Nevertheless the rate of growth in some product categories is exceptional, and whatever the problems all retailers now realize that the virtual marketspace is here to stay.

At the moment the '.com e-tailers' are struggling with some very real problems. Most Internet buying is done because of attractive stimuli in the form of low prices for products that are easy to compare with known alternatives. There is little evidence of any strong degree of loyalty developing towards these providers, and in most cases the costs of switching to an alternative supplier are very low. There are problems of security when using credit cards for e-purchases, and a recent spate of multiple hacking has done much more damage than any brick thrown through a shop window. Most worrying is the US experience where typically two thirds of people complaining about missing products and wrong delivery never received a reply to their e-mails. Astonishingly over half of all problems were not resolved. This will have to change if the .com e-tailers are to achieve their ambitious objectives.

One advantage of a purchase from a local store is the re-assurance that if anything goes wrong a quick visit should resolve the matter, and in the case of continuing problems there is often a remedy under the 'Sale of Goods' legislation. When considering the success of an established, major high street retailer it can be seen that shoppers have completely 'bought' into the value proposition offered, and trust that store to deliver its promises regarding goods, service levels and value. The issue is more complex with e-commerce, but unless it is resolved there will be many potential shoppers who will reject this way of trading. Trust is developed over time, and many .com e-tailers are still too new in this respect. The successful online retailers in the future will be those that are perceived as able to meet their promises regarding the supply of specific types of products, and are thus able to develop a 'virtual community' of loyal shoppers.

Of course fixed-site retailers are determined to retain their share of business. There are initiatives such as 'holiday hypermarkets' which combine the advantages of a physical location with the excitement of multi-media, and claim to offer prices that match those from the e-tailers. Several large retail groups are experimenting with hybrid channels offering choice to customers, but backing their Internet business with their established brand image and reputation. Such operators include banks and grocers, booksellers and record stores. With these retailers the customer feels more secure because of a familiarity with the company from past experience. New and unknown operators will have to earn the confidence of shoppers, and such trust takes time to develop. But the 'wheel of retailing' will continue to turn. It is difficult to be precise as to new forms of retailing, as Lord MacLaurin found in 1986 when he speculated that 'by the early twenty-first century "tele-shopping" could well account for a fifth of the *affluent* market and, once established, the practice will spread' (emphasis in original). It is obvious now that such a prediction was well wide of the mark.

Different forms of retail, giving rise to different purchase behaviour modes will continue to evolve. At present less than 10 per cent of all purchases are from the alternatives to retail stores, although for some categories of product the .com e-tailers are claiming higher shares. It is, perhaps, instructive to consider the advantages and disadvantages of each of the current modes with respect to the various utilities offered by retailers. Table 1.3 illustrates some key criteria and has been adapted from work in the area of experimental psychology.

Table 1.3 Forms of Retail Marketing

Utility	Physical stores	Mail-order catalogues	Internet retailing
Form			
Types of product	All types	Speciality	Most types
Alternative brands	Almost all	Some	Many
Place			
Shopping effort	Often high	Low	Usually low
Time			
Purchase time	Moderate	Low	Low
Possession			
Wait for delivery	Seldom	Yes	Yes
Other Issues			
Potential for fun	High	Some	Moderate
Delivery charges	Seldom	Sometimes	Often
Ease to complain	Usually easy	Some	Can be difficult

The Essence of Successful Retailing

This is, of course, the key question facing all retailers: *How to succeed in a dynamic marketplace?* Perhaps the most important issue is to 'create' enough customers to ensure profitable trading. For this to happen it is obviously necessary to satisfy those customers so that they might recommend the store to others, and also visit the outlet again for their own future purchases.

The concept of the *right* product, price and time is at the centre of all successful marketing exchanges. A profitable transaction between a willing supplier and a willing customer should generate benefits for both parties. If the positive aspects of whatever was received exceed the costs or sacrifices in obtaining them, there will be a degree of satisfaction regarding the exchange. From a retailer's perspective this is measured in hard currency with the achievement of profit levels and appropriate margins at the centre of most calculations. Customers have a different '*value equation*' but it is still necessary for a consumer to experience some positive feelings regarding a purchase if satisfaction is to be achieved. Perhaps this is most prevalent when a shopper has been to a sales event and bought at a particularly good, *bargain*, price. Here the perception of value is most intense and leads to feelings of great satisfaction.

But the level of satisfaction is also affected by the expectations that a party might have prior to the transaction. These will also be compared with the perceived benefits received. The issue of satisfaction will be considered more fully in subsequent chapters, but one measure of successful retailing should be based upon the creation of satisfied customers. It is as true today as it, probably, was in 1000 AD that 'there is only one valid purpose of a business .... To *create* a satisfied customer... . It is the customer who determines what the business is' (Drucker 1968, emphasis in original).

But customer satisfaction should not be seen as the sole determinant of retailing success. It is necessary to outperform other retail competitors as well. This will be achieved only if a customer *values* one supplier above all others. The value to a customer has as much to do with the perceived benefits derived from the services performed by the 'retailer' as it has to do with the prices charged. Customers will use their personal value assessments in order to decide where to obtain any *considered* purchase. This is likely to involve the comparative assessment of acceptable offerings within a customer's own decision making framework. This is not always the case with *emergency* purchases, as these could require the closest, most available, supplier because this category describes those items, goods or services, that must be acquired without any delay. For such products the value derives from the ease of availability of the item. There is a further category, the so-called *impulse* purchases that occur when an offering looks so good that a customer feels driven to react immediately without evaluating competitive offerings.

In most classes of product, however, it is likely that the items desired are available from more than one retail outlet (competing local stores, mail order and even the Internet). In some categories of consumer durables, such as stereo systems or washing machines for example, this will almost certainly involve shopping around for the 'best' deal (value). All the aspects of the *total offering* and the *promotional extras* will be considered before a buying decision is made. It is obvious that only that retailer who actually achieves the final sale can be considered as successful. All others could have incurred costs with no immediate return. Remember that retailers have to fund their stockholding, and retailer profitability is a function of stock turnover and margins realized. If turnover is low then there is little revenue to set against the costs, and this is the most common factor in retail failure.

Retailers have to take strategic decisions regarding where they wish to operate. These will include decisions on the *target customers* that they hope to attract, as well as the *product/service assortments* that they intend to offer. Strategic options also extend to decisions on whether to *position* themselves as a high-quality, high-price, high-margin company or to adopt the 'pile it high, sell it cheap!' philosophy of low-margin, discount retailers. There is also the so-called '*category killer*' position, such as Toys 'Я' Us who are distinguished by the unusual width and breadth of their range within a specific category. By offering an enormous range, and promising prices that reflect their enormous buying power, these retailers effectively dominate their segment.

These choices will affect all other decisions regarding the marketing of any specific retail operation. Directly dependent on the strategic choices will be the tactical decisions within the retailer's marketing mix. These are the short-term options that determine competitive success in day-to-day operations. Both are critical and will be considered in this book. The elements of the Retail Marketing Mix are set out in Table 1.4, and the elements are all considered in more detail in Chapter 2.

Table 1.4 The Retail Marketing Mix

Element	Description
Location	Physical or virtual placement of outlets
Image, Reputation	Managing and encouraging demand (traffic/shopper visits)
Store design/Environment	Interior and exterior design (layout, display, atmospherics)
Range/assortment	Mix of items offered for sale
Pricing	'Shelf' prices relative to competitors
Promotion	Store-based and market-based communication
Customer service	During and post-sale
Relationship management	Building loyalty and positive shopper perceptions

Conclusions

The retail sector is a vibrant, dynamic and ever-changing marketplace. Retailers are re-sellers of goods and services, adding value to them and making them *available* 'close' to, and convenient for the final shopping customer. This closeness is not necessarily a geographical proximity as can be seen by considering Internet retailers. But even these '.com e-tailers' are creating an 'emotional' closeness through the Web link. They are making it easier for a chosen customer to find and acquire a specific product and are thereby *adding value* through an increase in the convenience factor for that customer. In fact, all retailers increase this dimension for their customers. It is, therefore, possible to sum up the role of the retailer as making an *acceptable* and *affordable* combination of goods and services *available* to given customers at the *right* time and in the *right* place.

The way a retailer might achieve success has evolved over many centuries. As new initiatives are introduced and new technologies developed, creative retailers have found ways of utilizing them, and have benefited accordingly. The various theories of retail evolution, such as the 'wheel' and the 'accordion' illustrate the dynamic nature of the retail environment. It is crucial that anyone hoping to succeed in a retail market understands these developments and puts together market-led strategies that offer customers a real reason to visit their retail outlet in preference to all the others.

References and Further Reading

Alexander, N. (1988) Specialist Retailers and General Stores: A Marketing Life Cycle, University of Edinburgh, *Working Paper*, 88/2 quoting from *The Times*, 26 May 1885.

Carlzon, J. (1987) *The Moments of Truth*, Ballinger, Cambridge, Mass.

Davies, G. (1994) The Delisting of Products by Retail Buyers, *Journal of Marketing Management*, 10, 473–93.

Dawson, J. (1999) Retailing at Century End: Some Challenges for Management and Research, University of Edinburgh, *Working Paper*, 99/8.

De Kare-Silver, M. (1998) *e-shock: The electronic shopping revolution*. Macmillan, London.

Dennison, T. and Knox, S. (1993) Pocketing the change from loyal shoppers: the 'Double Indemnity Effect', in M. Kirkup, et al. (eds), *Proceedings on Emerging Issues in Marketing*, 221–233.

Dibb, S., Simkin, L., Pride, W.M. and Ferrell, O.C. (1997) *Marketing*, 3rd European edn, Houghton Mifflin, Boston.

Drucker, P. (1968) *The Practice of Management*, Pan Books, London.

Dunne, P. and Lusch, R.F. (1999) *Retailing*, 3rd edn, Harcourt Brace & Co, Orlando, FL.

Ferry, J.W. (1961) *A History of the Department Store*, Macmillan, New York.

Geist, J.F. (1983) Arcades: The History of a Building Type, in J. Dawson, *Retailing at the Century End*, Edinburgh University Press, 1999.

Ghosh, A. (1994) *Retail Management*, 2nd edn, The Dryden Press, New York.

Gummesson, E. (1991) Marketing Orientation Revisited: The Crucial Role of the Part-Time Marketer, *European Journal of Marketing*, 25, 2, 60–75.

Henley Centre Report (1995) *The loyalty paradox*, Henley Centre, London

Hollander, S.C. (1960) The Wheel of Retailing, *Journal of Marketing*, 25, 37–42.

Hollander, S.C. (1966) Notes on the Retail Accordion, *Journal of Retailing*, Summer, 29–40.

Jefferys, J.B. (1954) *Retail Trading in Britain 1850–1950*, Cambridge University Press, Cambridge.

Jones, T.O. and Sasser, W.E. (1995) Why Satisfied Customers Defect, *Harvard Business Review*, November–December.

Keynote/Business Monitor (1998), PA1003 'Retailing in the UK, Keynote, London.

Lancaster, B. (1995) *The Department Store*, Leicester University Press, Leicester.

Levy, H. (1948) *The Shops of Britain*, Trench Trubner, London.

Levy, S.J. and Zaltman, G. (1975) *Marketing, Society and Conflict*, Prentice Hall, NJ.

MacKeith, M. (1986) *The History and Conservation of Shopping Arcades*, Mansell, London.

Powell, D. (ed.) (1987) *The Tesco Papers 1975–1987*, Tesco Stores Holdings Plc/Hallam & Mallen, London.

Reichheld, F.F. (1996) The Satisfaction Trap, *Customer Services Management*, December, 51–3.

Reichheld, F.F. and Sasser, W.E. (1990) Zero defections: quality comes to Services, *Harvard Business Review*, Sept-Oct, 105-111.

Ries, A. and Trout, J. (1983) *Positioning: The Battle for your Mind*, McGraw Hill, New York.

Schlesinger, D. and Hesketh, D. (1991) The Service-Driven Service Company, *Harvard Business Review*, September–October.

Shostack, G.L. (1987) Service Positioning Through Structural Change, *Journal of Marketing*, January, 34–43.

Marketing and the Retail Environment in the Twenty-First Century

CHAPTER 2

This chapter:

- Defines the dynamic and competitive retail environment
- Defines marketing strategy
- Delineates the macro environment and the micro environment

Marketing and the Retail Environment in the Twenty-First Century

Introduction

Retail in most Western countries is a dynamic and very competitive area of business. As described in Chapter 1, there are continual changes and new initiatives always being tried in order to keep trading with existing customers and to win new ones. The failure rate amongst small retail businesses is high, but even the established giants can have problems. In the first year of the twenty-first century there have been:

- Trading problems at both Marks & Spencer and J Sainsbury
- Arcadia closing its Richard Shops and Principles for Men outlets
- Uno/World of Leather going into receivership
- Both Boots and W H Smith turning in lower profits
- Storehouse/Mothercare/Bhs ripe for a takeover
- Coop Homeworld & Living closing all stores
- Do it All taken over by Focus DIY
- Somerfields issuing a profits warning
- Barclays Bank closing 171 branches (10 per cent of all its retail branches).

There are numerous reasons for the difficulties experienced by the companies listed above. Nevertheless these problems have occurred in a period during which total consumer spending has risen. The question that must be asked is 'did these companies fail in their marketing, or was there some other reason for the trading problems?'

In order to answer this question it is necessary to understand the retail marketing and the environment in which marketing strategy is both formulated and implemented.

Marketing has already been defined as 'everything undertaken by a retailer in order to satisfy the needs and wants of customers'. This is consistent with the view that the purpose of a business is to create a customer. However it is not a very tight definition and that is deliberate because marketing activities are so diverse, and there are probably as many definitions of marketing as there are textbooks on the subject. While many have common elements, the very fact that there are so many serves to create confusion rather than clarity. Perhaps the most important thing to remember is that there is no *one correct* way of 'doing' marketing, there is no *prescription*, no *set of rules* that guarantees success. What there is is only a way of thinking, and a focus for activity, that is targeted at customers and markets.

Marketing strategy is just as difficult to pin down. Fifield (1992) offers 10 definitions, each from an eminent academic, and each emphasizing that person's own specific premise regarding strategy. This leads to confusion, and Fifield seeks to reduce this. Rather than produce his own definition he opts to suggest what marketing strategy *does*, and on this there is a much greater consensus:

> Marketing strategy is the process by which the organisation translates its business objectives and business strategy into market activity.

Of course this does not tell us what is a good strategy and what a poor one. Perhaps that is because strategy is about taking decisions for the future, and the future is uncertain. Most of us have 20/20 vision when it comes to hindsight. We can all hope to identify a successful strategy from the past, analyse the reasons for that success, and applaud the organization concerned. But when it comes to the future we are short of feedback, while any decisions that are taken should be based upon the most appropriate or rational predictions, the outcome resulting from any activity is still unknown.

This does not mean that we should not try to create a profitable future for our organization. If we accept that strategy translates 'objectives into activities', then it is important to have some framework for testing any proposed strategy in a real, practical situation. The crucial test is whether the strategy appears to be *feasible* given the three key determinants of every market situation. These are:

- The *competitive market environment* in which the activities have to be performed.
- The *customers* who are the target of the marketing activity.
- The *capabilities and competencies* of the retailer to undertake those activities.

Chapter 3 will concentrate on issues of customer behaviour, and the impact of marketing activities on customers can be assessed throughout the book. The resources, capabilities and competencies of an individual retailer, and whether they are adequate, is a matter of judgement that will be discussed when considering the planning and control of marketing. This chapter will be concerned with the first issue, the *competitive retail environment*. This comprises the *external*, uncontrollable factors that affect a retailer in their normal business and marketing decisions.

Kotler (2000) suggests that the *marketing environment* can be divided into 'a macro environment and a micro environment.' Both need to be understood and there are opportunities and threats in each of them. This distinction between the macro and the micro environment is useful and it can be easily and specifically applied in retail markets.

The *macro environment* 'consists of the larger societal forces that affect the whole market' – political, economic, demographic, social, cultural, ethical and technological. Of course the greatest recent change in the macro environment is the development of electronic retail (.com e-tailers), and the opportunities and threats posed by the use of new technology. But another important factor is the saturation in some markets, and an excess capacity that exists due to an oversupply of retail space.

The *micro environment* 'consists of the forces close to the company that affect its ability to serve its customers' – such as the trends in the product/market chosen by a company, its publics, suppliers and competitors, etc. For a retailer this will include issues such as how big a group should be to benefit from economies of scale and critical competitive mass while remaining responsive to the needs of customers.

The Macro Environment

Adcock (1991) suggests that

> One traditional way of considering the external environment is to examine the four major component parts:
>
> **P** Political and legal factors
>
> **E** Economic factors
>
> **S** Social and cultural factors
>
> **T** Technological factors.
>
> This group makes up the mnemonic PEST. There are a number of equally good and widely used mnemonics such as STEP, PCDENT, SPELT, and SLEPT, which are also used. However it is not the identification of the issues but the evaluation of the impact they might have which is critical to future success....These factors only become a 'PEST' if an organisation fails to identify those that are likely to have a significant effect on future business. There is a difference between the small '*evolutionary*' changes that can be accommodated within a developing strategy, and the major '*revolutionary*' changes that require significant shifts to remain competitive.

Every retail organization will need to monitor its macro environment, and continually assess the potential effect of changes in that environment.

They will endeavour to identify the major *issues*, and will then forecast the *impact* of that particular factor so that relevant actions can be undertaken. One technique used by some organizations is to build different scenarios that describe the future – a '*most likely*' scenario, or '*worst case*' scenario, for instance, so that strategy can be evaluated against different predictions of the future. Such analysis is particularly important with respect to all the macro environmental factors.

The Political and Legal Environment

The *political environment* includes all the actions of governments that impact on a retail business. This can be via formal legislation such as the Sales of Goods Act, as well as through competition policy and planning regulations. Recent influences such as initiatives regarding food safety and the marketing of genetically modified (GM) produce also both influence and limit activities.

As Fifield (1992) says: 'It is supremely important that the organisation understands the role of government in the marketplace, be it as regulator or participator.... We must also understand which of the vast array of legislation impacts on our organisation and our marketing activities.' The impact will not be the same for every type of retailer and it is beyond the scope of this book to list every possible political factor. However it is important to realize that many regulations are introduced in order to protect consumers from abuse, and these are often discussed well in advance of government action. Those organizations that are sensitive to the political climate will be able to anticipate changes and implement appropriate actions. In the long run the government has power over business and, as in the debate over high prices and 'rip off Britain', sometimes retailers can be their own worst enemy.

There can be some issues that impact on more than one of the macro environmental categories – one recent example is the minimum wage legislation which has increased employment costs and is, therefore, also a factor within the economic environment.

The Economic Environment

Economic issues affect business in two ways. First the impact of disposable incomes and inflation on consumer spending; and second the effect of taxes, rents, employee costs and other expenses that are involved in running a retail business.

Economic issues are not restricted solely to the local economy in which a retail store is operating. The *globalization* of retailing via the Internet means that international competition, much of it based on price, is now a reality in many markets. There has also been a great deal of publicity regarding the opportunities for consumers to purchase cars in continental Europe and thus save against UK prices. Another example is the increasing popularity of 'booze cruising' to purchase beer and wine in France where taxes and prices are lower. The impact of a single European currency will definitely have an impact on UK businesses in the future.

Globalization is an issue that affects business costs but it is uncertain what the trend is in retail industries. There has been the takeover of Asda by Wal-Mart, UK companies such as Tesco now operate in many countries and foreign companies such as Aldi and IKEA are also expanding internationally. But as shown by the withdrawal of Marks & Spencer from Germany, there can be problems, especially if the retailer brand is unknown and has little value in the new market.

In the UK the dramatic growth of discount clothes retailer Matalan has, in part, been blamed for the problems of Marks & Spencer in the UK, and the decision of the Dutch-owned department store C&A to close its UK operation.

The key question is which types of retailers can derive really significant economic benefits from globalization in the same way as manufacturing companies. For some retail businesses there is merit in small, local, personal service. For others such as McDonald's the use of franchizing is an attempt to 'think global but act local'. However the term 'McDonaldization' is increasingly being used in a rather derogatory way to imply unblinkered standardization of an offering. This says something about the perception of customers regarding a major global retailer.

The Sociological and Cultural Environment

In Fifield's (1992) view 'This aspect of the environment is probably the most difficult to understand, quantify, and predict, dealing as it does with people and human behaviour'. While purchasing behaviour is discussed in Chapter 3, there are some wider issues that impact upon retail activities. One important trend is the 'ageing' of the population and this *demographic shift* is creating new opportunities for some retailers, and proving a threat to others. The increasing *multi-ethnic mix* in UK society, linked to the high levels of mobility and international travel, has dramatically altered the knowledge and consumption of a wide range of exotic foodstuffs. Retailers who fail to anticipate changes in taste and demand will be left behind. This is well understood by fashion retailers, who make extreme efforts to predict trends in colours and style as well as trying to lead rather than follow their customers' needs.

There are again areas of overlap affecting both the sociological and the political environments. Current concerns about the quality of food are prompting government action. The 1998 *Eurobarometer* survey covering all 15 EU countries showed that only 39 per cent of respondents thought pre-cooked meals safe to buy. But the figures showed an enormous national variation ranging from 71 per cent in Sweden down to 7 per cent in Greece. The survey also reported that only 34 per cent of Germans believed fresh meat was safe, and with the current regulations in the wake of the BSE and foot and mouth crises, this shows how such attitudes might drive both government action and affect retailing activity.

The Technological Environment

Technological developments often lead to 'revolutionary' discontinuities in a market. But as Aaker (1998) commented, 'new technologies start by invading sub-markets, but they then tend to create new markets instead of simply encroaching on existing ones'. He goes on to suggest '[new technologies] can represent an opportunity to those in a position to capitalise... [but] could also prove a significant threat'. This is obvious, as shown by the explosion in e-commerce since the late 1990s.

It is not at all clear whether the new opportunities to use the Internet will become a serious threat to 'bricks and mortar' stores in all product categories, but it is certainly here to stay and will be a significant player in a number of areas. In some markets the established stores might offer the e-retail services alongside existing operations, in others new suppliers will take the initiative. E-retail (.com e-tailing) is still in the early stages of its development and there is uncertainty as to the future direction and application of the technology. What is certain is that the Internet and the opportunities for electronic retailing are likely to change forever many of the traditional ways of doing business, having a far greater impact than the move to out-of-town shopping which was fuelled by the increasing use of cars. Retailers who have invested heavily in fixed tangible assets such as buildings are likely to have to review the relevance of those assets in the new environment of marketing hyperspace.

While the Internet is creating a revolution in retail, other technological developments help retailers incrementally, so that they can carry out existing tasks more efficiently. The use of article numbering (barcodes) has changed stock control and re-ordering, as well as improving merchandising balance and speeding up the checkout operation. Small, plastic 'loyalty cards' utilize encoding technology and the mass of information they provide can drive many aspects of retail marketing strategy. Advances in chilled food technology (the 'chill chain') have created opportunities to expand product ranges and lengthen shelf lives. There are many other examples from the past; what is important for retail is what are going to be the new technological developments that will improve or change activities in the future.

The Micro Environment

The micro environment, sometimes termed the 'task' or 'proximate' environment, includes all the forces close to the company that *affect its ability to serve its customers*. One classic model that looks at the structure of an industry is Michael Porter's 5 forces model, which dates from 1980. More recently Morgan and Hunt (1994) have produced a diagrammatic summary of the influences on an organization; this retains the buyer and supplier links but widens the other factors studied to include many internal and external factors. Morgan and Hunt's original model was designed for any type of organization but it has been slightly adapted here to focus on retail companies. Both models are shown in Figures 2.1a and 2.1b.

For this text the four headings of Morgan and Hunt will be used.

External Influences

There are many external influences on a retailer, ranging from direct and indirect competition through to the financial and other stakeholders who

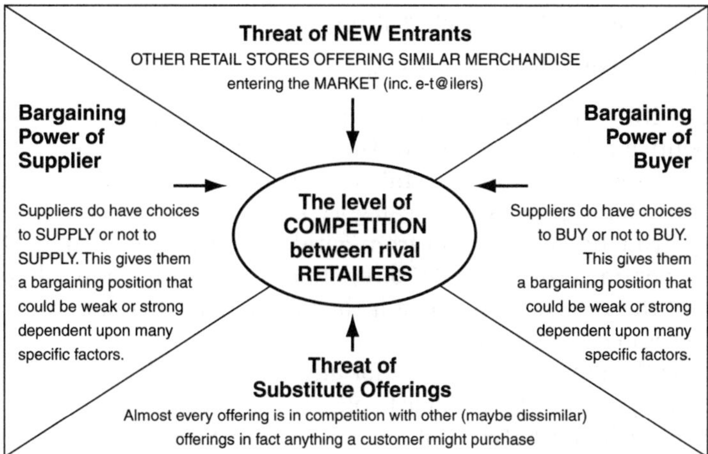

Figure 2.1a Porter's 5 forces model (1980)
Source: Porter, M., *The Competitive Advantage of Nation*, 1990, Macmillan, reproduced with permission of Palgrave.

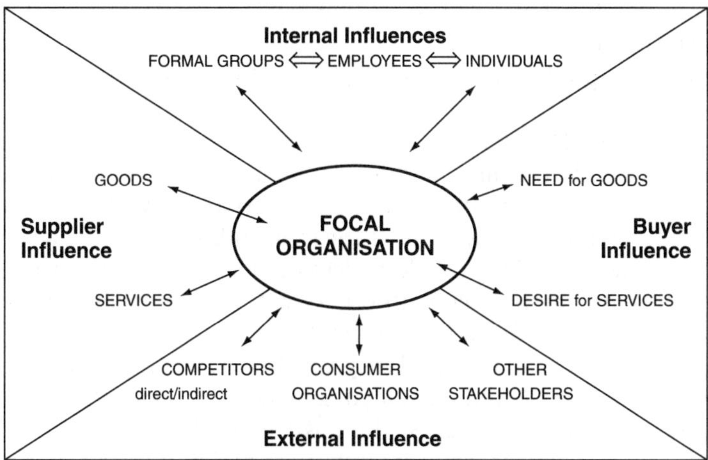

Figure 2.1b Morgan and Hunt's model (1994)
Source: Reprinted with permission from *Journal of Marketing*, published by the American Marketing Association, Hunt and Morgan, 1994, Vol. 58 (3), pp. 20–38.

can directly limit activities by the use of the power they hold. But it is obvious that the major external influence, apart from the customers themselves, comes from the competitors who are making offers to those same customers.

Competitors: Direct and Indirect

There are three aspects of competitive activity that can affect a retailer. These are drawn from three of Porter's 5 forces and are:

- The *existing interfirm competition*

- The threat of *entry by new competitors*
- The threat of *substitute offerings*.

Kotler (2000) is quite incisive in his evaluation of changes in the competitive retail environment. He writes that there is an 'oversaturation of retailing': 'Small retailers are succumbing to the growing power of giant retailers and "category killers". *Store-based retailers* are facing growing competition from catalog houses; direct-mail firms; newspaper, magazine, and TV direct-to-customer ads; home shopping TV; and the Internet. As a result they are facing shrinking margins' (emphasis in the original).

While the most obvious focus for any retailer will be on the existing direct competitors who are able to offer comparable goods or services, it must never be forgotten that customers make the buying decisions. What a customer perceives as comparable might not concur with a retailer's view. For instance a customer out shopping for some new clothes might see an attractive handbag on offer and decide to purchase that instead. As most customers have limited financial resources, there is often a real and difficult decision that has to be made with regards expenditure at any point in time (although, of course, the use of credit cards and other extended deals can help as part of the retailer's marketing mix).

When two product offerings are identical they become *equivalent to commodities* and the obvious reaction of a consumer is to buy the cheapest. It could be said that it is the task of marketing to ensure that no two offers are that similar, perhaps by adding extra value. This could involve levels of customer service, or increased availability, or an extended warranty, or any other of the multitude of ways that a product can be augmented. Many retailers carry out local surveys to ensure that their offers are comparable with others within their radius of competition. Some even offer to refund the difference (or more) if the same product is found cheaper within given limits. Such guarantees are designed to provide confidence for customers and to expedite a purchase decision. Kotler (2000) suggested a possible marketing response could include 'entrepreneurial retailers [who] are building *entertainment* into stores with coffee bars, lectures, demonstrations, and performances. They are marketing the "*experience*" rather than the product assortment' (emphasis in the original).

It is certainly important for retailers to study other organizations within the competitive market space in which they are operating. That is a retailer's *radius of competition*. A limited geographical area once defined this, but the development of international travel and the World Wide Web means the boundaries are now extensive. However for some low-involvement products, and those areas where remote supply is impossible, such as the choice of petrol retailer, the locality remains the competitive domain. But in many markets, from the supply of insurance to the purchase of computers, there is direct competition between fixed 'bricks and mortar' stores and telephone or Internet providers.

Many new entries are based on new ways of reaching customers. However, whether a new market entrant uses traditional or new technology, that newcomer has to develop its customer base, and encourage shoppers to switch suppliers. This can take time as during the initial period after a launch many customers are unaware or reluctant to use the new supplier. But it important that a retailer finds out about any new entrants as early as possible, because if this happens then the threat can be evaluated and relevant action can be considered in an effort to destroy a competitor before it becomes established. It might be possible to do this by heavy promotion and thereby hope to stop the competitor reaching a break-even situation quickly. This is sometimes the reason why it is so difficult for new independent stores to get started.

Of course Internet competitors are proving less easy to match. But the classic model of the *diffusion of innovation* (Rogers 1962) suggests there is a difference in a customer's readiness to try any new product (or retailer). 'Innovators' and 'early adopters' might now be using the Internet for purchases, but there are still many in the categories of 'late majority' and 'laggard' to be convinced of its advantages.

With existing competitors, and with new entrants, the basic questions that must be asked are:

- *Where* and *how* is the competitor competing with our organization?
- Does their strategy *affect our performance?*
- What are the *capabilities* and *resources* of the competitor?
- Which are the *comparative strengths* and which the *weaknesses?*
- How should we *respond* to this competitor?

The first two questions can usually be answered by intelligent observation, it is the more detailed aspects of a competitor's operation that require real insight. It is important that any competitive evaluation is as objective and complete as possible. If an organization knows both its own and its competitor's strengths and weaknesses, the development of appropriate strategies will be better grounded in fact.

Warning: A word of warning is necessary regarding Strength and Weaknesses, and the more general SWOT (Strengths, Weaknesses, Opportunities and Threats) analyses. The identification of the factors is only a first step, the SWOT is a tool of analysis that is deceptively simple, widely used and too often misused. It must not result in *uncritical* listings of the many issues. It must be concise and must focus on the *key* factors only. These will be the crucial *differential* strengths and weaknesses, *vis-à-vis* the competition, that require attention. Each will be accompanied by an assessment of the impact that that factor is likely to have on future performance. At the end of the analysis there should be an objective assessment of the competitive position of the business, one that could be confirmed by external customers, if asked. The achievement of a good, critical SWOT can be the foundation of a good strategy.

Consumer Organizations

While consumer organizations may seem less dangerous than direct competitors, they can be a strong external influence on retail businesses.

Major organisations such as the Consumers' Association are able to exert great influence over shopping behaviour, especially through the pages of their highly respected *Which*© magazine. Intense lobbying by the Disability Alliance (and by many high-profile charities) has had a real impact on legislation regarding access to buildings for people with disabilities.

There are other organisations, sometimes formed to campaign on a single issue, that can also affect retailing in general or a local issue in particular. For instance the 'Save our Sundays' group fought very hard to restrict the legal trading hours for shops to open on Sundays. The current arrangement in the UK is a result of a compromise in the 1990s, although prior to the legal agreement on shopping hours, many major retailers actually flouted regulations and risked financial penalties. As Dennis Landau, then CEO of the Co-op (CWS), said 'I'd rather break the law and remain in business, than obey the law and go bust.' Perhaps he knew that general public opinion was heavily in favour of Sunday shopping and the risk was worth it. On a local level, ecological protestors campaigned to stop a new Tesco store being built near Bristol; while they were ultimately unsuccessful, their actions were costly for Tesco and led to a great deal of adverse short-term publicity.

Many retailers, of course, realize that there are positive benefits from being a good corporate citizen. Support for local charities, or providing a free community notice board, or offering small incentives to local events all help to increase goodwill and provide opportunities for good public relations at very low cost. Many retailers understand that they have a responsibility within the community in which they operate to maintain or if possible enhance the environment, and this can be made more effective by working in partnership with local organizations. In some cases support can be more than a local activity. The larger multiple stores will consider the advantages of 'societal marketing' as one component in their overall promotional plans.

Other Stakeholder Influences

There are a large number of diverse stakeholders each having a legitimate interest in a particular retail organization. They include the investors in that organization (shareholders, banks and private owners), the retail employees (managers and staff), the customers, the suppliers (who depend upon the retailer for their livelihood) and the wider community where the retailer's activities have an impact. Many of these will be discussed elsewhere, such as consumer organizations (see above), or local and national governments, or trade unions such as USDAW (the shop workers' union).

It is imperative that every retailer understands that it is involved in an *exchange relationship* with each and every stakeholder. The importance of the particular relationship with an individual stakeholder, and the advantages of fully satisfying that interested party, will need to be assessed and compared. The presence of multiple stakeholders will possibly lead to a number of conflicting objectives, and it will be unlikely, therefore, that all stakeholders can be fully satisfied, so certain compromises will have to be made.

Supplier Influences

There was a time when manufacturers considered retailers as a passive conduit to the final consumer. These times have passed in most markets, and retailers now possess much of the power and ability to control events. But that should not eliminate the influence of suppliers both to ensure stocks of existing products are *available* as and when required, and to act as an *innovator* developing new products for the future.

Most retail goods are supplied in a finished state to the store, or to a central warehouse that supplies several stores. Even when vertical, backward, integration occurs, the supplier is usually considered as a separate profit and operating centre and thus similar to independent suppliers. Retailers are more often involved with a single supplier for each item they wish to offer. This is true for branded manufactured items which only the brand owner can supply, although alternative brands could be available, and for many own-label items where the economies of a single supplier can be exploited. However this means that the retailer is especially vulnerable to supplier problems, and thus must keep closely in touch with all suppliers but particularly those supplying the key 'traffic-building' products that attract shoppers into the store.

In particular unanticipated increases in price can damage retail sales, so long-term contracts at known costs can be advantageous. Unexpected developments affecting a supplier can have major impacts on retailers, stock shortages might lead to dissatisfied customers who will complain to the retailer not the supplier; inadequate quality is another problem, and again it rebounds onto the retail store. Good partnerships between supplier and retailer can be developed, but it is crucial they should not be abused. Situations are now developing where the retailer is often a larger organization than their suppliers. As Dawson (1999) suggests:

> Large size in retailing gives the retailer potential power over many aspects of the buying relationship. Having this power also brings the responsibility to use or not use it. A challenge of size is to establish to what extent, for what purpose and how should the channel power be used in relationships with suppliers. Managing these power relationships requires a level of managerial sophistication, which sometimes takes time to evolve.

The decision of Marks & Spencer to dramatically reduce its orders from some of its UK suppliers was detrimental to both the parties involved. In another area the support given by Rover car dealers (retailers) to the rescue bid for Rover Cars in May 2000 illustrates the mutual dependency of retailer and supplier.

With regards new product offerings, there has been an increasing involvement of retailers with the development activities of suppliers. However it is still the suppliers who are most likely to carry out the development, whereas it is the retailer, in a position of closeness to the final customer, who is best able to identify trends. The activities of retail buyers, and the way they source merchandise and work with suppliers, affects good range selection, relevant pricing and promotion and the overall success of the retailer. Therefore the influence of a supplier and the way they work with one retailer in preference to another could be a crucial factor in success.

Internal Influences

There are four key aspects of internal influences that are part of the retailer's micro environment:

- *Front-line employees*, who directly interact with customers
- Other employees who contribute to the *effective operating* of a retailer
- Formal groups, such as *trade unions* or *staff associations*
- *Non-human resources* available to the retailer.

This book is not a management text, nor is it concentrating on human resource management. These topics require specialised study and there are many appropriate books available. However one relevant point needs to be made about managing a retail operation, especially a nascent, small outlet. Many people dream about the freedom of managing their own business, setting up a restaurant, or investing in a store to offer goods to fill an apparent gap in the market. The statistics are bleak, many new retailers fail because they do not have the necessary combination of marketing and managing skills. There are fewer failures when the 'new' retailer is a franchise because the franchisor can supply much of this knowledge as part of the overall package, although the new entrant should beware, since not all franchises are as attractive as they are sometimes made out to be.

Most retailers, even small shops, will require both management and service staff in order to ensure they are open at the right times and can serve customers without unacceptable delays. Employees, especially service assistants, become a prime stakeholder group in every organization, and there is a vicious circle of activities that runs:

- *Employee:* 'The company doesn't look after me why should I bother with customers'
- *Customer:* 'These people don't seem to care, I'm not coming back to this store'
- *Retailer:* 'Our staff aren't doing their job they need to be sorted out!'

This emphasizes the importance of internal staff in retail operations, and in particular the importance of people in the achievement of marketing objectives. In some retail operations, a majority of the service employees are part-time workers trying to earn a little money, and in reality do not always feel totally committed to a large organization. In fact, many view themselves as in 'dead-end' jobs: this can be a recipe for disaster.

There was a lot of interest in the 1990s as to what marketing people could contribute by directing their focus internally into an organization. This is now termed *internal marketing*, and involves the application of marketing skills and techniques in order to create appropriate relationships with employees.

There are three closely related internal areas where marketing can be beneficial:

- The first is to act directly on the relationship between an *organization and its employees*. This involves the use of research techniques to understand employees, and of communications and promotions to disseminate corporate plans and other relevant information.
- Secondly there is the need to propagate the concept of the *part-time marketer* and to create a customer orientation within the organization. Evert Gummesson (1991) proposed that all employees whose major job is not primarily marketing but, by virtue of their direct customer contact, can influence the interactive encounters with customers, should be considered as part-time marketers. This is obviously a critical area for retail because of the close contacts involved. The ability of these contact staff, and their understanding of their role, can be enhanced by being in direct contact with the full-time marketers.
- Third is the understanding of the *organization structure* and, in particular, the internal supplier–customer relationships that exist inside a company. If every employee, whatever their role, considers that they are customers of other people and departments from within, as well as being suppliers to yet more internal departments as a result of their job, then the idea of an *internal supply network* becomes apparent. It is then only a small step to getting internal departments to try to act as 'quasi-independent' business units and to utilize marketing thinking and techniques to ensure that their 'internal customers' are satisfied. This will then lead to a real marketing orientation internally, and by extension out to the external customers as well.

For the larger retailers there is a distinct possibility that some employees will be members of a union. USDAW, the shop workers' union, has campaigned tirelessly for workers' rights, minimum wage levels and maximum working hours. Formal groups, whether recognized or not by the employer, can have an affect on some important aspects of what is, and what is not, possible with regards to retail operations. Their influence should not be ignored.

The influence of non-human internal resources within the micro environment is quite different. The most important issues are the financial resources available to the organization, and the fixed assets it owns. *Inadequate capitalization* is a feature of many small retail organizations, and the failure to invest sufficiently in merchandising, coupled with real limits on promotions, is a cause of failure for many new entrants.

But, as the 'wheel of retailing' theory implies, retailers should continually re-invent themselves if they wish to remain relevant to the changing needs of customers in a dynamic market. This can mean renewing internal layouts and fittings, as well as reassessing the location of a store. Decisions made in the past to invest in fixed assets could leave a retailer with unsuitable resources for the future. This is particularly relevant where a 'bricks and mortar' store is owned, maybe in a high street area, but the development of a new shopping centre, perhaps out-of-town, has reduced the regular shopping traffic. For this reason, and to keep down costs, many retailers prefer to rent premises rather than own them. After all, the retailer is in a very different business from the property developer who builds and manages shopping locations.

The critical role of retail marketing and management is to ensure that the store and the offerings evolve in response to future consumer needs. As Peter Salsbury, then CEO of Marks & Spencer, said (*Economist* 1999) 'We lost touch with our customers, and forgot about the competition'. Customer responsiveness has to be at the strategic marketing and organizational level. It involves the systems used to serve customers as well as the more obvious fixed assets. There are many functions that a retailer can contract out – for instance, invoicing, warehousing, security or even shelf-filling. The question of sub-contracting of some operations is beyond the scope of this book, but whenever they have an impact on the customer experience, there is a role for marketing to ensure the performance standards are consistent with the overall strategy.

Buyer Influences

The influence of customers upon a retail business, or any business, is obvious: No customers = No business. But it goes further than that. Customers must be attracted into the store, or retail marketspace, then they have to be encouraged to spend. If they are satisfied, these customers might return to buy again. They might also tell their friends and acquaintances about the retailer: good 'word-of-mouth' endorsement is worth far more than paid-for advertising. Successful retailing requires a critical mass of regular customers, and retail marketing should be aimed at achieving this objective.

Not all customers will return to buy, perhaps the merchandise offered is a one-off, say a new bathroom which will then not be replaced for many years. For this type of product, recommendations from past customers can make the difference between just trading and trading profitably. Even if the merchandise being offered is a type to be repurchased, say flowers being bought to give to a friend, the customer, although satisfied, is possibly just not the type to either become a loyal shopper or to recommend the specific retailer. This is no problem if the retailer understands the differing behaviour and influence of its various customer groups, and responds accordingly. Customer behaviour is discussed in more detail in Chapter 3.

The worst retail scenario is when a customer is not satisfied with an offering and then tells friends, or even contacts one of the media consumer programmes such as 'Watchdog'. It has been suggested that dissatisfied customers tell between 10 and 20 others of their experience. This type of negative publicity is very damaging and there is a need to encourage customers to enter into a dialogue with the retailer before too much damage is done. There is evidence to suggest that customers do acknowledge that mistakes sometimes occur and, if the complaint is handled quickly and well then the customer relationship can be recovered. This aspect of retail marketing is further discussed in Chapter 11.

The strength of a relationship between a buyer and a retailer can be seen through the *positive brand images* that can develop. Retail branding has moved from generic products, into 'own-label' offerings, and to effective, and all-embracing, retail brands. Organizations such as IKEA, B&Q, Comet and Toys 'Я' Us, are all strong store brands with positive associations. This has been facilitated by the customer influence on the retailer's image, which is now going further, into brand extensions. Tesco has launched Tesco Bank, Marks & Spencer offer life insurance and investments and Boots have extended into opticians and beauty-care parlours. The Co-operative movement has always offered many services, from travel agencies to funerals, thus extending their brand. Successful brand extensions rely on strong buyer influences that enable positive images to be transferred into other area of business.

Analysis of the Retail Environment

This text is not concerned with analytical techniques, there are many books specifically written for that. However it is crucial as a foundation for good marketing that environmental influences are studied, and that any decisions as to future operations are made based on the probable impact of such factors.

All marketers will need to make decisions as to how widely they should explore their environment. This so-called '*surveillance filter*' is a measure of the breadth of study that is undertaken. The surveillance filter determines which categories should be studied, which of those in great depth and which, such as some of the macro factors, require only a quick look. There is no good answer to this dilemma, all data-gathering involves some cost and extra data analysis involves both cost and time. In general, each retailer will decide what information they need, although for those working in a particular retail situation it is surprising how data that have not been specifically sought suddenly become noticeable because they affect the business. Good, market-focused retailers have a heightened sense of what is happening around them.

When it comes to analysing environmental data it is important to reduce the large number of issues to a limited number of *really important issues* that could have a *major impact* on the organization for the future. Again there are many ways of tackling this, but be aware of the warning about the much misused SWOT analysis made earlier in this chapter. In predicting the *future impact* (scale, direction and timing) of a particular issue there is a high degree of personal opinion. There is also personal judgement in deciding which issues are really crucial and thus require attention in any future strategy. This introduces another filter, the '*mentality filter*', which means that people involve decide on the basis of their own views which particular issues are to be included and which left out. The best advice is to try to avoid the worst subjective bias by involving outsiders in the process. Also if you are unsure about any issue, it is better to include it rather than ignore it.

A Brief Look at Different Retail Formats

There are many different ways of categorizing retail organizations:

- With reference to the type of customers served – *consumer, industrial* or *re-seller*.
- With reference to the type of premises and the market space occupied – *fixed store, mobile* or *non-store*. The fixed store category can be further sub-divided into type of location; *primary site, secondary site, urban, rural, remote*. It could also include the distinction between *multiple retail outlets* and *single outlet retailers*. With *non-store*, this covers everything from vending machines, market stalls, through mail-order and onto <.com e-tailing>.
- In terms of the *type of merchandise offered, range and assortment, price position*, and *level and type of service* available.

Each of these can provide an insight into the role of a retailer and can help to explain the large number of marketing options available.

Type of Customers Served

Consumer Markets

Consumer markets are those where the purchase is made to supply the needs of an *individual or a small group*, maybe a family or household. Products are often bought in small quantities and there are typically many millions of customers in these markets. There is a retail emphasis on providing an effective offering and service that is geared to the way individuals behave while shopping.

Even within consumer markets there can be a distinction based on the categorization of the merchandise offered. The so-called '*shopping goods*' – those durables that are usually selected after shopping around to compare price, quality, features, etc. (maybe washing machines, cars or computers) – are very different from the markets for the *fast-moving consumer goods* (FMCG).

For consumer markets it is likely that the *location* of a retailer and the *environment* in which the offering is made will be more important than in, say, an industrial market.

Industrial Markets

In these markets the products are bought by a *commercial organization*. They will require some items as capital investments to use in order to carry out their business, others as components used as part of a finished product being produced, or even as a consumable, something that is necessary to keep the business going (maybe a lubricant, or some office stationery). Some of these will be sourced directly from the actual manufacture, but this sometimes takes place at a 'trade counter' attached to a factory and other items will be purchased from an industrial retailer. Where a retailer is involved it will be because the service provided offers better value than buying direct.

Industrial customers tend to be more interested in the value of any offering they buy, this includes its comparative price, quality and the reliability of the 'on-time' supply. There are fewer opportunities for promotions and other emotional appeals, although there are occasions where such actions can be effective. Another feature of industrial markets is that regular supplies ultimately depend on the performance of the customer in their own markets. This is termed 'derived demand', and it causes some industrial markets to fluctuate and be subject to cycles of activity that can be difficult to predict.

Re-Seller Markets

There are some organizations that buy goods and/or services in order to *sell them on* at a profit. Wholesalers or cash and carry outlets will serve many of these re-seller organizations, but they also purchase from other types of retailers. The re-sellers could be hotels and restaurants purchasing food, or market stallholders buying anything that could be sold on or, maybe, a local convenience store. The basic retail activities of a 'cash and carry', or any other type of 'restricted customer' store, are not dissimilar to general retailers. However this type of outlet, dealing with re-seller customers, is often able to build up an effective database of its customers, and will use many more promotional offers than an industrial retailer.

Type of Premises and Market Space Occupied

Fixed-store, Mobile or Non-Store Retailing

Fixed-store, 'bricks and mortar', retailing is still the dominant format as we enter the twenty-first century. The benefits are obvious, a known location and a familiar layout, the ability to browse and to actually see and handle the merchandise all being important. While some stores are small offering restricted merchandise, others can cover 100 000 or more square feet of sales space and display thousands of lines. There are even some 'catalogue stores' offering a wide range in a relatively small space. The major point with 'fixed-store' operations is that location is critical, and customers have to travel to the store in order to make a purchase.

Some grocery retailers, such as Iceland and Tesco, are now offering home-delivery services. This has been a feature of electrical and furniture retailers for many years. However it is also possible to use a *mobile store* to visit a customer at home. Many years ago mobile greengrocers were common, home milk delivery is another activity that is now used less, the reasons being that consumers can compare the increased cost of this type of service with the benefits (i.e. price on the doorstep compared to price in a shop). However there are still some product classes where mobile retailers thrive. One is the supply of fresh fish – this comes direct to many locations from the ports and the mobile shops used are a feature that seems to enhance the consumer's perception of 'freshness'. Another example is the retailing of sandwiches to a major office complex; the service offered is very convenient to the customers and in many instances the costs are no different from fixed-store suppliers. While mobile retailing is unlikely to feature strongly in most markets, it does have some advantages and is an acceptable option in some situations.

The early development of retail did not involve fixed stores. It is important to remember what retailing is, rather than what are the existing, popular formats. Retailing is aimed directly at customers and there is no requirement for a 'bricks and mortar' building. All the talk today regarding *non-store* operations is focused on retailing via the Internet and this is certainly revolutionizing the market. However there are other types of non-store formats that are already well established, although they do not offer the vast range of opportunities that can be found on the Net. Industry reports (*Keynote* 1998) suggest that mail order sales are around £7 billion per year, and sales via direct selling, market stalls and other non-store outlets a further £4 billion per year.

Retailing can take place through automatic vending machines, which allow transactions to occur at times, and in places where the use of staff is not feasible – for instance, a confectionery machine on a railway platform. Some automatic machines are used to actually extend the service of a fixed-store operator, such as the provision of a bank cash machine in a town where no retail bank exists. Although not really stores, these retail formats are still fixed in location. Another form of non-store operation is the 955 or so market stalls registered for VAT (*Business Monitor* PA 1003), although there may be many more traders who are unregistered. These outlets still offer an attractive range of merchandise, often at competitive prices, and they bring variety into the towns where they operate.

Direct retailing is another way of reaching customers. This is when the retailing takes place in the home or at a club or in the workplace, maybe through a party plan but often on a personal basis. It is also possible to include the activities of door-to-door retailers in this category, for instance the Betterware company leave a catalogue but actually visit customers again to discuss the goods required. Sometimes direct retailing is carried out via clubs or affinity groups, for instance Age Concern Insurance has been very successful in targeting one specific segment and reaching them through a variety of direct channels. Although this type of retailing is not very common in the UK, Dunne and Lusch (1999) estimate that 'world-wide direct sales are $50 billion, with Japan being the largest country. Major products sold include personal care items, decorative home products, cookware and encyclopaedias'.

The major advantage of direct, non-store selling is the emphasis on the person-to-person contact with time devoted to imparting knowledge about and demonstrating the products. While there is no reason for this to be absent in fixed stores, the in-home contact has lower overheads and often involves a commission salesperson who is prepared to spend more time with a customer.

The most common form of the established non-store retailing before the advent of the Internet was the mail-order catalogue. The Target Group Index (BRMB International©) survey reported that 49 per cent of all UK women purchased from a catalogue in 1997. This is an indication of the wide penetration of this form of retailing. Whether the transaction involved a general catalogue, or a more focused 'specialogue', mail-order companies try to place a visual representation of a range of merchandise into a customer's home. The photographs used are critical in attracting buyers, although as the Managing Director of a well-known company once said 'it is sometimes possible to make a cheap dress look a million dollars in a picture, but then the customer gets the product'. He stressed the careful balance necessary, as well as the need to develop an efficient process for the return of unsatisfactory items.

The market for mail-order in the UK in 1997 was estimated at some £6.8 billion. Although it has not grown in volume terms it matched inflation during the 1990s. The UK market is dominated by Great Universal Stores (GUS) (33 per cent of market share) and a few other large companies who produce major catalogues (Littlewoods, Grattan and Empire Stores). It also includes the special catalogues produced and managed by companies like Fine Art Developments on behalf of many of the major UK charities. In all there are over 2000 registered mail order businesses in the UK.

Dunne and Lusch (1999) suggested that some of forces contributing to the growth of non-store retailing are:

- The consumers' need to *save time*
- The *erosion of fun* in some shopping experiences
- The lack of *qualified sales help* in stores to provide information
- The explosive development of the *telephone*, the *computer* and telecommunications in general
- The consumers' desire to *eliminate the middleman's profit and reduce prices.*

These of course lead directly into the conditions that are helping the development of electronic retailing (.com e-t@iling). At present it is impossible to predict whether or not e-commerce will become a significant competitor for all types of fixed-store retailing. What is certain is that it will change the way retailers think and act. The developments are currently being driven by suppliers and technology, but for real success they must become consumer-led. However *Keynote* (1998) reports that:

> Whilst the future points strongly towards electronic home shopping, the rate of its development will be heavily influenced by the service providers. Before consumers can be attracted in large numbers to the use of home shopping services, the network needs to provide realistic low-cost access, and to improve the security of online payment practices.

There are many relevant questions regarding the future of Internet retailing and the topic is therefore covered in more detail in Chapter 16.

Type of Offering Made

Discussion of the different components of an offering is covered in Chapters 5–13. The choice is vast, as can be seen by any visit to any shopping area, or online shopping site. Decisions about what should be offered are usually taken in a logical sequence, hence the type of merchandise has to be decided before the range and assortment decisions are taken. This can then be followed by price and service considerations.

This is generally echoed when retail statistics are collected so that figures on the number of stores offering a specific type of merchandise will be available and within that category there will be sub-divisions into the other variables.

Conclusions

It is obvious that the external environment can have a major effect on marketing performance and success. Many external variables are not within the direct control of individual retailers, although it is sometimes possible to utilize public opinion to bring about change. This happened with the laws allowing shops to open for trade on Sundays that were achieved after much lobbying. It will be interesting to see if public pressure in the future can bring about a reduction in the tax on retail petrol sales, for example. Many factors cannot, however, be changed and thus retailers must endeavour to design their strategies in ways that are suitable given the prevailing environmental conditions, and feasible given the competitive nature of the market. This is especially true in an economic recession, or during a period of rapid social or technological change. The dramatic growth in Internet retailing is an obvious example of current changes.

Most changes within the macro environment are likely to affect all retailers in some way. However, by effective planning it is possible for an individual operator to mitigate the actual effect of a negative factor, and to benefit to a greater degree than competitors when positive factors are present. Success does not come from adapting to the given uncontrollable environment, but by doing this better than competitors. The study of an organization's *competitive marketspace* is therefore a key factor in the achievement of success. It is not possible to define the boundaries of any environmental study, and it is very easy to review a series of past events with the benefit of hindsight and then to say that a particular issue was not studied, or was not considered as important as it subsequently became. There is no answer to the problem of what to consider in order to make better decisions for the future, the only advice is to try to get a reasonable balance and to make the process as objective as possible. Certainly a trade off exists between the breadth and detail of the data gathered in order to assess the competitive environment, and the importance and cost of acquiring relevant information. In the effort to assess the impact of particular issues there is also a high level of personal opinion, and thus a risk of *subjectivity*. These dilemmas will always be present for marketing professionals, and it is inevitable that some will be able to predict the future environment more accurately than others.

References and Further Reading

Adcock, D., Halborg, A., Bradfield, R. and Ross, C. (1991) *Marketing: Principles and Practice*, FT Pitman, London.

Aaker, D (1998) *Strategic Market Management*, Wiley, New York.

Dawson J. (1999) *Retailing at Century End: Some Challenges for Management and Research*, University of Edinburgh, *Working Paper*, 99/8.
Dunne, P. and Lusch, R.F. (1999) *Retailing* 3rd edn, Harcourt Brace & Co, Orlando, FL.
Fifield, P. (1992) *Marketing Strategy*, Butterworth-Heinemann, London.
Gummesson, E. (1991) Marketing Orientation Revisited. The Crucial Role of the Part-Time Marketer, *European Journal of Marketing*, 25, 2, 60–75.
Keynote/Business Monitor (1998), PA 1003 'Retailing in the UK, Keynote, London.
Kotler, P. (2000) *Marketing Management*, Millennium Edition, Prentice-Hall, Englewood Cliffs, NJ.
Morgan, R.M. and Hunt, S. (1994) The Commitment–Trust Theory of Relationship Marketing, *Journal of Marketing*, 58, 3, 20–38.
Porter, M. E. (1980) *Competitive Strategy*, The Free Press, New York.
Rogers, E. (1962) *The Diffusion of Innovations*, The Free Press, New York.

Shopping Behaviour

CHAPTER 3

This chapter:

- Shows how retailers aim to maximize sales
- Reviews influences on shopping behaviour
- Defines the SOR model

Shopping Behaviour

Introduction

Like any other business, retailers aim to *maximize sales* (and more importantly profits) from each and every customer, both retained and new. This process of maximization is based on a clear understanding of how the system works – i.e. what makes a shopper purchase or, more importantly for long-term success, repurchase? An essential ingredient of the answer to this fundamental question is a detailed knowledge of that shopper's behaviour both in-store and beyond. Armed with this knowledge, a retailer can begin to design retail strategies and their associated tactics to fit seamlessly with the shopper, thus making the shopping process as easy and as satisfying as possible. The idea being that the more easy and satisfying the process, the more sales and profit will be generated. This chapter will begin to explain why this might be so.

The first step in understanding shopping behaviour is to consider all the factors that will have a direct affect on the shopper – i.e. *external influences* and *internal processes*. Verification of these two basic categories can be found in a fundamental behavioural principle that states that an animal's behaviour can be represented as a function of that animal's physiological and psychological make-up, and that animal's immediate environment. To give an example, suppose an individual was walking alone and at night along a narrow passageway when a sound was heard behind that individual's back. It would be natural for the individual to turn round (usually very quickly), for adrenaline to be produced and for a certain amount of stress to be experienced. In this case, adrenaline production would be a physiological response whereas the need to turn round and the development of stress would be psychological responses. The nature of the responses was affected by the environment – i.e. had the noise been heard in a crowded area during the day it is likely that a different response would have been made to the same sound. The model that can be developed from this starting point is known as the *SOR model*, or Stimulus–Organism–Response.

The SOR Model of Buyer Behaviour

The SOR model (see Figure 3.1) states that an organism (a shopper, in this case) is exposed to a variety of environmental stimuli (anything sensed by that shopper), will process those stimuli in a uniquely individual way and will then respond (behave) accordingly. The more in-depth an understanding a retailer has of the shopper's stimulus processing, the greater the accuracy of predicting likely behaviour in the face of controlled stimuli. Or, put more simply, the retailer can design the environment such that the *right stimuli* are received by the shopper to elicit the *right type of response*. 'Stimuli' in this case could be anything seen, heard, smelt, tasted or touched in the shop itself. The right type of response would be either purchase or positive attitudes about the store or its products within the shopper's mind. It should be noted, however, that the complex nature of the human being means that the probability of accurately predicting behaviour is far less than 100 per cent. Having said this, great value still exists in merely being able to influence shopper behaviour.

Consideration of *buyer decision making* can add more detail to the basic SOR model – i.e. can illuminate the processes used to decide on a response to a given strategy. Buyer decision making covers the mental and physical processes that the buyer undertakes when considering a prospective purchase. While decision making models differ depending on the type of purchase, all follow the same basic three-stage format of *need recognition*, *investigation* and *action*.

Is it accurate to say that an individual's approach to buying is the same for all products? Consider the purchase of a house and a loaf of bread, for example; the former involves lengthy deliberation while the latter can be over in seconds. Buying a house is a much more important decision with a high level of risk attached. The same cannot be said for a loaf of bread. The idea can be developed by examining the concept of *involvement*, or the degree of interest an individual has in a purchase. Involvement depends on *familiarity* and *risk*. A frequently made purchase will usually be treated in a very different way to a first-time purchase. The level of perceived risk, mainly financial and social, will again have an affect on the nature of

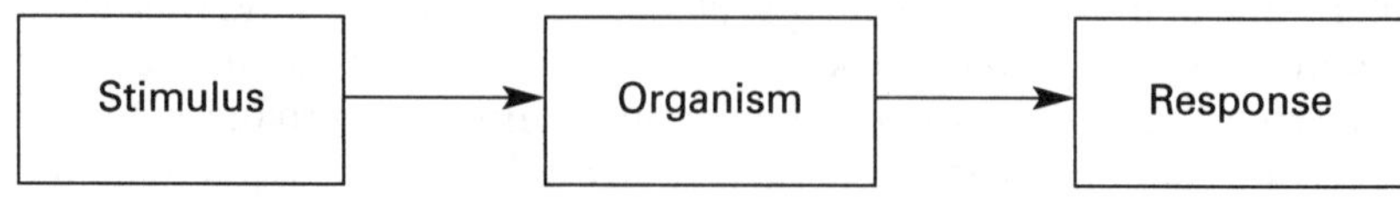

Figure 3.1 The SOR model of buyer behaviour

purchase behaviour. In the previous example, the house purchaser would be highly involved as the purchase involves a high degree of financial and social risk, and is usually infrequently undertaken. The bread buyer would show a low level of involvement as the loaf is cheap, has few social connotations and is usually bought often.

A second element that can be considered is *perceived product differences*. If a buyer perceives that all possible purchase options are very similar, it is likely that the decision process will involve less options analysis – i.e. if products are the same, why bother gathering information on every single one of them? In this case, it is probable that a simplified decision process will be used. If, however, the buyer perceives all purchase options as very different, the benefits of options analysis will increase. In this situation, it is likely that a more complicated decision process will be used. Considering the previous example, houses differ greatly whereas all bread is seen by most to be very similar. It would be expected that a more complicated process will be used to buy the house and a more simplified one will be used for bread.

Combining involvement and perceived product differences allows a number of different types of behaviour to be identified (see Table 3.1).

Table 3.1 Four Types of Buyer Behaviour

Product differences	High involvement	Low involvement
Large perceived	Complex behaviour[1] 'I got information on all the makes and compared all the figures. It wasn't until I was convinced that I made the purchase'	Variety-seeking behaviour[3] 'I'm not really concerned which product I buy, but they're all different so I normally try a different variety each time'
Small perceived	Dissonance-reducing behaviour[2] 'It's an important purchase, buy they're all the same these days aren't they?'	Habitual behaviour[4] 'I know that brand and I know it works, so I always buy it'

Note: Examples may include:
1 Houses, fashion items, cars, wedding rings; 2 Car tyres, PCs, home insurance;
3 Biscuits, standard beers, pasta; 4 Deodorant, petrol, washing powder.

Before discussing these four types of buyer behaviour it is necessary to consider the buyer decision process – i.e. need recognition, investigation and action (as discussed earlier). More detail can be added to this simple process (see Figure 3.2) by considering the elements of the investigation and action stages. Investigation can be seen as an information-gathering and evaluation process, while action can be at the point of purchase and post-purchase. Adding this extra detail gives a process that begins with *need arousal* (recognizing a want), leads on to *information-processing* (what are the alternatives?), *evaluation* (which alternative is best?), *purchase* (buy or not buy, what product, quantity, timing) and *post-purchase evaluation* (was this a good purchase?).

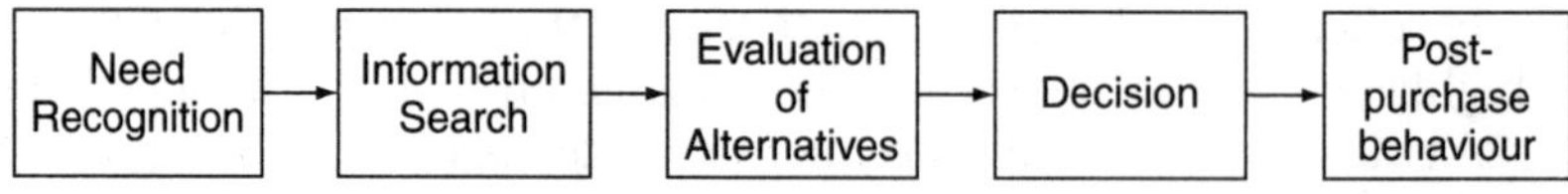

Figure 3.2 The buyer decision process

Need arousal can be triggered by *external stimuli* (from the environment) or *internal stimuli* (from the buyer). Needs themselves arise from either physiological (*biogenic*) or psychological (*psychogenic*) states. Biogenic needs are usually triggered automatically by the body and include hunger, thirst, etc. whereas psychogenic needs arise from psychological states of tension such as pride, love, anxiety, jealously, etc. Biogenic needs are often seen as harder to influence than psychogenic. Once a need has been aroused, the buyer will then seek out ways to satisfy it. An information search is undertaken to gain all the details perceived as important by the buyer. This search can involve information retrieval from the buyer's memory (internal) as well as external search if 'internal' information is insufficient. Once the required information is available, the buyer will begin to evaluate each purchase option with the aim of gradually reducing the list of possible purchases to one. This process of *option reduction* can be made on either a compensatory or non-compensatory basis. The *compensatory model* (also called the Expectancy-Value Model) assumes that buyers evaluate each brand across all product attributes and pick the product that scores highest overall. The *non-compensatory model* assumes that buyers rate brands one attribute at a time. Table 3.2 gives an example to illustrate the two methods.

Table 3.2 Compensatory and Non-Compensatory Decision Making

A buyer is considering purchasing a hi-fi system and considers power, cost, reliability and features as the most important attributes. The choice will be made from four options – *A*, *B*, *C* and *D*. Each option is assessed on the four key attributes already mentioned, with each being rated on a 10-point scale where 1 is low and 10 high.

Option	Power	Cost	Reliability	Features
A	5	6	5	3
B	9	5	8	5
C	3	5	8	9
D	5	9	4	6

A non-compensatory decision would see *B* chosen if power were the most important attribute, *D* if cost dominated and so on. A compensatory decision requires the buyer to rank each option on each attribute, set a weighting factor indicating the importance of each attribute, then produce an overall score for each option. If the buyer had assigned weightings of Power 5, Cost 9, Reliability 7 and Features 7, then Option *B* would be selected as it produced the highest overall rating (see below) (on a 10-point scale where 1 is low and 10 is high).

Option	Power	Cost	Reliability	Features	Score
A	5 × 5 = 25	6 × 9 = 54	5 × 7 = 35	3 × 7 = 21	135
B	9 × 5 = 45	5 × 9 = 45	8 × 7 = 56	5 × 7 = 35	181
C	3 × 5 = 15	5 × 9 = 45	8 × 7 = 56	9 × 7 = 63	179
D	5 × 5 = 25	9 × 9 = 81	4 × 7 = 28	6 × 7 = 42	176

The evaluation process will develop a strong *purchase intention* within the mind of the buyer. This purchase intention is a strong indicator of product choice and it is likely that the buyer will make the expected purchase. Problems can occur in the period between intention development and final purchase, owing to unexpected situation factors (more urgent purchases arise, money problems, stockouts, etc.) and reference group influences (other individuals whose opinion is seen as important – see later). Both factors may lead to purchase decision postponement or modification. The greater the risk associated with the purchase, the more likely it will be postponed or modified. Assuming that purchase takes place, the buyer must make purchase sub-decisions on what specific product to buy (the *brand* decision), where to buy it from (the *vendor* decision), when to buy it (the *timing* decision), how much to buy (the *quantity* decision) and how to pay (the *payment* decision). Once the purchase has been made, evaluation continues so that the buyer can ensure that the purchase has met expectations. *Post-purchase satisfaction* occurs when the buyer's product expectations meet the product's perceived performance while if expectations are not met *post-purchase dissatisfaction* occurs. It should be noted that perceived, rather than actual, performance is assessed – i.e. the buyer makes a judgement that will often support the decision even if the product itself is deficient in some way. This is due to the buyer not wanting to admit that they have made a mistake. Satisfied buyers are more likely to buy again whereas dissatisfied buyers are unlikely to re-purchase and may communicate their dissatisfaction to friends and relatives. This word-of-mouth information source is usually highly respected by the friends and relatives, so they may not consider the same product if they have to make the same purchase in the future.

Having considered the various stages of the buyer decision process it is apparent that differences will emerge between the four types of buyer behaviour detailed earlier – i.e. complex, dissonance-reducing, variety-seeking and habitual. *Complex behaviour* will be the most extensive process as both involvement and product differences are high. The buyer will, therefore, seek out a lot of information as all options will appear very different. Evaluation will also be extensive as will the purchase decision and post-purchase evaluation. *Dissonance-reducing behaviour* will see the buyer initially follow complex behaviour, but soon realizing that the various options are all similar (small product differences). The information search will be curtailed, as will evaluation when compared to complex behaviour. Post-purchase evaluation will be extensive as the buyer realizes that an important purchase (high involvement) has been made with limited information and evaluation. *Habitual and variety-seeking behaviour* involve more limited information search and evaluation owing to the reduced level of involvement – i.e. shoppers see the costs of more extensive search and evaluation exceeding the benefits. Post-purchase evaluation will also be more limited for the same reason. Habitual behaviour exhibits the most limited information search, evaluation and post-purchase evaluation, as the costs of such activities way exceed the benefits. Variety-seeking behaviour sees a higher level of information search, evaluation and post-purchase evaluation as different choices need to be considered.

Developing the SOR Model for a Retail Setting

The SOR model can be adapted to more accurately fit the shopping situation by the consideration of a number of environmental factors, shopper types, purchase behaviour and more detailed theories. Important environmental factors relate to physical and social surroundings, temporal (time) factors, task definition (shopping purpose) and the shopper's psychological state. Two extremes of shopper can be identified as those largely driven by the process (*hedonists*) and those concerned primarily with the outcome (*utilitarians*). Three broad types of purchase behaviour can be considered, based on the characteristics of the purchase process. Shoppers with a quite rigid approach are seen as *planners*, while those who have a degree of flexibility in decision-making are either *semi-impulse* or *impulse* purchasers. Two useful theories that extend the SOR model in a retail context are the Mehrabian–Russell (MR) model (1974) and the Elaboration Likelihood Model or ELM (Petty and Cacioppo 1986). The MR model adds greater detail to the response side of the SOR model by introducing positive or negative responses to the environment. The ELM model can be used to characterize the ways that shoppers are persuaded (influenced) both inside and outside the store.

Retail Environment Factors Affecting the SOR Model

Table 3.3 details the main environmental factors that can be used to add greater detail to the SOR model and apply it more effectively to the shopping situation. The first three factors largely relate to external stimuli while the two remaining factors are more concerned with the shopper.

Table 3.3 Environmental Factors Influencing Shopping Behaviour

Factor	Description
Physical surroundings	Location and physical characteristics of selling space
Social surroundings	Other shoppers or store personnel
Task definition	The shopping purpose
Psychological state	Internal characteristics of the shopper
Temporal perspective	Time factors

Source: Adapted from Belk (1975).

Physical Surroundings

Shoppers may be affected by the *physical nature of the retail environment*. It is well known that a product's packaging can convey impressions of quality, indeed packaging is often referred to as the 'the silent salesman'. The same effect may be observed for the physical characteristics of a retailer's store – i.e. size, design, cleanliness, etc. Important issues in the physical nature of a store relate to the design and appearance of the store's exterior and interior. *Exterior design* aspects such as architecture, signing and appearance maintenance have an important role to play in the formation and development of store quality perceptions, and whether the shopper visits the store or not. Indeed, a perception of poor quality may cause the shopper to postpone a store visit entirely. *Interior design* aspects relate to the overall plan for the arrangement of selling displays (layout), the presentation of the assortment (display) and background factors such as colours, textures, lighting, etc. (atmospherics). All these factors, both external and internal, will be discussed in depth in Chapter 7 on Store Design.

Social Surroundings

An individual's social surroundings comprise all *interactions* (e.g. physical, emotional, etc.) *with other members of society*. In the retail environment, this would tend to mean other shoppers or store personnel, but could also relate to non-store interactions such as those within a family or society, for example. Considering the nature of the shopping process allows two broad groups of interactions to be addressed, namely *intra-unit* and *inter-unit*. 'Unit' in this case refers to the shopping unit, or the collection of people (or the individual for a sole purchaser) involved in the shopping process. Intra-unit interactions are those that take place within the shopping unit while inter-unit interactions take place between this unit and other individuals or units. Factors affecting both types of interaction are culture, social class, reference groups and lifestyle. A specific area of research involves crowding, or the effects of a large number of shopping units on shopping behaviour. This area is covered in detail in Chapter 14 on Retail Demand Management.

Culture

Culture is the pattern of life adopted by people to help them interpret, evaluate and communicate as members of society. Behaviour is strongly influenced by culture as the 'pattern of life' also usually determines the boundaries of *acceptable behaviour*. In the retail context, cultural factors will influence shopper behaviour both inside and outside the store. Values, attitudes and beliefs may influence the perception of stores and shopping in general, as well as consumption habits. To understand the specific nature of this influence on a given group of shoppers it is necessary to realize that sub-cultures exist and have an important role. A sub-culture exists within a social group that shares the overall cultural norms of the society but retains an associated set of more tightly defined norms that allows it to be differentiated, usually on the basis of geography, ethnicity, religion or demographics. To give an example, a clothes retailer should be aware that very different behavioural norms and consumption habits exist between the young and the old. Youth culture 'imposes' a very different set of values and acceptable behaviour that must be reflected in the retail marketing approach. On a basic level, assortments will differ while more subtle differences may exist in other tactical areas such as store design and promotion, for example.

Social class

Some sort of social class system exists in most societies. The Romans divided people into 'classis' based on property and taxation, and feudal England was similarly segregated. Social classes are relatively homogenous and enduring divisions in a society, which are hierarchically ordered and whose members share similar values, interests and behaviour. In this sense, a social class is also a *sub-culture* (as described above) and can be treated in the same way. Again, common behavioural norms typically exist that have implications for retail marketing tactics. Many researchers have identified strong links between behaviour and social class, with elements such as shopping habits, choice of media and advertising exposure all being linked to class membership.

Reference group

A reference group is a group of individuals that has a direct or indirect influence on a person's attitudes or behaviour. As such, the group shares *common norms* (beliefs, attitudes and values) that regulate behaviour. In this sense, reference groups can also be considered as sub-cultures and can again be treated in the same way. Many researchers have addressed the issue of the reference or social group, classifying them on the basis of membership status, degree of formality and nature of interaction. Membership groups are those to which the individual belongs either automatically (*ascribed groups*) or has sought membership to (*acquired groups*). Individuals may wish to join other groups (*aspirational groups*) or not be associated with others (*dissociative groups*). Formal groups have a clearly defined purpose and roles while informal groups have a more casual nature. Groups with close emotional contact and face-to-face communication are primary groups while secondary groups are more impersonal and often larger.

One of the most important reference groups is the family, that can be classified (in most cases) as an ascribed primary membership group that is formal in nature. The influence of the family is considerable owing to the close interaction between members. Behaviour and attitudes are learned and reinforced, with uniformity encouraged through the family's role as a consumption unit, a purchasing unit, a financial resource, a source of information and a source of physical and emotional satisfaction. Family shopping behaviour can be highly complex, although research shows that roles tend to be adopted in both overt and covert ways. In general, all shopping units (the family is a shopping unit) contain one of five broad roles, namely influencers, deciders, buyers, users and gatekeepers. The *influencer* has a large impact on what purchases are considered, the *decider* makes the actual purchase decision, the *buyer* makes the purchase, the *user* uses the product and the *gatekeeper* controls the flow of purchase information. To give an example, suppose that a family was engaged in buying a new mobile phone for their youngest daughter. The youngest daughter would be the user, so would have a big say in what was required, but it is likely that the decider and buyer would be the parents. The eldest daughter may already have a mobile phone hence may be seen as a source of expertise and product knowledge so would be an influencer. The eldest daughter may also have an interest in ensuring that a certain type of mobile phone is purchased (maybe one of a lesser standard than her own) so may choose to be selective in the product information passed on to her parents. In this sense, the eldest daughter is acting as a gatekeeper. A retailer, therefore, has a difficult task in directing marketing efforts at a number of different, yet important, members of the family unit.

To simplify the process it is possible to show the family member that has the biggest impact on any shopping decision. This member is often referred to as the *prime mover*. Table 3.4 shows the prime mover for a range of purchases involving a husband and wife shopping unit.

Table 3.4 Prime Movers in Husband and Wife Shopping

Husband is prime mover	Joint decision	Wife is prime mover
Insurance	Furniture	Washing machines
Car	Holidays	Carpets
TV and video	Houses	Kitchenware
Meals out	Loans (mortgage)	Food
Drinks (bar or at home)	Fuel	Clothes, hers
DIY products	Holidays	Purchases for the children

Family shopping also changes over time in line with changes in needs, aspirations, relative disposable income and family composition. The family life cycle concept can provide insights into shopping habits, and is shown in Table 3.5.

Table 3.5 The Family Life Cycle

Stage in cycle	Behaviour pattern
1 Singles Young, single, not living at home	Few financial burdens, recreational spending high, basic household equipment is bought also cars
2 Childless couples Young couples, no children	Quite well off, high purchase rate, practical spending plus recreational
3 Full Nest I Youngest child under six	Home buying, little money, buy practical things and children's products
4 Full Nest II Youngest child six or over	Financial position better, buy practical goods in large pack sizes plus children's products
5 Full Nest III Older couples with dependent children	More money still, some wives work, buy better household goods and more recreational spending
6 Empty Nest I Older couples, children moved out	Home ownership at peak, money situation good, recreational spend increases, home improvements and luxuries bought
7 Empty Nest II Older couples, head of household retired	Drastic cut in income, spending reduced to replacement only
8 Solitary Survivor I One partner left, still working	Income steady, likely to sell home, spending much more limited
9 Solitary Survivor II One partner left, retired	Drastic cut in income, spending for attention, affection and security

Lifestyle

Lifestyle is an individual's pattern of living in the world as expressed by activities, interests and opinions. This pattern of living will incorporate shopping habits as well as purchasing habits in general and may be understood by a process of lifestyle modelling. The aim of lifestyle modelling is to identify those different lifestyles that exist, discover their characteristic features, determine the population groups concerned, and ultimately link products, brands or retailers to given lifestyles. Typically, an activities, interests, opinions (AIO) inventory is developed with groups of like individuals gathered together in clusters. Clusters, or *lifestyle groups*, can then be targeted with specific retail marketing tactics. In the example shown in Table 3.6, very different approaches were taken by the same women's clothing retailer to the 'Dash with cash' and 'Ritz with glitz' groups. The former were typically younger and single, desiring clothes to make an impression while the latter were older, usually married and seeking a more timeless style. Assortments, prices, location and store designs were developed accordingly.

Table 3.6 The National Magazine Clusters

Men	%[1]	Women	%[1]
Timid traditionalists	21.8	Cosy and comfortable	20.0
Brash with cash	17.1	Harassed housewife	19.6
Bullseye and beerguts	13.2	Well dressed but not obsessed	15.6
Business class	11.3	Dash with cash	14.7
Fast-lane free-stylers	10.0	Flamboyant fortysomething	9.9
Man at his best	8.5	Ritz with glitz	8.8
One foot in the grave	5.8	Forever frumpy	6.3
Beethoven and books	5.8	Grannies but not glamorous	5.3

Note: 1 Approximate percentage of the UK population.

Crowding

Crowding is the state of psychological stress that results when one's demand for space exceeds the supply (Stokols 1972). It is a subjective experience of an excessively high rate and amount of environmental stimuli leading to the belief that task performance (the shopping process) is being restricted by others or from intrusions by others into one's own personal space. The subjective element of the experience means that *perceived crowding* is a more accurate term to use as, in Stockdale's words (1978), 'crowding is in the eye of the beholder'. The most common behavioural changes under conditions of crowding are adjustments in shopping time, deviations in shopping plans, reduced levels of social contact, greater conformity to store traffic patterns, reduced levels of exploratory behaviour and the use of buying process shortcuts. Typical behaviour under conditions of crowding involves reduced shopping time, curtailed shopping plans (low-priority items ignored), limited interaction with other shoppers or staff, movement in the same direction and at the same speed as other shoppers, limited information search on potential new decisions and the use of shortcuts (e.g. brands as a cue for product quality) to speed up the purchase process. These changes in behaviour are known as *behavioural adaptation strategies* (Milgram 1970) and are covered in more detail in chapter 14, on Retail Demand Management.

A number of researchers have suggested strategies to deal with perceived crowding based largely on increasing consumer choice. Retailers could, for example, give shoppers a number of potential store starting points when consumer density is high. Other strategies relate to the provision of information, distraction and store design. Making information more easily available may allow shoppers to simplify their shopping process by cutting down the time spent on information-searching. If this simplification is enough for the shopper to regain sufficient control over the situation, the amount of purchases may not be reduced to such a large extent. Distraction aims to affect a shopper's judgement of crowding. If, for example, music is played in the store shoppers have been found to have a different perception of the environment (see Chapter 7 on Store Design for details). It can be argued that the effect of the music is to change the shopper's level of perceived control. Store design can also be modified to allow threshold consumer density to be increased and shopping to be easier under conditions of perceived crowding (see Chapter 7).

Task Definition and Psychological State

Task definition (shopping purpose) and psychological state can be dealt with together as they share similar foundations – i.e. the internal characteristics of the shopper. Shopping purpose is closely linked with involvement with different shopping tasks exhibiting different behaviour dependent on the degree of importance attached to a given task. Kahn and Schmittlein (1989) found that shoppers are habitually regular or quick in their shopping behaviour. *Regular shoppers* typically make fewer larger shopping trips and tend to spend more per trip, whereas *quick shoppers* are the opposite, typically making more trips but spending less per trip. In addition, it was suggested that two broad types of shopping trip (or task) exist that are closely linked to the regular and quick theory. *Major trips* tend to be longer in duration, less frequent, involve higher levels of expenditure, satisfy a range of shopping needs and incorporate a mix of planned, semi-impulse and impulse purchase behaviour (see later in this chapter for more details on purchase behaviour). *Fill-in trips* are shorter in duration, more frequent, involve lower levels of expenditure, tend to satisfy a more limited range of needs (usually pressing) and primarily involve more planned purchase behaviour – i.e. planned and semi-impulse.

Involvement will have a large impact on observed behaviour and is closely linked to the shopping task. Typically low-involvement situations such as grocery retail (high purchase frequency, low perceived risk) see different shopping behaviour to a high-involvement situation such as expensive jewellery retail (low purchase frequency, high perceived risk) – i.e. as involvement increases shoppers move to increasingly 'complex' behaviour. It is still likely that shoppers will be habitually regular or quick in their behaviour but the time frame will tend to lengthen as involvement increases. Financial pressures may also preclude major trip behaviour as expensive purchases may need to be spread over a period of time rather than dealt with at the same time. As an example, a shopper looking to upgrade all their white goods (cooker, fridge, dishwasher, washing machine, etc.) may choose to spread those purchases over a one-year period rather than buy all items on the same day. In Kahn and Schmittlein's framework this would mean that shoppers tend towards fill-in behaviour as involvement increases. In reality, major and fill-in shopping behaviour is best used to explain low- rather than high-involvement shopping.

Psychological state has already been mentioned in the coverage of the SOR model (see psychological factors) and relates to the fundamentals of perception, learning, motivation, personality and attitudes. Sociological factors are also a part of the psychological state and have been covered earlier in this section.

Perception

Perception is important as it relates to *stimulus detection and reception* – i.e. how well the individual can detect and decode a given stimulus. To give an example, if a retailer were to display a special offer sign, its effectiveness would depend on how easily the shopper could see it (stimulus detection) and then understand what it meant (stimulus decoding). Clearly if the sign could not be seen and/or understood the special offer sign would have failed to fulfil its purpose. Individuals have different levels of detection (eyesight differs, for example), and tend to be selective in what they decode. Typically, individuals are more likely to decode a stimulus if it is relevant to them – i.e. is linked to a need that they currently have.

Learning

Learning relates to the way that individuals simplify the task of responding to the multiplicity of things that are going on around them. As individuals, we are constantly bombarded with a huge number of stimuli that we cannot possibly hope to treat on a conscious individual basis. To deal with this situation, we store up a *memory bank* that allows us to quickly categorize a stimulus and adopt a previously successful response, thus minimizing thinking time. The task is then to consider if the stimulus is the same as before or different (these processes are linked to the concepts of generalization and discrimination, respectively). If different, no previous successful response exists, and the full SOR process is adopted. To give an example, the majority of food shoppers when visiting their regular supermarket tend to follow the same route, give or take a few exceptions, around that store. Over time, the shopper will have built a *mental map* of that store, linking store areas and product assortment areas. Rather than wandering around the store aimlessly, shoppers will work to a mental route map that takes in all those areas of the store that are necessary. The shopper has 'learned their way around the store', or built up a memory bank of responses to past searches for particular items. Now consider a shopper new to a given store, or more annoyingly a situation where the shopper's regular store has had a layout change. An accurate mental map is not available, so the shopper has to go back to square one and search the entire store. The process is often frustrating for many shoppers and may not build the positive attitudes about the store that the retailer would like.

Motivation

Motivation is based on motives, or needs that are sufficiently pressing to drive the individual to act. Two sorts of motive exist, *biogenic* and *psychogenic*. The former arise from physiological states of tension such as hunger, thirst and discomfort. The latter arise from psychological states of tension such as pride, esteem, love and belonging. Much of the theory of motivation was developed from the early work of a number of psychologists such as Freud, Maslow and Herzberg. Freud stated that a person's behaviour was driven at a subconscious level by the many repressed urges amassed through the formative years and thereafter in the process of social conformation. Maslow stated that human needs (motives) could be divided into groups and ranked in order of importance. The *basic survival needs* (hunger, thirst) were the most important and would always have top priority. The remaining needs could then be ranked in importance, forming a total of five levels. Maslow stated that an individual would be motivated by the most basic need that remained unsatisfied, moving to a higher level only when satisfaction had occurred. Herzberg developed the *two-factor theory of motivation*, proposing that motivation resulted from combinations of positive and negative influences, satisfiers and dissatisfiers respectively. Put simply, an individual would be drawn to satisfiers and repelled by dissatisfiers. In the Western retail system, biogenic or survival needs are usually satisfied, so shoppers tend to be motivated by psychological factors.

Personality

Personality can be defined as those distinguishing psychological characteristics that lead an individual to respond in a relatively consistent way over time to the surrounding environment. Theories of personality are numerous and often conflicting. Two important areas for the retailer are *personality traits* and the shopper's *self-concept*. Traits are identifiable personality characteristics that relate directly to response, for example, extrovert or introvert versus sociable. Every individual's personality is made up of many traits although a smaller group of traits dominate. These key traits are relatively stable, are assumed to influence behaviour and can be identified through personality testing methods. Retailers' assortments, prices, promotions and store designs can reflect certain personality traits, thus encouraging a certain sort of behaviour (i.e. purchase). A shopper's self-concept is linked to a quote by Martineau (1958), 'everything we buy helps us to convey to others the kind of people we are, helps us identify ourselves to the world at large'. The self-concept is an individual's mental picture of themselves based on the traits that the individual thinks she or he has. If a product fits this mental picture, purchase likelihood increases. It is also the case that individuals have a mental picture of how others see them (*others' self-concept*) and how they would like to be seen (*ideal self-concept*). All three mental pictures have a strong influence on shopping behaviour and the purchases made.

Attitudes and Beliefs

Attitudes and beliefs are thoughts based knowledge, opinion and faith, and influence the way that any stimulus (a retailer's assortment, price, store, etc.) is processed by providing a short-cut – i.e. responses are either based on *generalization* or *discrimination* (see section on perception). Attitudes and beliefs are developed on a wide range of issues both serious and trivial. Attitudes and beliefs, like personality, are enduring and take a long time to change. For this reason, attitudes and beliefs tend to lead individuals to behave in a fairly consistent way towards a range of stimuli. From a retail perspective, attitudes and beliefs may relate to types of location ('out-of-town stores are better'), retail format ('discount retailers have sub-standard assortments'), price ('retailer *X* always has higher prices then retailer *Y*') as well as any other part of the retail tactical mix or strategic considerations. An understanding of attitudes and beliefs, leads to a better understanding of behaviour and certainly identifies shoppers who have a negative view of a given retailer.

The Temporal Perspective

The temporal perspective is concerned with issues relating to *time*. The main areas of research cover shopping times, trip duration, trip frequency and time constraints. Retailers are keen to discover if shoppers have habitual shopping times in order to map out demand at all times throughout the day. Knowledge of this 'demand map' can then assist in retailing issues such as stock replenishment, staffing levels and store design. *Trip duration* and *frequency* are also important factors in assessing the nature of shopper demand and can have benefits in similar areas to demand mapping. Time constraints are important as they have a fundamental effect on shopper behaviour. Shoppers in a rush exhibit different characteristics to those with plenty of time. As always, retailers are keen to understand shopper behaviour in order to develop an appropriate set of retail marketing tactics.

Shopping Times

Research has shown that shoppers are often habitual in their choice of shopping time. Influential factors in the development of this habit are personal commitments, shopper perceptions of crowding, financial issues and the level of involvement. East *et al.* (1994), in a survey of grocery shopping, found, for example, that 89 per cent of shoppers habitually chose the same day to shop with work commitments being cited as the major reason in 21 per cent of these cases, financial issues 18 per cent, proximity to the weekend 34 per cent and crowding 16 per cent. Habitual days earlier in the week (Monday–Wednesday) were associated mainly with crowd avoidance, whereas the end of the week (Thursday and Friday) was linked to financial issues and the proximity to the weekend (pay or pension days). Weekends were selected mainly because of non-working days. Interestingly, 80 per cent of shoppers were able to change the day but the vast majority chose not to. East also found that 67 per cent of shoppers habitually shopped at the same time of the day, with work commitments accounting for 18 per cent of cases, fitting in with other journeys or shopping trips 24 per cent and crowding 25 per cent. Shopping early in the day avoided crowds and fitted with work or other journeys. Early or late afternoon shopping times were selected to fit with other journeys or work commitments. Again, the majority of shoppers could change their shopping time (71 per cent) but most chose not to.

Personal commitments may develop habits, particularly if shoppers seek to incorporate their shopping trips into a daily or weekly routine. Shoppers may fit shopping trips around work commitments and may visit stores by stopping off on the way to or from their place of work, or may make trips during break periods (e.g. midday). Store location decisions may be affected by this factor as a site close to major employment areas or close to major routes serving these areas may increase shopper traffic. Perception of crowding is another important factor in the selection of shopping times. Shopping trips to low-consumer-density retail situations (see Chapter 14 on crowding) are heavily influenced by knowledge of the busiest times.

Financial issues relate primarily to personal disposable income – or, more accurately, the availability of personal disposable income. Shopping trips are often made on a certain day or at a certain time in the month owing to the effect of income cycles. Shoppers relying on income related to work commitments or state benefits usually receive payments on a regular but infrequent basis. Shopping behaviour may, therefore, be influenced by these income cycles, with trips scheduled at times when money is available. In the UK, it was historically the case that many benefits or salaries were paid weekly, often on a Thursday or Friday. This being the case, shopping trips were often scheduled for these two days, or afterwards, thus accounting for high shopper traffic from Thursday to Saturday. While it is true that this situation has changed in recent times, East's survey mentioned above still found that 64 per cent of grocery shopping trips were made in this period.

Trip Duration

A number of factors affect the time spent on any given shopping trip, many of which have already been discussed in this section – i.e. psychological state, sociological issues, task definition (and involvement), shopper profile (demographics). Research by McDonald (1994) identifies three broad categories of shopper on the basis of trip duration (see Table 3.7).

Table 3.7 Shoppers' Temporal Characteristics

Shopper category	Search time (hr)	Purchase time (hr)	Post-purchase time (hr)	Characteristics
Routine manager (50% of sample)	0.3	2.6	0.2	Moderate sense of purpose, organized, seek convenience and time savings
Aimless wanderer (37% of sample)	4.1	3.3	0.8	Little purpose, not organized, not routine-orientated
Purposeful organizer (13% of sample)	0.1	2.3	0.1	Strong sense of purpose, highly organized, goal-orientated

Table 3.7 shows that aimless wanderers tend to make the longest shopping trips, the majority of the difference with routine managers and purposeful organizers being accounted for by pre-purchase activity – i.e. information search and evaluation. Aimless wanderers also have the most random approach to shopping, that may account for the longer trip duration. Purposeful organizers are the most efficient shoppers, so tend to have the shortest trip duration. Routine managers lie between the other two categories although they have more in common with purposeful organizers owing to their level of planning and organization. The key factors determining the profile of a given category are the same as those mentioned earlier (psychological state, sociological issues, task definition/involvement, shopper demographic profile), although accurate profiling of each is very difficult owing to the complex nature of the shopping process. Retailers should, therefore, be aware of the different categories and prepare appropriate strategies to accommodate them. Purposeful organizers will require high levels of convenience and will seek to minimize time inside the store. This means that the retailer only has a limited time in which this category of shopper can be influenced, although it is a less important issue, as this category of shopper will tend to buy to a shopping list and be largely resistant to influence. Retailers have considerably more time to influence aimless wanderers as the largest part of their shopping time is spent on search activity. In this case, the retail tactical mix will potentially have a big influence, so aspects such as store design, in-store promotion, assortment width and depth will be important. As before, routine managers tend to lie somewhere between purposeful organizers and aimless wanderers.

Trip Frequency

Trip frequency is determined by many of the same factors identified for trip duration. Purchase frequency is strongly linked with involvement, with infrequent purchases typically attracting higher levels of involvement. Taking the reverse argument, it is reasonable to assume that low-involvement retail situations such as grocery will see significantly higher trip frequency than high-involvement situations such as furniture, cars, etc. Useful concepts can also be drawn from research on shopping task definition (see earlier in this chapter), particularly that relating to major and fill-in trips, and regular and quick shoppers. To recap, regular shoppers typically make fewer larger shopping trips whereas quick shoppers are the opposite, typically making a larger number of smaller trips.

Time Constraints

A range of adaption behaviour is observed for shoppers under time pressure that shares many similarities with behaviour under conditions of crowding. In the case of crowding, shoppers found it difficult to deal with the shopping trip in its original format, so sought to make simplifications. In the case of time pressure, shoppers also cannot deal with the shopping trip as originally planned and look to make similar simplifications. The major simplifications made are to *abbreviate exploratory behaviour* (information search and evaluation) and disregard non-essential purchases. The results of these simplifications are that purchases are often made by memory, so only the most frequently purchased or most urgent items are considered. Purchase accuracy often falls as quantities may be incorrect or products are bought that are not required but are in the shopper's memory. Many of the same issues apply as already covered for crowding and retailer approaches to managing time-constrained customers also share marked similarities.

Shopper Types

Two distinct shopping behaviours can be identified, namely purely *hedonic* and purely *utilitarian*. The two are opposite ends of a spectrum of behaviour that describes how the population as a whole behaves when shopping. It should be noted that few shoppers will exhibit such extremes of behaviour but will tend to lie towards either the hedonic or utilitarian end of the scale. Observed behaviour can be compared only on a retail situation-by-situation basis, but it is certainly true that individuals tend to favour one end of the scale or the other. The difference can be summed up in a useful, if simplistic, manner as joy versus pain. Utilitarians tend to see shopping as a chore that must be undertaken whilst hedonists tend to see shopping as an enjoyable activity in itself. Hedonists can often be said to buy to shop whilst utiliarians shop to buy. Quotes made by shoppers add extra detail to these definitions,

> Utilitarian: 'I like to get in and out with a minimum amount of time wasted ... shopping is like a mission, if find what I'm looking for, I'm satisfied – mission accomplished.' (Babin, Darden and Griffin 1994)
>
> Hedonist: 'It's a high ... it's a thrill. It gives you a lift to buy something fun'. (Babin, Darden and Griffin 1994)

Table 3.8 summarizes the key characteristics of the two shopper types.

Table 3.8 Characteristics of Utilitarian and Hedonist Shopper Types

Utilitarian	Hedonist
► A means to an end	► An end in itself
► Seen in the same light as work	► Seen in the same light as leisure
► Usually deliberate and effective	► Can be unstructured and inefficient
► Information collected in thorough manner if no purchase made	► Experience valuable and enjoyable even if no purchase made
► Shopping has rational worth (benefits of products purchased predominate)	► Shopping has emotional worth (freedom, fantasy, escapism)
► Often shorter trip duration	► Often longer trip duration
► Expenditure levels vary, as do levels of loyalty, trip frequency and shopping group composition	► Expenditure levels vary, as do levels of loyalty, trip frequency and shopping group composition

Source: Adapted from Babin, Darden and Griffin (1994).

Purchase Behaviour

The actual nature of the purchase itself can also provide valuable insight into shopper behaviour. Rather like the earlier section on shopper types, extremes of purchase behaviour can be identified as impulse and planned or largely unconsidered and largely considered acts, respectively. Cobb and Hoyer (1986) classify such purchase types using the two measures of intent to buy the product category and intent to buy the specific brand or product type. On this basis, impulse can be classified as an absence of either intent, while planned is the opposite case where both types of intent exist. An intermediate type, called 'semi-impulse', can also be identified, where an intent to buy the product category exists without an associated intent to buy a specific brand or product type. In more simple terms, an impulse purchase happens when a purchase decision is made entirely *within the store itself.* A planned purchase occurs when a buyer's mind is largely made up *before entering the store,* while a semi-impulse purchase occurs when the buyer had decided to buy a given type of purchase outside the store then makes the final decision of specifically what to buy in the store. Figure 3.3 illustrates Cobb and Hoyer's classification.

Given that impulse, semi-impulse and planned acts relate to actual purchasing or decision making, consideration of buyer decision making theory can add extra detail to the description of the three purchase types. The basic buyer decision process, as discussed earlier in this chapter, contains the five stages of problem recognition, followed by information search, evaluation of alternatives, purchase decision and post-purchase behaviour. The nature of the three purchase types means that different weight will be given to these five stages. These weightings along with other features of impulse, semi-impulse and planned purchasing are detailed in Table 3.9.

Table 3.9 Characteristics of Planned, Semi-Impulse and Impulse Behaviour

Impulse	Semi-impulse	Planned
▶ Problem recognition in-store ▶ Information search very limited ▶ Evaluation of alternatives brief ▶ Purchase decision made with limited information ▶ Post-purchase behaviour varies ▶ Low/medium point-of-purchase time ▶ Medium/high brand preference ▶ Moderate purchase frequency ▶ Often pick first brand seen ▶ Little time spent searching in-store ▶ Low/medium level of in-store deliberation	▶ Problem recognition outside store ▶ Information search and evaluation varies in extent (both in-store and out) ▶ Purchase decision usually made with more information (than impulse) ▶ Post-purchase behaviour varies ▶ Highest point-of-purchase time ▶ Weakest brand preference ▶ Lowest purchase frequency ▶ Rarely pick first brand seen ▶ Longest time spent searching in-store ▶ Highest level of in-store deliberation	▶ Problem recognition outside store ▶ Information search and evaluation varies in extent (largely outside store) ▶ Purchase decision usually made with more information (than impulse) ▶ Post-purchase behaviour varies ▶ Lowest point-of-purchase time ▶ Strong brand preference ▶ Highest purchase frequency ▶ Often pick first brand seen ▶ Least time spent searching in-store ▶ Lowest level of in-store deliberation

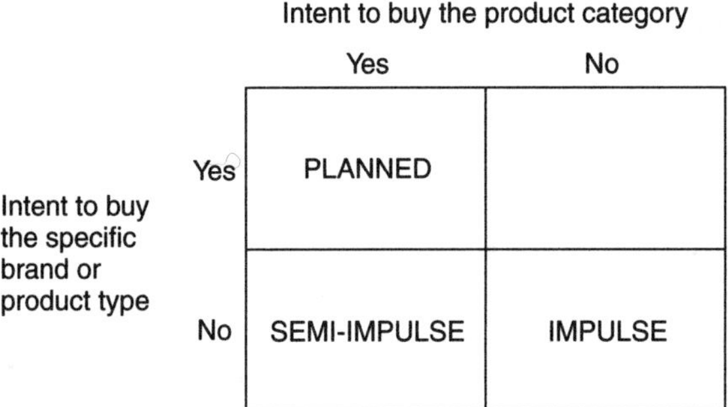

Figure 3.3 Cobb and Hoyer's classification (1986)
Source: Adapted from Cobb, C.J. and Hoyer, W.D., Planned Impulse Purchase Behaviour, *Journal of Retailing*, Vol. 62, No. 4, pp.384–409. Used by permission.

As an example of the three purchase types, suppose three shoppers set out to buy something to wear. The planned purchaser would have a specific item of clothing in mind before the shopping trip (Levi jeans, for example) and would seek out shops that offered that item. The semi-impulse purchaser would have a type of clothing in mind (a jacket, say) but would not know which type or brand. The shopper would then look in shops that sold jackets. The impulse purchaser may or may not even have thought about buying clothes, but would certainly have no idea what type of clothes were required. The shopper would then visit a wide range of stores and decide in the store if or what to buy.

More Detailed Theories

Three main areas of research can be considered to build upon the shopper behaviour material presented to this point. The Mehrabian–Russell model (1974) introduces the concepts of approach (positive) and avoidance (negative) behaviour, as well as the precursors of pleasure and arousal. Environmental stimuli trigger levels of pleasure and arousal that in turn lead to either approach or avoidance behaviour. The Elaboration Likelihood Model (Petty and Cacioppo 1986) can be used to explain shopper persuasion and, hence, is linked to decision making. The central route involves persuasion based on a systematic consideration of the facts while the peripheral route concerns persuasion based on less systematic consideration. Both routes are influenced by environmental (e.g. store) factors, although the nature and extent of influence varies. Mood states (e.g. Swinyard 1993; Donovan *et al.* 1994) are present in virtually all retail situations, have a huge impact on shopping patterns and become increasingly important as involvement increases. More specifically, mood states can affect buying patterns, purchase type and timing, level of expenditure, shopping trip duration and the level and nature of information search and evaluation. More detailed consideration of the Mehrabian–Russell and Elaboration Likelihood Models, as well as mood states, is contained in Chapter 7 on Store Design.

Conclusions

> During the 1980s, shopping had become a national sport, a recreational pursuit grounded in a consumer culture characterised by conspicuous consumption, frivolous spending and demands for instant gratification. (Betts and McGoldrick 1996)

The above quote stresses the importance of shopping in the national culture of many Western countries. The behaviour of shoppers is no less important to the retailer as it fundamentally affects both tactical and strategic marketing decision making. The basic behavioural models such as Stimulus–Organism–Response (SOR) show that shopper behaviour is influenced by both internal (shopper characteristics) and external (environmental stimuli) factors. In essence, the shopper is confronted with a barrage of stimuli from the environment (the store) and reacts in a uniquely individual way. The retailer can control environmental stimuli to a certain extent and can discover a number of shopper characteristics. Taking these two factors together, it can be seen that retailers may be able to influence behaviour.

Taking a step back, shoppers can be characterized on the basis of their observed behaviour and attitudes. The hedonic–utilitarian continuum states that all shoppers can be placed between the two extremes of 'shopping to buy' (utilitarian) and 'shopping to shop' (hedonic) or outcome and process orientations, respectively. It is apparent that these two extremes exhibit vastly different shopper behaviours and present very different challenges to the retail marketer. Looking in a little more detail, shopper behaviour can also be affected by the store itself, the people within that store and time factors. The effects of the store are discussed later in this text (see Chapter 7 on Store Design), while social factors relate to store personnel, other shoppers and the shopping group itself. Issues relating to store personnel will be discussed later, interaction with other shoppers can relate to reference group effects or crowding. In both cases, shopper behaviour can be altered. Other shoppers may influence behaviour owing to the desire to fit in or be different, while crowding can increase feelings of dissatisfaction and pressure. Time also has an effect, with many shoppers exhibiting habitual shopping times and/or days, different behaviour under time pressure and typical shopping trip durations and frequencies.

Purchase behaviour is also an important issue for retailers owing to the revenue implications. Three broad types of purchase behaviour exist ranging from little (if any) thought (impulse), moderate thought (semi-impulse) and extensive thought (planned). The implications for the retailer relate again to retail marketing and more specifically decision making. Planned decisions are usually made outside the store, semi-impulse both outside and inside and impulse usually inside. If retailers wish to influence these decisions, such knowledge is valuable. Influence is possible via all the tactical elements that will be discussed later in this text. The nature of this influence can be considered by utilizing more detailed behavioural theories such as the Mehrabian–Russell model (see

Chapter 7 on Store Design). What is undoubtedly true though, is that shopper behaviour *is* highly complex, *is* difficult to accurately predict and definitely *is* of great importance to the retailer.

References and Further Reading

Babin, B.J., Darden, W.R. and Griffin, M. (1994) Work and/or Fun: Measuring Hedonic and Utilitarian Shopping Value, *Journal of Consumer Research*, 20, 4, 644–57.

Belk, R.W. (1975) Situation Variables and Consumer Behaviour, *Journal of Consumer Research*, 2, 157–63.

Betts, E.J. and McGoldrick, P.J. (1996) Consumer Behaviour and the 'Retail Sales' – Modelling the Development of an 'Attitude Problem', *European Journal of Marketing*, 30, 8, 40–58.

Cobb, C.J. and Hoyer, W.D. (1986) Planned Versus Impulse Purchase Behavior, *Journal of Retailing*, 62, 4, 384–409.

Donovan, R.J., Rossiter, J.R., Marcoolyn, G. and Nesdale, A. (1994) Store Atmosphere and Purchasing Behaviour, *Journal of Retailing*, 70, 3, 283–94.

East, R., Lomax, W., Willson, G. and Harris, P. (1994) Decision Making and Habit in Shopping Times, *European Journal of Marketing*, 28, 4, 56–71.

Eroglu, S.A. and Machleit, K.A. (1990) An Empirical Study of Retail Crowding: Antecedents and Consequences, *Journal of Retailing*, 66, 2, 301–21.

Hui, M.K. and Bateson, J.E.G. (1991) Perceived Control and the Effects of Crowding and Consumer Choice on the Service Experience, *Journal of Consumer Research*, 18, 2, 174–85

Kahn, B.E. and Schmittlein, D. (1989) Shopping Trip Behaviour: An Empirical Investigation, *Marketing Letters*, 1, 1, 55–64.

Martineau, P. (1958) The Personality of the Retail Store, *Harvard Business Review*, 36, 47–55.

McDonald, W.J. (1994) Time Use in Shopping: The Role of Personal Characteristics, *Journal of Retailing*, 70, 4 345–66.

Mehrabian, A. and Russell, J.A. (1974) *An Approach to Environmental Psychology*, MIT Press, Boston.

Milgram, S. (1970) The Experience of Living in Cities, *Science*, 167, 1464–8.

Petty, R.E. and Cacioppo, J.T. (1986) 'The Elaboration Likelihood Model of Persuasion', *Advances in Experimental Social Psychology*, 10, ed. L Berkowitz, Academic Press, New York.

Stockdale, J.E. (1978) Crowding: Determinants and Effects, *Advances in Experimental and Social Psychology*, 11, Academic Press, New York, 197–245.

Stokols, D. (1972) On the Distinction Between Density and Crowding: Some Implications for Future Research, *Psychological Review*, 79, 275–7.

Swinyard, W.R. (1993) The Effects of Mood, Involvement, and Quality of Store Experience on Shopping Intentions, *Journal of Consumer Research*, 20, 271–80.

Key Marketing Factors in Retailing

CHAPTER 4

This chapter:

- Explains how an organization is market-led
- Defines the factors in customer buying decisions
- Delineates retailers' strategic decisions on the retail offering

Key Marketing Factors in Retailing

Introduction

There are a lot of very good reasons for suggesting that an organization should be *market-led*, that is all its activities should be planned with due cognizance of the market conditions that exist at any time. But in order to be successful it is usually necessary for an organization to be proactive with regards to its *marketing*. This means that all decisions that are made regarding those elements that the company can control should be effective in attempting to lead rather than follow market trends. It is not enough to simply be in tune with a market, successful organizations also offer something extra, that is the difference between attracting customers and thriving rather than just surviving. In particular new retailers who do not offer any reasons for shoppers to switch from existing suppliers are never likely to succeed.

The buying decisions made by customers will involve a complex group of factors. They will certainly include issues regarding the perceived match between an offer and the underlying needs of that purchaser. But customers are likely to become more deeply involved in some purchase decisions while giving little attention to others. From the retailer's position it is necessary to gain the *attention* of the customer and at least ensure that an offer is included in the customers' *evoked* set of acceptable alternatives.

There are times where the *choice of retailer* is more important than the actual choice of product. This is because there are many occasions where customers wish to buy more than one product and therefore have to consider groups of purchases rather than a single item. This is certainly true with regards choice of a particular supermarket (Asda, Tesco, Sainsburys or ...) as a source of major grocery purchasing. Of course there are other situations where the product choice is critical, but even then the choice of retail supplier often becomes an important issue within the overall buying decision.

In Chapter 1 it was stated that retailers have to take strategic decisions regarding where they wish to operate. These will include decisions on the target customers that they hope to attract. Directly dependent on the strategic choices will be the tactical decisions within the retailer's marketing mix. Both are critical, and both of these can be considered within the concept of a '*Total Product Offering*'. There are many definitions of a 'product' as an all-embracing concept within marketing. Perhaps the most useful is Dibb *et al.* (1997), who suggest that:

> A product is everything, both favourable and unfavourable, that is received in an exchange. It is a complexity of tangible and intangible attributes, including functional, social and psychological utilities or benefits.

Retail marketing can be focused on any of the elements that make up a total retail product offering. The emphasis has moved since 1970. In the 1970s *location* and *price*, 'the *right* place at the *right* price', were considered critical. In the 1980s *design, branding,* and *service* were promoted although location remained a priority. In the 1990s *loyalty schemes* became prominent. Further initiatives will, undoubtedly, occur in the future, but all the previous aspects remain important areas in the complex attempt of retailers to achieve success for themselves and satisfaction for their customers.

For a retailer the 'total product offering' includes the following eight elements that were listed at the end of Chapter 1. These form four natural groupings:

1 LOCATION AND PERCEIVED IMAGE
- Physical/virtual location
- Retail image, position and reputation

2 INTERNAL ENVIRONMENT AND CORE PRODUCT
- Internal atmosphere/ environment
- Range/assortment of goods offered

3 IN-STORE STIMULI
- Relative price/value perception
- Promotional effectiveness
- Service levels, both during and after sales

4 RELATIONSHIP ISSUES AND BUILDING LOYALTY
- Strength of any on-going relationships that might exist.

From a retailer perspective every aspect of the total product must be evaluated, although some are strategic decisions with long-term consequences, and others more short-term tactics. It could be said that the level of customer satisfaction is affected by everything in the total offering, which covers everything that takes place in the *interaction between a buyer and a supplier*. Every retail purchase is as much a feature of the retail environment and the people involved in delivering the service, as it is dependent upon the benefits provided by the 'core' product offered. In particular, the quality of any relationship encounter must be included in any consideration of a total offering. This could be almost as important to the satisfaction received as the actual tangible purchase item.

While it is the complete offering that is of importance to a customer, they might allow one positive feature to compensate for a less good attribute. For instance there could be a trade off in that some customers are happy to receive a basic service, maybe buying from an impersonal out-of-town warehouse if they can benefit from low prices. Other customers would prefer to have more attention at the point-of-sale accepting that this might involve paying a higher price. It is interesting to consider the success of companies such as IKEA when evaluating the important factors in the retail marketing mix. All retailers should compare the cost of providing each specific element of their marketing mix with the effect that element has in enhancing the total offering as perceived by customers.

Example

The decisions taken in April 2000 by Barclays Bank to close 171 branch offices in rural areas (representing less than 1 per cent of retail customers) received a lot of adverse publicity. While it is probable that these were low-profit assets that did not fit in with a strategy for the twenty-first century for an international banking group, the effect on the total image of Barclays Bank was, at least in the short-term, highly damaging.

Location and Perceived Image

Physical/Virtual Location

Retail history shows how many developments took place because retailers located close to potential customers. This action was in response to the retailers' role as the final link in the supply network providing *place* and *time* utility to consumers. There is no doubt that a well-chosen location can lead to increased numbers of shoppers and also have a significant effect on consumer purchasing behaviour. As has already been mentioned, the need for retailers to chase customers and locate near to large groups has now changed. It is now sufficient to attract customers into a particular retail location and, because of the availability of cars and other flexible transport, many consumers will travel to dedicated places to seek out specific retail outlets. In addition, both old technology (mail and telephone) and new technology (the Internet), have brought countless opportunities for customers to shop from remote locations.

It would be wrong to assume that *all* potential shoppers are able to participate in *all* such developments. There are consumers who do not own cars, or for some reason cannot travel long distances to shop. The penetration of computer ownership might be growing fast, but there will always be some consumers who cannot afford the hardware or who do not wish to utilize a virtual shopping location. In addition, for certain classes of product, there are reasons why some new channels are not necessarily the best way of obtaining an item.

The traditional retail marketing mix was described as '*Place; Place; Place; and Place.*' It is still necessary for a product to be 'conveniently' accessible as a prerequisite for a trading exchange to be possible. However the concept of '*Place*' must be redefined. When a shopper visits a Web site location it must be viewed as similar in many ways to the act of going to a retail market in the nearby town. It is not the need for a local 'marketplace' that is crucial but it is the existence of an accessible 'marketspace' that is now required. This 'marketspace' must be compatible with the *lifestyle* and *behaviour* of the target customer.

Greater understanding of a customer and their 'activity cycle' will lead to a wide definition of *Place* based on the test of availability for that specific customer. Such an understanding should ensure that the correct attention is given to this key factor in retail success. But this knowledge must be compared with the *type of product* that is to be offered. The examples below should indicate why this must also be considered:

- For a 'shopping good', e.g. a new CD player, consumers might 'go to shop', visiting many different locations, including the Internet.
- For an 'emergency item', e.g. a replacement windscreen for a car, the retailer must be contacted, often by telephone, but will usually have to 'come to supply' at the scene of the problem.
- Finally, for an 'impulse purchase product', say a chocolate bar, it is essential that the item is widely available in convenient (physical) locations at the specific time when a desire could be present. For some impulse products the location could be a 'virtual' market, as a bargain offer of (say) a cheap airflight could easily be advertised on an e-mail home page.

Each of these categories requires a different definition of '*Place*' in order to lead to retail success.

There is a further consideration with regards the physical location of retail outlets that does not affect either mail-order or Internet retailing. This is the general perception of the *neighbourhood* in which the store is situated. Some small stores might find it advantageous to be near outlets that attract appropriate shoppers, especially as there is some evidence to suggest that many shopping trips are made as part of a more general outing maybe to/from work or while taking children to school. The image of the area and the surrounding retail and other businesses are just as important as the accessibility. It could be beneficial because of a sense of identity, perhaps being located near other similar outlets such as the Savile Row area of London known for exclusive tailoring, or the Sparkbrook area of Birmingham where many of the best Balti restaurants are to be found. Alternatively it could be a decision to find premises in a new retail development such as Bluewater in Kent, where the overall quality of the stores attracts a desired segment of shoppers.

Location choices are the most strategic of all retail marketing decisions. Once a location has been chosen it will be retained for some period of time. This is especially true for a multiple retailer trying to grow by opening new stores in new locations. There are a number of key issues that should be considered:

- For instance the decision may focus only on *certain kinds of sites*. For this, the retail organization would narrow down the choice of potential sites to identify those that fit certain criteria – e.g. size (selling space), type (city centre, satellite, new), nature (incremental, planned) or prior usage (pre-existing, brownfield, greenfield).
- Alternatively the decision may be based on an attempt to *avoid direct competition* and thereby acquire a 'local monopoly'. This so-called *'avoidance'* strategy might involve trade agreements, joint ventures or other co-operative approaches. In many new retail parks and shopping centres the developers often offer attractive financial incentives to high-profile retailers who can help build traffic (customer visits). Generally these are accepted but with the additional assurance that no directly competing store will be allowed in; hence a particular grocery supermarket (e.g. Tesco) or department store (e.g. Debenham) might gain a real advantage. But a local monopoly might also arise simply by being the first company to set up in a location, as in the example below.

Example

During the 1980s the Early Learning company, who offer educational toys and other items in the UK, was trying to move from its initial mail-order style of operating to establishing retail shops in every major conurbation. The company postulated that there was room in the market for only one company such as theirs, and decided to be the first to any appropriate location. They believed, with real evidence, that if there was an Early Learning shop in a town then they could dominate the niche market and no competitor would set up in close proximity to them, so they were able to 'own' the marketspace.

- Location decisions may be taken for strategic reasons related to *competitive issues* rather than totally 'rational' reasons. A retailer might adopt a quite aggressive approach in order to increase its market share or decrease the share of a competitor (e.g. new stores located close to the flagship stores of a competitor may affect that competitor's sales performance). Defensive approaches may also be undertaken in response to competitors' actions.

But, as suggested by Bennison, Clarke and Pal (1995), locations should be reviewed regularly to check whether they are still *appropriate to the future*:

> locational decision making involves not only the planning of new sites, but also the management of existing ones to maximise the effectiveness of a store portfolio.

Multiple retailers must be concerned with maintaining or improving the *overall collective performance* from all their stores (i.e. the *store portfolio*).

Key decisions have to be made at the strategic level concerning the breadth and depth of the overall store portfolio. Specifically, store portfolio size considerations relate to selling space increases or decreases. Increases may be achieved by adding further stores to the portfolio, either by acquisition or the construction of new stores. Decreases can be achieved by store closures or divestment of less profitable outlets.

Sometimes it is very difficult to find suitable new locations that improve the competitive position and help achieve organic growth. However it is sometimes possible to *acquire* stores from other retailers or to *take over* a smaller rival. Acquiring existing stores not only facilitates growth but it also overcomes some planning permission problems. However it may not produce sites of an ideal size, nature or location. Looking at the UK grocery retail sector again, it can be argued that the problems faced by Somerfields after their acquisition of Kwik Save were directly related to the poor locations of many of the new stores. On the other hand, one of the main reasons for Tesco's ascent to market leadership was the take over of the William Low supermarket chain, following on from a series of well-chosen acquisitions over the previous decade.

Retail Image and Positioning

Positioning has famously been described as the 'battle for a customer's mind' (Ries and Trout 1983). 'Positioning' is the marketing term that is used to describe the view a customer has regarding the *image of a particular offering*. It is important to take a cognitive approach when considering the issue of retailer image/positioning. The image relies more on the perception of the customer than it does on the messages put out by the supplier. The overall perception that a customer has regarding a particular retail organization will have a significant effect upon the purchasing behaviour. If a retail store is thought to be rather 'basic' it might attract customers who equate that with no frills, low price. Alternatively the Harrods department store in Knightsbridge has an upmarket image that leads to a subjective opinion regarding the products offered and the level of prices charged.

A retailer's image will be affected by an amalgam of the physical environment; apparent atmosphere; convenience; types of shoppers using the stores; merchandise available; service levels; and many other dimensions both real and perceived. One of the most important cues for shoppers, at both a conscious and an unconscious level is the prices that are being charged. For instance it is common for people looking for a restaurant to study the menus and prices displayed outside before venturing in. In many cases the position/image will be based on a combination of fact, experience, knowledge, opinion and rumour. It is as likely to be the result of 'word-of-mouth' comments from friends or acquaintances as it is based on personal experience. In fact personal experience can be a poor determinant since it might be based on a single visit. The possible variability that can occur in the service encounters on any visit could lead to widely different views about a single store.

The image of any retail outlet is very personal to each individual customer. It is developed over time, with the retailer giving inputs in the form of both communications and actions that are then interpreted by the customer. The customer evaluates these messages in a subjective way, adds other personal or acquired knowledge and then forms or modifies an opinion regarding the retailer.

In the early stages of a multiple retailer's development, expansion typically takes the form of rolling out the same store concept (retail offering/fascia) throughout a defined geographic area. This will benefit the retailer by building on its positive features in a consistent manner. It will also help the development of the retailer's image by reaching a greater number of potential customers. To give an example, Morrisons, the Yorkshire-based grocery retailer, is currently developing duplicate stores outside its traditional area of strength in the north of England.

A *'retailer image'* can evolve into a strong 'brand identity' in the same way as other products develop into brands. Retail groups are recognized by their '*store brand name*', and this reflects the values and personality associated with them. There is no doubt that Tesco, IKEA, Next and Dixons have really strong identities in the minds of customers and non-customers. These brands can be used as an umbrella for several sub-brands, for instance Tesco now offer Tesco Superstores; Tesco Compact; Tesco Extra; Tesco Metro; and Tesco Express, as well as Tesco Direct for home delivery.

The Burton's group once ran an advertisement in the financial press that stated that 'the secret of successful retailing was giving the market what it wanted'. The graphics emphasized the target marketing approach utilizing segmentation of the Top Shop, Principles, Dorothy Perkins, Evans and Burton's group of clothing shops. Accurate targeting is an important issue in the development of a *multiple fascia strategy* that utilizes a store portfolio with several different retail approaches. In this situation, the store portfolio is managed to ensure that the right sites are available for each given fascia. Decisions regarding multiple operations are usually considered by retailers that have reached an effective saturation point with their existing approach. This could arise because the addition of existing stores using the original concept would result in a disproportionately lower increase in sales. Many examples exist of such an approach, the current saturation in the UK grocery retail sector provides a good illustration. Availability of large sites is now restricted. As mentioned above, Tesco, the market leader, has adopted a multi-fascia approach in terms of store image and size. Tesco's store portfolio now contains a range of store sizes from superstores (approximately 26 000 sq. ft in size) to small convenience stores (approximately 1500 sq. ft.).

Extension into unrelated areas of business, for instance Sainsbury's Bank, or Boots Opticians, can also exploit the brand equity. Such extensions rely on the customer transferring the same values from the original store to the new ventures.

It is the customer who is always right, in that their opinion is the only one that really matters. However, every retailer has to endeavour to achieve a strong, favourable image in the minds of their preferred customers. There are many actions that can be undertaken and all will be part of the retail marketing activities of the organization.

Internal Environment and Core Product

The Internal Environment/Atmosphere

There is a progression that links the overall image of a retailer, through the accessibility and perception of the location and then goes further, focusing on the appropriate environment inside a store so that it is conducive for a customer to consider a purchase. It obviously then continues through to the other elements of the '*total retail offering*' which include the range of goods, aspects of price/value, service levels and other factors. Researchers have commented that retail store environments are relatively closed and this can impact on shoppers' affective, cognitive and behavioural states.'

In all retail environments there are a large number of influences that can affect shopping activity. These include the activities of salespeople; the colour, lighting, noise, smell and temperature within the store; shelf space, display and merchandising; even the behaviour of other shoppers. Each of the above elements is also part of the *total offering* and is important and any one could affect the likelihood of a sale. If a customer has been attracted into a specific retail location it is then essential that they must also feel comfortable once inside. The ambience has to be appropriate and consistent with the in-store layout and all other elements. In a survey of an early shopping centre comments from the shopping public such as 'It's hot in here, there's no fresh air!' and 'It gets so crowded that it's really uncomfortable' led the owners to redesign that centre.

It is obvious that if potential customers feel unhappy, they are less likely to spend, and there is a high probability they will not visit again. However, the environment that upsets one customer might be attractive to another. A Top Shop manager told one of the authors that they deliberately played young person's music, chose vibrant colours and placed racks of clothes close together. This was because it seemed attractive to the young customers they wanted and would probably deter older people (undesirable) from entering the store. This helped to ensure the right segment was encouraged.

The store environment actually starts with the shopfront, or the cover of a mail-order catalogue, or the first page of a Web site. It then moves inside to the internal shape/layout, the colours, fitments and finishes used, the lighting, sounds and smells: in fact a *complete sensory experience* in a physical store, rather less in a virtual one. There is much evidence to suggest that a positive ambience complemented by appropriate merchandising will actually enhance sales. This critical aspect of retailing success is discussed in more detail in Chapter 7.

Store layout and atmosphere is also important with regards how long a shopper will stay in a store, and how many products they will see during their visit. In grocery hypermarkets the layout is designed to maximize the number of items that are easily visible, and to ensure that customers are encouraged to stop at counters serving high-margin produce such as fresh meat and prepared meals. Use of sound and smell is also utilized to complement the internal environment. In department stores with several sales floors offering different merchandise the traditional layout has the up-escalator going from the front of the store but coming down often involves walking to the back and passing many more products on the way. Another tactic involves placing high-demand impulse items near the entrance to encourage shoppers to come into the store or near the checkout to promote extra sales. Furniture giant IKEA also uses layout to encourage additional spending, and having walked all around the sales floor there is a restaurant and then the bargain offers to tempt even more purchases.

Range and Assortment of Goods Offered

Retail success is dependent on satisfying customers. Once a customer has been attracted into a retail outlet, the important issue is to maximize the spending during each visit. This depends to a large extent on the range of merchandise offered. Ghosh (1994) states that 'central to a store's success is the merchandise selection that matches the tastes, preferences and expectations of its target customers'.

Davies (1994) suggests that 'Range management involves two major activities, selection of the range components and the subsequent management of the range by the addition and deletion of individual products.' Decisions need to be taken regarding what assortment of products should be stocked, the breadth of the range and the depth of supply of each item. The quantity stocked (*depth of supply*) is important to avoid out-of-stock situations, since these have a double impact, first leading to loss of sales, secondly upsetting customers who may not return on subsequent occasions. However, regular review should be undertaken regarding all aspects of the range, and retailers should not be scared of deleting any item that is not fulfilling its role within the assortment offered.

Retail buyers will want to offer a range of merchandise to meet a number of differing objectives. There will be some products stocked because they help to build store traffic. Examples could include '*must stock*' lines such as newspapers in convenience stores, or '*loss leader*' products such as cheap bread in some grocery supermarkets. These items are chosen to ensure that customers visit the store. Other goods may be stocked to enhance the store image. While sales of such lines could be low, offering designer clothes, for example, could increase the reputation of a department store by association. Marks & Spencer introduced designer ranges to counteract the negative comments made about their general range in the 1999–2000 season. There are other reasons for choice of merchandise but it should be obvious that good choices will help achieve success.

The complexity of product selection decisions involves marketing, merchandising, buying and financial input. However the achievement of a well-balanced range of goods is more an instinctive skill than an exact science, but decisions must be taken in the light of the best information available. Studying the rise and fall (and rise again?) of companies such as Laura Ashley and MFI shows how critical product assortment is to retail success.

In-Store Stimuli

We now look at the key factors that lead directly to purchases being made, or not taking place.

Prices Charged and Value Offered by Retailers

Sir John Cohen, founder of Tesco, started trading from Hackney market. His trading philosophy in the development years of the supermarket was based on the maxim 'pile it high, and sell it cheap'. The lure of low prices is very strong as customers are always looking for bargains or at least good-value offerings. Tesco has now changed its marketing position to one of quality products at affordable prices. Other groups trade on a more unashamedly price basis: Asda promote their price promises, and John Lewis is 'never knowingly undersold'.

There is a link between price levels as perceived by customers and value to that customer, but *price and value are not the same*. As in all marketing situations it is critical to manage the expectation of customers, especially with regards the simple equation of 'what value have I received from my purchase, and what did it cost me?'. Customers are likely to be satisfied if they believe the value of the benefits received exceeds the sacrifice or cost of obtaining the item.

The pricing policies of a retailer are a *statement of position*. They should reflect the value expected by the chosen target customers. However it may be possible for an organization to charge 'above market' prices if it offers exclusive items or speciality merchandise, or additional services, or even if the retailer is in a more convenient location or is open at times when competitors are closed. Usually customers act as though there is a 'zone of tolerance' with regard to pricing, allowing it to be evaluated against other elements in the retailer marketing mix, but prices are powerful stimuli and are almost always compared to those for alternative offerings.

For the retail supplier the price that is charged to customers is also the revenue received by the store. But it is not simply an exercise in ensuring that selling prices exceed product costs, as gross profitability is a function of the *margin* (between selling price and cost) *multiplied by the number of items sold*. If you pile high, and sell cheap there will be low margins but high stock turn. This might or might not be better than a higher margin with a lower volume of sales. In both cases the gross profit will still need to be compared to the running costs of the store as many retail failures are related to problems in this respect, rather than selling goods at less than the cost of acquisition.

Recent offers from e-retailers have often been at heavily discounted prices. This reflects the very different cost structure of such retailers. It is still unclear which areas of e-commerce will grow to threaten fixed-location stores, but it is likely to include many product categories where selling prices offer wide margins and volume sales are not common. Pricing policies are obviously vital to financial success, but the comparative level of prices is a key variable when attracting and satisfying customers, competing effectively and managing demand. Pricing levels require marketing judgement and balancing the short-term and long-term needs of an organization.

Traditionally prices and sales volume are linked in economic theory by the so-called *demand curve*. While there is some validity in the link when considering a single product purchase when all other conditions are constant, many retail purchases involve a number of products bought at the same time. Some may be 'loss leaders' offering very good value, other 'full price' items, and yet more 'impulse' buys (see Chapter 3). Most retailers consider the overall pricing and promotional policy to ensure that there is a good balance across the whole range of merchandise offered. In doing this it is important to understand the role of *price* in the purchase behaviour of potential customers.

Retailers must be careful that they do not deceive customers in a way that could cause resentment and bad publicity. What is deceptive and sometimes illegal is offering a product at a low price although the availability is unfairly restricted, or if the retailer has no intention of selling the product. Some packaged holiday offers have been very close to illegal trading in this respect. There is some legislation designed to protect consumers regarding deceptive pricing and good retailers take care to ensure they deal fairly with their public, while still trying to use price as a very effective marketing tool.

Promotional Activity and Other Communications

It was suggested in Chapter 1 that there are two specific roles of retail marketing,

- *First* to attract customers into the retail environs (store/virtual location)
- *Second* to persuade those shoppers to make a purchase from the store.

Promotions and other communications could be aimed at either of these roles. In general the objectives of promotions and communications will include one or more of the following three categories:

- *Informing* Giving information, building awareness that a retailer exists, what that retailer offers, where it can be found
- *Persuading* Creating a favourable attitude, providing a stimulus to favour one store over another and offering a deal to purchase now
- *Reinforcing* Dispelling doubts about an action already taken, building support/loyalty for a return visit, ensuring a good climate for future sales.

Some retailers think that advertising and promotional activity are restricted to specific campaigns, but all elements from the retail marketing mix offer cues and messages to shoppers. For instance the way prices are expressed can give out messages. A high price with a discount is very different from a permanent low price. If a retailer stocks an exclusive brand of merchandise this will offer other messages to customers. Even the act of running a sales event with specially bought-in merchandise can allow customers to speculate about the motives of the retailer. What is important in managing the communications mix is that *all messages are consistent*, and that they are all considered with regard to the *communications objectives of the store*. An often-quoted model from general communication theory is DAGMAR (Defining Advertising Goals for Measured Advertising Results). This can be widened to include all promotions and communications.

The DAGMAR model is related to the sequences in the so-called *conviction* models that consider the process of moving from an initial position through to taking some action, hopefully making a purchase. There are a number of not dissimilar sequences including the classic AIDA model which can be found in most marketing texts. These are illustrated in Table 4.1.

Table 4.1 Stages of Conviction Model (1998)

	Information stage	**Persuasion stage**	
Awareness	Comprehension	Conviction	Action
Attention	Interest	Desire	Action

Source: Adapted from Adcock *et al.* (1998).

Both the sequences in Table 4.1 show a progression through to some form of action by customers which illustrates that the ultimate test of any communication is whether the *resulting action is the one the retailer wants*. Advertising and promotion are important aspects of retail marketing and a great deal of money is spent both directly by retailers and indirectly as a result of suppliers contributing to promotional allowances in exchange for a product being stocked. It is therefore essential to ensure the money is spent effectively.

It is impossible to differentiate in a general way between the various forms of advertising, suggesting that one is more appropriate for a specific use. Main media television adverts can be used to inform and build awareness for a store group, but can just as easily be utilized to deliver a stimulus that persuades customers to buy based on a price promotion or other offer. The same could be said about a direct-mail or a poster campaign. There are many different techniques open to creative communicators and an ever-increasing number of media that can be used. However in-store promotions and point-of-sale communications must be seen as primarily aimed at persuading a customer to buy, although they can also inform – for instance, the leaflets placed in certain supermarket stores describing their policy with regard to genetically modified (GM) food and other environmental issues.

The results of communication will be seen in many guises. These range from simple carrier bags showing the store logo, through to multi-million pound TV campaigns and even into sports sponsorship. During the 1990s the Italian company Benneton sponsored a Formula 1 motor racing team. These issues are discussed further in Chapter 10. However it is not always necessary to advertise to achieve retailing success; word of mouth is probably the most effective promotional tool. But, of course, it is difficult to control. Few stores setting up in today's competitive markets can rely on word of mouth alone, but when it is achieved, often assisted by effective PR and good editorial comment in important media, it can be very powerful indeed.

Service as a Competitive Factor in Retail

All retailers provide a service to their customers. As stated by Dunne and Lusch (1999) they 'collect products, arrange for their delivery, prepare the goods for use if needed, provide a store for the transaction, and provide information consumers need to make purchase decisions'. This is not an exhaustive list as there are many other activities that are also carried out, such as the opportunity to view an item before purchase, the provision of credit and after-sales service as required. A good service provider will enhance the feeling of security for a customer regarding a transaction, and will make that transaction a really satisfying experience.

The term 'moments of truth' was coined by Jan Carlzon of SAS Airways to describe the contact encounters between a customer and a representative of the supplier. During those encounters, if viewed from a customer perspective, the shop assistant or retail employee is *acting on behalf of the whole organization*. The encounter might be very short but such direct interaction can have a dramatically large effect on the customer's satisfaction. Unless these 'moments of truth' are 'positive' there will be little chance of good sales today, and bad experiences will certainly deter the customer in the future.

However, as every retailer knows, *service* costs *money*. Service employees are often low-paid staff, and it is difficult to raise productivity, but that does not alter the fact that *service costs*. But it can cost in more ways than cash. Poor service reduces sales and alienates customers; most customers who defect from a service business blame indifferent or unhelpful employees, according to Schlesinger and Hesketh (1991). These authors emphasize the importance of good design of the service tasks to be undertaken by employees and due consideration to the economics of service provision. They criticize the industrial approach to service provision that treats employees

> as though they were machines. Front-line customer contact jobs designed to be as simple and narrow as possible so that they can be filled by almost anyone – idiot proof jobs.

The example offered is Sears, a retail giant in the USA at the time:

> Sears has consistently followed the basic tenet of the old industrial mind-set to keep labour costs as low as possible. During the 1970s and early 1980s, Sears shifted the composition of its sales force from 70 per cent full-time employees to 70 per cent part-timers. In the short run, this change undoubtedly reduced the aggregate wage bill dramatically. Over time, however, it led to rising rates of staff turnover and a sharp drop in customer satisfaction.

In most retail organizations staffing policies and training are not part of the marketing brief. There is an assumption in many that location strategies, merchandising and promotion are enough to influence trading levels. It is the unit operational managers who are usually responsible for cost control, and that includes staffing. What this forgets is that the staff who interact directly with customers play a key role in *delivering customer satisfaction*, and that this is key to retail success.

The Scandinavian school of marketing coined the term 'part-time marketer' (PTM) (see Chapter 3). It describes those large numbers of employees who don't have a primary marketing role but interact with customers. Anyone in an organization who might influence customer relations, customer satisfaction, or customer perceived quality is a PTM. Gummesson (1991) suggests that:

> Marketing-orientation (customer consciousness) does not occur because management preaches its gospel; it occurs when a customer notices the difference between now and before. Marketing-orientation only becomes alive when all members of an organisation have asked themselves 'How do I contribute to customer relations and to revenue?', [and they] have answered the question, and implemented the answer.
>
> It has to reach the firing line in each specific department, function and organisational tier (emphasis in the original).

Because the service provided by retailers is so visible the pay off from good service is high. The SERVQUAL model of service quality stressed the dimensions of Assurance, Reliability, Responsiveness and Empathy. All of these can contribute to a good interaction and this, in turn, will actually enable a retailer to achieve a real competitive advantage over others offering lower levels of service. In fact, the economic equation suggests that a study embracing all aspects of service and the decision to offer appropriate service where it can best add value to the shopping experience is very important in the attempt to achieve retail success.

For instance most grocery hypermarkets are 'self-service' for the customer selecting goods to purchase. However, if there are long delays at the check out, or if the shelves are not full of the required product, the customer will have real reason to complain about the service. The move to 'self-service' is comparatively recent and, at the time, stores were unsure about the reaction of shoppers who were used to being served over a sales counter. Events have proved that this particular service activity was not critical – provided the customers were able to see a compensating benefit. In the case of grocery supermarkets it came in the form of lower prices, with Tesco, the pioneers of 'self-service' in the UK, cutting prices dramatically and gaining several points of market share at the time. In this case most competitors followed suit, although there is still a market for more traditional outlets. Interestingly the moves to Internet shopping, for instance the launch of Tesco Direct, has heralded a return to increased service in putting together a customer's order and delivering it to the home address. For this a flat rate fee is charged, which reflects again the trade off between levels of service received and price paid.

Relationship Issues and Building Customer Loyalty

It has already been mentioned that there are two distinct aspects in retail marketing – first *attracting customers* and then persuading those customers to *spend as much as possible* when in the retail location. All the factors previously discussed are aimed at creating satisfied customers. This occurs if the expectations of customers are met (or exceeded). Satisfied customers might return to buy again, or they might tell their friends about the experience, but in any case they will be content with the transaction. While the emphasis in the past has often been more biased towards short-term selling aspects, successful traders have always been the ones who have built up significant levels of long-term repeat business. It is usually more difficult to attract a customer to make a first visit to a retail outlet than it is to persuade a satisfied existing customer to return.

However satisfaction does not automatically lead to repeat business, although it usually helps. Loyalty to a specific retail outlet requires a commitment by the shopper that often has *emotional overtones* in addition to the economic aspects. Most customers certainly know that they have the power of choice in highly competitive retail markets. There is usually *no* cost penalty for the customer should they decide to switch to an alternative supplier. The prevailing attitude seems to be 'If I am to spend my money with you, you've got to make it worth my while'. It could be that some pressures exist on a particular shopper, maybe time or the need for convenience. These could drive that customer to use a specific location, but this clearly will not apply in all situations. In fact the Henley Centre loyalty report (1995) suggested that only 17 per cent of consumers were loyal to their supplier in over half the product categories purchased. Many more were categorized as 'Shop Arounds' (loyal in only 25 per cent–50 per cent of the categories) or 'Promiscuous' (little loyalty in most categories).

Most consumers are sophisticated, confident, experienced and demanding when considering a retail purchase. Buying decisions are usually well thought through and deliberate, although 'impulse purchasing' is still present in specific situations. The Henley report (1995) explores the major reasons for a repeat purchase in different product categories. These are shown in Table 4.2.

Table 4.2 Repeat Purchases

Category	(%)	(%)	(%)
FMCG packaged goods	Quality (46)	Price (35)	Trust in supplier (15)
Financial services	Service (46)	Trust in supplier (25)	Price (20)
Electrical goods	Quality (36)	Price (30)	Service (19)

Source: Henley Centre loyalty report (1995).

The results in Table 4.2 are not surprising, but it is obvious that previous experience of a supplier, and the levels of satisfaction, are bound to influence such factors. Jones and Sasser (1995) describe four types of customers:

- *Advocates* who are both loyal and satisfied

- *Mercenaries* who have no loyalty to a supplier even though they are satisfied
- *Hostages* who are loyal but only because they feel trapped to purchase from a specific source
- *Terrorists* who are neither loyal nor satisfied and could possibly do damage by speaking up against a supplier.

These are shown on a matrix in Figure 4.1

	LOYAL	DISLOYAL
SATISFIED	Advocates	Mercenaries
DISSATISFIED	Hostages	Terrorists

Figure 4.1 Types of customer (1995)
Source: Jones and Sasser (1995).

The 'mercenary' type of customer will exhibit no loyalty to a previous supplier. They will consider every new shopping occasion as a *separate event*, re-evaluating the comparative offers on each occasion. This type of customer is to be found in most retail situations; however, while this type of behaviour might apply to some categories of product it is not certain it will apply to every one.

It is obviously important to continue to satisfy these 'mercenary' customers because no supplier wants dissatisfied 'terrorist' shoppers. But loyalty requires a customer to forsake alternative suppliers and to restrict the freedom to choose. It is naive to suggest that they could be easily persuaded to give up their freedom of choice and become loyal 'advocates'. Understanding how and when to attempt to *develop loyalty by investing in customer relationships* is important for retail success.

Many of the so-called 'loyalty schemes' run by retailers are really worth very little in terms of developing loyalty among the customer base. Initiatives such as repeat-purchase coupons will attract some customers, but they are really short-term promotions. It is important that the retailer appreciates the needs of customers and offers relevant incentives in order to develop loyalty where appropriate. Piercy (1997) warns that:

> There is an element of spuriousness about the relationship offering made by some companies. From the customers' perspective, the Tesco and Sainsbury relationship does not offer more than a bribe to come back next time. The only tangible aspects of the customers' relationship with these companies seems to be becoming the target of large quantities of junk mail, selling financial services.

Retailers need to consider the purpose of their 'loyalty schemes' and to design ones that do reward 'loyal' behaviour, offering increased benefits, *economic and emotional*, as a customer becomes more committed to a relationship. Of course, retailers do not want 'hostage' customers who feel trapped to purchase from an outlet although they are dissatisfied with it. It could be the local newsagent is the only one delivering newspapers to your street. You might stick with this supplier in spite of problems, for instance missed deliveries or regular mix-ups on the bill, because there is no choice. If an alternative were to become available you would change immediately and become a 'terrorist' in respect of the previous supplier.

Reichheld (1996) put the marketing task into perspective when he wrote 'It's not how satisfied you keep your customers, it's how many satisfied customers you keep!' Both customer satisfaction and consumer loyalty are crucial issues in successful retailing, although it is important to realise that *satisfaction* is not the same as *loyalty*. There is no doubt that satisfaction is important in order to avoid 'terrorist' customers who tell, on average, some 20 others about their problems. However, as Reichheld continues to suggest, 'there's nothing wrong in measuring satisfaction. The problems begin when satisfaction scores become a goal unto themselves, independent of customer loyalties.'

There is no doubt that loyal customers are the most valuable customers, especially when measured over a lifetime of trading. Pizza Express speaks about the $3000 pizza, a measure of the 'spend' by a single regular customer over an average buying life. Reichheld and Sasser (1990) stress the importance of lifetime values. Extending the period over which a customer remains loyal to a supplier can result in a dramatic increase in profitability. Obviously any increase in the number of loyal customers has a similar effect, and those companies with the highest retention rates tend to be the most profitable. But exclusive loyalty is not easily attained, in fact customers are often 'loyal' to more than one retailer in a particular class, exhibiting a form of 'polygamy'.

Any loyal relationship from a customer will involve a commitment to voluntarily restrict choice and to give up the freedom to shop anywhere. Why should a customer want to accept such a constraint? The only answers are that either they perceive that they will receive additional 'value' by remaining with a single supplier, or the costs of termination, and switching to an alternative source, are too high to accept. Dennison and Knox (1993) developed a matrix not unlike Figure 4.1 (Figure 4.2). They considered loyalty in a balance between few stores shopped at, and many stores, utilizing the dimension of commitment to a particular store rather than the satisfaction received from shopping there. While the two matrices are not identical they both indicate the fact that loyalty is not an automatic reaction even if satisfaction and commitment are present.

	FEW stores	MANY stores
HIGH COMMITMENT	Loyals	Variety Seekers
LOW COMMITMENT	Habituals	Switchers

Figure 4.2 The loyalty matrix (1993)
Source: Dennison and Knox (1993).

The work of Dennison and Knox accepts that exclusive loyalty is rare, but it obviously can exist under certain conditions. Loyalty is also variable, as they state: 'it is potentially misleading to assume that individual consumers are equally loyal across all retail sectors'. In fact loyalty levels vary depending on both individual motivation and marketplace characteristics, such as product type, purchase frequency, expense involved and competitive issues. It might be that shoppers require a 'change of pace' to give some variety to their purchasing, or it might be a genuine desire always to obtain the best value available. Whatever the behaviour of a customer, it is important that a retailer tries to understand the *motives* of the individual shopper and responds in an appropriate way in order to increase loyalty.

Conclusions

It is possible to consider the task of retail marketing in the role of someone attracting a customer into a store, and to be more involved the deeper they enter. Consider first a customer with a desire to go shopping for some kind of product. Their initial decision will be about which marketplace to visit. It could be the local high street, or a new out-of-town shopping centre, or an in-home market made possible by a home-shopping catalogue or Internet Web site.

The decision on which location to visit will be influenced, of course, by previous knowledge, current motivation and the accessibility of the location in the light of the type of shopping to be undertaken. Some locations will be acceptable, others rejected, and there will be others that are not even considered because the shopper does not know they exist. In any event, a decision will be made based on a perception of which is the *most appropriate*, and so a location will be chosen. Obviously the first role of retail marketing is to ensure your outlet is positioned in a location where the relevant shoppers are likely to visit, and that there is an *awareness* of your store.

The next decision the shopper makes is which particular store to enter, this is especially crucial if there is more than one outlet offering a particular class of product. When considering grocery products it could be there is only one supermarket at a specific location, but this is not always so. With many products there could be a choice available, and an opportunity for comparing different offerings and different prices. This is certainly true in the virtual Internet marketplace. A decision to visit or not visit a particular store will probably be influenced by its image, perceived position and reputation.

Once inside, the internal environment becomes critical – it could be inviting, but equally it could be a objectionable or just neutral. It can be seen that at each stage it is necessary for the customer to be drawn in deeper, but it is just as easy to stop the progression and to put the shopper off from venturing further. For example a poorly designed Web site might have really good visuals but if these take forever to download the potential customer could get irritated – or, worse, get bored and leave. The same can apply in a traditional 'bricks and mortar' store. Again it is the responsibility of the marketer to ensure the right customers continue to be *interested.*

Continuing the analogy of entering a store, it will be obvious that the *desire* to purchase will depend upon the range of goods offered and the various in-store stimuli of price/value, promotion and service, each becoming important in their turn.

All the above factors are crucial for retailing success, but the most crucial event is an actual purchase. It is only the *action* of purchasing that actually concludes the process and all previous 'window-shopping' is redundant without it. Retail marketing involves all the factors both before and up to the time of a sale, in addition it continues *after the sale,* as it is crucial to ensure customer satisfaction and to create the right conditions for possible repeat purchases.

It will be seen the sequence neatly fits the well-known conviction model:

attention → interest → desire → action

The usual retail maxim is

- ▶ First get a customer *into your store*
- ▶ Then encourage that customer to *spend.*

Obviously in the later category some promotional activity is aimed at maximizing transactional spend. This could involve cross-selling insurance cover to someone who has just bought a washing machine, or utilizing the best impulse purchase locations to offer additional items such as chocolate bars near supermarket check outs. Many retailers monitor the in-store behaviour of shoppers, sometimes resorting to hidden cameras to do so. The information can be used effectively to improve store layouts and the merchandising of products. Internet retailers also undertake analysis of customer reactions to different parts of a Web site, especially the time spent in each area. The term 'stickiness' is often used to describe how well a site keeps a customer 'sticking around'. The more time spent on the site, or in a store, the more chance of cross-selling or an impulse buy. In addition, if a customer is really involved there is also less chance of that user visiting a competitor's site, and an increase in loyalty.

The best retail marketing strategies are built on the *psychology of a customer's shopping behaviour.* But retail today is not solely about a single transaction, even a large spend can be seen in the light of future potential spending. In fact, the cost and effort of attracting a customer to make an initial purchase is generally far greater than the cost of encouraging them to make a further purchase in the future. For that reason more and more retail marketing activities are being aimed at *retaining* customers and developing a degree of loyalty in shopper's *buying cycles.*

Most retailers would like to have a hard core of loyal customers who continue to frequent their outlet. Generally this is achieved but whether there are enough of these customers, and whether they are the right customers, will be explored in chapters 11 and 12. It is also important to remember that it is very easy for customers to switch from one retail supplier to another for most classes of products: there are just too many suppliers available in today's marketplaces. Therefore it is necessary to evaluate the cost of a loyalty programme to decide if the benefits are really worth it. Safeway, the supermarket operator, did this in 2000 when it discontinued its ABC loyalty card scheme. However the other side of the equation is whether an operator can afford not to offer a competitive loyalty programme. If such a scheme is expected by customers, and there are no compensating benefits to make up for the absence of such a programme, then it is likely that a competitive disadvantage will lead to lower sales. This is a key decision area for retail marketing.

References and Further Reading

Adcock, D., Bradfield, R., Halborg, A. and Ross, C. (1998) *Marketing Principles and Practice*, 3rd edn, FT Pitman Publishing, London.

Bennison, D., Clarke, I. and Pal, J. (1995) Locational Decision Making in Retailing: An Exploratory Framework for Analysis, *International Review of Retail, Distribution and Consumer Research*, 5, 1, 1–20.

Carlzon, J. (1987) *The Moments of Truth*, Ballinger, Cambridge, MA.

Davies, G. (1994) The Delisting of Products by Retail Buyers, *Journal of Marketing Management*, 10, 473–93.

Dawson, J. (1999) *Retailing at Century End: Some Challenges for Management and Research*, University of Edinburgh, *Working Paper*, 99/8.

De Kare-Silver, M. (1998) *e-shock: The Electronic Shopping Revolution*, Macmillan, London.

Dennison, T. and Knox, S. (1993) Pocketing the change from loyal shoppers: the 'Double Indemnity Effect', in M. Kirkup, et al. (eds), *Proceedings on Emerging Issues in Marketing*, 221–233.

Dibb, S. Simkin, L. Pride, W.M. and Ferrell, O.C. (1997) *Marketing*, 3rd European edn, Houghton-Mifflin, Boston.

Dunne, P. and Lusch, R.F. (1999) *Retailing*, 3rd edn, Harcourt Brace & Co., Orlando, FL.

Ferry, J.W. (1961) *A History of the Department Store*, Macmillan, New York.

Geist, J.F. (1983) *Arcades: The History of a Building Type*, in Dawson, J., *Retailing at The Century End*.

Ghosh, A. (1994) *Retail Management*, 2nd edn, The Dryden Press, New York.

Gummesson, E. (1991) Marketing Orientation Revisited. The Crucial Role of the Part-Time Marketer, *European Journal of Marketing*, 25, 2, 60–75.

Henley Centre Report (1995) The Loyalty Paradox.

Hollander, S.C. (1960) The Wheel of Retailing, *Journal of Marketing*, 25 July, 37–42.

Jefferys, J.B. (1954) *Retail Trading in Britain 1850–1950*, Cambridge University Press, Cambridge.

Jones, T.O. and Sasser, W.E. (1995) Why Satisfied Customers Defect, *Harvard Business Review*, November–December.

Keynote/Business Monitor, (1998) PA1003 'Retailing in the UK', Keynote, London.

Lancaster, B. (1995) *The Department Store*, Leicester University Press, Leicester.

Levy, H. (1948), *The Shops of Britain*, Trench Trubner, London.

Levy, S.J. and Zaltman, G. (1975) *Marketing, Society and Conflict*, Prentice-Hall, Englewood Cliffs, NJ.

MacKeith, M. (1986) *The History and Conservation of Shopping Arcades*, Mansell, London.

Piercy, N. (1997) *Market-Led Strategic Change* (2nd ed), Butterworth-Heinemann, Oxford.

Powell, D. (ed.) (1987) *The Tesco Papers 1975–1987*, Tesco Stores Holdings Plc/Hallam & Mallen, London.

Reichheld, F.F. (1996) The Satisfaction Trap, *Customer Services Management*, December, 51–3.

Reichheld, F.F. and Sasser, W.E. (1990) Zero defections: quality comes to services, *Harvard Business Review*, Sept-Oct, 105–111.

Ries, A. and Trout, J. (1983) *Positioning: The Battle for Your Mind*, McGraw-Hill, New York.

Schlessinger, D. and Hesketh, D. (1991) The Service-Driven Company, *Harvard Business Review*, Sept–Oct, pp 71–81.

Shostack, G.L. (1987) Service Positioning through Structural Change, *Journal of Marketing*, January, 34–43.

Retail Location

CHAPTER 5

This chapter:

- Explains the importance of retail location
- Shows how retail locaction may be classified
- Defines key location factors

Retail Location

Introduction

A well-known saying in retailing, usually attributed to Sir Charles Clore (the founder of Sears), states that the three most important factors in retailing are *location, location,* and *location.* George Davis (once of Next) supports this viewpoint stating that 'you can be the best retailer in the world, but if you set up your shop in the wrong place, you'll never do much business'. Both these quotes refer to the importance of location in terms of the status, population and infrastructure of the area, as well as the large effect it has on the success or failure of the store. Collins (1992) states that 'at least 85 per cent of store performance is determined not by internal management control, but by local and external factors'. Put another way, Collins' work shows that only a small part of store performance (15 per cent in this case) can be attributed to internal factors.

The reasons for the importance of retail location lie in the nature of retailing and the retail environment. Retailing is a business that *relies on traffic* – i.e. a steady flow of potential customers into the store. The more convenient the location, the more likely it is that shoppers will visit the store. The other side of this argument is probably more revealing, in that shoppers will be less motivated to visit if they find it difficult to get to the store either because it is a long way away from their home (or place of work) or because transport links are poor. In the modern competitive retail environment, it is unlikely that a shopper will have to look very far for an alternative store that is in an altogether more accessible location. Research by Foxall *et al.* (1994) adds extra detail to this argument stating that '80 per cent of shopping trips begin and end at home; more than half are made on foot, the rest involve car travel'. The importance of a location close to home or conveniently accessible by car is therefore apparent.

The importance of location in ensuring successful operations means that the majority of retailers put location first on their list of tactical considerations. Select the optimum location and the rest can then follow.

Select a poor location and expect store performance to be equally poor, irrespective of other tactical elements. Practical reasons also support this approach, as aspects such as store size and orientation will have an effect on other tactical areas, such as store design, for example.

Classifications of Location

Retailers have two broad choices of location to choose from. *Incremental developments* are those retail areas that have developed gradually over a period of time and are typified by the high street or city/town centre development. *Planned developments* are those that have been planned prior to construction and include newer retail concepts such as the shopping centre or mall and retail park. Planned or incremental developments can be further divided on the basis of the specific placement of the area in relation to population centres. *City centre sites* are situated in close proximity to centres of population while out-of-town sites may be located on the outskirts of towns/cities (satellite areas) or in an area away from domestic and commercial zones (new areas). A final division of planned and incremental developments can be made by considering the usage of the site prior to retail development. *Pre-existing* sites are those that have already been built upon and are typically based in incremental developments. *Brownfield* sites are those that have seen prior usage (usually commercial) but have been cleared prior to retail development. *Greenfield* sites are those that have not previously been built upon.

Planned locations usually occur in either satellite or new areas owing to land availability – i.e. sufficient available land must exist so that planning is not compromised. Land availability also dictates that planned locations are typically brownfield or greenfield sites. Road access to the location is usually good, as is parking capacity and convenience. Accessibility by foot can be good for satellite sites, but is often poor for new areas. Public transport links are variable depending on the site's displacement from areas of population or proximity to existing transport routes. The level of on-site competition is usually low as the mix of retail offerings is usually pre-planned or managed on an ongoing basis. The number of *complementary stores* (non-competing stores that positively affect demand – see later in this chapter for a fuller explanation) can be high, owing again to the mix of retail offerings providing shoppers with the 'one-stop shop' – i.e. a wide array of different retail purchases can be made in the same location. *Incremental locations* can occur anywhere but are typically seen close to population areas where shops have been located for a number of years. The city centre is, therefore, the most common site for incremental locations so pre-existing sites dominate. Good pedestrian access and public transport links are the norm, although access by car is often more of a problem owing to potential traffic congestion and low-capacity, inconvenient parking. The number of competing and complementary stores can vary, depending on the nature of the individual site. In some city centres, certain areas are dominated by a given retail offering (jewellery, department stores, etc.)

hence competition is high and the number of complementary stores is low. In others, a mix of retail offerings may exist so competition is reduced and the number of complementary stores increases.

The Location Decision Process

Location assessment methods used by retailers range from simple 'paper-based' approaches to highly complicated computer-based modelling. All methods do, however, share the common features of *search* (all sites), *evaluate* (each site against set criteria) and *select* (the best site). Differences emerge between methods in the nature and complexity of these three stages. Research by Clarkson, Clarke-Hill and Robinson (1996) identify the five most common location methods used by UK supermarket retailers as *checklist, analogue, financial, regression* and *spatial interaction*. These and other methods are discussed later in this chapter.

Two good starting points for the discussion of location assessment are the methods put forward by Berry and Parr (1987), and Bowlby, Breheny and Foot (1984). Berry and Parr put forward a four-stage process, comprising selection of market area, identification of feasible sites, site selection and determination of store size. Bowlby, Breheny and Foot consider three stages, namely search (geographic areas), viability (find the best sites) and micro (evaluation of specific sites). Combining these two related approaches produces a useful location assessment method with three simple stages:

1 Macro location evaluation

2 Micro location evaluation

3 Site selection.

Macro Location Evaluation

This stage of the process is essentially a *country* or *regional screening process*. The process shares many parallels with export market screening theory drawn from international market entry strategy. The first step is to carry out a detailed *external marketing audit*, analysing areas such as the macro environment (political, economic, social, technical factors), customers, competition and the retail market itself. The analyst is looking for any positive or negative factors that will affect the suitability of the proposed country. Assessment can then be made either by a *sequential hurdle* (non-compensatory) or a *multi-factor* (compensatory) method. The sequential hurdle method isolates the most important factors to the company – e.g. level of customer spending, personal disposable income (PDI), degree of competition, availability of sites, planning regulations, etc. – and ranks each country on this basis. Minimum acceptable levels for each factor are then set, and only those countries that meet the minimum acceptable levels are selected for more detailed assessment. The multi-factor method rates each country against a number of factors that could be similar to those mentioned for the sequential hurdle method – i.e. level of customer spending, etc. Each factor is first assigned a weighting to account for its relative importance to the company. Next, each country is scored on all factors and an overall rating for each calculated by multiplying each individual rating with the weighting factor then adding all these scores together. Only those countries achieving a certain score will make it through the screen and pass on to the next stage of assessment. Table 5.1 gives examples of both processes.

Table 5.1 Examples of Sequential Hurdle and Multi-Factor Assessment Methods

The following data have been gathered on countries *A*, *B*, *C*, *D* and *E*:

Country	Market development	Level of competition	Site availability	Level of PDI
A	3	3	8	2
B	8	8	3	6
C	6	5	5	7
D	8	6	4	8
E	6	3	5	7

The retailer then decides that the factor weightings and minimum acceptable levels are as follows:

	Market development	Level of competition	Site availability	Leval of PDI
Factor weighting	3	5	7	8
Minimum acceptable level	3	4	5	5

(a) Using a *sequential hurdle* method:
Hurdle 1 (Level of PDI) – *A* excluded (rating less than minimum)
Hurdle 2 (Site availability) – *B* and *D* excluded
Hurdle 3 (Level of competition) – *E* excluded
Result – Country *C* accepted

(b) Using a multi-factor approach:
Country *A*'s score = 96 (3 × 3 + 3 × 5 + 8 × 7 + 2 × 8)
Country *B*'s score = 133 (8 × 3 + 8 × 5 + 3 × 7 + 6 × 8)
Country *C*'s score = 134 (6 × 3 + 5 × 5 + 5 × 7 + 7 × 8)
Country *D*'s score = 146 (8 × 3 + 6 × 5 + 4 × 7 + 8 × 8)
Country *E*'s score = 124 (6 × 3 + 3 × 5 + 5 × 7 + 7 × 8)
Result – Country *D* accepted

Once the country screen has been completed, a second screen takes place based on particular regions within the 'accepted' countries. This screen is undertaken in essentially the same way as the country screen, although much more detailed local data are used. Again, a marketing audit is used to collect these data and either sequential hurdle or multi-factor approaches may be used.

Micro Location Evaluation

For each selected region, the assessment process is now required to identify and screen potential sites. Four key factors can be identified that affect the suitability of any given site, namely *population, infrastructure, retail outlets* and *costs*. Population is important as it is desirable for a sufficient number of suitable shoppers to be living a convenient distance from the store. Infrastructure is also important as it dictates how accessible the store will be to its potential shoppers. Retail outlet analysis is important as it identifies the level of competing and complementary stores – competing stores usually decrease the attractiveness of a site while complementary stores may have the opposite effect. Finally, the development and operational costs are as important, as in any business. High start-up (development) or ongoing (operational) costs will affect store performance.

Population Analysis

As has already been mentioned, the vast majority of shoppers choose the *most convenient acceptable store*. In the increasingly competitive retail environment, the need to differentiate becomes more important as shoppers usually have a number of convenient stores to choose from. Like any other business, retailers must decide which segments of the total population they intend to target – i.e. what body of target shoppers the retailer will consider when designing its retail offering (assortment, pricing, store design, etc.). When the target shopper has been identified, the retail offering can be designed to fit their requirements, thus meeting their needs better than a competitor with a different target shopper. Armed with a knowledge of the store's target shopper, the retailer can measure the number of target shoppers residing in the neighbourhood containing any given potential site. Sites with higher numbers of target shoppers will score more highly than those where numbers are low. This process of shopper analysis is often referred to as *Trade Area Mapping*.

Trade Area Mapping

Trade area mapping comprises the steps of definition, analysis and demand estimation. *Trade area definition* seeks to identify the trade area's boundaries. Defining the extent of the trade area is essential as it will have implications for potential demand patterns and will allow the number of target shoppers to be measured. The process is analogous with a goods manufacturer deciding if their market is local, regional, national, international or global. *Trade area analysis* is the detailed study of the population using a detailed customer (shopper) audit. The audit is an essential first step in gaining an understanding of the population as a whole – or, more importantly, the retailer's target shoppers. This understanding can then be used to assess *potential demand* and ultimately in the development of the retail offering or tactical mix.

Trade Area Definition

Retailers have a number of tools at their disposal to assist in trade area definition, the most commonly used of which are central place theory, land value theory, minimum differentiation and spatial interaction theory. More simplistic methods include the concentric zones approach and the shopper mobility/time constraints matrix (for further reading see Clarkson, Clarke-Hill and Robinson 1996).

Central place theory

Central place theory (Christaller 1966) seeks to define trade area boundaries by building a hierarchy of *competing retail stores*. The hierarchy implies that given patterns of shopper visits can be predicted based upon the attractiveness of the given store. The key determinant of attractiveness is the required travel distance to the store. Additional determinants include the size of the selling space and the nature (extent) of the overall retail offering. The theory assumes that in a trade area with a suitable level of competition, shoppers will visit the store with the best cost/benefit outcome. Costs are the travel distance to that store, the time involved and the required financial outlay. Benefits relate to the perceived outcome of the visit as measured by a utility judgement – i.e. how well will the store provide for the shopper's needs? The theory also takes into account the concept of the *threshold* of a good or service, defined as the required level of demand for a store to be economically viable. Threshold is important as it allows a distinction to be made between different categories of retail offering. High-threshold items are those that are expensive and infrequently purchased, such as cars, furniture, jewellery and white goods (fridges, cookers, etc.) whereas low-threshold items are the opposite, being relatively inexpensive with a higher purchase frequency, such as groceries. The assumption made here is that as threshold increases shoppers will be more motivated to travel longer distances (also longer travel time and greater travel cost). This being the case, central place theory predicts significant local demand for low-threshold items as shoppers will be motivated to travel only short distances (low travel time and costs). A large number of locally-based 'low-threshold' retailers would, therefore, exist in the trade area. The theory also predicts that only a limited number of regionally based 'high-threshold' retailers will exist and that shoppers will be motivated to travel longer distances (greater time and cost) to make such a purchase. Actual trade area boundaries are to be found at that point where the probability of shoppers visiting the store tends to zero.

A number of researchers have either criticized or attempted to modify the original model based on the following points:

1. The assumption that all customers are *identical and behave in a totally rational way* is flawed
2. The notion of an *even population distribution* is an oversimplification
3. The model is based on *single-purpose trips* only
4. Factors such as *store image, price, assortment*, etc. are not sufficiently considered in the measurement of attractiveness.

Central place theory, even with these subsequent modifications, is not an accurate enough model to be solely relied upon. The theory does certainly give an insight into the choice behaviour of shoppers given a number of competing stores but does not provide the full answer to the question. *How far will shoppers travel to make their desired purchase?*

Land value theory

Lane value theory (Haig 1926) is based on the assumption that as the supply of land for use is inelastic, site occupation, in the long run, will go to the highest bidder – i.e. the activity that can *afford to pay the highest rental* will occupy that site. In retail terms, land value theory states that prime sites tend to be occupied by those retailers that can afford to pay the high rent while less 'attractive' sites are left for the remaining retailers. The theory assumes that 'market forces' will set the rents for all sites, so the original definition of a prime site as a central (city-centre) location can be accounted for, as can the more modern out-of-town site. Refinements to the theory by Firey (1947), among others, broaden the criteria to include equal accessibility from all directions, perfect knowledge on the part of the retailer and no legal, physical or social constraints. Even accounting for these refinements, land value theory is too inflexible to deal with more complex environments. Brown (1993) points out that planned shopping centres often rely on 'household-name' stores to increase interest and stimulate shopper visits. In this case, such retailers often pay a lower rent than others that are less well known. Land value theory would certainly not predict this outcome. In addition, land use may not be truly rational in nature – i.e. sites may be occupied by non-conforming or outmoded land uses that interfere with the logic of land value theory (Clarkson, Clarke-Hill and Robinson 1996). Put in more simple terms, the modern retail environment is significantly more complex than land value theory assumes it to be. In much the same way as central place theory, land value theory gives a useful but incomplete trade area definition.

Minimum differentiation

The principle of minimum differentiation (Hotelling 1929) states that a number of competing stores will achieve superior performance if they are *clustered together*. The concept is based on the assumption that a store will gain access to a larger market area, or body of target shoppers, if it is located nearer to a competitor. To give a simple example, suppose a petrol station was located 5 miles due east of its nearest competitor. Business would be almost guaranteed from all areas away from its competitor and it can be assumed (*ceteris paribus*) that the petrol station would gain approximately half the sales from the area between the two petrol stations – i.e. it would gain all sales up to 3 miles away. Now consider what would happen if the petrol station was to locate 2 miles to the east of its competitor. Sales would still be guaranteed from all areas away from the competitor, but this area would now include an extra 4 miles of trade area. In addition, the petrol station would also gain all sales up to 1 mile towards its competitor. Clearly, the petrol station has improved its performance by clustering.

Minimum differentiation has been used to explain the apparent clustering of certain types of store, particularly in city centres. In this case, if a city centre area becomes known as the centre for a given type of retail outlet or offering, shoppers will maximize choice and minimize inter-store travel by visiting the area in question should they require the particular products or services. This clustering has been observed for retailers such as clothing and department stores but is rare in retailers such as convenience stores (Brown 1989, 1993; Houston and Stanton 1984). The relatively poor predictive ability of minimum differentiation is highlighted by Brown's research, and it is true to say that the approach needs modifying if it is to have any practical use. What can be said is that the theory is more likely to apply to higher-threshold retail types (see the section above on central place theory) such as jewellers, antique dealers, clothing stores or department stores than to lower-threshold retail types such as convenience stores or supermarkets. For this reason, the theory, like central place and land value, is useful but fails to be totally accurate in defining the trade area.

Spatial interaction

An additional tool available to the retailer relates to spatial interaction, or the way that *competing retail areas affect shoppers in intermediate residential areas.* As an example, suppose town *A* lies between *X* and *Y*, two retail areas with similar shops. The retailer would like to know whether the residents of *A* are more likely to visit *X* or *Y* so that the store could be located in the right area. Many spatial interaction models have been developed with a view to answering such a question. The most commonly used are detailed in Table 5.2.

Table 5.2 Spatial Interaction Models

Model	Comments
Reilly's Law (1931)	Early model based on physical laws of gravity
Huff's Law (1964)	Development of Reilly's Law based on customer utility
Lakshmanan–Hansen/MU (1965–6)	Further development of Reilly's Law based on index of specific store types
MCI models	Development of Huff's Law to include competitive factors
MNL models	Individual shopper choice measured

Reilly's Law is one of the oldest spatial interaction models dating back to Reilly (1931). The law identifies the boundary between two retail areas or towns based on the population of the towns and the distance from the towns to the area concerned. In its full form, the law states that the 'frequency with which the residents of an intermediate settlement trade with two towns is directly proportional to the populations of the two towns and inversely proportional to the square of the distances from the two towns to the settlement'. The boundary that the law identifies is known as the *break-point*. This break-point allows the limits of a retail location's potential catchment area to be identified (see Figure 5.1). In mathematical form, the law can be represented as:

$$BP_{01} = \frac{d_{12}}{1 + \sqrt{(A_2 \div A_1)}}$$

BP_{01} = distance or journey time of the break-point from point 0 to town 1
d_{12} = distance or journey time between towns 1 and 2
A_1, A_2 = measures of the attractiveness of towns 1 and 2.

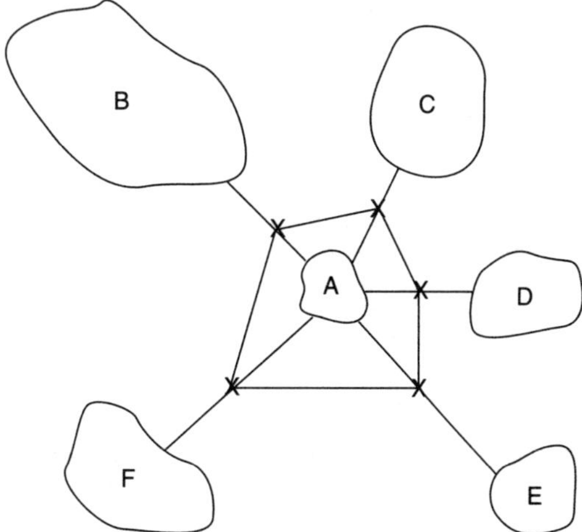

Figure 5.1 Example of Reilly's Law
Note: Town *A*, with a population of 30 000, is surrounded by five other towns *B*, *C*, *D*, *E* and *F*. Town *B* (population 500 000) is 55 miles away, town *C* (population 110 000) is 45 miles away, town *D* (population 75 000) is 20 miles away, town *E* (population 65 000) is 60 miles away and town *F* (population 125 000) is 75 miles away. Using Reilly's Law, the break point between A and the other towns can be calculated, this identifying town *A*'s catchment area. On this basis, town *A*'s catchment area extends 10.8 miles towards town *B*, 14.4 miles towards *C*, 9.0 miles towards *D*, 28.9 miles towards *E* and 31.4 miles towards *F*.

The example of Reilly's Law given in Figure 5.1 highlights the need for a certain amount of interpretation to make the law work. Huff (1964) recognized a number of problems with Reilly's approach, namely that the model does not successfully handle more than two centres, does not make allowance for different shopping trips and is absolute rather than graduated in nature. Put more simply, if a shopper has a choice of a large number of retail areas Reilly's Law will be very difficult to apply. In addition, it is highly probable that shoppers will make different choices of retail area for different types of shopping trip – e.g. the regular grocery shopping trip would be considered in a different light to a shopping trip aimed at purchasing a more expensive item, such as a personal computer, for example. Finally, the notion of a point where shopper choice changes from one area to another is a little simplistic as, in reality, the boundary would be graduated, based on the probability of choice – i.e. something approximating to a normal distribution (bell-shaped curve) would exist where the highest probability would be at the break-point, with decreasing levels of probability for points on either side. Huff's response to these limitations was to consider the attractiveness of each retail location as a *utility function* where utility is the ability of a commodity to satisfy human wants. Utility was based on the size (floor space) of each centre. In addition, a parameter was introduced to allow for different types of shopping trips, the probability of shopper choice was measured and the model was designed to handle a number of different retail areas (see Table 5.3). The law can be represented as,

$$Pi = \frac{Fi \div (Ti^{B})}{\Sigma Fj \div (Tj^{B})}$$

j $= 1 \rightarrow n$
Pi = probability of a shopper travelling to shopping centre i
Fi, Fj = floor space in shopping centre i or j
Ti, Tj = travel time to shopping centre i or j
n = the number of shopping centres in the area
B = parameter allowing for the type of shopping trip

Table 5.3 Example of Huff's Law

Retail area	Travel time[1] (min)	Selling space (sq. ft)	Probability $B = 2.7$[2]	Probability $B = 3.2$[3]
W	4	50 000	64.7	73.8
X	6	18 000	7.8	7.3
Y	10	100 000	10.9	7.9
Z	12	250 000	16.6	11.0

Notes:
1 Travel time from a specified point.
2 Typical value for furniture retail.
3 Typical value for clothing retail.

Many researchers have developed models that refine the early work of Reilly and Huff (see Figure 5.2). Lakshmanan and Hansen's model (1965) adds greater sensitivity to the measurement of attractiveness by expanding the number of variables used. The multiplicative competition interaction (MCI) model (Nakanishi and Cooper 1974) incorporates a wider range of variables (e.g. competitive factors), while the multinomial logit (MNL) model (e.g. Arnold and Tigent 1980; Miller and Lerman 1981) is an alternative approach that has been extensively used in analysing transport type usage.

Multiplicative Competitive Interaction (MCI) Model (Nakanishi and Cooper 1974)

$$Pij = \frac{\prod_{h=1}^{m} X^{bh}{}_{hij}}{\sum_{k=1}^{n} \prod_{h=1}^{m} X^{bh}{}_{hij}}$$

Pij = probability that shopper *i* chooses shopping alternative *j*
Xhii = any of $h = 1 \rightarrow m$ attributes of alternative *j* and *k* for shopper *i*
B = parameters that determine the effect of each attribute on choice probability

Multinomial Logit (MNL) Model

$$Pij = \frac{\prod_{h=1}^{m} e^{Xhij\beta hij}}{\sum_{k=1}^{n} \prod_{h=1}^{m} e^{Xhij\beta hij}}$$

Figure 5.2 Refinements of Reilly's and Huff's Laws

Concentric zones

Trade areas can also be analysed using the concentric zones approach. Survey data are collected that allow the area surrounding a given retail location to be classified on the basis of the likelihood of inhabitants visiting that location. Three bands (or zones) are identified that comprise a range of visit probabilities from high (primary-zone), medium (secondary-zone) and low (tertiary-zone). The bands are represented as concentric circles centred on the retail location itself (see Figure 5.3). A typical example of the concentric zones approach would show approximately 60 per cent of customers being accounted for by the primary zone, 25 per cent by the secondary zone and 15 per cent by the tertiary zone. The figures will vary, depending on the level of competition and the type of retail offering.

Shopper mobility/time constraints

The mobility/time constraints approach seeks to classify shopper visit behaviour into one of four generic categories (see Figure 5.4). The method is less sophisticated than many of those mentioned earlier in this section but useful insights can still be gained. Mobility has already been seen to be important as it dictates what potential range of shopper movement exists – i.e. how far a shopper will travel to shop. Central place theory aims to answer this question using determinants of *attractiveness*. The mobility/time constraints method takes a more *customer-based* approach. A shopper profile is developed from market research that is used to predict

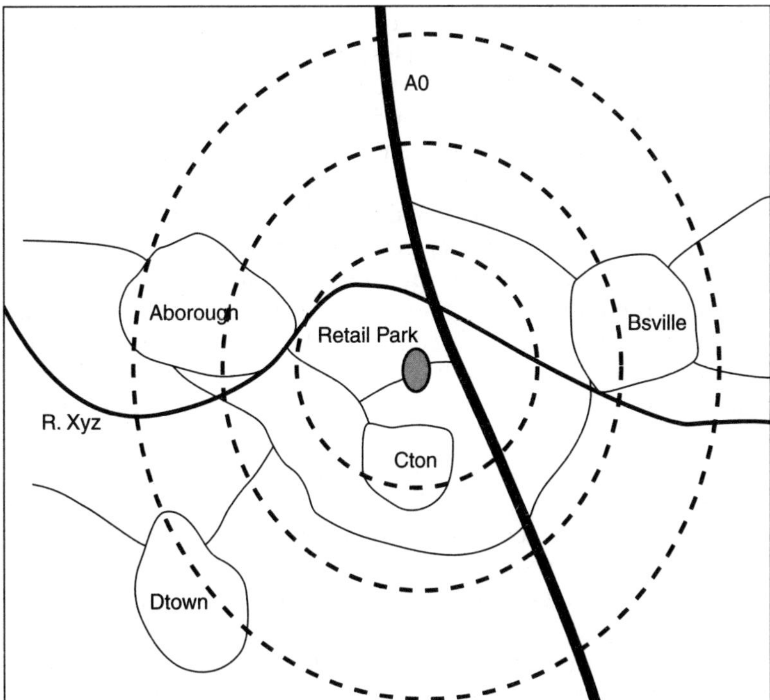

Figure 5.3 Example of the concentric zones approach

likely behaviour. A process of managerial judgements is used to consider factors that will affect mobility or time constraints, with a bipolar scale used for classification. Suppose a retailer was analysing an area characterized by low levels of income and limited car ownership. It is reasonable to assume that local shops will be favoured even if they are not seen as providing the best offering. In this case, shopper mobility is limited, thus decreasing the likely distance of any shopping trip. Considering time constraints provides an extra level of detail given the notion that more time-constrained shoppers will look to minimize overall shopping time, usually by favouring shops closer at hand (Figure 5.4).

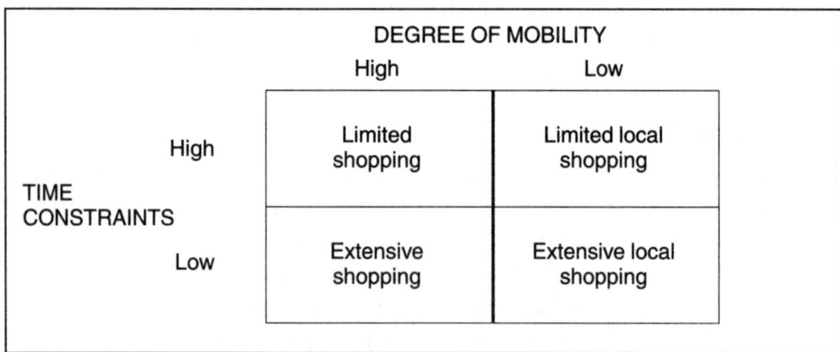

Figure 5.4 Shopper mobility/time constraints matrix

A *limited local shopping area* would be characterized by few local trips probably of a short overall duration. Trade areas of this composition would require store locations as close as possible to the target group's home or place of work. Travel to the store would also need to be quick and convenient. At the other end of the scale, *extensive shopping* comprises many or more lengthy shopping trips both to local and more distant shopping areas. Store location in this case does not need to favour proximity and easy access although both will still be an issue for shopper. *Extensive local shopping* sees shoppers with the time to shop but hampered by poor mobility. In this case, shopping trips will be numerous or lengthy and local in nature. The final condition is limited shopping where the shopper is constrained by a lack of time. Mobility is high but time does not permit a large number of trips or a long trip duration. Local shops would be favoured if, and only if, they provided the required offering.

A similar approach is that developed by CCN (now called Experian) and reported by Davies and Clarke (1994). In this case, the matrix uses the variables of time (convenience) versus leisure (comparison) and bulky versus portable purchase (see Figure 5.5). The assumption underlying the model is that *available time* and the *nature of the purchase* are the key variables explaining shopping trip choices. The similarities with the mobility/time matrix are apparent, with mobility substituted for purchase bulkiness in this case. On further consideration, it is apparent that mobility and purchase bulkiness are related – i.e. mobility will have an effect on the extent to which bulky purchases can be made.

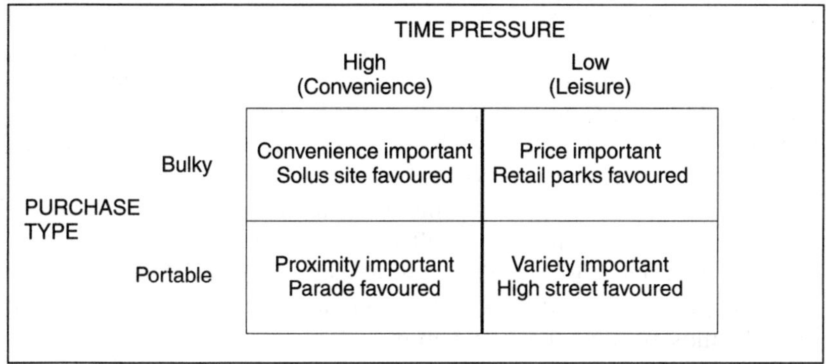

Figure 5.5 The Davies and Clarke model (1994)
Source: Adapted from Davies, M. and Clarke, I. (1994) A framework for network planning, *International Journal of Retail and Distribution Management*, Vol. 22, No. 6, pp 6–10, with permission.

In this case, the time-constrained shopper will seek convenience and will tend to shop on the basis of *proximity* for portable items and *accessibility* (convenience) for bulky items. Shops located close to the shopper's place of work or home (shopping parades) are favoured by proximity shoppers, while convenience shoppers will seek out easily accessible stores that are often large and located away from other retail areas (solus stores). The less time-constrained shopper seeks enjoyment, so shopping is more of a leisure activity. Such shoppers seek comparison (want to shop around) and favour retail parks for bulky items and the high street for more portable items. Again, the model has provided the retailer with an insight into trade area definition.

Trade Area Analysis

Detailed analysis of the trade area begins with a detailed *trade area audit* covering topics such as population size and growth rate, demographics, disposable income, lifestyle, neighbourhood analysis, current shopping patterns, media habits, main employers and seasonal factors. All customer groups are analysed initially to provide an overall picture of the trade area. More in-depth analysis is then undertaken on the appropriate target shoppers – i.e. the shoppers to which the retailer is directing its offering. Identification of this target group is achieved by analysing profile or classification data such as demographics and lifestyle. This data includes age, occupation, social class, disposable income and the shopper's way of living (lifestyle). Population (target shopper) size and growth rate is then used as a rough indicator of sales potential, both now and in the future. A more detailed estimate of sales potential can be obtained from a behavioural profile based on *shopping pattern data*, such as store patronage, shopping frequency and level of expenditure. *Seasonal factors* should also be considered, as they may lead to fluctuations in target group size throughout the year. This is particularly apparent in holiday areas such as seaside resorts or winter sports areas. Consideration of the main employers in the area and their relative stability can also assist in projections of likely future demand, but prediction in areas of unstable employment, for example, is liable to be highly dubious. On a more practical level, *media habits* are measured to provide retailers with information that can be used to increase the effectiveness of communications with shoppers. 'Media habits' refer to the media that given people are exposed to – i.e. what newspapers or magazines are read, what TV programmes are watched, etc. Shopping pattern data are also used to assess the effects of *competing* or *complementary* stores in the area. It is essential for a retailer to identify the competitors that must be accounted for and the complementary stores that might have the most positive effect on demand.

Geodemographic packages such as Mosaic (Experian) or ACORN (CACI) are widely used by retailers to gain much of the required trade area audit data (Clarkson, Clarke-Hill and Robinson 1996; O'Malley, Patterson and Evans 1997). Specific examples in the UK include IKEA (Bradford 1995), Tesco (Moore *et al.* 1991) and the Nationwide Building Society (Beaumont and Inglis 1989).

Such packages work by collecting shopper data with a geographical marker (e.g. postcode) and combining all data into geographic groups. The more different data sources that can be combined the more detailed a picture is built up of the geographic groups. The resultant data base provides a wide range of data based on a given postcode area and is very useful in building up a picture of the typical trade area residents. The usage of such systems does not stop with commercial operations like Experian. Many retailers are now developing their own proprietary data base systems, or geographic information systems (GIS) that 'blend tabular data with digital maps and then print or display the results' (Robins 1993). The GIS will manage data with a geographic marker from a wide variety of different sources, both internal and external to the company. The advances in EPOS (electronic point of sale) systems mean that a retailer has detailed sales information for any given period of the day, month or year. Add to this the increasing use of loyalty or store cards (see Chapter 12), and the retailer has customer information that can be combined with EPOS data – i.e. a postcode associated with a given card holder can be tagged to a given sales receipt. Additional data sources may be the geodemographic data bases mentioned above, other data bases, published surveys and the retailer's own surveys. The benefits of such a system are clear, fast and accurate data on any given site or trade area in a retailer's sphere of operation.

Demand Estimation

Once mapped, the trade area must be assessed for potential customer demand. Marketing research can be used to measure existing spending levels of all customer groups located in the trade area. A number of methods can then be used to predict demand for a new retail outlet at a given location, ranging from simple ratio methods to more complex modelling/simulation approaches. Two commonly used methods are the Index of Retail Saturation (ratio) and regression (modelling/simulation).

The *Index of Retail Saturation (IRS)* is based in the notion that retail saturation occurs at the point where a given trade area can *just support the number of competing stores* located within its boundaries. All stores are economically viable before and at the saturation point, whereas past this point customer demand is insufficient to make *all* competing stores viable. Retailers can use the IRS to predict the potential demand of a given trade area, based on a specified level of competition (expressed in selling space) and a measure of shopper expenditure. It should be noted that the IRS assumes that stores will take a share of the total sales proportional to the selling space of that store. Other factors such as retail brand popularity, accessibility (see later), tactical effectiveness and costs (see later) are not included in the calculation. For this reason, the IRS should be seen as a useful starting point to demand estimation rather than a means of accurate prediction. Table 5.4 gives an example of the use of the IRS, the equation for which is given below.

$$IRSi = \frac{Ci \times REi}{RFi}$$

$IRSi$ = IRS for trade area i
Ci = number of customers in area i for the given retail offering
REi = retail expenditures per customer in area i for the given retail offering
RFi = total retail selling space (sq. ft) in area i allocated to the given retail offering.

Table 5.4 The Use of the IRS

Using the same situation as discussed for Huff's Law (see Table 5.3) with a proposed new store of 10 000 sq ft size and customer numbers/spend as indicated, IRS figures can be calculated for each trade area, as below. In addition, the break-even point for the new store is calculated as a sales figure of £75 per sq. ft.

Factor	Trade area 1	Trade area 2	Trade area 3	Trade area 4
Number of customers per year	25 000	45 000	65 000	100 000
Average annual purchase per customer (£)	100	65	150	200
Existing selling space (sq. ft)	50 000	18 000	100 000	250 000
Total selling space (sq. ft)	60 000	28 000	110 000	260 000
IRS figure (£ per sq. ft)	41.67	104.46	88.64	76.92

Trade areas 2, 3 and 4 would meet the break-even criteria, although Trade area 2 would give the best viability as the IRS exceeds the break-even by the largest figure.

Result: Trade area 2 selected.

Regression is based on an assumption that analysis of a similar store can provide predictions for the new store in question. Analysis is undertaken to find the key factors that affect demand and the equation that links them together. The mathematical relationship between demand and these key factors can then be used as a model for predicting demand for similar stores in a similar situation. Key factors typically include population size and composition, level of personal disposable income, store selling space and competitive intensity. The section on site selection later in this chapter gives a more detailed explanation of the regression process.

Infrastructure

The most important aspect of *infrastructure*, or the physical assets and attributes associated with a retail area, is accessibility (i.e. the ease with which potential shoppers can get to the retail area). Simply measuring the population in a given trade area is not enough to predict likely sales volume. Retailers must check how many shoppers will *physically be able to get to the store* using any of a number of modes of transport (e.g. on foot, by road vehicle, or on public transport). Poor accessibility will deter shoppers, thus lowering the likely sales volume, whereas excellent accessibility may have the opposite effect. *Accessibility studies* usually concentrate on factors such as pedestrian flow and entry routes, public transport, site access, the road network, parking and visibility. It is important to note that the type of retail outlet or area will affect the relative importance of these accessibility factors, as will the type of shopper. In general terms, though, the research by Foxall *et al.* (1994) quoted earlier in this chapter is important as it states that 'more than half [of shopping trips] are made on foot, the rest involve car travel'. Clearly, accessibility by foot and car are of vital importance. Public transport is also important, as this was included in Foxall *et al.*'s definition of 'on foot'.

- *Pedestrian flow and entry routes* relate to the volume of footfall in the vicinity of the store. Flow relates primarily to the volume of pedestrian traffic while entry routes provide an insight into the likely direction of those traffic flows. These factors are important for city-centre stores where vehicular access is limited, as well as those stores targeting a less affluent shopper where a low level of car ownership exists. Small local convenience stores also tend to rely heavily on pedestrian traffic.
- *Public transport* is assessed by considering the types available, their convenience and cost to the shopper, their capacity, and links to other forms of transport. The types of public transport available will tend to influence a number of the other factors, especially cost and convenience, and capacity. Traditional rail services are typically inconvenient for the majority of shoppers as stations tend not to be numerous while bus services have more pick-up and set-down points and a greater variety of routes. *Capacity* indicates the maximum shopper traffic in any given time period and links show how multiple public transport trips can be made. Public transport tends to be important for many of the same stores and locations as listed for pedestrians.
- *The road network* is an increasingly important factor in accessibility studies owing to the increasing usage of the car generally and for shopping trips in particular. Important points to be considered here are restrictions to traffic flow (traffic congestion, limited access zones, one-way streets) and links to major routes. The car is particularly important for retail areas situated outside the town centre (satellite or new) where cars are the dominant form of transport used by shoppers. In addition, shopping trips where purchases are sizeable favour the car. Such sizeable purchases could be due either to multi-store shopping trips where many different items are bought or single-store shopping trips where a single large item is bought. An example of the former would be a trip to a large diverse retail park while the latter could be the purchase of a large electrical good.
- *Parking* is obviously linked to the road network as it directly affects the ease of using the car. The road network itself may present no access

problems, but car access overall may be restricted by parking capacity and convenience. Parking can be a difficult issue for the retailer to handle, as it has serious space implications. Consider the size of the car park in relation to the overall store size in modern retail parks and it is apparent that parking space is both expensive and accounts for a lot of potential selling space. Analysis of the available research points to an ideal selling space to parking space ratio of between 6 and 12 places per 1000 sq.ft of selling space.

- *Visibility* refers to how noticeable the store or retail area is to the passer-by. Suitable promotional campaigns can build awareness for a new store or retail area, but it is still the case that a significant proportion of first time visits are triggered by actually seeing the store or retail area in question.

- *Site access* relates to access for staff and deliveries, so it is derived from a number of the accessibility factors already mentioned. *Delivery access* usually relates to the road network but may, in isolated situations, relate to public transport. *Staff access* may relate to pedestrian issues as well as public transport, the road network and parking. Both issues are important as poor access for either staff or deliveries will impair the efficient operation of the store.

Retail Outlets

The number of retail outlets in a given trade area will have an effect on potential demand, levels of required marketing activity, site availability, ease of obtaining planning permission and customer choice. The overall number of retail outlets will certainly affect site availability and planning permission as a given retail area will have a maximum number of sites or land area. This being the case, as the number of stores increases so the number of available sites will decrease and the difficulty of gaining planning permission for a new site will increase. Customer choice will also be affected by the overall number of stores as shoppers can increasingly 'one-stop-shop' – i.e. can make all their retail purchases in one shopping area. In addition, as the number of similar stores increases so shoppers have a greater degree of choice for each of their different retail purchases.

The concept of *total store numbers* and the number of *similar stores* is an important distinction when considering potential demand and the level of required marketing activity. Measurement of the overall number of stores in a given retail area fails to take into account either the positive effects of some non-competing stores, referred to as *complementary*, or the negative effects of *competing* stores. Competing stores can be defined as those whose retail offerings overlap while complementary stores are those that positively affect demand, are usually part of the same shopping trip but whose retail offerings are different. As an example, suppose that a small retail park contains one grocery retailer (supermarket) and two home and garden (DIY) stores. The two home and garden stores would be classed as competing whereas the grocery retailer could be seen as complementary to the other two. Clearly shoppers would have a direct choice to make between the two competing stores but may choose to make both their grocery and home and garden purchases in the same shopping trip. This being the case, the presence of one store has had a positive effect on demand for the others by increasing traffic flow to the retail area, thus increasing the number of potential shoppers for all retailers.

To look at this in more detail, analysis of retail outlets must take into account the number of outlets in the trade area, both currently and in the future. As has already been noted, retailers are interested in the total number of stores, as well as the number of competing and complementary stores. Current numbers can be easily assessed via a simple survey, while prediction of future numbers can be assisted by considering *planning applications* (increase in numbers) and likely *disposal/divestments* (decrease in numbers). Competing stores should then be analysed further to quantify the nature of the competitive threat, with factors such as the degree of retail offering overlap, company size/strength, selling space of store(s) and customer attitudes being considered. The key question concerning complementary stores is their likely effect on *demand*. An answer to this question can be found by assessing the probability of shoppers visiting both stores in the same trip. Two factors affect visit probability, *degree of fit* and *proximity*. Degree of fit is the extent to which two types of retail purchase can be jointly considered by the shopper, while proximity relates to the travel distance or time between the two stores. Complementary stores exhibit a high degree of fit and a close proximity.

Site Selection

The retailer now has detailed trade area information (definition, analysis and demand estimation) for a number of individual sites. The final stage in the location decision making process is the selection of the actual site or sites for the new store(s). Three common approaches to site selection are the checklist method, the analogue approach and regression modelling.

Checklist method

The *checklist method*, developed over 40 years ago, is a simple listing process that addresses all the categories and types of data required for accurate site assessment. Early work by Nelson (1958) identified eight categories and 36 types, whereas Pope (1984) analysed Boots plc (a UK retailer) and found two categories, external and internal. *External* covered data types such as population totals and composition, income, unemployment, inflation, retail sales, trade area composition, competition and store position. *Internal* included sales forecasts, sales areas, sales productivity, stock and stock areas, and tenure type. Combining Nelson and Pope's work with a number of other checklist approaches (e.g. Applebaum 1965; Eisenpris 1965; Kane 1966) allows a comprehensive, if not exhaustive, list of checklist categories and data types to be developed. The four key categories are population, retail outlets, costs and infrastructure (these categories have already been discussed in detail earlier in this chapter). Table 5.5 illustrates the proposed checklist.

Table 5.5 Checklist of Location Factors

Population	Retail outlets	Costs	Infrastructure
Size and growth rate Demographic profile PDI *per capita* Lifestyle profile Neighbourhood analysis Shopping patterns Main employers Seasonal effects	Number of stores (total, competing, complementary) Planning applications Disposals Demand effects of competing Demand effects of complementary	Start-up costs including purchase or lease price, site preparation, store construction, development concessions Operational costs incl. rates, maintenance, security requirements, delivery and staff costs, cannibalization costs	Pedestrian flow and entry routes Public transport types, convenience capacity, cost and links Site access for staff and deliveries Road network congestion and access Parking capacity and convenience Visibility

Analogue approach

The analogue approach (Cohen and Applebaum 1960; Applebaum 1968) seeks to base site suitability decisions on a comparison with an equivalent store. The approach involves the identification of suitable comparable or analogue stores, quantification of key store and trade area factors, and estimation of the performance level for the new store based on an extrapolation from the analogue.

To give a simple example, suppose a retailer had identified a potential site (*S*) and a suitable analogue (*A*). A concentric zones analysis (see earlier in the chapter) could be undertaken for site *A* which could then be used to make predictions for site *S*. The proportion of each zone's total sales gained by site *A* would be measured, along with the total weekly *per capita* sales from each zone. Measurement of the population within each corresponding zone for site *S* could then be used in combination with site *A* data to predict likely weekly demand per zone and hence total demand for site *S*. Table 5.6 contains an example of this method with figures.

Table 5.6 Example of the Analogue Method

Zone	Proportion of sales site *A* (%)	Per capita sales site *A* (£)	Population site *S* (£000)	Estimated sales site *S* (£000)
Primary	65	3.50	25	56.9
Secondary	23	3.25	60	44.9
Tertiary	5	2.85	100	14.3
Total				116.1

Regression

Regression (see earlier in this chapter) is a more rigorous approach to site selection that involves the development of a model to explain the performance of a store on the basis of a number of determinants. Such an approach is usually multi-determinant-based, hence should be called *multiple regression*. Selection of the determinants is an important process, particularly in relation to the predictive accuracy of the subsequent model. The basic model (Clarkson, Clarke-Hill and Robinson

1996) typically uses five determinants, namely competition (C), trade area composition and characteristics (T), site accessibility (S), store physical attributes (A) and catchment area (or trade area) demographics or customer profile (D). Potential store turnover (T/O) is then expressed as the equation

$$T/O = f\ \{C, T, S, A, D\}$$

Data are then fed into an appropriate regression software package that will calculate the regression coefficients for each determinant. These coefficients show how each determinant affects turnover, while an additional measure (beta) gives the relative importance of each determinant. The regression method has been successfully applied to a number of retail offerings including hotels (Hanson 1983) and grocery stores (Cottrel 1973).

Conclusions

Location is typically the first area considered by the retailer because of the simple fact that retailers make sales when shoppers are in the store. The increasing level of retail competition means that shoppers have a wide choice of local stores to visit for a given purchase, so why should they bother to make the extra journey to a store further away? Unless a retailer is highly differentiated, the answer is that many shoppers will not bother to make that extra journey. Retailers must, therefore, choose a location close to their shoppers. Retailers also need to consider competition, costs and infrastructure.

Location assessment involves the three stages of macro and micro location evaluation, and site selection. Macro location evaluation takes all the possible regions and screens out those that are unsuitable. A number of factors such as level of customer spending, degree of competition and site availability are used to make this decision leaving a small number of suitable regions. A simple screening process is used that may use compensatory or non-compensatory elements. A more detailed, although essentially similar screen is now used to narrow down the list of suitable sites to the best prospects only. Analysis undertaken to make this second screening covers the population, infrastructure, existing stores and projected costs.

Population analysis involves trade area mapping or the detailed characterization of a given area, comprising definition, analysis and demand estimation. Defining the trade area can be a complicated process owing to the complex nature of shopping patterns. A number of methods exist to allow a trade area to be defined, all of which seek to explain *shopper visit behaviour* – i.e. where a shopper from this area will go to buy a particular item. Early theories used either travel time as the key factor (central place theory, Reilly's Law) or were based on economic principles (land value theory and minimum differentiation). Retailers increasingly realized, however, that travel time or economics did not fully explain shopper visit behaviour, and sought refinements based on more accurate measures of attractiveness (incentives to visit a given site). Huff's Law considered selling space and particular types of product while later models (MCI and MNL) sought to use a much wider range of variables. Approaches were also developed based on survey data (concentric zones) and shopper mobility. Once definition has been achieved, analysis is undertaken using a detailed *trade area audit* covering a wide range of areas (e.g. population size and growth rate, demographics, disposable income, etc.). Finally, demand is estimated using methods such as the Index of Retail Saturation (IRS) or regression.

Infrastructure is analysed to allow accessibility to be assessed. As has already been noted, shoppers usually have sufficient choice of competing stores and can select the most accessible. 'Accessibility' refers to any mode of transport, so access by foot, public transport or car is important. The car is clearly the preferred mode of transport for a majority of shoppers, so the road network (congestion, ease of access) and parking are particularly important. The presence of other retail outlets may affect the shopper's view of accessibility, as a more difficult or time-consuming trip may be justified if a number of different purchases can be made. *Competing* stores offer the shopper more choice but reduce the attractiveness of the site for retailers. *Complementary* stores are those that fit together to provide an enhanced shopping trip. Retailers can benefit from such stores as demand may be encouraged.

Once a trade area has been selected, an individual site can be chosen. Three methods are commonly used to make this selection based on a consideration of factors affecting site attractiveness (checklist), comparison with an equivalent store and site (analogue) and the mathematical modelling (regression).

Location is a process of data collection and detailed analysis because it needs to be. Whether a site is chosen in the city centre or out of town (satellite or new), or is planned or incremental, a sufficient number of the right shoppers must be nearby or within easy reach, competition must be manageable, access must be unhindered and the site must fit the retailer's offering. Even the best retailers in the world, to paraphrase George Davis, must set up their shop in the right place or risk never doing much business.

References and Further Reading

Applebaum, W. (1965) Can Store Location Research be a Science?, *Economic Geography*, 41, 234–7.

Applebaum, W. (1968) *Store Location Strategy Cases*, Addison-Wesley, Reading, MA.

Arnold, S.J. and Tigert, D. (1980) Conditional Logit Versus MDA in the Prediction of Store Choice, *Advances in Consumer Research*, 8, 665–70.

Beaumont, J.R. and Inglis, K. (1989) Geodemographics in Practice: Developments in Britain and Europe, *Environment and Planning A*, 21, 587–604.

Berry, B.J.L. and Parr, J.B. (1987) *Market Centers and Retail Location: Theory and Applications*, Prentice-Hall, Englewood Cliffs, NJ.

Bowlby, S., Breheny, M. and Foot, D. (1984) Store Location: Problems and Methods I, *Retail and Distribution Management*, 12, 5, 31–3.

Bradford, G. (1995) Targeting Technology, *Admap*, January, 32–4.

Brown, S. (1989) Harold Hotelling and the Principle of Minimum Differentiation, *Progress in Human Geography*, 13, 4, 471–93.

Brown, S. (1993) Retail Location Theory: Evolution and Evaluation, *The International Review of Retail Distribution and Consumer*, 3, 185–229.

Christaller, W. (1966) *Central Places in Southern Germany*, Prentice-Hall, Englewood Cliffs, NJ.

Clarkson, R.M., Clarke-Hill, C.M. and Robinson, T. (1996) UK Supermarket Location Assessment, *Internal Journal of Retail and Distribution Management*, 24, 6, 22–33.

Cohen, S.B. and Applebaum, W. (1960) Evaluating Store Sites and Determining Store Rents, *Economic Geography*, 36, 1–35.

Collins, A. (1992) *Competitive Retail Marketing*, McGraw-Hill, London.

Cottrel, J. (1973) An Environmental Model of Performance Measurement in a Chain of Supermarkets, *Journal of Retailing*, 49, 51–63.

Davies, M. and Clarke, I. (1994) A Framework for Network Planning, *International Journal of Retail and Distribution Management*, 22, 6, 6–10.

Eisenpris, A. (1965) An Evaluation of Current Store Location Research, paper presented at the National Conference of the American Marketing Association.

Firey, W. (1947) *Lane Use in Central Boston*, Greenwood Press, New York.

Foxall, G. and Goldsmith, R.E. (1994) *Consumer Psychology for Marketing*, Routledge, London.

Haig, R.M. (1926) Towards an Understanding of the Metropolis: I and II, *Quarterly Journal of Economics*, 40, 402–34.

Hanson, D. (1983) The Effect of Location on Hotel Performance: A Case Study of Manhattan, unpublished thesis, Columbia University.

Hotelling, H. (1929) Stability in Competition, *The Economic Journal*, 39, 3, 41–57.

Houston, F.S. and Stanton, J. (1984) Evaluating Retail Trade Areas for Convenience Stores, *Journal of Retailing*, 60, 1.

Huff, D.L. (1964) Defining and Estimating a Trading Area, *Journal of Marketing*, 28, 34–38.

Kane, B.J. (1966) *A Systematic Guide to Supermarket Location Analysis*, Fairchild, New York.

Lakshmanan, T.R. and Hansen, W.G. (1965) A Retail Market Prediction Model, *Journal of the American Institute of Planners*, 31, 134–43.

Manchester University (1966) *Regional Shopping Centres in North West England Part II: A Retail Shopping Model*, University of Manchester, Manchester.

Miller, E. and Lerman, S. (1981) Disaggregate Modeling and Decision of Retail Firms: A Case Study of Clothing Retailers, *Environment and Planning A*, 13, 729–46.

Moore, S. and Attewell, G. (1991) To Be and Where Not to Be: The Tesco Approach to Location Analysis, *OR Insight*, 4, 1, 21–4.

Nakanishi, M. and Cooper, L.G. (1974) Parameter Estimation for a Multiplicative Competitive Interaction Model – Least Squares Approach, *Journal of Marketing Research*, 11, 303–11.

Nelson, R.L. (1958) *The Selection of Retail Locations*, McGraw-Hill, New York.

O'Malley, L., Patterson, M. and Evans, M. (1997) Retailer Use of Geodemographic and Other Data Sources: An Empirical Investigation, *International Journal of Retail and Distribution Management*, 25, 6, 188–96.

Pope, M.P.R. (1984) 'Developing a Strategic Planning Data Base', in R.L. Davies and D.S. Rogers (eds), *Store Location and Store Assessment Research*, Wiley, Chichester, 181–94.

Reilly, W.J. (1931) *The Law of Retail Gravitation*, Knickerbocker Press, New York.

Robins, G. (1993) Retail GIS Use Growing, *Stores*, 1, 44–50.

Retail Image, Positioning and Reputation

CHAPTER 6

This chapter:

- Defines retail image
- Shows how positioning is crucial to the customer image of the retail offering
- Defines the factors in a customer's perception of a retailer

Retail Image, Positioning and Reputation

Introduction

Ries and Trout (1983) have famously described positioning as the 'battle for a customer's mind'. *Positioning* is the marketing term that is used to describe the view a customer has *regarding the image of a particular offering*. There is an obvious link between *Image, Positioning* and *Branding*, as all of these terms describe essentially the same thing. Of course a store image and branding are, to quote Birtwistle and Freathy (1998), 'More than just a name above the shop', they are the very essence of what a potential customer believes and as such a crucial influencing factor regarding store choice and customer purchasing behaviour. It is easy to understand that a favourable image will lead to real trading advantages while an unfavourable image will affect decisions in an adverse way. The marketing positioning of a retail store has nothing to do with its geographic location, but is the positive image that an organization wishes to achieve. However the only position that really matters is the *perception* about a particular retailer that is 'lodged' in the mind of a potential customer. This could be described in terms of a brand that is the link between the store name or logo and the values a customer ascribes to it, together with the beliefs they hold regarding the supplier.

One problem facing customers is that they can receive a great deal of information about a supplier, coming from many different sources both personal and impersonal, direct and indirect. It can lead to a real overload whereby it becomes impossible for the customer to evaluate effectively all the relevant factors. The reaction of most customers to this situation will almost inevitably lead to a very subjective view being formed regarding that supplier. This perception regarding a particular retailer will therefore emerge from a complex jumble of impressions, together with some relevant facts. The resulting image or position will build in the mind of a customer in spite of the efforts of retail marketers.

However, that does not mean that retailers should not try to persuade its target customer and to improve any image or correct any misconceptions, but, as already mentioned, it is the customers view that is paramount when it comes to a purchase decision.

Retail Image and Positioning

A retailer's *image* has always been viewed as a critical factor affecting both store choice – and, equally importantly, store loyalty. This has been supported by classic studies by Doyle and Fenwick (1974) in the grocery market, Nevin and Houston (1980) on urban shops and Osman (1993) who researched issues of loyalty. The image formed regarding a specific store will be affected by an amalgam of its physical environment, apparent atmosphere, convenience, types of shoppers using the stores, merchandise available, service levels and many other dimensions both real and perceived. Over a quarter of a century ago Oxenfeld (1974) argued that 'store image is a concept which is more than the sum of the parts ...., it represents interaction among characteristics and includes extraneous elements ...., it has some emotional content ... a combination of factual and emotional material'.

Lautman (1993) was more specific when he suggested that the positioning of an offering could be expressed in terms of:

- *Attributes*
- *Benefits*
- *Claims.*

This easy to remember: 'ABC' suggests that the interaction that leads to a perceived position, or image, is derived from the actual *attributes* of, say, a retail store such as its location, decor and merchandise. These will then be considered in the light of the *benefits* that a customer might expect to receive. Benefits can be expressed in terms of actual or perceived value, or in the way a purchase might meet a specific need of the shopper. Affecting both the actual attributes and the expected benefits are the *claims* made, usually in the form of advertising or word-of-mouth communication that can influence potential consumers.

It must be remembered that the major source of competitive advantage for a retailer will come from the way its operations are perceived to add 'real' value for a customer. To do this a retailer must make the merchandise offered more *affordable* or more *available* to shoppers than is the case from competitive suppliers, alternatively it must do so in a more *acceptable* way. Therefore this 'added-value' could come from the services performed or from the merchandise actually being more accessible in a particular store or from some other aspect of a retail operation. The evaluation of these attributes by potential customers, and in particular the balancing of all aspects of a retail offering, both positive and negative, will be a major factor in the development of an image regarding the retailer.

Example

In the retail car market there are typically both main dealers who have a formal franchise contract with a specific manufacturer (e.g. Ford or Rover), and there are non-franchise outlets that can also retail new cars. Often the franchised dealers are constrained regarding their offering by the terms of the agreement with the manufacturer. They cannot offer some deals whereas the non-franchise retailers have more freedom.

The franchisee still has some advantages because many customers believe the service back-up and guarantee carries more credibility from the official dealers and this is a form of added value that is relevant to many potential purchasers.

The situation has become even more complex because cars can now be purchased over the Internet, as well as being available from abroad at very different prices to those charged in the UK.

One of the most important cues for shoppers, at both a conscious and an unconscious level, is the level of *prices* that are being charged. For instance, it is common for people looking for a restaurant to study the menus and prices displayed outside before venturing in. In many cases the position/image will be based on a combination of fact, experience, knowledge, opinion and rumour. It is as likely to be the result of 'word-of-mouth' comments from friends or acquaintances as it is based on personal experience. In fact personal experience can be a poor determinant since it might be the result of just a single visit to the shop. The possible variation that can occur in the service encounters on any visit could lead to widely different views about a single store.

It is important to take a cognitive approach when considering the issue of retailer image/positioning. The image relies more on the perception of the customer than it does on the messages put out by the supplier. The overall perception that a specific customer has regarding a particular retail organization will have a significant effect upon the decision of that customer to visit or not to visit, and to purchase or not to purchase. If a retail store is thought to be rather 'basic' it might attract customers who equate that with 'no frills, low price'. Those customers who feel comfortable in this type of store will visit it and are likely to make purchases from it. Alternatively the Harrods department store in Knightsbridge, London has an upmarket image that leads to a subjective opinion regarding the products offered and the level of prices charged. Harrods will obviously attract a different type of shopper, as well as deterring others because of its image.

The image of any retail outlet is very personal to each individual customer. It is developed over time but, as mentioned above, the retailer should not leave the development of a position entirely to chance. Retailers should continually offer inputs in the form of both communications and actions, and then will trust that different, potential customers can interpret these in an acceptable way. Customers evaluate all the messages received in a subjective way, then add other personal or acquired knowledge, and finally form or modify an opinion regarding that retailer. Achieving the *most appropriate position* is a crucial aspect of retail marketing. It is not only important with regards to a single store and a single location but it is also important when a multiple retailer wishes to roll out coverage into new areas while building on what has been achieved in existing locations. In fact the image of many retail, 'bricks and mortar' stores has also been vital to success when such operations are extended into the virtual location of the Internet.

Branding of Retail Stores

A 'retailer image' can evolve into a strong 'brand identity' in the same way as other products develop into brands. Retail groups are recognized by their 'store brand name', and this reflects the values and personality associated with them. There is no doubt that Tesco, IKEA, Next and Dixons have really strong identities in the minds of customers and even non-customers. What is important is whether or not the position that is encapsulated in the brand identity is appropriate to the right customers. This could mean that a specialist niche operator, maybe a specialist town centre boutique in a large urban area, might target its activity to a very closely defined segment across a wide catchment area. Conversely a large grocery supermarket must try to attract as large a proportion of the potential shoppers within its immediate locale as is possible. The supermarket must therefore position itself to appeal equally to many disparate groups. This could mean a stronger emphasis on the functional aspect of the brand, as opposed to the emotive feelings that could be evoked by stylish retailers such as Gap.

It is the *customer's opinion* that is the only one that really matters. If shoppers do not have enough information about a particular retailer they will make their own assumptions based on the facts they possess and their perceptions as to its relevance to their requirements. Therefore every retailer has to endeavour to achieve a strong, favourable image in the minds of their preferred customers, and this will lead to a specific position that might also be understood in the form of a *recognizable identity* and *brand name*. A brand has been defined by Doyle (1998) as a 'specific name, symbol or design – or, more usually combination of these – which is used to distinguish a particular seller's product'. The term can also be applied to the retail seller organization as a whole. The brand is therefore a more specific representation of the store image and positioning. However a brand is still *intangible*, although the brand name can be more accessible. The image is a combination of tangible attributes and subjective perceptions, and while all marketing cues help to develop a brand it is the customer who actually gives life to the brand by virtue of the beliefs ascribed to it.

Real comparable advantage can flow from a strong brand image since it is almost impossible for a competitor to match the set of beliefs held by customers about a specific retailer. Sometimes the term 'brand equity' is used to describe the positive and negative associations that are linked to a brand name. Aaker (1991) describes brand equity as 'a set of assets and liabilities that add or subtract from the value provided'. He suggests that these assets and liabilities will depend on the context in which they are to be found. For instance, a low-priced discounter located in an up-market high street will be evaluated differently in another more suitable location. Aaker suggests that there are four categories of factors that can affect the strength of a brand's equity:

- Its level of *awareness*
- Its *perceived quality*
- Anything *associated with the brand*
- The level of *brand loyalty*.

All of these add or subtract from the total equity, and all benefit from the same equity. *Awareness* is crucial in retailing – all too many new stores fail because they are unable to achieve early recognition after opening. The offering could well be absolutely right to meet customer needs but the delay in making those customers aware of the store can lead to initial losses which are impossible to sustain. This has certainly been the case with some of the Internet failures such as Boo.com.

Obviously the perception a shopper has regarding the quality of merchandise and the quality of service will affect the brand image of a retail store, but associations go further. There are many things connected to a brand that have been transferred directly or indirectly into the perception of customers. Such associations are important in developing an image. Maybe the fun of Ronald McDonald, or the links between the hamburger chain and children's charities, could be beneficial. Alternatively it could be the Asda 'price promise' or the perennial John Lewis strap line 'never knowingly undersold'. Just as powerful is the link between Richard Branson and those organizations carrying the Virgin name; this is continuing even though not all Virgin companies are fully owned by the flamboyant entrepreneur. Traditional services such as the 'no-quibble' returns policy at Marks & Spencer also enhance the brand equity by association.

The real objective of any marketing programme is to achieve high levels of *loyalty*, to the brand and to the store. Perhaps the example of Marks & Spencer is appropriate as that organization scores very highly on the measures of awareness, perceived quality and association, but recently has lost out badly in terms of loyalty and levels of repeat purchasing. The Marks & Spencer store name and the St Michael brand continue to be well respected in the UK, there is still a high degree of brand equity but the retention of traditional customers, the category of store loyalty, is paramount. In this respect Marks & Spencer is not performing at all well.

It is important to be careful when studying links between brand image and brand (store) loyalty. In any case there are two forms of loyalty – true and spurious. Bloemer and Kasper (1995) suggest that loyalty which is due to inertia, or habit, where alternatives are not properly considered, is classed as 'spurious'. True loyalty is more *proactive*, a behavioural response nevertheless, but one based on the feelings a customer has for a specific store. In true loyalty the shopper is likely to go further than simply repurchasing themselves, they will also recommend the store to others, becoming an advocate for the retailer. However in a study of department store customers in the USA, Sivadas and Baker-Prewitt (2001) failed to establish a firm link between favourable attitudes and repeat patronage. They suggest that department stores are more likely to fall into the 'always-a-share' category of retail suppliers, with the acceptable ones always standing a chance of getting a share of the available business.

Perhaps Marks & Spencer has now fallen into the same category. It is no longer sufficiently distinct, and it does offer a wide range of merchandise. It might still have a quality image, but then, in a not too dissimilar way, so do the House of Fraser, Debenhams and other multi-category stores. Marks & Spencer will always get a share of the available business, but it no longer has a monopoly on certain categories, nor on certain customers. In the changing retail marketplace other general stores can now compete for a wide range of goods, and specialist, niche retailers can supply the traditional products such as underwear that was once a dominant part of the St Michael brand business. In fact the wheel of retailing has continued to turn, and Marks & Spencer have suffered because the unique position, developed over a century of trading, has now lost its focus and relevance to some segments in the market.

Aaker (1991) suggests that 'brand loyalty reduces marketing costs, creates barriers to competitors, provides leverage, affects the brand image, and provides time to respond to competitive threats'. However as the example of Marks & Spencer shows, the perception that the merchandise offered is both right and offers superior value in all ways is still vital in a retail marketplace.

As with all branding, there are different levels, for instance an overall company name such as Tesco, or a stand-alone name indicating a particular focused operator within a larger retail group, e.g. Top Shop. Company brands can also be used as an umbrella for several sub-brands, for instance Tesco now offer Tesco Superstores; Tesco Compact; Tesco Extra; Tesco Metro; and Tesco Express, as well as Tesco Direct for home delivery. Each of these sub-brands benefits from the image of the parent company, yet each reflects a specific type of retail operation. Of course, with retail supermarkets, and many other stores, the branding goes even deeper with many items of merchandise branded under the store name, such as Tesco baked beans or Sainsbury's Classic Cola. These retail products will benefit from, as well as reinforcing, some of the components in the parent brand name.

Extension into unrelated areas of business, for instance Sainsbury's Bank, or Boots Opticians, can also exploit the brand equity and position of the parent brand. Such brand extensions offer immediate *awareness* for the new offering, and this should lead to earlier trial and perhaps higher levels of acceptance. Extensions rely on the customer transferring the same values they hold about the original store onto the new ventures. It is necessary, however, to be very careful and continually measure whether any particular extension is affecting the original brand. This can be more apparent in related areas than in unrelated ones. In the USA it has been reported that when the Gap clothing store was under intense competition from similar fashions at lower prices it launched a new venture 'Gap Warehouse', offering fashions at both lower price and lower quality. The resulting confusion hurt the parent brand more than the competitors because of the continued use of the Gap name. The warehouses were then re-branded as the Old Navy Clothing Company, and as such have become very successful without any obvious link to the Gap organization.

If the retail outlet and the target market chosen do not have any obvious overlaps, then it will be more appropriate to use a multi-branding approach. Hence decisions will be taken to develop different positions for each separate store type within the same overall group. The Burton's group once ran an advertisement in the financial press that stated that 'the secret of successful retailing was giving the market what it wanted'. The graphics supporting the advert emphasized the target marketing approach utilizing segmentation of the Top Shop, Principles, Dorothy Perkins, Evans and Burton's group of clothing shops. Accurate *targeting* is an important issue in the development of a multiple-fascia strategy that utilizes a store portfolio with several different retail approaches. In this situation, the store portfolio is managed to ensure that the right sites are available for each given fascia.

Brand Image and Retail Expansion

When a retailer is thinking about expanding into a new location, say another geographic area or even the Internet, it is vital they evaluate the strength of their position with regards to the potential new customers. *Brand equity* is very specific in that it is a measure of what is present in the minds of each and every customer. Those in existing areas will have the benefit of continuing experience regarding a particular supplier and this will obviously affect awareness, perceived quality and loyalty. In the new locations the prior experience of many customers will be lacking although other perceptions might be present. If there are strong positive feelings already in the minds of these new target shoppers then there will be real advantages in replicating the existing format and brand. This could have occurred owing to the mobility of customers, the wide nature of some mass-media communications or simply word of mouth between consumers. It needs to be confirmed by careful research. In such situations the development of a multiple retailer might be achieved by rolling out the same store concept (store name/retail offering/fascia) throughout a defined geographic area. This will probably benefit the retailer by building on its positive features in a consistent manner. It will also help the development of the retailer's image by reaching a greater number of potential customers. Thus the positioning of a retailer can become a real competitive advantage in the new area, but only if that concept fits easily into the new location. To give an example, Morrisons, the Yorkshire-based grocery retailer is currently developing duplicate stores outside its traditional area of strength in the north of England.

Example

During the 1980s the Early Learning Company marketed its educational toys and other products exclusively through mail order catalogues. In order to extend the operation the company studied their data base to establish clusters of existing customers in particular towns. This was based on customer postcodes. Where a large enough cluster was found it was believed that an opportunity would exist for a physical retail store. Suitable locations were investigated and stores were then opened in those locations. The existing mail-order customers were targeted by direct mail to encourage them into the new stores and incentives were used to encourage them to bring friends along.

It was thought, correctly, that those locations were ones where the equity of the 'Early Learning' brand was strong enough for more development. The strategy was extremely successful and the company became the leader in its market niche.

However this strategy might work in closely related geographic areas but it is far less certain in wider, say international, expansion. It is crucial that there is consistency in any development and if the store format has to be significantly modified then the use of established brand names, and reliance on an established position will not be possible in the new area. The dilemma for retailers wishing to move into other areas is whether the economies of scale from standardized operations, coupled with the positive image in an established location, are really appropriate without adaptation in a new marketplace. Often a period of time is necessary to allow any new development to really prosper in a new market; this could be because shoppers will take time to change their purchase behaviour, even if they respect the image of a new entrant.

Brown and Burt (1992) posed the key question 'does a retail brand mean the same to a group of customers in one country as it does to customers in another?' In some categories the answer is 'yes'. For instance, McDonalds is well understood and recognized across the globe. In fact Jain (1989) argues that 'the worldwide marketplace has become so homogenised that multinational corporations can market standardised products and services all over the world, by identical strategies'. A real case of 'McDonaldization'! Category killers such as Toys 'Я' Us and IKEA have both achieved international success, overcoming any problems with large investments and appropriate marketing activity. In another way, designer fashion companies have been able to expand beyond the capital cities of New York, London and Paris based on the high profile of the parent brands. Others have been moderately successful, such as Laura Ashley and Benetton in the clothing market. In other cases the answer is definitely 'no'. It is important to study local conditions and local needs and revise the offering in line with the existing conditions. The announcement by Marks & Spencer that it intended to close all its stores within continental Europe was supported by the fact that these operations were not profitable despite some of the stores having quite a long history following the original expansion.

Example: Tesco Ireland

Tesco first bought a chain of discount stores in Ireland (Eire) in 1978, and re-branded them as Tesco. However the venture did not prove successful, even with the retail expertise of the parent company. One problem was that they were more like the Tesco operation in the 1950s and 1960s and yet the market in both Ireland and the UK had moved on. These stores were sold off in 1986 and for the next 11 years Tesco had no operation in Eire.

Then in 1997 as part of a strategic decision to expand operations across Europe, Tesco again entered the Irish market. Again it achieved this by acquisition. This time it was able to acquire the Quinnsworth and Stewart group of stores. The advantages were that these stores were closer to the current image/position of Tesco in the UK, and by taking over an Irish business the company acquired many contacts with local suppliers. In fact, the Irish government put pressure on Tesco to continue to use such links and this in turn has meant that the company is viewed more favourably in the new marketplace.

Although the new company is now distinctly Tesco, very similar in image and operation to the UK parent, it has also been able to offer some local customization. The company undertook a very wide research programme as to what Irish consumers wanted and how they viewed the only foreign-owned multiple in Eire. The commitment to offer products predominately sourced in Ireland was found to be very important, so now Tesco offer a specific guarantee, promoting the fact that well over half its product is from local suppliers. It also highlights the level of Irish-produced items exported for sale in other Tesco stores in other countries.

It now has over 100 stores in Ireland and the expansion is proving very successful.

The reasons for expanding retail operations are often based on a simple push/pull motivation. The *push* could come from such factors as saturation of existing markets or adverse trading in those markets. This could happen where developing additional stores using the original concept would result in a disproportionately lower increase in sales. A good example of this is to be found in the saturation in the UK grocery retail sector, made more acute because the availability of new large sites is now restricted. The *pull* factors arise from a view that there are real opportunities in new markets where a particular retail formula has yet to be established. Whatever the motivation it is crucial to establish a real competitive position in the new marketplace.

It does not matter whether the expansion is geographic or just into a new segment within an existing area, the retailer must evaluate the strength of its brand and then decide whether to build on the parent brand or develop an entirely separate identity. Within the UK it can be seen that the Burton/Arcadia group have utilized stand-alone 'brands' for each of their group of stores – Top Shop, Principals, Dorothy Perkins, Evans, etc; in contrast Tesco have used an 'umbrella' branding policy.

Their multi-fascia approach differentiates stores in terms of both image and size. Tesco's store portfolio now contains a range of store sizes from superstores (approximately 26 000 sq. ft in size) to small convenience stores (approximately 1500 sq. ft), but all presented under the same umbrella brand.

Building Strong Brands

It is one thing to discuss the benefits of a strong brand or a suitable position as perceived by potential customers – it is quite another to set about *building such a position*. As already mentioned, brand images develop in the minds of customers, the resulting subjective positioning depends on the way an individual shopper evaluates all the cues they receive. Certainly a brand is much more than a simple name. As Kotler (1999) says:

> having just a brand name is not enough. What does the brand name mean? What associations, performances, and expectations does it evoke? What degree of preference does it create? If it is only a brand name, then it fails as a brand.

Nevertheless the *name* or *logo* is a starting point for building a brand, although this must be viewed in conjunction with the core offering from a particular store. It could be considered that this starting point is a 'naked' product offering, and that over time it will become 'clothed' with the values and beliefs of customers. In order to achieve the right 'clothing', a retail marketer must try to ensure that all messages received by the customers are *consistent* and *appropriate*. These messages are not solely from advertising, in fact Doyle (1998) suggests that 'Brands are rarely created by advertising. This is often misunderstood because the advertising is generally much more visible than the factors that create the differential advantage'. However, advertising boss Gary Duckworth (1996) does admit that 'the role of advertising is to *manipulate* the meanings connected with the brand to the brand owner's advantage' (emphasis in the original).

Other inputs to the customer will be received through many other sources such as:

- *Experience* in visiting the store, including its appearance
- *Satisfaction* felt when, perhaps, purchasing from it
- Appearance and attitude of *staff*
- A subjective evaluation of the *other shoppers* seen in the store
- Opinions and expressed views from *third parties* such as friends
- Anything in the *media* a customer might see regarding the store.

The above list is not complete because there are many *indirect sources of information* that will influence the perceived image of a store. Earlier in this chapter positioning was expressed in terms of *attributes*, *benefits* and *claims*, and the input to the development of a brand in the customer's mind can be expressed similarly. An important marketing role is to ensure that most relevant attributes are obvious to the customers. In addition, regarding those messages that can be controlled, marketing should strive to confirm that they are appropriate given the stage of development that the brand has achieved. In order to achieve this it is important to research the strength of any brand image on a regular and continuous basis and then to ensure any new attributes and all future messages actually do 'manipulate' meanings in a positive way. In communications terms this will involve *adding information* where necessary and *providing corrections* to any misconceptions. Aaker (1991) warns that 'too often the brand message is weak, confusing, irrelevant or worst of all indistinguishable from the competition.' However, there are many other factors apart from the communications that contribute to brand building. Every promotion, additional feature, or change in presentation will affect the brand image: it is, therefore, critical to review the importance of such factors in any research being carried out concerning developments.

The task is not as easy as it might sound, as the only weapons open to the marketer are those under his/her direct control. There are a plethora of uncontrollable stimuli from third parties making the issue much more complex, and the target customer will also have a mind of his or her own with regards the matter. However the retail marketing task should involve the responsibility for *directing* and *influencing* all those aspects of a store's presentation that impinge on its customers, either directly or indirectly. Perhaps the key marketing objective should be to achieve an image that is *robust*, *unique* and *relevant* to the target shoppers.

Activities aimed at increasing levels of awareness among the target group will be implemented in conjunction with initiatives that ensure the perception of quality, merchandise and service, are right for a chosen image. While perceived quality will be a strong influence on brand equity the converse is more problematic. Brand associations are not necessarily a good predictor of the actual quality of an offering.

Example

McDonald's is one of the strongest brands in the world. Its fast-service hamburger outlets are present in most countries, so much so that the term 'McDonaldization' has been used to describe a particular form of global standardization. In considering quality of service there seemed to be an implicit assumption that McDonald's were synonymous with good, efficient service even if the actual hamburgers do not compare to a gourmet meal. But as Donkin reported: 'Customers ... told McDonalds they were loud brash, American, successful, complacent, uncaring, insensitive, disciplinarian, insincere, suspicious and arrogant. ... We thought we knew about service. Get the order into the customer's hands in 60 seconds – that was service. Not according to our customers. They wanted warmth, helpfulness, time to think, friendliness and advice. ... We had failed to see ... that our customers were now veterans in the quick-service market and their expectations had gone through the roof. What was revolutionary in the seventies was ghastly in the caring nineties.

Remembering Aaker's (1991) categories regarding brand equity, anything that affects the *associations* connected to the brand are also part of the marketing task. This could be to ensure that the 'wrong' type of customer is deterred from entering a store, for instance Top Shop claim that the in-store music and atmosphere is designed to deter the older consumer while appealing to younger ones. Obviously associations with major personalities through store visits or advertising reinforce such associations. In this respect many companies utilize their PR skills to gain the maximum benefit from all other types of relevant association.

Paul Feldwick (1996) suggests that:

> a brand may have a personality but it is not a person. You cannot talk to it and it cannot answer back. In fact it has no absolute or objective existence.

In spite of this, a *brand personality* will develop over time and, remembering that a retail store is a service organization dependent on its employees to interact with shoppers, it is vital that any communications with those employees are consistent with the brand personality desired. When considering customer care it is crucial to understand that when a customer talks with a member of the retail staff, then during those 'moments of truth' that member of staff is 'the retail store' in the eyes of the customer. Such encounters require training as well as direction from marketing if the resulting perception of the store is to be developed in a consistent way.

The following chapters of this book will look at the many individual activities that are all part of retail marketing. While each is presented separately, the customer receives them all as a *complete package*, positive as well as negative. A brand is more than the sum of its individual parts, and it is built by more than a single form of input. These inputs will inevitably involve some contradictions, but the more the consistency in all the messages the greater the chance of successful development of the brand over time. Striving for consistency in all areas is, perhaps, the most important marketing contribution to the building of a strong brand.

Brands, Positioning and Competition

There is only one reason for the emphasis on building brands in marketing. It is because brands are very different from commodities and by 'de-commoditizing' an offering the emphasis of competition switches to include all the components of the retail marketing mix, with less emphasis given to the price being charged. Branding is aimed at making an offering both distinctive and desirable. In a highly competitive marketplace it is critical to achieve a position where a retailer is seen to be offering a *comparative advantage*, adding value in a way that other competitors cannot match. The brand is both the expression of such a position and, when successfully established, the proof that the position achieved is relevant to customers. From a customer perspective a successful brand must offer:

- *Easy recognition* within a crowded marketplace
- A guarantee as to the *type* and *quality* of the offering
- A statement of values and beliefs that appeal on a *personal level.*

The first test of a successful brand or position is that it should be seen as *distinctive* within a particular category. Being recognized as different from other retailers will mean that a specific store will be considered in a purchase situation rather than the selecting of a supplier being left to chance. Of course, there are risks in being different, it is possible that the differences actually put off some customers, especially the location, atmosphere or perceived quality of some stores. This is not a problem as long as the target customers still find the store desirable, in fact it can be beneficial to deter unwanted shoppers. However if the factors that lead to a different distinct image are not valued by the target customers then the differentiation is irrelevant and worthless.

This leads directly to the second test of a successful brand. It should be recognized as *desirable* by the target group of customers. This will encompass both the guarantee as to the offering and the personal statement of values desired by consumers mentioned above. The development of a brand, the 'clothing' of the 'naked' product, adds layers of beliefs and values to the core offering. These can be positive, in terms attractive to shoppers, or negative, deterring them. Consider the type of shopper likely to be attracted to a warehouse type store such as Matalan, and contrast with those attracted to a designer fashion store. Of course the distinctions between store images are very marked, and in some cases so are the distinctions between the regular shoppers at each type of outlet. However, some distinctions are actually very blurred with the same customer being attracted to both types of store but for a different type of purchase. In fact Theodore Levitt (1992), writing about what he called the 'pluralization of consumption', suggested that:

> In all product categories and places, people increasingly occupy many and often disparate segments, and circulate among varied brands. Customer segments are no longer tightly discrete or distinct. Segments have become porous and coincident. Customers are now segment migrants, possessed of multiple segment preferences at the same time. They've become heteroconsumers, as in a cafeteria, leading lives of seemingly idiosyncratic consumption.

For these shoppers there will be a number of acceptable brands and each could be chosen depending on circumstances. However if a store image is unacceptable under any circumstances then it will not be a successful brand.

Conclusions

Image and *position* are interchangeable as marketing terms. Both must be evaluated from a customer perspective, but those that become implanted into the mind of a customer are the key components in what can be called a *brand*. Retail stores will acquire a brand image in just the same way as any other product. Brand image is a lot more than a brand name, it includes a complex mixture of beliefs and values that a customer ascribe to the brand, in fact everything that a customer perceives, both positive and negative.

The strength of a brand – its *brand equity* – will develop from all the 'messages' received. This development will take place over an extended period of time, with every new input being interpreted by every customer. Customers can receive hundreds of inputs related to just one retail store, and there will be many messages, possibly conflicting, for the shopper to interpret. Retail marketing must continually research the effect of all messages, as well as trying to reduce any inconsistencies that might be uncovered.

The factors that contribute to a strong brand include *awareness, quality, associations*, and *regular loyal purchasing behaviour*. Nevertheless the evaluation of any retailer will include more than the specific attributes, in fact it is the beliefs and perceptions that are the key elements in any assessment. That is why it is crucial to monitor customer attitudes on a regular, continuous and objective basis. It is possible that general retailers such as department stores and other multi-product retailers will have great difficulty in achieving a really focused position owing to the wide-ranging nature of its operations.

While a strong brand and position are important in existing areas of trading, helping to differentiate one retailer from its competition, it is not always certain that the brand equity will transfer into new areas of trade. When a retailer is expanding its operations it would be very naive to assume that the brand image is directly transferable to the customers in the new location. In some cases the awareness exists, but even that is not really enough, so a programme of extensive research will be required before any development. The continuous researching and regular monitoring of the 'health' of a brand should be undertaken in all areas of operations as a matter of course. The information gathered will then be used to plan future 'manipulation' of customers by the use of marketing. However, where a store is operating in several locations, it might be discovered that the brand is at different stages of development, and with perhaps different meanings in each separate location.

References and Further Reading

Aaker, D. (1991) *Managing Brand Equity*, The Free Press, New York.

Adcock, D., Halborg, A. and Ross, C. (2001) *Marketing Principles and Practice*, 4th edn, FT Pitmans Publishing, London.

Birtwistle, G. and Freathy, P. (1998) More Than Just a Name Above the Shop, *International Journal of Retail and Distribution Management*, 26, 8, 318–23.

Bloemer, J.M.M. and Kasper, H.D.P. (1995) The Complex Relationship between Consumer Satisfaction and Brand Loyalty, *Journal of Economic Psychology*, 16, 311–29.

Brown, S. and Burt, S. (1992) Retail Internationalisation: Past – Imperfect, Future – Imperative, *European Journal of Marketing*, Special edn, 81–2.

Dibb, S., Simkin, L., Pride, W.M. and Ferrell, O.C. (1997) *Marketing*, 3rd European edn, Houghton-Mifflin, Boston.

Donkin, P. (1994) No Relish for Cheese and Pickle Sandwich, *Financial Times*, 28 October.

Doyle, P. (1998) *Marketing Management and Strategy*, 2nd edn, Prentice-Hall, Englewood Cliffs, NJ.

Doyle, P. and Fenwick, I. (1974) How Store Image Affects Shopping Habits in Grocery Chains, *Journal of Retailing*, 50, 4, 39–52.

Duckworth, G. (1996) in D. Cowley (ed.) *Understanding Brands*, Kogan Page, London.

Dunne, P. and Lusch, R.F. (1999) *Retailing*, 3rd edn, Harcourt Brace & Co, Orlando, FL.

Feldwick, P. (1996), in D. Cowley (ed.), *Understanding Brands*, Kogan Page, London.

Ferry, J.W. (1961) *A History of the Department Store*, Macmillan, New York.

Gurhan-Canli, Z. and Maheswaran, D. (1998) The Effects of Extensions on Brand Name Dilution and Enhancement, *Journal of Marketing*, November, 464–473.

Jain, S.C. (1989) Standardisation of International Marketing Strategy: Some Research Hypotheses, *Journal of Marketing*, 53, 1.

Kotler, P. (1999) *Kotler on Marketing*, The Free Pres, New York.

Lancaster, B. (1995) *The Department Store*, Leicester University Press, Leicester.

Lautman, M.R. (1993) The ABC of Positioning, *Marketing Research*, Winter, 12–18.

Levitt, T. (1992) *Levitt on Marketing*, Harvard Business Review Paperback, Cambridge, MA.

Moore, C.M., Fernie, J. and Burt, S. (2000) Brands without Boundaries, *European Journal of Marketing*, 34, 8, 919–37.

Nevin, J. and Houston, M. (1980) Image as a Component of Attractiveness to Intra-Urban Shopping Areas, *Journal of Retailing*, 52, 1, 77–93.

Osman, M.Z. (1993) A Conceptual Model of Retail Image Influences on Loyalty Patronage Behaviour, *International Journal of Retail Distribution and Consumer Research*, 2, 133–48.

Oxenfeld, A.R. (1974) Developing a Favourable Price–Quality Image, *Journal of Retailing*, 50, 4, 8–14.

Powell, D. (ed.) (1987) *The Tesco Papers 1975–1987*, Tesco Stores Holdings Plc/Hallam & Mallen, London.

Ries, A. and Trout, J. (1983) *Positioning: The Battle for your Mind*, McGraw-Hill, New York.

Sivadas, E. and Baker-Prewitt, J.L. (2000) An Examination of the Relationship Between Quality, Satisfaction and Store Loyalty, *International Journal of Retail and Distribution Management*, 28, 2, 73–82.

Vignali, C. (2001) Tesco's Adaptation to the Irish Market, *British Food Journal*, 103, 2, 146–63.

Store Design

CHAPTER 7

This chapter:

- Explores the shopper's patronage decision
- Defines how store design creates a controlled environment for the shopper
- Defines the ambient, social and design dimensions of the store environment

Store Design

Introduction

A key factor in the shopper's patronage decision concerns their perception of the store itself, or more importantly the *experience of shopping* at that store. This Perceived Store Shopping Experience (PSSE) has been seen to have more influence on a shopper's store selection than assortment quality/type and price level. Indeed, PSSE has been found to directly influence a shopper's perception of assortment quality, price levels and the overall value of the store. With this in mind it is clear that a retailer should pay close attention to any factor that will affect a customer's PSSE. Tactical elements such as those presented in this text (assortment, price, location, customer service, loyalty building, promotion, etc.) all influence the PSSE, but it is apparent that the store itself has the major role to play. This fact makes the whole area of *store design* very important.

Store design is also important as it creates the *controlled environment* within which shoppers shop. The basic SOR (stimulus–organism–response) behavioural model presented earlier (see Chapter 3 on Shopper Behaviour) shows that a shopper's behaviour is influenced by all the stimuli sensed by that shopper. The Mehrabian–Russell model developed this concept to address behaviour within a specific environment. Environmental stimuli are processed by the shopper in a uniquely individual way, generating a certain mood state that is the precursor to behaviour. If the retailer can develop the right controlled environment, shopper moods may be influenced. If moods can be influenced, so can behaviour.

Baker's framework for store design (1986) identifies three critical dimensions of the store environment, namely the *ambient* dimension, the *social* dimension and the *design* dimension. The ambient dimension covers all the 'background' effects in an environment usually referred to as atmospherics, the social dimension covers all the people in an environment and their interactions and the design dimension covers the physical appearance and nature of the environment. A successful overall store design must take all three dimensions into account. A typical store design process would begin with the design dimension to set the proportions and nature of the physical selling space. The selling space itself is then refined by the development of the social and ambient dimensions. Accordingly, the three dimensions will be covered in this order. Before moving on to discuss store design in greater depth, it is necessary to expand upon the 'more detailed theories' introduced at the end of Chapter 3 on shopper behaviour, namely the Mehrabian-Russell model, mood states and the Elaboration Likelihood model.

The Mehrabian–Russell Model

The Mehrabian–Russell (MR) model (1974) developed the basic SOR model in an environmental psychology context. The basic premise of the model is that a shopper's perceptions of, and behaviour within, a retail environment are the result of *emotional states* created by that environment (Baker, Levy and Grewal 1992). Put more simply, a shopper's behaviour is affected by the immediate environment – i.e. the store. The model contains three elements – *environmental stimuli, emotional states* and *behaviour* (see Figure 7.1). Stimuli from the store (images, sounds, smells, etc.) are perceived by the shopper and processed in a uniquely individual way. The first level of response to the stimuli is the development of an emotional state or the modification of an existing one. The shopper's emotional state is described by two variables, *pleasure* and *arousal*. Pleasure can be defined as the extent to which a shopper feels good in the store while arousal can be defined as the extent to which a shopper feels excited or stimulated. The second level of response to the stimuli is behaviour based on the shoppers' emotional state. This behaviour can be either *approach* or *avoidance* orientated, positive or negative, respectively. Approach behaviour includes a willingness to move towards the environment, participate more extensively and an increased propensity to buy. Avoidance behaviour is the opposite, with an intent to move away from the environment, reduce participation and a decreased propensity to buy. Research by Donovan and Rossiter (1982)

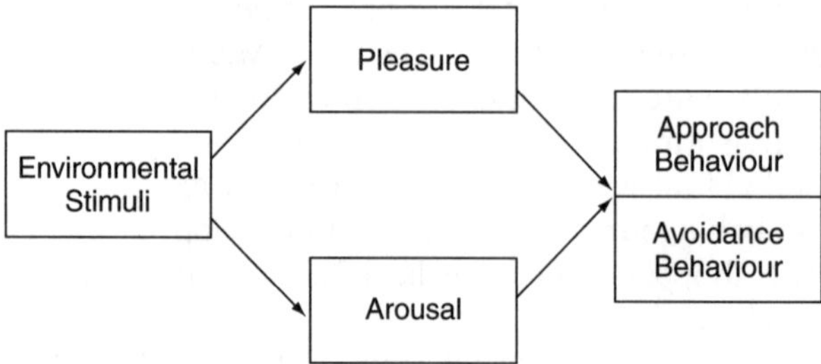

Figure 7.1 The Mehrabian–Russell model (1974)
Source: Mehrabian, A. and Russell, J.A., *Retail and Distribution Management: an approach to environmental psychology* (1974). Reprinted with permission from MIT Press.

found that store-induced pleasure was positively associated with willingness to buy and store-induced arousal influenced the time spent in the store and the willingness to interact with sales personnel.

The main use of the MR model is in the design of *store environments*. If the retailer understands the way shoppers react to certain store design elements (layout, display, atmospherics), the correct environmental stimuli can be created to build the correct emotional state that will trigger the most appropriate behaviour (approach). The process is not an exact science, however, as predicting shoppers' emotional states and behaviour is difficult, not least because an existing emotional state 'developed' outside the store may have a significant influence on that shopper's emotional state within the store and, hence, their behaviour. Even allowing for this caveat, the MR model is a very useful tool in predicting and influencing a shopper's in-store emotional states and behaviour.

The concept of *mood states* is linked to the MR model by virtue of the similarity with emotional states. A mood is a subjective reaction to a given situation (environment) that is transient (Isen, Clark and Schwartz 1976), not an intense emotion and not directed at specific target objects (Clark and Isen 1982). Moods have a significant effect on behaviour, with a good mood encouraging more prosocial behaviour, more resistance to temptation and more willingness to delay self-reward. A bad mood, however, discourages prosocial behaviour and reduces both resistance to temptation and willingness to delay self-reward. Moods are present in virtually every retail situation and, as a mood state is the same as an emotional state, the MR model shows that they have an influence on behaviour. To be specific, moods have an impact on the perceived store shopping experience, buying patterns, expenditure, trip duration and frequency, information search and evaluation (Swinyard 1993; Donovan *et al.* 1994). Swinyard (1993) goes on to propose a three-way relationship between involvement, mood and perceived store shopping experience. *Involvement*, or the degree of personal importance attached to a purchase, has an effect on the importance of mood effects in judgements of the store shopping experience. As involvement increases, *mood effects* become more pronounced with the mood effects of high involvement amplifying good or bad store experiences. Low involvement shoppers, on the other hand, are affected little by their moods.

The Elaboration Likelihood Model

The Elaboration Likelihood Model or ELM (Petty and Cacioppo 1986) was originally developed to explain cognitive responses to promotional stimuli. The model can, however, be applied more widely to retail environments if the concept of *persuasion* is considered. Persuasion is the process by which shoppers move towards a final purchase decision and can take two routes under the ELM treatment. *Central route persuasion* occurs if the shopper has both the ability and motivation to digest the arguments offered in a careful and critical manner while *peripheral route persuasion* occurs without any systematic consideration of the facts (DeBono 1992). Both routes are affected by environmental factors although shoppers taking the central route tend to be affected on a more conscious level than those using the peripheral route. The ELM adds, therefore, an extra level of detail to the MR model by considering the mechanism by which an environmental stimulus may invoke a certain response.

The Design Element

Store design concerns the control of the more *tangible* (foreground) elements of a store's interior to create the appropriate shopping environment for a given body of target shoppers. 'Appropriateness' in this case refers to both shopper and retailer considerations. Shoppers may develop positive or negative perceptions of a store owing to its appearance, ease of use and the overall shopping experience. Retailers must make the most productive use of their available selling space, as this is typically a scarce resource (capacity restraint) – i.e. retailers work with a finite selling space so must seek to gain the maximum return on this selling space if overall returns are to be maximized. The balance between retailer and shopper considerations is known as the *design fit*. Hasty and Reardon (1997) see the design fit as the satisfaction of shopper needs via interior and exterior design elements that produces an operationally efficient store, the desired store image and a central location that effectively displays merchandise.

A number of approaches to design exist, all of which aim to maximize the design fit. The most time-consuming and expensive method is based on test marketing and is known as the *Prototype method*. A prototype design is developed, either for the entire store or a given store area. Shoppers are then introduced into the prototype store design and their reactions measured by observation and more direct data collection methods. This approach is expensive, as investment is needed to convert a given store or store area and a significant amount of time is required in the design, build and testing phases. The approach does, however, produce highly accurate findings that are directly applicable to the actual store in question. The key reason for this accuracy and applicability is that the actual store is being used in the testing rather than a more artificial environment. Shopper behaviour within this test environment is, therefore, as close to real life as is possible.

Less expensive and faster approaches attempt to simulate the retail environment using *computer aided design (CAD)* or laboratory experimentation. The CAD approach builds a virtual store design that quickly and cheaply allows a design to be tested. Shopper reactions can be gained to all aspects of the design, although current hardware and software does not allow the real-life setting to be exactly duplicated – i.e. sensory data (smells, textures, etc.) cannot adequately be replicated in such an artificial environment. For this reason, the CAD approach is not as accurate or applicable as the prototype method. Laboratory experimentation can be used to test specific design elements in an artificial setting – e.g. display types (shelving, racking, etc.). Shopper reactions to the specific design elements can be accurately measured quickly and relatively cheaply. The findings of such an experiment are accurate but apply to the laboratory setting rather than the actual store environment, hence applicability is significantly lower than the prototype method.

In practice, retailers are advised to use a combination of the store design approaches mentioned above in order to achieve the best and most cost effective design fit. Cheaper and faster approaches such as CAD or laboratory experimentation should be used to produce a provisional or rough design that can then be refined using the prototype approach. If the store design is successful in the prototype store or store area, the design can be rolled out to all the retailer's stores (for more in-depth coverage of store design approaches, see Baker, Levy and Grewal 1992).

A number of elements are addressed in a given store design – namely, style, architecture, layout and display. The *style* of the design is driven by the overall store concept or image and is the theme to which all elements of a store's design must conform. To give an example, a high-fashion clothing store would have a very different style to a discount clothing store. The *size* and *exterior* of the store would probably be very different (architecture), as would the usage of the *selling space* (layout) and the way that the clothes themselves were *presented to the shopper* (display). Style has been covered throughout this text; architecture, layout and display will be covered in more detail below.

Architecture

Store exterior and size are usually the first design elements to be considered. The reason for this is that they are also often the first things considered by a potential new shopper standing outside the store. The impression conveyed by a store's *outward appearance* can influence a shopper's judgement on the benefits to be gained from visiting that store. In much the same way as a product's packaging is known as the 'silent salesman', so a store's exterior can help shoppers to evaluate the nature of the store in terms of the assortment on offer, the price levels concerned and the likely shopping experience. A good *exterior design fit* is, therefore, important to the retailer. Retailers may either use the low-cost approach of locating a site where the existing architecture is appropriate or the higher-cost approach of building a new store to a specified architectural blueprint.

The size of a store is fundamental to the retailer, as it dictates the parameters of operation. The amount of *selling space* places a limit on the size of the assortment that can be presented effectively to the shopper. The amount of storage space has implications for retail management areas such as assortment availability and restocking efficiency. On a more general level, size can influence shopper judgements on style and hence store image. A retailer seeking to build the image of wide choice and the 'one-stop-shop' would expect this image to be more believable as the store size increased. Retailers looking for an image of exclusivity, however, should opt for a much smaller store if shoppers are to build the correct image perceptions.

As has already been noted, store *architecture* must fit with store style and image. Store exterior design relates to the nature of a store's appearance or the first impressions gained by a shopper when approaching that store. Design elements such as the materials used, the architectural styles adopted, the colours, textures and lighting applied, window display (see Chapter 10 on Retail Promotion), and signage have an important role in the creation of this impression. To give an example, an antique shop would create the right first impression if it were located in a store with old architecture. A supermarket, by contrast, may not create the right first impression in such a location and may look for a building with architecture of a much more modern appearance.

Layout

The layout of a store defines how the total selling space will be divided into specific selling areas. It is also the master plan upon which other elements of the store's design are based – e.g. atmospherics, display, etc. A layout design must facilitate the easy flow of traffic throughout the store, handle the required traffic capacity, allow all products to be displayed effectively to the customer, utilize the available selling space as efficiently as possible given the type of store and assortment and incorporate safety and security features. Most layout designs utilized by retailers are based on one or more of three generic layout designs known as *grid pattern*, *free-flow* and *boutique*.

Grid Pattern

The grid pattern layout is typically associated with supermarkets and is arguably as old as the supermarket itself. The design was developed in 1916 by Clarence Saunders for the Piggly Wiggly store (in Memphis, USA) that is acknowledged as one of the first, if not the first, self-service supermarket in the world. Shoppers visiting the museum that now occupies this site would be struck by the similarity with modern supermarkets. The grid pattern layout comprises a number of long fixtures arranged in parallel to produce a number of *aisles*. Access to the aisles is usually limited to the two ends, so shoppers often move through the store using a quite predictable route. The positive aspects of the design are high space utilization, low effective cost, high traffic control and capacity and high assortment exposure. On the negative side, shoppers find the store experience to be quite limited and the retailer will find it difficult to effectively deliver customer service or provide a personal selling approach.

Looking at the layout in more detail (see Figure 7.2), it is apparent that shoppers have quite a limited choice of routes owing to the similarly limited number of aisle entry and exit points. This limited choice of shopper routes leads to a high degree of *traffic control*. In addition, *high assortment exposure* is possible as shoppers have little choice but to walk past a large percentage of the assortment on offer. The layout also leaves little space unused, so *space utilization* is high. Add this to the possibility of standardised fixtures and a *low effective cost* is common. High space utilization and predictable shopper routes also lead to a potentially high traffic capacity, as shoppers are encouraged to move through the store in a given direction rather than by a more random route. A good analogy would be a pipeline, where shoppers are continuously entering at one

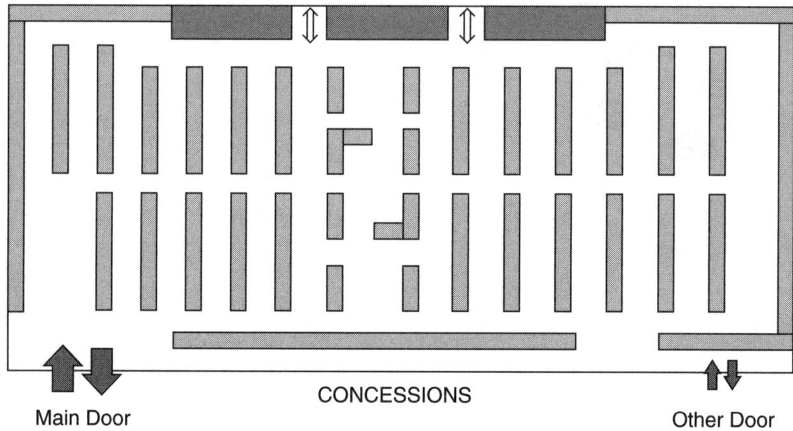

Figure 7.2 The grid pattern layout

end, passing through then emerging at the other end. A larger number of shoppers can fit into the store space (pipeline) at any given time, as the speed of shopper movement tends to be high.

The high efficiency of the grid pattern layout also produces a number of weaknesses. Shoppers tend to find the shopping experience quite limited, as the design does tend to 'herd' shoppers in given directions rather than giving them freedom of movement. In addition, aisle space is quite limited so many shoppers find browsing quite uncomfortable owing to the awareness that they are probably blocking the way for other shoppers. Contact between shoppers and sales personnel is also difficult, as visibility across the store is very limited. This leads to great problems in the provision of either customer service or personal selling. Consideration of the strengths and weaknesses of the grid pattern layout shows that it is mainly used by retailers wanting to maximize selling space utilization for predominantly low POP (point of purchase) time purchases. The main users tend to be supermarkets and potentially any high-volume 'low-involvement' retailer.

Free-Flow

The free-flow layout is the typical high street shop design, for clothing especially, incorporating combinations of different fixtures (wall shelving, racks, table displays, etc.) and space for shoppers to move around the store in a quite unstructured way. Unlike the grid pattern layout, access to all parts of the store is easy and can be achieved by many different routes. The positive aspects of the design are the greatly enhanced shopping experience and the ability to provide customer service and personal selling easily and effectively. Negative aspects are low control of traffic, limited traffic capacity, poor space utilization, potentially low levels of assortment exposure and a high effective cost.

Looking at the layout in more detail (see Figure 7.3), it is evident that shoppers have great freedom of movement, with plenty of available shopper routes and large areas of open space. Shoppers tend not to feel pressured, so can take as much time as they want over their purchase

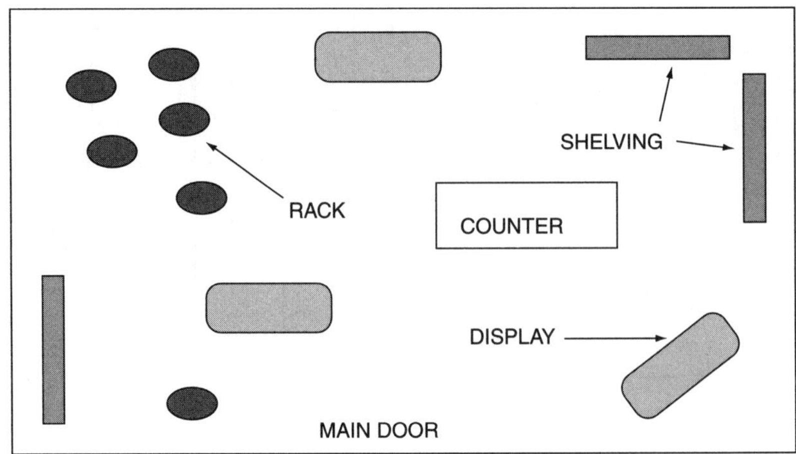

Figure 7.3 The free-flow layout

decision. The overall shopping experience is, therefore, greatly enhanced when compared to the grid pattern layout in particular. The high level of open space also lends itself to the provision of *customer service* or *personal selling*. Sales staff can move freely around the store and can use the high degree of shopper visibility, owing to the relatively open store layout, to assess a shopper's need for personal attention. Providing an enhanced shopping experience inevitably leads to losses in *efficiency*. A large amount of open and, therefore, unused space leads to *poor space utilization*. Add to this the greater shopper freedom of movement and *traffic capacity* becomes limited. Greater freedom of movement also means that the number of routes available to the shopper increases, thus limiting the ability of the retailer to control traffic flow and potentially lowering the level of assortment exposure – i.e. unlike a grid pattern layout, the retailer cannot guarantee that the majority of shoppers will actually see a certain display area. Bearing in mind these positive and negative aspects it is apparent that a free-flow layout is appropriate for retailers seeking *store experience* rather than efficiency. Such retailers would typically be offering a more limited assortment of higher-involvement products where a high degree of purchase consideration is required (high POP time).

Boutique

The boutique layout lies somewhere between the grid pattern and free-flow. The store is divided up into *selling areas* where a specific category of products will be located. The design is often known as the 'shop within a shop' concept (see Figure 7.4). Space inside the selling areas is utilized quite effectively with display fixtures appropriate for the specific type of category. Open space exists between the selling areas although not to the same extent as the free-flow layout. The layout is something of a compromise between *store experience* and *efficiency*, so tends to provide only moderate levels of *space utilization*, *traffic control* and *traffic capacity*. Effective cost and assortment exposure vary,

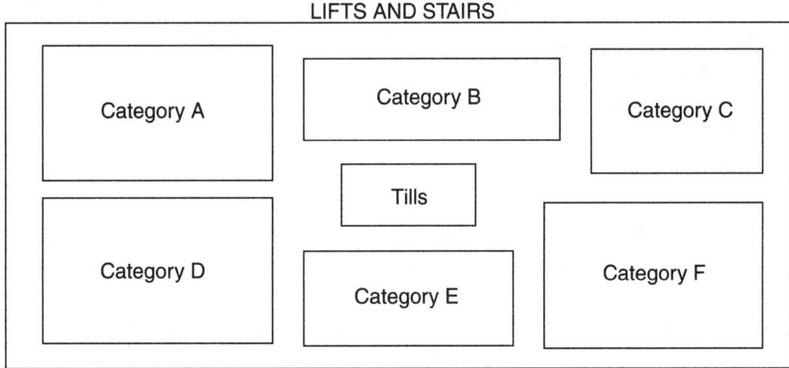

Figure 7.4 The boutique layout

depending on the design of the individual selling areas – i.e. a collection of selling areas with standardized fixtures and limited open space would lead to higher levels of assortment exposure and a lower effective cost. Provision of customer service and personal selling is much easier than for a grid pattern, although this is dependent on the design of the individual selling areas. The appropriate retail usage of this layout would be for an assortment comprising a wide range of product categories with typically moderate to high POP times or the 'store within a store' concept mentioned earlier. The classic example would be a department store.

A modern development of the boutique layout is often called the 'racetrack' (see Figure 7.5). Here, the store is designed so that shoppers follow a *set path around the store* with a large number of potential *stop-off points* (individual selling areas) en route and no obvious shortcuts. *Traffic control* increases as does *traffic capacity*, although usually not at the expense of a reduced store experience. *Assortment exposure* also

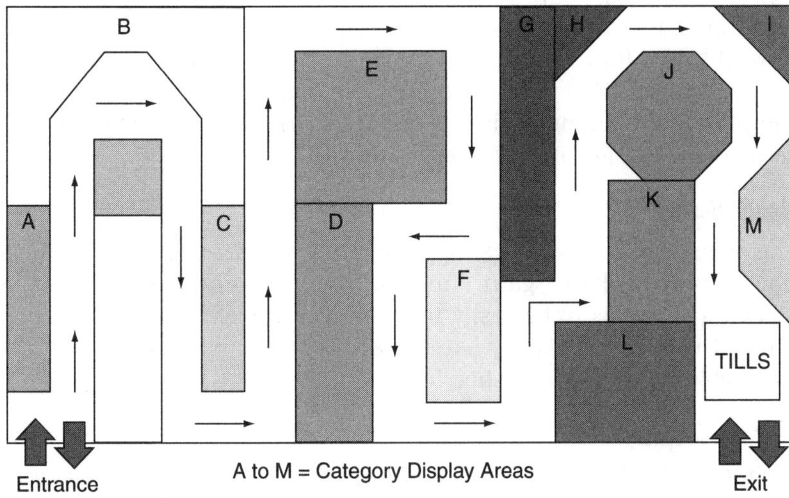

Figure 7.5 The racetrack layout

increases as shoppers are exposed to the vast majority of the individual selling areas. A good example of the racetrack layout is that used by IKEA in the UK.

The key features of the three generic layouts are summarized in Table 7.1.

Increasingly, though, combinations of the three generic layouts are being used. A study by Hart and Davies (1996) showed that supermarket retailers should change their layout approach for non-food items added to the assortment. Clothes and entertainment products were found to be best displayed by a separate boutique layout outside the main selling area while household, health and beauty and stationery products were found to be best displayed on grid pattern layouts separated from food items but in the main selling area.

Table 7.1 Features of the Three Generic Store Layouts

Factor	Grid pattern	Boutique	Free-flow
Traffic capacity	Highest	Moderate	Lowest
Control of traffic flow	Highest	Moderate	Lowest
Assortment exposure	Highest	Variable	Usually lowest
Space utilization	Most efficient	Moderate	Least efficient
Cost	Usually lowest	Variable	Usually highest
Store experience	Limited	Better	Enhanced (confusion?)
Provision of service and personal selling	Difficult	Easier	Easy
Typical POP time	Low	Higher	Highest
Typical retail usage	Supermarkets	Department stores	Clothes stores

Display

Once the layout has been finalized, designers need to consider display. Display is simply the method by which a retailer's assortment is presented to the shopper. The primary goal of a display is to present the assortment in such a way that *sales are maximized.* Other goals can be identified such as gaining the shopper's attention, fulfilling shopper demand, communicating and reinforcing store image and helping to control traffic flow (Buttle 1984). A number of display methods have been developed, most notably Rosenbloom's classification (1981), which identifies five different display types called *open, themed, lifestyle, co-ordinated* (or *project*) and *classification dominance.*

Open Display

The open display gives the shopper *free and easy access* to the products. The display seeks to gain shopper attention and involvement by allowing products to be easily touched or sampled. Clothing retailers utilize this form of display extensively, typically with racks, but also with tables or easy-access shelving.

Themed Display

A themed display is aimed at building a *connection between an event, activity, season or other feature* and the shopper. The style and physical characteristics of the display are dictated by the theme itself – e.g. a summer holiday display in a chemist store may feature umbrellas and sand, as well as the products themselves such as sun creams, etc. Sales are achieved by shoppers seeing the display, making the association with the event, and considering a range of purchases that may not have been in the forefront of their mind.

Lifestyle Display

Lifestyle displays seek to present products that fit with the way the *shopper lives*, or what Plummer (1974) describes as the shopper's activities, interests or opinions. Fashion retailers use this method extensively to show that a given assortment or category is right for the individual shopper. Pictures, video, sound or objects are often important parts of such a display as they both gain the shopper's attention and communicate the lifestyle much more effectively via role models, opinion leaders, etc. Nike uses this method extensively and very successfully within its Nike Town stores, for example.

Co-Ordinated or Project Display

Shoppers often purchase a number of items together if they are to be used together. A project display brings all products required for such a purchase together in one place, allowing the shopper to purchase the *finished solution* rather than just a number of constituent parts. As an example, interior decorating products are often organized to present co-ordinating designs of wallpaper, curtains, rugs and cushions, thus allowing the shopper to decorate an entire room rather than just the walls or floors. Shoppers tend to feel more confident purchasing the solution and are generally happier with their purchase. Shoppers are also prone to buying additional products for that solution that perhaps were not considered originally. As an example, a supermarket project display for an Italian meal may include pasta, pasta sauce, bread sticks and garlic bread. The shopper may have considered buying the first two items but not the last two. Should the shopper purchase all four items the display will have succeeded in increasing sales.

Classification Dominance Display

A classification dominance display is designed to present the shopper with a large amount of choice in a given area. If a retailer's store concept is to provide that choice, such a display is appropriate and will communicate this feature to the shopper. An additional feature of the classification dominance approach is that it can build a perception of quality and price levels in the mind of the shopper, this feature being an integral part of *category pricing*, for example (see Chapter 9 on Retail Pricing). The display of instant coffee in supermarkets is a good example of a classification dominance approach. A wide range of alternatives are presented, with price points increasing in bands from the cheapest (usually coffee powder) to the most expensive (so-called 'super-premium' products). A shopper may be impressed by the wide array of choice and may make their judgements of value based on relative price rather than a more detailed assessment of product quality. Care must be taken in ensuring that quality levels are obvious to the shopper, as presenting a product with another of comparable quality often creates conflict in the shopper's mind, thus decreasing the likelihood of a purchase of either product (Tversky and Shafir 1992).

Display Location

In addition to the type of display, retailers can utilize a number of display locations to increase the effectiveness of product presentation. Three general locations can be identified, namely *window*, *on-shelf* and *off-shelf*. Window display is an important promotional issue and is covered elsewhere in this text (see Chapter 10 on Retail Promotion) while on-shelf display has been discussed above.

Off-shelf display can be used to meet peaks in demand, enhance store image, sell non-standard lines (high-margin, bulk purchase or excess stock) and control traffic movement (Buttle 1984). Many retailers find that demand fluctuates throughout the year owing to non-controllable factors such as seasonality and controllable factors such as retail promotions. In such situations, retailers can utilize temporary off-shelf displays to allow a greater volume or breadth of items to be displayed. Typical methods include dump bins, cut-case displays, self-supporting stacks or pallets. Store image may also be affected by off-shelf display by conveying the impression of a bargain or exclusivity. In the first case, many discount retailers use off-shelf display to convey low prices and frequently utilize dump bins and pallet displays. In the second, separate off-shelf displays may be used to present exclusive items that deserve to stand apart from the rest of the assortment and place high-quality display units throughout the store.

The Social Element

The social element of a store's design relates to people – or, more accurately, store personnel and other shoppers. Design in this sense relates only to store personnel, as this is the only social element that the retailer can control to any significant extent. The effect of other shoppers has already been discussed earlier in this book (see Chapter 3 on Shopper Behaviour), so this treatment will focus on store personnel only. Designing the social element with respect to store personnel relates to the provision of customer service. A wide body of research exists to show that contact with store personnel can influence the shopper's perception of the store as a whole, particularly as involvement increases. Two main benefits may be gained by the shopper when contact with store personnel is made. *Social benefits* relate to friendship or intimacy, while *functional benefits* relate to time and effort, and specialist advice. Three types of service environment – *low-*, *moderate-* and *high-contact* – can be identified that relate to differing levels of contact between the shopper and store personnel.

A *low-contact* social environment is one where the retail concept is largely self-service in nature (e.g. a supermarket). In this case, social contact is limited to transaction processing or the collection of money at the till or checkout. Contact in this case leads to very limited benefits to the shopper, usually of a functional nature. A *moderate-contact* social environment is one where a degree of service is required by the shopper as part of the shopping process. It may be that items are not on self-service display, so must be asked for at the counter. Contact between the shopper and store personnel may be limited to quite simple functional benefits in excess of the low-contact situation. High-contact environments involve a high degree of service, making the shopping process highly participative in nature. Contact is extensive and is an integral part of the buying process with the shopper gaining both functional and social benefits. More details can found on the social element in Chapter 11 on Customer Service.

The Ambient Element

Study of the ambient dimension of store design was driven by the realisation that a store's appeal was due to more than just its obvious physical characteristics. Martineau (1958) stated that 'a store's personality is that way in which the store is defined in the shopper's mind, partly by its functional qualities and partly by an aura of psychological attributes'. The ambient element in a store's design can be viewed as part of that *aura of psychological attributes* and it is from this beginning that the field of atmospherics, or the manipulation of the ambient dimension, developed.

Atmospherics can be defined as 'the effort to design buying environments to produce specific emotional effects in the buyer that enhance purchase probability' (Kotler 1973). Atmospheric elements are often viewed as *background* or *peripheral* stimuli – i.e. they tend to influence the shopper on a more subconscious level. If we consider the Elaboration Likelihood Model (ELM) discussed earlier, it can be said that atmospherics tend to persuade via the peripheral route – i.e. persuasion not based on a systematic consideration of the facts. This ability to persuade subconsciously has led many commentators to view atmospherics as quite sinister or dishonest in nature. In reality, atmospherics can place the shopper in the right mood for purchase, but can rarely be seen to actually persuade them to buy. Clearly, a combination of all the other tactical elements discussed in this text is the means by which retailers aim to persuade shoppers to buy. In the terms of the ELM, retailers use a combination of both central and peripheral routes to persuasion.

In listing the various atmospheric elements it is first necessary to refine the original definition of atmospherics put forward by Kotler. Atmospherics are peripheral stimuli that can be sensed by the individual, hence they relate to a variety of *sensory cues*. Considering the Mehrabian–Russell Model discussed earlier, atmospherics concerns the manipulation of peripheral stimuli with the aim of utilizing the individual's sensory perception to produce the correct combination of pleasure and arousal that will encourage approach-orientated behaviour. The sensory cues or peripheral stimuli mentioned earlier comprise those related to sight, touch, hearing, taste and smell.

Atmospherics comprises, therefore, *visual*, *aural*, *olfactory*, *tactile* and *taste* elements, as described in Table 7.2.

Table 7.2 The Five Atmospheric Dimensions

Dimension	Description
Visual	Colour, lighting levels, appearance of objects (size and shape)
Aural	Volume, pitch, tempo and style of sounds
Olfactory	Nature and intensity of scent
Tactile	Temperature, texture and contact
Taste	Nature and intensity of taste sensations

Only the first three of these dimensions has been researched in any detail. The use and nature of these atmospheric elements is discussed in detail later in this chapter. Work has also been done to measure the range over which the peripheral stimuli can be altered to produce noticeable effects. The inverted 'U'-shaped relationship best describes this range of effects, as is illustrated in Figure 7.6.

Figure 7.6 shows that peripheral stimuli have an effect over the range from the threshold of *stimulus awareness* to *stimulus overload*. As an example, colour has an effect over the range of visual perception. If intensity is below the level of perception the effect becomes very limited. As the intensity of the colour increases so does the scale of the effect until a maximum is reached. After this point, increases in intensity lead to perceptual overloading, or the individual being dazzled, which in turn lessens the scale of the effect. In short, peripheral stimuli have a positive impact over the range of perceptual reception and comfort, sounds can be too quiet or too loud, scents too faint or too intense, lighting too dim or too bright. In addition, all individuals do not possess the same perceptual abilities – i.e. eyesight varies, as do hearing abilities, sense of smell, etc. For this reason, it is more appropriate to consider a zone of maximum effectiveness rather than an absolute maximum level. Given the negative effects of stimulus overload, retailers would be advised to select

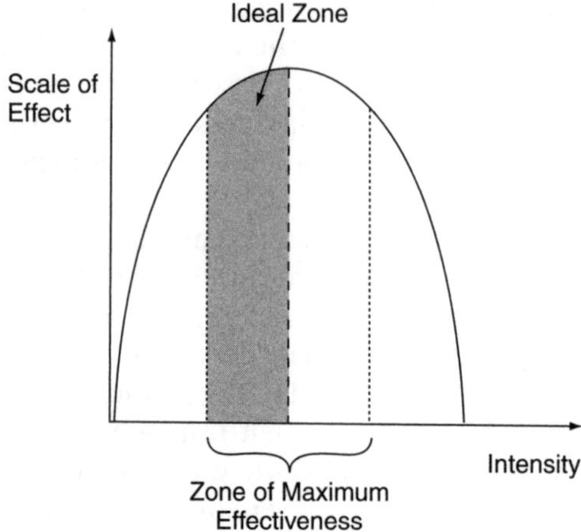

Figure 7.6 The inverted 'U' curve

maximum intensity levels that are towards the low-intensity end of the zone of maximum effectiveness (represented by the shaded area).

The Visual Dimension

The visual dimension encompasses *colour*, *lighting levels* and the *appearance of objects* (size and shape).

Colour

Colours can be divided into light (high white content), warm, cool, neutral (shades), bright (intense warm colours) and new. For simplicity, colours will be referred to as 'warm' or 'cool' in this text. *Warm colours* are those at the red end of the spectrum, while *cool colours* are at the blue end. Colour has been found to attract attention, assist evaluation and highlight certain product or store features. In addition, colour can be used for informative reasons, to improve mood and direct emotions and to increase arousal or excitement. Looking in more detail, colour can be seen to have both a *physiological* and a *psychological* effect on the individual. The first case relates to an unthinking or instinctive physiological reaction to a colour such as red, for example – i.e. the perception of danger or excitement seen in both humans and animals. In the second case, the psychological effect is based on the link between colour and mood. Both physiological and psychological effects will be covered separately below, although it should be noted that the overall effect of colour on the shopper is more than likely to be a combination of both types of effect.

Physiological effects

The physiological effects of colour have generally been measured in a laboratory setting, rather than in a retail environment. Retailers can use the research findings, however, as physiological effects are seen as being largely instinctive, so individuals will react in the same way irrespective of the environment they are in. Measurements made in the lab include blood pressure, respiratory rate and eye blink, under the blue and red extremes of the visual spectrum. The findings (e.g. Gerard 1957; Wilson 1966; Clynes 1977) show that *red* is inherently exciting and physically stimulating to the human brain – i.e. blood pressure and respiratory rate may increase, and eye blink may increase in frequency. At the other end of the spectrum, *blue* is found to be much more relaxing in its effect.

An interesting study was carried out by Ott (1973), who kept two groups of wild mink under either blue or pink light. Wild mink are very aggressive and certainly far from tame. Ott found that the mink that were kept under blue light became much less aggressive and were easier to tame. The mink that were kept under pink light became highly aggressive and were virtually impossible to tame. Ott's findings support the theory that animals tend to be excited by warm colours and relaxed by cool colours. These findings are also supported by anecdotal examples such as prisons using blue walls to relax inmates and dentist surgeries using blue to relax patients prior to what many see as an 'ordeal'. Retailers may use these findings to either excite or relax shoppers at the appropriate time and location. As an example, shoppers probably need to be excited when walking through the entrance in order to put them in the shopping mood, but may need to relaxed whilst in the store to allow them to fully consider all the products on offer.

Psychological effects

The psychological effects of colour can be seen as being due to a combination of *learned* and more natural responses. The *learned* response relates to the associations an individual makes between colours and other elements (people, places, occasions, etc.). These are gained by experience and so are learned by the individual. The *more natural* response is based upon the concept that an individual's psychological make-up – personality, for example – affects the way that colours are perceived.

Learned responses to colours are dictated by the individual's pattern of *socialization* – i.e. the way that individual has lived. This means that aspects such as nationality, culture, family and peer groups will have an effect on an individual's learned responses. As an example, in the UK and much of the Western world the shade white is associated with weddings. Individuals grow up being exposed to weddings both personally or in the media and gradually make the connection between the shade and this event. In some parts of the Eastern world, white is actually associated with funerals. The difference is due to differences in national culture and so in an individual's pattern of socialization. Other examples from the UK and the Western world include red for danger, black for funerals, purple for royalty, yellow for the sun or summer months and green for nature or health. Retailers can clearly use these learned associations and responses to provide a cue to the shopper on the nature of the store or the particular area of the selling space. Health food products may benefit from a green display to convey health and naturalness, summer products may be assisted by yellow colours and luxury products may benefit from purple colours (the association with royalty).

More natural responses relate to the individual themselves, or more accurately that individual's *psychological profile*. Consideration of the SOR model of buyer behaviour (see Chapter 3 on Shopper Behaviour) shows that an individual's response to a given stimulus (an object of a given colour, for example) is partly due to a range of psychological factors. These psychological factors include learning but also attributes such as personality and motivation. A body of research (e.g. Jaensch 1930; Rickers-Ovsiankina 1943) exists that suggests that individuals fall along a continuum from totally warm colour dominant to totally cool colour dominant. *Warm colour dominants* tend to be visually orientated, outwardly integrated, have faster reaction times, be more open, more adaptable and have a more positive attitude to need gratification. *Cool colour dominants* are seen to be emotionally cold, detached and reserved, less adaptable, less distracted and more selective in responses to stimuli. The research goes on to state that warm and cool colour dominants will tend to react to colours in a different way owing to their different psychological profiles. The accuracy of this approach can certainly be questioned, although it does provide more insights into the possible effects of colour on the individual shopper.

A more widely acceptable area of research concerns the psychological meanings and associational themes attributed to certain colours (e.g. Bjerstedt 1960). The concept is based on the idea that a given colour exhibits a different meaning or association, and that these meanings or associations will affect the individual, causing different attitudes or behaviour. Warm colours are seen as brighter, more negative (tense), more associated with up-to-date merchandise and equally as lively as cool colours. Shoppers were also seen to be more drawn towards warm colours than cool. Making the association between a colour and attitudes/behaviour allows store colour schemes to fit the individual and the product assortment or retail type. Again, this approach fails to completely explain all the psychological effects of colour, but does provide additional insights.

Looking at the retail applications of colour as an *atmospheric factor*, a number of in-store uses can be identified based on the three main types of response – physiological, learned psychological and 'more natural' psychological. In general, warm colours are used where the shopper needs to be excited or where shopper consideration is not important. Examples include a store's exterior, window displays, entry points, impulse situations and low-involvement or short point of purchase (POP) time products, such as frequently purchased or low-price items. Cool colours are favoured when the shopper needs to be relaxed or where shopper consideration is more important. Examples include store interiors, planned purchase situations and high-involvement or longer POP time products, such as expensive, infrequently purchased or high-perceived risk (financial and social) products.

The reasoning behind the applicability of warm and cool colours to certain situations is based on the nature of warm and cool colour environments. Warm colour environments are seen as being quite tense owing to the observed physiological and psychological effects described earlier, and may cause shoppers to become too 'aroused' to be able to make realistic judgements about potential purchases or the environment in general. Any small problem with the environment may lead the shopper to react in quite an extreme way blowing the issue out of all proportion. This being the case, any problem encountered within the warm-colour store may lead to a reduced perceived store shopping experience, if not a delayed purchase. The only real exception to this could be for retailers selling fashion- or technology-related products, where warm colours convey a more up-to-date image. Care should be taken in this circumstance, however, as a warm-colour environment tends to encourage shortened shopping times (i.e. less browsing and consideration) which may clash with a shopper requiring more decision-making time.

Cool colour environments, on the other hand, can be described as more attractive and pleasant. Shoppers are less likely to become aroused, so can make more considered purchase and store-related decisions – i.e. the perceived store shopping experience tends to be more favourable. To summarize, warm colours draw shoppers into the store, cool colours provide the enhanced store shopping experience.

Lighting Level

A large body of research, drawn mainly from environmental psychology, has been undertaken to investigate the effects of lighting level on the individual. Little substantive research has been carried out in the retail setting although much of the research done can be applied to such an environment. Studies into the effects of lighting levels on behaviour (e.g. Festinger, Pepitone and Newcomb 1952; Hopkinson, Petherbridge and Longmore 1966; Boyce 1973) have found that *task performance improves with increased brightness* – i.e. individuals were found to perform better when lighting levels were increased. This can be explained by the fact that individuals tend to feel more self-conscious under bright lighting, so it can be argued that they feel more pressured to adopt appropriate behaviour (i.e. more effort is given to the central task or issue). Darkened lighting leads to a reduction in self-consciousness and an associated weakening of the pressure to adopt appropriate behaviour. The inverted U-shape relationship was found to apply here also, with performance levels increasing over a narrow range of light intensities. Too dim and individuals couldn't perform the task, too bright and individuals found the situation too uncomfortable. While a number of different viewpoints exist to explain the effects of lighting levels, it is true to say that certain behaviours and perceptions are encouraged or facilitated by different levels of brightness. Typically, increased brightness leads to increases in the perception of cleanliness, traffic flow and shopper self-awareness/self-consciousness.

A major implication for the retailer concerns *browsing*, or the extent to which a shopper will actively seek out additional information before making a purchase decision. Research discussed earlier shows a relationship between the levels of browsing and brightness. Within a quite narrow range of light intensity (where sight is possible), browsing is negatively related to brightness – i.e. greater brightness leads to reduced levels of browsing. Failure to match the level of brightness to the nature of the purchase and type of shopper may lead to an environment not conducive to browsing, which may in turn lead to an unsatisfactory purchase experience and a potential sale that may be lost or reduced in value. Shoppers predisposed to browsing will feel more comfortable in slighter dimmer lighting, particularly for products that require a high amount of purchase deliberation time. Shoppers with little predisposition to browsing may be put off by dim lighting, especially for limited purchase deliberation items. As a result, standard lighting should be possible throughout the store only for retailers with homogeneous customers and/or appropriate purchase types. In all other cases, retailers should vary lighting to fit customers or purchase types. Retailers need to decide if this is practical for their own particular selling space.

Size and Shapes

Little research has been carried out into the effect of altering the size and shape of store design elements such as point of sale (POS) materials, display units or store infrastructure. Theory on the physiology of the visual system shows that the contrast and size of objects (design elements) affect their impact on the individual (Hering 1868; Anstis 1974; Steinman and Levinson 1990). An object is interpreted as having more potential information value, and so will exert more competition for attention, as the degree of contrast with the surroundings and/or relative size increases. In such a situation, an object that lies on the periphery of the shopper's vision may gain that shopper's attention if it is noticeably different from the surroundings. If attention is gained, the object moves from the background to the foreground of that shopper's attention.

The contrast and size concept is linked to the theory of *selective attention* or the process by which only those personally appropriate or noticeable stimuli (objects) are noticed by the individual. To add more detail, contrast with the surroundings can be achieved by varying the *physical nature* of the object in terms of shape, dimension, appearance or location. An object with an unusual or unexpected shape will contrast with its surroundings, as will an object with an unusual or noticeable appearance (different colouring, for example). An object in an unexpected place may also achieve the same aim.

The Aural Dimension

The aural dimension concerns the *control of sounds* within the store environment. For the purposes of this text *music* will be considered as the key aural element, as the control of all sounds in an environment is almost impossible to achieve. Research in this area concerns the effects of music as well as the impact of music type, tempo, pitch and volume.

The bulk of research conducted into the effects of music on the individual has concentrated on advertising. Work in this area by Kellaris and Cox (1989) and MacInnis and Park (1991) shows no proof that music influences purchase, although it was found to influence via both central and peripheral routes of persuasion (elaboration likelihood model – ELM). Music was also found to evoke emotions by providing a link to *prior experiences* and was best viewed as a *message enhancer* – i.e. to enhance reception of the advertising message. Additional findings showed the need for music to *fit the environment or message*, and the effect of the type of purchase on the importance of this fit – i.e. as involvement increases, so do the positive or negative impacts of a good or bad fit. At low involvement levels, negative impacts may be limited to the loss of attention. This research, while in a related field, can provide a starting point to the use of music as an *atmospheric element*. The only difference is the environment, the basic effect on the individual should be very similar in nature. On this basis, important factors for the retailer to bear in mind are the ability of music to evoke emotions, to persuade (although not necessarily to influence purchase) and the importance of the fit between music and environment.

Moving to the use of music as an atmospheric element, research from a number of sources is important. The first area of research concerns the ability of music to *alter the mood of the listener*. The right mood has already been identified as a factor influencing purchase, hence measuring the ability of music to alter mood is of great importance to the retailer. Shatin (1970) draws parallels between the Iso principle of psychiatry and music as an atmospheric element. The Iso principle is based on the concept that music can evoke emotions and that the individual's attention can be gained by matching music to that individual's current mood state. Once attention is gained, the ability to influence increases. The retailer is also trying to gain the shopper's attention, either on a largely conscious or subconscious level. This could, therefore, be achieved by exposing the shopper to the correct music.

Bruner (1990) measured the effect of different aspects of music on emotions (i.e. mood) and found that a faster tempo was seen as happier than slow, firm rhythms were more serious than smooth, high-pitched music was more exciting and happy than low, minor keys were sadder than major and louder music suggested animation while softer music suggested tranquillity. Milliman (1982) found that tempo was related to traffic flow – i.e. a slower tempo decreased the speed of traffic flow. He also found that any music can distract shoppers' attention from the passage of time (see also Hui, Dube and Chebat 1997) and that enjoyment of the music can produce a more positive mood within the listener.

Bruner and Millman went on, in their separate studies, to measure the impacts of different music on an individual's behaviour. They found that as *volume increased*, so the total time spent in the store decreased, although volume had no direct effect on the total amount spent or the satisfaction level of the shopper. Music of any tempo was found to increase *approach behaviour* (the propensity to purchase), while a slower tempo was linked with an increased time spent in the store. Music of a type that didn't fit with the store or the assortment sold was found to increase avoidance behaviour (the propensity not to buy). Sullivan (2000) measured the impact of music in more depth, finding that for a restaurant setting the presence of any sort of music significantly increased the money spent on food and drink, and the time spent in the restaurant. Loud music significantly reduced expenditure and time duration when compared to soft, while tempo and popularity were seen to have little effect on behaviour except for popular music significantly increasing time duration when compared to unpopular music (Table 7.3).

Table 7.3 Summary of the Atmospheric Effects of Music

Characteristic	Effect
Music (any type)	Any music can affect perceptions of time Presence of any music may increase expenditure and time spent in store
Volume	Loud music more animated, soft music more peaceful Louder music may decrease expenditure and time spent in store
Tempo	Fast music more happy/pleasant than slow Fast music increases rate of in-store traffic flow Has little effect on expenditure
Pitch	High pitch seen as more exciting, low pitch more sad
Popularity	May have an effect only on time duration, more popular music increases time spent in store

The Olfactory Dimension

The olfactory dimension relates to the presence of *scents* in the store environment. The three main research areas are the *affective aspect* (how pleasant the scent is), *arousal* (the ability of a scent to evoke a response) and *intensity* (strength of the scent). The link between scents and pleasure is said to be due to the Limbic system of the brain. This system deals with both emotions and the processing of olfactory messages, so it has been suggested that a strong link exists between scents and emotions. Arousal can also be affected by the presence of scents, leading to differences in behaviour. Once again, the effects of the intensity of a scent were seen to follow the inverted U-shape curve (see Figure 7.6).

Pleasant scents have been found to increase alertness and performance on a range of tasks, facilitate recall of pleasant memories, increase prosocial behaviour and increase the time spent in store. No evidence exists, however, to suggest that pleasant scents increase the level of purchases made by the shopper (Baron and Bronfen 1994; Mitchell, Kahn and Knasko 1995).

The effects on behaviour of scents can be partly explained by the concept of *congruity*, or the degree to which a given scent is perceived to fit the immediate environment (Bone and Jantrania 1992). As an example, many shoppers associate the smell of leather with a furniture store, so would see this scent as congruent. Shoppers may not, however, associate the smell of leather with a grocery store, so this scent would be seen as incongruent. Research shows that congruent scents, if intense enough to detect, make shoppers more likely to use the peripheral route to persuasion and spend more time processing data on a wider range of factors, thus making improved evaluation. Incongruent scents, in contrast, make shoppers more likely to use central route persuasion and spend less time processing a narrow range of factors (Mitchell, Kahn and Knasko 1995; Spangenberg, Crowley and Henderson 1996). Practical examples of this effect date back to the 1930s when Laird (1932) found that women buying silk stockings scented with a pleasant odour believed them to be of higher quality than those scented with a more natural odour. Cox (1967) repeated these findings, comparing orange-scented nylon stockings to unscented ones. The vast majority (approximately 90 per cent) of women selected the orange-scented version over the unscented one. More recently, it was found that 22 out of 35 subjects liked a pair of Nike shoes better in a room with a floral ambient scent than one with no odour (Hirsch 1990; Miller 1991).

Summarizing the effects of scent, Spangenberg, Crowley and Henderson (1996) found that the nature and intensity of the scent was not as important as its *presence*, with many of the benefits associated with pleasant scents associated with any scent of an inoffensive nature. Neutral and congruent scents were found to provide the greatest benefits to the retailer with the shopper having an enhanced shopping experience. Rather like the presence of music, the presence of scent led to inaccurate perceptions of time, with shoppers believing that the time spent in store was shorter than it actually had been.

Atmospherics in Reality

A wide body of research has been discussed that points to the benefits of atmospheric elements to retailers. The presence of certain colours, lighting levels, sounds and smells has been seen to trigger *emotional changes* in shoppers that may lead to certain behaviours. Two factors need to be discussed to qualify the usage of such atmospheric elements in the retail environment. The first concerns the effects of *combinations of atmospheric elements* (e.g. colour and smell), the second concerns *perceptual differences* among shoppers.

The majority of the research on atmospherics has sought to isolate a particular element – colour, for example – and measure observed behaviour or mood changes when this element is varied (i.e. the effects of warm or cool colours). Retailers must be aware that the effects of a given atmospheric element can be 'accurately' predicted only in isolation. As an example, if colour and smell were used together, what would the combined effect be? A limited number of studies (e.g. Zellner and Kautz 1990) have attempted to answer this question, but with little success as far as the retail situation is concerned. For this reason, retailers would be advised to use atmospheric elements *individually*, to ensure that any unexpected negative effects from combinations of elements are avoided.

The concept of congruity was discussed for aural and olfactory atmospheric elements. Essentially, the atmospheric element had to be seen to fit the environment if a more positive effect was to be had on the shopper. Congruity is based on perception, which is in turn based on the individual shopper's psychological and sociological make-up. This being the case, different types of smell or music would be perceived in different ways by different shoppers, seeing them as either congruent or incongruent: what to one shopper was an appropriate smell may be totally inappropriate to another. The available research points to the concept of congruity covering all atmospheric elements not just aural and olfactory. Colours need to fit the environment, as do lighting levels, tactile factors and tastes. It is for this reason that as retailers target a broader body of shoppers, so the degree of difference in the perceptions of congruity increases. This fact has implications for both mass-market and more specialist retailers.

Mass-market retailers target a large number of different shoppers, hence finding one smell, sound, colour, texture or taste that was seen to fit the environment by all shoppers would be highly problematical. In this case, retailers should look towards *neutral atmospheric elements* that will appeal to all – or, more accurately, will not been seen as negative by all. More specialist retailers that target a smaller number of shoppers may find that the degree of differences in the perceptions of congruity decrease. Such retailers may, therefore, be able to select atmospheric elements that will be seen as congruent by the majority of shoppers and may be able to achieve some of the benefits outlined earlier in this chapter.

Conclusions

Retailers must be aware that *how* they sell to the shopper is just as important as *what* they actually sell (assortment, prices, etc.). The importance of the method of selling results from the importance of the shopper's perceived store shopping experience (PSSE) to that shopper's overall store patronage decision. In some circumstances, it is possible that a good PSSE may do more to convince the shopper to revisit a given store than the quality of the goods on offer or the prices charged. The PSSE can be maximized by an appropriate store environment covering design, social and ambient dimensions. A successful store design must also be practical for the retailer, allowing for the most effective balance between shopper satisfaction (PSSE) and store efficiency.

The *design dimension* covers all the physical features of the store, including architecture, layout and display. Architecture relates primarily to the exterior of the store and can convey certain impressions on the retail offering to the passing shopper in much the same way as a product's packaging. Stores located in a Victorian shopping arcade may, for example, convey a different impression to the shopper than those located in a new out-of-town development. *Layout* is the store blueprint, determining where display areas will be located, and is based on a combination of grid pattern, free-flow and boutique designs. Layout has an important role to play in controlling shopper movement and can affect areas such as assortment exposure, space utilization, traffic capacity, service provision and the overall shopping experience. *Display* concerns the way that products are presented to shoppers and can affect assortment exposure, traffic flow, store image and the store experience. A number of different display methods can be used, based on shopper access to the products (open display), the shoppers themselves (lifestyle display) and the products on display (themed, project and classification dominance display).

The *social dimension* relates to people – i.e. shoppers and store personnel. Other people have an important role to play in determining the quality of a shopper's store shopping experience. Shoppers can influence the behaviour of others (see Chapter 3 on Shopper Behaviour) while store personnel can provide shoppers with social benefits (friendship or intimacy) and functional benefits (time and effort, specialist advice). The relative importance of store personnel increases from low- (self-service supermarkets), to moderate- (DIY stores) to high-contact (jewellery stores) service environments.

The *ambient dimension* covers the more peripheral aspects of a store's design. These peripheral aspects, known as atmospherics, relate to the senses (colour and lighting, texture, sound, smell). Atmospherics influence the shopper on a more subconscious level hence can be seen to affect that shopper's mood rather than purchase decision directly. The Mehrabian–Russell model highlights the importance of these moods in determining the extent to which a shopper feels good about the store environment. Certain colours, sounds and smells can be used to trigger minor mood changes in shoppers by a combination of physiological and psychological responses. In this way, atmospherics can assist in stimulating the correct shopper mood, thus stimulating approach-orientated behaviour (positive feelings about the environment) and improving the store shopping experience. Atmospherics are perceived by shoppers, so each shopper will react in a slightly different way. For this reason, as a retailer's body of target shoppers becomes increasingly diverse, so it becomes increasing difficult to select the right atmospherics mix. Specialist retailers can, therefore, use atmospherics in a proactive way while mass-market retailers should consider a more neutral approach.

A number of store design elements have been discussed, but what makes a good store design? The answer lies in finding the correct combination of ambient (atmospherics), design and social characteristics that effectively communicates the retailer's *overall store image or concept* and provides the shoppers with an excellent store shopping experience while maintaining operational efficiency.

References and Further Reading

Anstis, H.F. (1974) A Chart Demonstrating Variations in Acuity with Retinal Position, *Vision Research*, 14, 589–92.

Baker, J (1986) The Role of the Environment in Marketing Sciences: The Consumer Perspective, in J.A. Cepeil *et al.* (eds), *The Services Challenge: Integrating for Competitive Advantage*, AMA, Chicago, 79–84.

Baker, J., Levy, M. and Grewal, D. (1992) An Experimental Approach to Making Retail Store Environment Decisions, *Journal of Retailing*, 68, 194–220.

Baron, R.A. and Bronfen, M.I. (1994) A Whiff of Reality: Empirical Evidence Concerning the Effects of Pleasant Fragrances on Work-Related Behavior, *Journal of Applied Social Psychology*, 24, 13, 1179–1203.

Bjerstedt, A. (1960) Warm–Cool Color Preferences as Potential Personality Indicators: Preliminary Note, *Perceptual and Motor Skills*, 10, 31–34.

Bone, P.F. and Jantrania, S. (1992) Olfaction as a Cue for Product Quality, *Marketing Letters*, 3, 3, 289–96.

Boyce, P.R. (1973) Age, Illuminance, Visual Performance, and Preference, *Lighting Research Technology*, 5, 125–44.

Bruner, G.C. II (1990) Music, Mood and Marketing, *Journal of Marketing*, 54, 4, 94–105.

Buttle, F. (1984) Retail Space Allocation, *International Journal of Physical Distribution and Materials Management*, 14, 4, 3–23.

Clark, M. and Isen, A. (1982) Toward Understanding the Relationship Between Feeling States and Social Behavior, in L. Berkowitz (ed.), *Cognitive Social Psychology*, Elsevier/North Holland, New York, 73–108.

Clynes, M. (1977) *Sentics: The Touch of Emotions*, Anchor, New York.

Cox, D.F. (1967) The Sorting Role of the Consumer Product Evaluation Process, in D.F. Cox, *Risk Taking and Information Handling in Consumer Behaviour*, Harvard University Press, Boston, 324–69.

DeBono, K.G. (1992) Pleasant Scents and Persuasion: An Information Processing Approach, *Journal of Applied Social Psychology*, 22, 11, 910–19.

Donovan, R.J. and Rossiter, J.R. (1982) Store Atmosphere: An Environmental Psychology Approach, *Journal of Retailing*, 58, 34–57.

Donovan, R.J., Rossiter, J.R., Marcoolyn, G. and Nesdale, A. (1994) Store Atmosphere and Purchasing Behaviour, *Journal of Retailing*, 70, 3, 283–94.

Festinger, L.A., Pepitone, A. and Newcomb, T. (1952) Some Consequences of Deindividuation in a Group, *Journal of Abnormal and Social Psychology*, 47, 382–9.

Gerard, R.M. (1957) Differential Effects of Colored Lights on Psychophysiological Functions, unpublished doctoral dissertation, University of California.

Hart, C. and Davies, M. (1996) The Location and Merchandising of Non-Food in Supermarkets, *International Journal of Retail and Distribution Management*, 24, 3, 17–25.

Hasty, R. and Reardon, J. (1997) *Retail Management*, McGraw-Hill, New York.

Hering, E. (1868) *The Theory of Binocular Vision*, Plenum, New York.

Hirsch, A.R. (1990) *Preliminary Results of Olfaction Nike Study*, Smell and Taste Treatment and Research Foundation Ltd, Chicago.

Hopkinson, R.G., Petherbridge, P. and Longmore, J. (1966) *Daylighting*, Heinemann, London.

Hui, M.K., Dube, L. and Chebat, J.-C. (1997) The Impact of Music on Customers' Reactions to Waiting for Services, *Journal of Retailing*, 73, 1, 87–104.

Isen, A., Clark, M. and Schwartz, M.F. (1976) Effects of Success and Failure on Childen's Generosity, *Journal of Personality and Social Psychology*, 27, 2, 239–47.

Jaensch, E.R. (1930) *Eidetic Imagery*, Kegan, Paul, Trench & Trubner, London.

Kellaris, J.J. and Cox, A.D. (1989) The Effects of Background Music in Advertising: A Reassessment, *Journal of Consumer Research*, 16, 113–18.

Kotler, P. (1973) Atmospherics as a Marketing Tool, *Journal of Retailing*, 49, 48–61.

Laird, D.E. (1932) How Consumers Estimate Quality by Subconscious Sensory Impressions: With Special Reference to the Role of Smell, *Journal of Applied Psychology*, 16, 241–6.

MacInnis, D.J. and Park, W.C. (1991) The Differential Role of Characteristics of Music on High- and Low-Involvement Consumers' Processing of Ads, *Journal of Consumer Research*, 161–74.

Martineau, P. (1958) The Personality of the Retail Store, *Harvard Business Review*, 36, 47–55.

Mehrabian, A. and Russell, J.A. (1974) *An Approach to Environmental Psychology*, MIT Press, Boston.

Miller, C. (1991) Research Reveals How Marketers Can Win by a Nose, *Marketing News*, 25, 1–2.

Milliman, R.E. (1982) Using Background Music to Affect the Behavior of Supermarket Shoppers, *Journal of Marketing*, 46, 86–91.

Mitchell, D.J., Kahn, B.E. and Knasko, S.C. (1995) There's Something in the Air: Effects of Congruent and Incongruent Ambient Odor on Consumer Decision Making, *Journal of Consumer Research*, 22, 229–38.

Ott, J.N. (1973) *Health and Light*, Simon & Schuster, New York.

Petty, R.E. and Cacioppo, J.T. (1986) The Elaboration Likelihood Model of Persuasion, in L Berkowitz (ed.), *Advances in Experimental Social Psychology*, 10, Academic Press, New York.

Plummer, J. (1974) The Concept and Application of Life Style Segmentation, *Journal of Marketing*, 38, 33–7.

Rickers-Ovsiankina, M. (1943) Some Theoretical Considerations Regarding Rorschach Method, Rorschach Research Exchange.

Rosenbloom, B. (1981) *Retail Marketing*, Random House, New York.

Shatin, L. (1970) Alteration of Mood Via Music: A Study of the Vectoring Effect, *Journal of Psychology*, 75, 81–6.

Spangenberg, E.R., Crowley, A.E. and Henderson, P.W. (1996) Improving the Store Environment: Do Olfactory Cues Affect Evaluations and Behaviours?', *Journal of Marketing*, 60, 67–80.

Steinman, R.M. and Levinson, J.Z. (1990) The Role of Eye Movement in the Detection of Contrast and Spatial Detail, in E. Knowler (ed.), *Eye Movements and Their Role in Visual and Cognitive Processes*, Elsevier, Amsterdam, 115–60.

Sullivan, M.N. (2000) Experiments in Atmospherics: Single and Multi-Variable Conditions, unpublished working paper, Coventry University.

Swinyard, W.R. (1993) The Effects of Mood, Involvement, and Quality of Store Experience on Shopping Intentions, *Journal of Consumer Research*, 20, 271–80.

Tversky, A. and Shafir, E. (1992) Choice Under Conflict: The Dynamics of Deferred Decision, *Psychological Science*, 3, 358–61.

Wilson, G.D. (1966) Arousal Properties of Red Versus Green, *Perceptual and Motor Skills*, 23, 947–9.

Zellner, D.A. and Kautz, M.A. (1990) Colour Affects Perceived Odour Intensity, *Journal of Experimental Psychology*, 16, 2, 391–7.

The Retail Assortment

CHAPTER 8

This chapter:

- Shows how the choice of retail assortment is a key strategic decision
- Explains the impact of scarce production capacity/selling space
- Examines retailers' assortment options

The Retail Assortment

Introduction

One of the key decisions a retailer has to make concerns *what goods (products) to offer the shopper*. The full product range on sale within a store is known as the *assortment*. The importance of a retailer's assortment lies in its primary job as a need satisfier. Shoppers will purchase a product because they have a need that can be satisfied by that product's benefits. Should a retailer not stock the correct need satisfiers, shoppers will look elsewhere. In addition, shoppers make store selection decisions based in part on the products on offer even if a purchase is not ultimately made. In this case, if shoppers perceive the assortment to be inappropriate a visit to the store is highly unlikely. Both these situations stress the need for careful thought about the precise make-up of the assortment. Clearly, retailers would like to be able to offer every need satisfying product but limitations on the size of an assortment exist owing to the finite amount of selling space contained in every store. This fact means that retailers have to decide on a 'limited' assortment that will most effectively meet target shopper needs. Online retailers do not have this constraint (see Chapter16 on Online Retail Marketing).

Retailers, like manufacturers, have to gain the highest returns from the resources at their disposal. For a manufacturer, this 'scarce' resource could be *production capacity* – i.e. only a certain number of units can be produced in any given period. Given this limitation, the mix of products sold will be adjusted so that sales or profits are maximized. This process requires decisions to be made on the mix of products to be produced and the quantities involved. Consideration of the likely demand and contribution for each product is also required before the final decision can be made. Retailers face a similar problem, although their scare resource is *selling space* – i.e. only a certain amount of space is available inside a given store. Retailers must, therefore, seek to maximize sales or profits by selecting the most appropriate range of products (assortment) to offer in the store. Clearly, shopper needs have to be taken into account (as has already been explained) but additional consideration of potential sales volume and contribution is also required. A number of additional areas can be identified that have an effect on the assortment decision, namely *retail image*, *competition* and *suppliers*. These factors, together with the target shopper, selling space considerations and profitability will be discussed in this chapter.

Retailers have a number of simple assortment options to choose from based on the nature of the products on offer. One view of assortments is that they can either be quite *homogeneous* or *heterogeneous*, and quite *extensive* or quite *limited*. A totally homogeneous assortment occurs when only one manufacturer's products are stocked and this may encompass either a large number (extensive) or small number (limited) of different products and varieties. A heterogeneous assortment occurs when either a large number (extensive) or small number (limited) of unrelated products are offered. The situation is obviously a little more complicated than this, although it does present a good starting point.

To add more detail to the composition of retail assortment, a number of assortment dimensions can be considered. *Assortment width* is the number of different product types offered by the retailer, *assortment depth* is the number of product varieties offered and *assortment consistency* is the degree of similarity between the products offered. Considering assortment width and depth identifies the four generic assortment approaches shown in Figure 8.1.

The grouping of individual products into a category is another assortment dimension and one that is commonly used by retailers. A *category* can simply be defined as a group of related products – e.g. a clothing retailer may group all trousers or skirts together. Categories are used as a means of simplification for retailers to allow groups of products to be analysed together rather than each one individually. This is particularly important when a retailer has a large assortment and is required to make a large number of product-related decisions.

An organization offering a wide range of products and a number of varieties of each is classed as a *full service retailer*: shoppers have a high degree of choice within categories and a large number of categories to choose from. Such a retailer is often referred to as offering a

ASSORTMENT DEPTH		ASSORTMENT WIDTH: Narrow	ASSORTMENT WIDTH: Wide
	Shallow	Niche Specialist	Full Convenience Retailer
	Deep	Category Specialist	Full Service Retailer

Figure 8.1 Four generic assortment approaches

'one-stop-shop'. At the other end of the scale, a *niche specialist* adopts a much more focused approach, usually to a much smaller body of target shoppers. Choice is limited in terms of varieties and categories, so shoppers will visit such a store for quite specific reasons. *Full convenience* retailers offer a large number of categories with little choice in each. This type of store is selling *convenience* rather than *choice*. *Category specialists* aim to provide high levels of choice within a limited number of categories. The appeal of such stores is unrivalled choice for a specific purchase.

To give an example from the grocery retail sector, supermarkets can be classed as *full service retailers* as they sell a large number of categories and offer a large amount of choice within each. The large average store size of such retailers is a result of the need to display such a large assortment. The high street greengrocer sells fruit and vegetables from a small store; the number of categories on offer is small, as is the degree of choice within each. This is a classic example of a *niche specialist*. Moving down the high street we may come across a delicatessen, selling quite a limited number of categories but offering extensive choice in each. The delicatessen is successful owing to its image as the only place to get real choice, and is a *category specialist*. A discount grocery retailer typically sells a large number of different categories but keeps costs down by limiting choice to a small number of varieties. Discounters are examples of *full convenience retailers*.

The overriding nature of an assortment is determined by the retailer's *retail concept* – e.g. a grocery retailer sells groceries, a furniture store sells furniture, etc. The assortment is also dictated by the needs of the target shoppers. Retailers must meet these needs with the right combination of products if they are to be successful. Factors affecting this 'right combination' include product types, brand types (manufacturer or retailer) and pack sizes. In addition, the retailer must be aware that competitors will also be trying to satisfy the same needs, so must give the shopper superior value. Shoppers also make judgements about choice and quality that have an effect on the assortment decision. Shoppers generally require enough choice to make a reasoned and satisfactory purchase decision in the time available. Too much choice often leads to confusion and the purchase may be deferred. Too limited a choice can cause the shopper to believe that better alternatives may be available leading again to deferral. Judgements about quality are based on a number of factors including price, product make-up (ingredients, content, materials, etc.), brand image (product), retailer image (perception of the retailer) and the shopper's past product experiences. The judgements can contain a significant *subjective element*, given that a shopper's opinions and attitudes are considered alongside more concrete facts about the product(s).

Once a retailer has developed an appropriate assortment, *product supply* is the next area to be addressed. Retailers generally do not manufacture products for themselves, preferring instead to buy from established suppliers. Those retailers that do manufacture (factory shops, specialized food and drink shops, etc.) have integrated backwards either because suppliers are not available or as a source of differentiation. Non-manufacturing retailers are in the majority, so it is necessary to briefly discuss retail buying and the retail buying function. The main reason for the importance of the buying function is that it directly affects the success of the business in terms of both customer satisfaction and profit. Products that are purchased from suppliers must be at the right cost and must be shopper need satisfiers. Order quantities must be sufficient to guarantee product availability and so ensure that sales potential is realized.

Assuming that the retailer has now planned and purchased the assortment, the ongoing *management of that assortment* must now be considered. It is likely that the assortment will change over time owing to changes in shopper tastes, seasonal factors and the availability of new suppliers. New products may be introduced, old ones deleted or order quantities changed. Retailers must have a system to ensure that the most appropriate assortment decisions are taken. This system is based on *stocking criteria* that detail the circumstances under which a given product is suitable for inclusion in the assortment. This inclusion decision becomes increasingly complex as assortment size increases, with numerous and interrelated cases to consider. Add in the limitations placed on selling space mentioned earlier, and the level of complexity increases still further. Only a certain number of products can be offered, based on the space occupied by each and the total available selling space. The inclusion decision now contains an allowance for the selling space allocated to a given product, as well as its financial performance. As an example, a typical grocery multiple (large supermarket chain) has at least 15 000 different products in its assortment, has suppliers offering new products on a regular basis and has a limited amount of selling space (25 000+ sq. ft). Decisions must be taken on assortment composition and order quantities, based on the prevailing target shopper needs, existing product performance, predicted performance of any new products on offer and the total selling space available.

The grocery multiple example presented above highlights the complexity of the assortment management process and the need to make the task more manageable. The introduction of the category allows the total assortment to be broken down into smaller units that can be controlled more effectively. The overall assortment composition decision can now be split into two levels. At the higher level, the *inclusion decision* (add new, delete old, change quantity) is on a *category-by-category basis*, with choices being made between alternative groups of related products. At the lower level, the *inclusion decision moves inside each category*, with decisions being taken (add new, delete old, change quantity) on the specific composition of this range of related products. This simplification is an example of category management.

Assortment Planning

The goal of assortment planning is to produce the most appropriate range of products to offer to target shoppers. 'Appropriateness' ultimately relates to satisfying target shopper needs better than the competition, while making the maximum sustainable profit. Retailers must achieve this with limited selling space, so appropriateness more accurately relates to satisfying target shopper needs better than the competition within the available selling area while making the maximum sustainable profit (usually measured per sq ft or metre). The process has two stages, *analysis* and *decision*. The analysis stage involves detailed analysis of all the factors that will have a major effect on the precise composition of the assortment – namely, the target shopper, competition, products and store capacity. The decision stage covers the total range of products to be offered – or, more usually, category number, type and composition. In addition, demand must be forecast to allow order quantities to be gauged.

Target Shopper Analysis

Any marketing person needs to answer a number of simple questions about customers – i.e. Who are they? What do they want? Why do they want it? How do they currently buy it (which products, purchased from where, how much purchased, purchase timing, etc.)? Retail marketers are no different, although customers are referred to as 'shoppers'. Target shopper analysis for assortment planning incorporates a number of these simple questions, although *customer identity* (Who are they?) has generally already been considered when developing the overall retail concept. *Needs* (Why do they want it?) and *benefits* (What do they want?) are the first areas to be considered, although it should be noted that only assortment related issues are considered. Aspects such as service levels, ambience and facilities, for example, are considered in connection with other elements of the retail tactical mix. In the case of assortments, satisfying shopper needs can relate to product composition, branding (manufacturer or retailer) and pack sizes.

Categories of Purchase

Three categories of purchase can be identified, dependent on the extent of decision making prior to purchase (see Chapter 3 on Shopper Behaviour). *Planned* purchasers shop with a specific purchase in mind, *semi-impulse* purchasers intend to purchase a type of product and *impulse* purchasers buy with little, if any, prior thought. Given that not all purchases are planned, many shoppers have to make a purchase decision inside the store. Indeed, even planned purchasers may briefly assess purchase alternatives in the store to seek reassurance that their original selection was the right one. For these reasons, all shoppers make *in-store judgements*, to a greater or lesser extent, about the products on offer. The two main factors that influence these judgements are choice and quality perceptions. An overall assessment of *value* is also important, which combines the quality judgement with the price element.

Degree of Choice

As has already been noted, shoppers require just the right amount of choice when considering a purchase. Too much choice often leads to confusion, too little leads to uncertainty over the quality of the decision.

Research by Kahn and Lehmann (1991) suggests that shoppers also look at flexibility for future choices – i.e. shoppers appreciate that their needs may change in the future, and assess an assortment on the degree of additional choice that is offered. Retailers must realize, though, that the addition of extra products to an assortment eventually reaches the point where *cannibalization* starts to occur. Cannibalization happens when a new product is added that fails to generate any new business and draws sales away from a retailer's existing products. To give an example, suppose a retailer offers products *A*, *B*, *C* and *D* in a given category and achieves combined sales of £10 000 per week. Product *E* is now added to increase choice and sales increase marginally to £10 050. Offering product *E* has caused cannibalization, as it has drawn sales away from the other products rather than causing new purchases to be made. The retailer has made a largely wasted investment in monetary terms and has tied up valuable shelf space in the process. Unless the addition of product *E* satisfied the shopper's present and future needs much better or responded to competitive pressures successfully, it was an inappropriate tactic (for further reading on cannibalization see Bultez *et al.* 1989). A retailer must, therefore, balance *customer choice* with *financial performance*. A limited number of purchase options leads to operational efficiencies for the retailer owing to buying power and space utilization, but may result in lower sales owing to a lack of choice for the shopper. A larger number of purchase options may increase sales by giving the shopper the right amount of choice for current and future needs, but may trigger operational inefficiencies at the point where cannibalization occurs.

Quality

Quality can simply be defined as the degree to which something is *fit for the purpose for which it is intended*. *Perceived quality* is a more accurate term to use, as quality assessments are uniquely individual in nature, being based on a combination of objective considerations and subjective judgements. *Perceived assortment quality* indicates how fit a range of products is for the purpose of satisfying that shopper's needs. Objective consideration can be made of the tangible elements of the products themselves (ingredients, content, materials, etc.) while subjective judgements can be made about more intangible factors such as brand image and retailer image. The shopper's past product experiences may also affect both objective consideration and subjective judgements. Competitor 'benchmarking' may also affect a shopper's judgement of quality, given the difficulty of absolute measurement of perceived quality. It is often easier for a shopper to assess the perceived quality of an assortment in relation to competitors' assortments than it is to consider one assortment in isolation. Judgements that rank each assortment on a range of factors, as already discussed, are typically easier to make than those made solely on an individual store's assortment.

Geographic Variations

An additional factor that must be considered is the impact of geographic variations. The shopper profile often changes from region to region, particularly if the retailer is operating in different countries. It is normally the case that retailers should adapt their assortment to fit the tastes of the local shopper. It is unusual that this adaptation will involve more than a small percentage of the total assortment, although this may not be the case in the multinational example mentioned above. Probably one of the most common areas for regional adaptation is grocery retail, where different parts of the UK, for example, exhibit slight differences in food preference. It should be noted, however, that shoppers are becoming increasingly homogeneous, so regional adaptation is becoming less of an issue. A related form of adaptation concerns *seasonal differences*. Just as shoppers in different regions have different tastes, so tastes at different times of the year may also vary. The most notable retail example is clothing, where climatic changes throughout the year cause assortments to change in many parts of the world.

Having understood shopper needs and, to an extent, behaviour, shopper numbers and expenditure need to be considered in order to assist in demand estimation. Trade area analysis (see Chapter 5 on Retail Location) provides the retailer with detailed information on target shoppers within a store's catchment area. This information will typically include both overall target shopper numbers and average (or cumulative) expenditure.

Competitor Analysis

Much of the information for an assessment of competitors' assortments already exists as part of a retailer's location evaluation data base. A specific factor that may require further research work is the *degree of assortment overlap* between competing stores in the same trade area. Research shows that the degree of customer overlap between competing stores increased in line with the degree of assortment overlap – i.e. shoppers who saw two assortments as similar would be more likely to spread their purchases over both stores. Developing this concept, it is apparent that *perceived assortment overlap* is also important, as detailed comparative analysis by shoppers can be impractical, especially in the case of large or complex assortments. Given the difficulties in the accurate determination of assortment overlap, shoppers are likely to make judgements (perceived assortment overlap) based on a limited data set. Both actual and perceived assortment overlap are important, as they indicate to the shopper which stores need to be compared and analysed for inclusion into their *store choice set* (the small number of stores from which the shopper finally selects).

Consider the example of a small speciality store offering a narrow and deep assortment in the same general product category area as a nearby mass-market retailer with a wide and shallow assortment. The actual assortment overlap will be relatively low, but the perceived overlap could be low or high, depending on that shopper's judgement. A low perceived overlap would mean a point of *differentiation* existed, so the mass-market retailer would not be seen as a threat to the speciality store and vice versa (no present threat). A high perceived overlap would be bad for the speciality store as the shopper would view the two retailers as in direct competition. In this case, a 'phantom' threat exists as the stores may be seen as competitors for as long as it takes the shopper to realize that the overlap is less than originally thought. Extending this example, suppose that a new speciality store was to open in the same trade area with an assortment with a high actual overlap. In the early stages it is likely that shoppers would have only a partial understanding of the store, so might perceive only a low assortment overlap. In this case, the new speciality store will present only a limited competitive threat for as long as shoppers have an inaccurate view of its assortment (future threat). Once a more accurate (high) perceived assortment overlap is developed, the new store will become a direct competitor (direct threat). Figure 8.2 illustrates the effects on competition of actual and perceived assortment overlap.

Product and Capacity Analysis

Products and store capacity can be covered together, as a certain amount of overlap exists between each area. It has already been noted that the assortment has to satisfy target shopper needs better than the competition within the available selling area. Product and capacity analysis is aimed at ensuring that this requirement is met – i.e. the available selling area is used as efficiency and effectively as possible. Issues covered in such analysis include the store area requirements and management and logistical issues for each product or category that may lie within the scope of the desired store image.

Store area requirements relate to the amount of selling space (measured in sq. ft or metres) required to effectively display a given product or category. The relative size of the product or products involved is clearly an important issue as large electrical goods (washing machines, cookers, etc.) obviously account for a larger amount of selling space than smaller electrical items such as a portable music system. An additional consideration concerns the total amount of display space required. Many products require a certain amount of additional display space, called an *open display* (see Chapter 7 on Store Design), to allow the shopper to carry out a full examination. Cars, for example, often require a significant amount of additional display space to allow shoppers to examine the products from all angles and 'get a feel' for

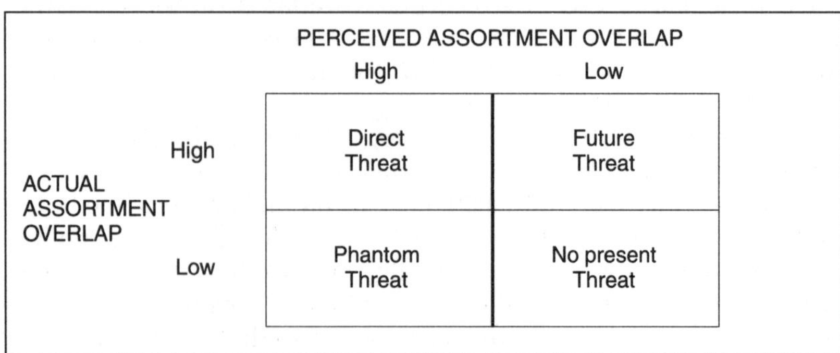

Figure 8.2 Actual and perceived assortment overlap

the styling. Retailers have limited physical store space, so must balance the required store space with the anticipated profit. A typical measure is to calculate the *projected profit per square unit of selling area* (ft or metres). A decision between two products (or categories) of equal importance to the shopper can therefore be made, on a sound financial basis. A common calculation used to aid decision making of this type is *Direct Product Profitability* (see Chapter 9 on Retail Pricing).

Management and logistical issues relate to the physical handling of the product or category. Certain products require more complex handling procedures, usually owing to issues relating to physical characteristics or buying. Important physical characteristics include perishability, fragility and weight, all of which require more care to be taken throughout the distribution, storage and selling process. Important buying factors relate to the ease of securing predictable supply and include the number of suitable suppliers and supply lead times. *Predictable supply* occurs when a sufficient number of suitable suppliers exist and supply lead times are short and/or regular.

The Decision Process

The decision stage covers the range of products to be offered as well as the relevant order quantities of each. In addition, decisions need to be made on product format – i.e. *manufacturer* or *retailer brand.*

Product Selection

The product selection decision is usually based on a number of *stocking criteria*, as listed in Table 8.1.

Table 8.1 Typical Stocking Criteria

Stocking criteria	Details
Shopper considerations	Value perception and choice
Financial considerations	Sales and profit potential
Store considerations	Shelf space, handling requirements
Buying considerations	Price and financial terms
Supplier considerations	Characteristics, marketing support
Category considerations	Width, depth and consistency
Physical distribution	Cost and difficulty
Strategic considerations	Longer-term factors

Source: Adapted from Doyle and Weinberg (1973) Effective new product decisions for supermarkets, *Operational Research Quarterly*, Vol. 24, No. 1, pp. 45–54 and reprinted from *Industrial Marketing Management*, Vol. 6, Nilsson, J, Purchasing by Swedish grocery chains, pp. 317–218, 1977, with permission from Elsevier Science.

Shopper and Category Considerations

Shopper considerations have already been discussed (see Target Shopper Analysis, above) and essentially relate to *need satisfaction*. Shoppers assess value on the basis of their satisfaction with the product or products (as well as other areas of the retail tactical mix) and the price to be paid. Issues such as *product composition* and *branding* will need to be considered, as will the degree of *choice* to be offered and shoppers' assessment of *perceived quality*.

An additional factor yet to be considered is *pack size*. Pack size has long been believed to affect product usage levels, especially for frequently purchased relatively low-price items. The belief is that large packs trigger higher usage volume than smaller packs. Much of the justification for this belief is anecdotal in nature – i.e. not based on suitable research. A number of possible explanations of the effect have been put forward, most notably concern about running out (Folkes and Gupta 1993), replacement cost (Lynn 1992), overpouring (Stewart 1994), scarce resource overvaluation (Lynn 1992) and perceived unit cost (Becker 1987). *Concern about running out* suggests that large pack sizes will encourage greater usage volume as customers are less concerned about finishing the pack. This becomes less true as the pack empties, of course, but overall usage volume still increases. The *replacement cost* idea is that smaller packages are used more sparingly to save the inconvenience of buying another pack, so usage volume is reduced as pack size decreases. *Overpouring* is the simple concept that larger packs are harder to handle, and so more difficult to control. In this case, as pack size increases, control decreases and usage volume increases owing to larger servings being poured. *Scarce resource overvaluation* suggests that scarce resources (smaller pack sizes) are conserved because they are seen as being less easily accessible and so become more valuable. *Perceived unit cost* is based on the common practice of pricing larger pack sizes at a lower cost per unit – i.e. a 100g pack may sell at £1.50 (£0.15 per g) whereas a 250g pack may sell at £3.00 (£0.12 per g). A lower unit cost leads to a reduction in perceived expensiveness and more liberal use. Research by Wansink (1996) identifies the perceived unit cost explanation as the most accurate, stating that 'package size increases usage volume only when accompanied by decreases in the product's unit cost'. It should be noted that these findings cannot be applied to higher-price less frequently bought items, where increases in purchase size are seen as largely unnecessary and uneconomical.

Category considerations are based on the key factors mentioned earlier – i.e. space utilization, width/depth/consistency, degree of shopper choice and quality perceptions. To a retailer, the ideal category is composed of products that satisfy shopper needs, make the maximum sustainable overall category profit per unit of selling space, give the shopper the right level of choice and allow for judgements of perceived quality to be made easily and appropriately. For this reason, a new product is assessed on its ability to give additional shopper satisfaction via an improvement in need satisfaction, a more appropriate level of choice or easier judgement of perceived quality. The space accounted for by the new product is then considered against the increase in need satisfaction. Should the product *increase need satisfaction per unit of selling space*, it seen as a suitable addition to the category.

Financial, Store and Physical Distribution Considerations

Financial considerations ultimately lead to a measurement of *product profitability*. Factors affecting this measurement include potential sales volume, selling price, buying price, handling costs and selling space utilization. Profit is determined by subtracting the selling costs (buying price + handling costs) from the selling price and scaling up for the total volume sold. Store and physical distribution considerations are then addressed to allow the profit per unit of selling space to be calculated and the handling requirements to be analysed. Profit per unit of selling space (per sq. ft or sq. m) is calculated by dividing the profit by the selling space required by the product. This process ensures that the store is making the maximum profit from the given selling space (this process will be discussed in more detail later). *Handling requirements* relate to the ability to handle the product within both the storage areas and the store itself. Some products may require specialist handling owing to product perishability (frozen products), fragility (fine china) and size/weight (furniture), for example. The ability to meet these handling requirements is assessed as well as the additional cost incurred. The direct product profitability calculation is relevant here (see Chapter 9 on Retail Pricing).

Buying and Supplier Considerations

Buying and supplier considerations tend to overlap, so will be covered together. The important factors relate to buying terms, marketing support, delivery and in-store services. *Buying terms* are the contractual or implied conditions that govern the supplier–retailer transaction. Buying price has already been mentioned, other conditions are volume discounts where retailers are 'rewarded' for reaching sales targets, usually with price reductions or occasionally additional product supply at reduced rates. Sale or return agreements allow the retailer to return unsold stock, thus eliminating write-offs while payment terms (credit facilities) may also be varied to give the retailer an accounting benefit, usually on a cash flow basis. To give an example, suppose a retailer negotiates a 30-day credit period with a supplier – i.e. payment for goods must be made 30 days after delivery. If the retailer can sell all the products within this 30-day period money is received before payment has to be made. In the case of some retailers (grocery, for example), products may be sold twice over before payment is due, so a significant cash flow boost is gained.

Marketing support is given by suppliers to ensure that their products sell effectively within the retailer's store. Support may be promotional, such as product advertising, in-store sales promotion and packaging development, or may involve staff training. *Delivery factors* primarily affect the flexibility of supply to allow for changes in shopper demand and the ease of supply. Flexibility covers supply lead times and small-order drops to individual stores, while ease of supply includes compatible delivery systems to simplify handling procedures. *In-store services* are made available to retailers to ensure that products are presented to shoppers in the most effective manner. Shelf replenishment may be undertaken by the supplier to guarantee that the right amount of product is on display at any given time – and, more crucially, that stock-outs do not occur. Assistance with product presentation (merchandising) is also given to ensure that shopper evaluation is both controlled and optimized.

Strategic Considerations

Strategic considerations are those that tend to favour the long-term position of the retailer over short-term performance. For reasons of store positioning or repositioning, competitive pressures, store image development or publicity, products may be stocked that fail to meet the considerations discussed above – e.g. financial performance may be below the required level, supplier selection may be less than ideal or selling space constraints may be overlooked. Common examples of such *strategic stocking decisions* include loss-leader products, competitor comparison products (CCPs), known-value items (KVIs) and special events (e.g. 'Robin Hood' campaigns).

Loss-leader products are offered at a low profit level in the knowledge that sales will be increased overall. The idea is that a loss leader will give excellent value for money, so will appear attractive to the shopper. New traffic will be encouraged and, once inside the store, these new shoppers will be exposed to the retailer's tactical mix and will be expected to buy additional higher margin products.

Competitor comparison products and *known-value items* are a small group of products that a shopper uses to assess value across different retailers. CCPs are used as a benchmark or point of comparison between stores, and will typically be standard products with a set level of quality. KVIs are items that a shopper has detailed price knowledge about and so are often used to estimate the overall store price level. Both CCPs and KVIs may be offered by retailers at low prices in order to gain favourable shopper perceptions. Fortunately for the retailer, CCPs and KVIs usually account for only a very small fraction of the assortment.

Special events cover situations where a retailer offers a product largely for publicity reasons. The UK has seen a number of such situations that have been connected to price maintenance or the setting of prices solely by manufacturers. Examples include books (Net Book Agreement), over-the-counter (OTC) pharmaceuticals and perfumes as well as branded clothing and footwear. In these cases, the retailer has either sold products at a lower price in contravention of price maintenance, or has obtained products from a cheaper source overseas and sold at a discount in the UK. Such campaigns, often referred to as 'Robin Hood' campaigns, don't necessarily make a profit for the retailer but do generate huge amounts of publicity.

Order Quantity

Order quantity determination is based on *accurate demand estimation* and impacts directly on store performance. McIntyre, Achabal and Miller (1993) consider accurate sales forecasts to reduce overbuying and hence reduce the need for clearance sales, to increase stock turnover and to maximize sales by reducing stock-outs. The right assortment, as has already been discussed, is one key to satisfying the shopper. Add to this constant availability and shopper satisfaction is likely to be high. Demand estimation or sales forecasting is used extensively for retail location decision making (see Chapter 5) and the same general approach can be used in this case. The methods will be the same (e.g. regression analysis) although data will be *assortment-specific*. By way of a reminder, regression is based on an assumption that analysis of a similar product can provide predictions for the new product in question. Analysis is undertaken to find the key factors that affect demand and the equation that links them together. The mathematical relationship between demand and these key factors can then be used as a means of sales forecasting. Sales forecasts for individual products may also be influenced by expert reasoning. McIntyre, Achabal and Miller (1993) describe a case-based reasoning (CBR) system that bases forecasts on the analysis of case histories (past examples of a similar nature). Expert judgement, usually by buyers, is then used to make the necessary adjustments from the case history to the current situation to allow sales figures to be estimated.

Brand Format Decisions

Having decided what product type to offer and the associated order quantity, a decision must be made on *branding*. Two broad options are open to the retailer – namely, brands attributed to the supplier (usually the manufacturer) and brands associated with the retailer (own-brand or own-label). *Supplier brands* typically account for a higher proportion of sales in the UK and Europe, although *retailer brands* are increasingly gaining market share. The split between supplier and retailer brand sales varies from retail sector to retail sector, but areas such as grocery and DIY see the highest retailer brand sales in the UK and, to a lesser extent, Europe. The shopper's decision between the different brand formats depends on a number of tangible and intangible factors. Product composition, uniqueness, pack size, price and availability are some of the typical *tangible* factors, while perceived quality, image and shopper confidence are typical *intangible* factors. The selection between supplier and retailer brands will now be discussed, followed by the specifics of retail brands.

An understanding of the reasons behind brand choice can be gained from an understanding of branding theory. All brands have tangible and intangible elements that combine to make up the *brand proposition*, or what is actually on offer to the shopper. Specifically, the proposition contains positioning and personality. *Positioning* relates to the product's position in the mind of the shopper, *personality* is the collection of intangible features that make up the brand's overall image. Positioning is communicated through tactical elements such as the product itself, price, distribution, advertising and possibly customer service. Personality, however, is much more difficult to define as it is an *opinion held by the shopper*. Historically, supplier brands were positioned towards the middle to top part of the market while retailer brands occupied the lower market positions. Supplier brands were also seen to have a quality-orientated personality while retailer brands were seen to be more price-conscious. In this case, the distinction between the supplier and the retailer brand buyer was quite easy to make on the basis of quality versus price. In today's retail environment, retailer brands have taken on a new dimension and have increasingly moved upmarket. The top of the market is still largely the domain of the supplier brand, but the middle market is being invaded by the retailer brand. This being the case, the distinction between the supplier and the retailer brand has become increasingly blurred.

Customer choice and need satisfaction are not the only factors considered by retailers when deciding on brand format. Internal issues such as financial performance, buyer power, control and store image must be taken into account, as must additional external issues such as competition. *Financial performance* is as important to a retailer as it is to any company. Factors affecting financial performance include the buying price, sales volume, handling costs (distribution, storage and display) and selling space. The level of *buyer power* also affects a retailer's financial performance, as high buyer power can allow lower buying prices to be negotiated and supplier promotional support to be increased (see co-operative promotion, in Chapter 10 on Retail Promotion). *Control* also affects financial performance owing to more effective planning and efficient operation. *Store image* may be enhanced by the quality and range of products that are offered, while competitive factors relate to differentiation and the generation of shopper traffic.

Financial performance must be balanced with shopper satisfaction. It is often the case that a highly popular but marginally profitable product brings shoppers into the store. Such loss leaders have strategic importance as they may increase sales overall. Given this fact, retailers actually seek to offer the best combination of supplier and retailer brands that meets shopper needs and makes the maximum sustainable profit. As has been noted, profit is influenced by costs such as the buying price and handling costs, as well as the selling price. Typically, retailer brands sell at a discount to supplier brands, have a lower buying price and comparable handling costs. Analysis of profitability shows that retailer brands often generate a slightly higher margin than supplier brands on a percentage basis. The reverse is often true of cash margins, where the higher selling price of supplier brands often means that cash generated per product is higher. To give an example, suppose that a retailer brand sold at £1.00 per pack with a buying price of £0.50, whereas a supplier brand sold for £2.00 with a buying price of £1.20. The retailer brand earns a higher percentage margin (50 per cent) than the supplier brand (40 per cent), but the cash margins are £0.50 and £0.80, respectively.

Financial performance is also linked to control and buyer power. Brand ownership has a large part to play in the level of control exercised by the retailer, with supplier brands being largely out of their control. A retailer brand is owned by that retailer so control is high. High control allows the retailer greater flexibility in pricing, better stock control, better product quality control and an ability to react to changing shopper tastes quickly. It is usually the case that retailers do not produce their own brand products, but the high degree of space capacity seen in many supply sectors means that retailers have a large number of potential suppliers to choose from. All other things being equal, when supply exceeds demand buyer power increases. Supplier brands, especially those with a high profile, are quite limited in number, so demand is much more in balance with supply. In this case, buyer power is much lower. Higher buyer power allows retailers to negotiate low buying prices or gain attractive buying terms, both of which lower costs. In addition, buyer power allows retailers to encourage promotional support from suppliers thus lowering the costs of a retailer's promotional campaign.

Store image and the competition are two further factors to consider. The products on sale within a store often influence shopper perceptions of store image. Retailers must be sure to match the balance of brands with their overall retail concept. Historically, as has already been noted, shopper perceptions of supplier and retailer brands were easy to gauge (quality and price, respectively). Currently, the position is more complicated and largely depends on the particular types of shopper. If a retailer's target shoppers are *supplier brand dominant*, too many retailer brands may start to damage store image. If they are *retailer brand dominant*, not enough retailer brands may cause problems. The type of brand format on offer may also allow a retailer to differentiate itself from its competition. This is particularly true for retailer brands where innovation can allow unique products to be offered or greater variety to be made available. In both cases, shopper traffic may be increased as uniqueness and/or variety may act as an inducement to use the store.

Retailer Brands

As has been already discussed, retailer brands may improve financial performance and store image, and give a competitive edge. A number of general points were also made about customer reactions to retailer brands, it is necessary to add more detail to this area before discussing retailer brands further.

Retailer brand buyers

Historically, retailer brands were seen as cheap lower-quality alternatives to supplier brands that represented good value for money. Purchasers of retailer brands saw that the risks involved in such a purchase were an appropriate trade off for the money saved on the purchase price. These less *risk averse shoppers* were found to be typically more secure, confident and often from higher socio-economic groups. Differences were found in the typical retailer brand buyer, probably owing to the nature of the retail situation. *Perceived risk* is a key component of involvement, and it is possible to consider some retail types as inherently low- or high-involvement. It follows that different retail types will trigger different levels of perceived risk and, so, different retailer brand purchasing patterns.

More recent times have seen a change in the perception of retailer brands. The reasons for this lie partly in the linked concepts of perceived risk and involvement mentioned above. Perceived risk can be said to depend on product performance, financial outlay and social acceptability. Perceptions of risk can also be affected by purchase experience and the shopper's judgement of the retailer in question. Retailers developed their own brands considerably at the end of the twentieth century with the move to cover more upmarket areas, the launching of highly branded products, the development of unique product types and varieties, and more supplier brand-like marketing support. Some retailer brands have, as a result, become much more like supplier brands in nature.

As retailer brands become more like supplier brands, shoppers' perceptions of the product performance differential between the two formats is likely to decrease as will any social issues concerned with the purchase of an 'inferior product'. The price of retailer brands is still typically below that of supplier brands, so perceptions of financial risk are still positive, if a little less so than in the past. These factors indicate a reduction in perceived risk and, therefore, an increase in the number of shoppers holding broadly positive attitudes about retailer brands. Add to this greater familiarity and experience with retailer brands owing to their increasing longevity in the retail environment, and perceived risk is even more likely to fall.

The final factor affecting shopper perceptions of retailer brands is the retailers themselves. Shoppers' perceptions of risk are influenced by their perceptions of the retailer or, put more simply: Can that retailer be trusted? Retailers have become considerably more sophisticated in image-building, utilizing a wide array of communications techniques such as advertising, public relations and personal selling (customer service) to get the right message across. *Perceived retailer rationality* (see Chapter 9 on Retail Pricing) can be interpreted as the extent to which the shopper trusts the retailer. Anecdotal evidence exists to suggest that perceived retailer rationality has increased, thus increasing trust and decreasing perceptions of risk. This being the case, it is likely that more shoppers will be motivated to consider retailer brands. Figure 8.3 summarizes the key characteristics of the modern retailer brand advocate.

Returning to the concept of involvement, it will still be the case that higher involvement retail situations will produce higher levels of perceived risk. This being the case, penetration of retailer brands will be lower as involvement increases. Typically low-involvement retail situations such as grocery retail should, therefore, see the highest acceptance of retailer brands while higher-involvement situations, such as luxury or fashion products, will see lower levels of acceptance.

He or she:

- Perceives retailer brands to *perform* just as well as supplier brands
- Believes that retailer brands are *cheaper* than supplier brands
- Sees no *image problems* associated with buying retailer brands
- Has confidence in ability to assess *value*
- Perceives the retailer to be *rational* and can be *trusted*
- Has *knowledge* and *purchase experience* of retailer brands.

Figure 8.3 Characteristics of the retailer brand advocate

Retailer brand approaches

The increasing development of retailer brands and their move upmarket has made the traditional classification of the own-label rather too broad. Traditionally, products on sale in stores could be classed into the three tiers of manufacturer (supplier) brand and two forms of retailer brand, namely own-label and generics. Own-label can be defined as 'an added value entity, produced by, or on behalf of a distributor [retailer]... targeted at specific customers and portray[ing] a unique relevant personality'; generics are 'items presented in commodity form, distinguishable by their basic packaging which is functional rather than aesthetic' (de Chernatony and McWilliam 1988). A more modern classification identifies seven different types of retailer brand (see Table 8.2), ranging from generics to premium.

Table 8.2 Seven Retailer Brand Approaches

Retailer brand approach	Description	Examples
Retailer-endorsed	Corporate name used	Tesco, IKEA, Boots
Pseudonym	Alias used	St Michael (Marks & Spencer), Winfield (F.W. Woolworth)
Generics	Brand free commodities	No Frills (Kwik Save)
Exclusive supply	Brand only produced for one retailer	Goodmans (Comet)
Stand-alone	Brand name more dominant than corporate name	Novon (J. Sainsbury)
Speciality	Unique or niche product	'Organic' range (J Sainsbury)
Premium	High-quality	Harrods

The *retailer-endorsed* approach describes the traditional own-branding method adopted by retailers. The company name is displayed on all products along with a product identifier (e.g. bath soap). The advantages of this method involve brand extension and promotional efficiencies. *Brand extension* is the stretching of an existing brand name to cover a new product. In the case of a retailer-endorsed approach, the company name may cover a huge range of products, so the launch of a new product is a low-cost undertaking. In addition, promotion of that company name effectively promotes all the products in the range making the process highly cost effective.

The *Pseudonym* approach is essentially the same as the retailer-endorsed approach although in this case a brand name is used that is often derived from the company name but is not the same. The benefits of such an approach also relate to brand extension and promotional efficiencies, a major weakness is the time required to build awareness of this new brand name.

A *stand-alone* approach is a modern development of the retailer-endorsed approach and could equally be applied to the pseudonym approach. In this case, the retailer produces a brand that has a brand name rather than simply a product identifier. The company name (or alias) is typically lower profile than this brand name, so the brand stands apart (alone) from the retailer's other own brands. This approach is extremely close to a supplier brand and demonstrates an increasing movement from retailer to retailer/brand builder. On the positive side, stand-alone brands present a unique image so are hard to copy. On the negative side, marketing costs increase (packaging and promotion mainly) and the benefits associated with brand extension may be reduced or lost altogether.

Generics have already been defined as brand-free commodity items and are still produced today, particularly by grocery retailers.

The *exclusive supply* approach involves a retailer offering a branded product that is produced only for that retailer. The brand may technically be a supplier brand, but is effectively a retailer brand. In a sense, this is a pseudonym approach applied to a single product or category. For this reason, the same strengths and weaknesses apply.

Speciality retailer brands are associated with unique products or those aimed at a small target shopper group (niche) while *premium* retailer brands are positioned towards the high-quality end of the market. Both speciality and premium retailer brands may be retailer-endorsed (Harrods), pseudonym, exclusive manufacture or stand-alone.

The seven retailer brand approaches mentioned above highlight a change in the means of differentiation used by retailers when launching their own brands. The traditional point of differentiation was on the basis of price, with retailer brands ideally selling at a 15 per cent discount to supplier brands (Dore 1976). More modern retailer brand theory offers a number of additional points of differentiation such as quality, uniqueness, variety and value for money. Shoppers may choose a given type of retailer brand because of high perceived quality at an affordable price or indeed moderate perceived quality at a value for money price. Shoppers may also make retailer brand selections owing to the availability of a product type or variety not available elsewhere. The success of non-price based differentiation is likely to aid the development of retailer brands that increasingly encroach on the territory of the supplier brand (mid-market and upmarket).

Conclusions

The assortment must be viewed as more than just a collection of products; it is a *need satisifier*. Shoppers tend to frequent stores where the products on offer fit their requirements, so the wrong assortment seriously affects traffic. In an ideal world, retailers would be able to offer every product that shoppers require. In reality, store constraints mean that only a limited assortment can be offered. This means that retailers must take some very difficult *inclusion/exclusion decisions* on a regular basis. A number of factors affect these decisions – namely, the shopper, competition, finances, the store, distribution, buying and suppliers and category composition or choice.

Shoppers require products that meet their needs by offering *superior value* – i.e. provide greater benefits than competitors' products. This judgement is typically made by comparing a small number of products common to every retailer. Such competitor comparison products (CCPs) are vital as are known-value items (KVIs). CCPs are compared without an equitable price in mind, whereas KVIs have a 'market price'. After successfully dealing with the competition, the retailer must then consider the shopper's behaviour within the store. Choice must be sufficient for an adequate number of options to be considered, but should not reach the point where too many options lead to confusion. *Pack sizes* should also be appropriate, as should the *brand format*. The increasing sophistication and diversity of retailer brands has increased their appeal and narrowed the perceived quality gap with supplier brands.

Having given the shopper superior value, internal factors must then be considered. *Profitability* must be ensured (using methods such as DPP) and *physical considerations* such as buying, suppliers and distribution/storage must also be considered. It is not enough for retailers to just give superior value to shoppers, they must also maximize profits from a limited selling area and must ensure that the management issues have been taken care of.

Having considered all these issues the retailer must also adopt a strategic approach. The retailers' *image* or *corporate brand* is important, and is based in part on the products making up the assortment. An image based upon quality own-label products (such as Marks & Spencer in the UK) has implications for the composition of the assortment. Similarly, a price-fighting image implies a certain assortment comprising of value for money items.

It is apparent, therefore, that many conflicting factors influence the assortment decision. The perfect assortment probably does not exist, and if it did it would change on a regular basis in line with changes in the market. *Optimizing the assortment* is the key and requires detailed data collection and analysis. Striking the right balance between customers, competitors, financial performance, internal management factors and strategic issues has led to four successful generic approaches. When considering their assortment, retailers would be advised to start with width and depth, and the options of full service, full convenience, category specialism and niche specialsim.

References and Further Reading

Becker, G. (1987) Economic Analysis and Human Behaviour, in L. Green and J.H. Kagel (eds), *Advances in Behavioural Economics*, Ablex, Norwood NJ, 143–72.

Bultez, A., Naert, P., Gijsbrechts, E. and Abeele, P.V. (1989) Asymmetric Cannibalisation in Retail Assortments, *Journal of Retailing*, 65, 2, 153–93.

De Chernatony, L. and McWilliam, G. (1988) Clarifying the Difference between Manufacturers' Brands and Distributors' Brands, *Quarterly Review of Marketing*, 13, 4, 1–5.

Dore, B. (1976) Own Labels – are they Still Worth the Trouble to Grocers?, *Advertising and Marketing*, 13, 2, 58–63.

Doyle, P. and Weinberg, C.B. (1973) Effective New Product Decisions for Supermarkets, *Operational Research Quarterly*, 24, 1, 45–54.

Folkes, V. and Gupta, K. (1993) When to Say When: Effects of Supply on Usage, *Journal of Consumer Research*, 20, 467–77.

Kahn, B.E. and Lehmann, D.R. (1991) Modelling Choice Among Assortments, *Journal of Retailing*, 67, 3, 274–300.

Lynn, M. (1992) Scarcity's Enhancement of Desirability: The Role of Naive Economic Theories, *Basic and Applied Social Psychology*, 13, 67–78.

McIntyre, S.H., Achabal, D.D. and Miller, C.M. (1993) Applying Case-Based Reasoning to Forecasting Retail Sales, *Journal of Retailing*, 69, 4, 372–99.

Nilsson, J. (1977) Purchasing by Swedish Grocery Chains, *Industrial Marketing Management*, 6, 317–218.

Stewart, B. (1994) *Can you Trust a Tomato in January?*, Bantam Books, New York.

Wansink, B. (1996) Can Package Size Accelerate Usage Volume?, *Journal of Marketing*, 60, 1–14.

Retail Pricing

CHAPTER 9

This chapter:

- Defines price
- Examines customers' price analysis behaviour
- Delineates how prices can be set
- Defines the concept of price sensitivity

Retail Pricing

Introduction

Price can be defined as 'the monetary value assigned by a seller to something purchased, sold or offered for sale, and on transaction by a buyer, as their willingness to pay for the benefits the product and channel service delivers' (Gilbert 1999). Like any other business, price levels, along with buying price, costs and sales volumes, have a major impact on a retailer's profitability. Price has not always been an issue for retailers in the UK, however, as the post Second World War years saw the continuation of the practice of *resale price maintenance* (RPM). RPM essentially meant that prices in-store were set at a fixed level, so all retailers had to sell at the same price. Under these circumstances, retailers had to concentrate on *non-price tactics* such as the assortment, location, promotion, etc. When RPM was largely abolished in 1964 (a few notable exceptions remained, such as the net book agreement), UK retailers had the freedom to vary prices at will, utilizing any scale economies or improved management practices to offer products at a lower price while still making a profit.

Over the next few decades shoppers became increasingly used to variations in price for comparable items and the need to 'shop around' for the best price grew. As shoppers became used to variable prices so they became increasingly knowledgeable and adopted more sophisticated *price analysis behaviour*. The increasing level of retail competition seen since the 1980s has produced a greater number of comparable stores and a wider range of prices for shoppers to analyse. As a result, the modern shopper has become more *value sensitive* – i.e. more able to assess if a product is worth the money charged for it. Retailers have had to react to the increasingly sophisticated shopper and have a number of strategies and tactical approaches at their disposal. Before discussing these issues, it is necessary to consider a number of basic pricing theories.

Simple economic theory can provide some basic points about the impact of price on demand. Clearly, retailers have to balance *price* and *sales volume* (demand) if profit is to be maximized and stock is to be managed effectively. The simple *demand curve* expresses the relationship between price and the number of units demanded by shoppers. The nature of this relationship is moderated by *elasticity*, which can be defined as the extent to which the quantity demanded changes as price is increased or decreased. Demand is considered to be elastic if the percentage change in demand is greater that the percentage change in price, while inelastic demand is the reverse situation. Table 9.1 contains an example of both elastic and inelastic demand.

Table 9.1 Elastic and Inelastic Demand

Demand (units) and price for products *A* and *B* were measured over a two-week period. Using the data presented below, product *A* is exhibiting elastic demand ($E > 1$) while product *B* is inelastic ($E < 1$). From the retailer's perspective, decreasing the price of both products by a similar percentage has stimulated increased demand for *A* but has had little effect on the demand for *B*. When considering future pricing for these two products, the retailer should note that pricing can have an effect on sales of *A* but not of *B*.

Product	Week 1	Week 2	Change (%)	Elasticity
A				
Price (£)	4.59	3.99	13.1	
Demand (units)	1000	1200	20.0	E = 1.53
B				
Price (£)	8.99	7.99	11.1	
Demand (units)	500	510	2.0	E = 0.18

The traditional demand curve/elasticity theory is somewhat simplistic, and it would be incorrect to assume that the sales will increase solely based on demand elasticity – i.e. the example presented in Table 9.1 fails to account for all the factors that affect demand in a retail situation. An improvement to the basic demand elasticity can be made if the concept of *price sensitivity* is introduced. Price sensitivity is the degree to which shoppers are affected by the price of an item and is influenced by factors such as the importance of the product to the shopper, the shopper's income characteristics, the relative price of the product and the availability of attractive substitutes. Sensitivity usually increases in line with increases in the availability of attractive substitutes and/or the relative price and/or importance to the customer and/or personal disposable income. In the retail context, customer loyalty, competitive factors and quality preferences can add to the shopper's price sensitivity. High loyalty may decrease sensitivity, while competitive pricing tactics and quality preferences may increase or decrease it.

The discussion of price sensitivity and demand elasticity highlights the importance of the shopper in the price decision. Other areas of importance are competition and the retailer itself. *Shopper factors* cover sensitivity and elasticity, as previously mentioned, as well as value evaluation and price comparison. *Competition* is important as prices are generally assessed by shoppers on a *comparative basis*, so alternative prices for the same item may be used in the shopper's value evaluation process. In this case, any pricing actions taken by competitors may affect the comparisons made by shoppers and may affect their purchase choices. *Retailer factors* cover internal issues such as costs and profits, space utilization and strategic considerations. Space utilization has already been discussed in connection with assortment decisions (Chapter 8) and strategic considerations cover longer-term price factors such as store image and shareholder pressure.

Shopper Value Evaluation

Value evaluation is the process of price/quality comparison where the shopper considers whether the price charged for a product is reflected in that product's quality. If price and perceived quality are in line, the shopper believes that value is appropriate. If the price exceeds perceived quality, poor value results while perceived quality in excess of price results in extra value. It is important to note the difference between *perceived quality* and *actual quality* (see Chapter 8 on The Retail Assortment). Shopper perceptions of quality may not be accurate, so the relationship between price and quality may not necessarily be linear – i.e. it is not always the case that a increase in price will lead to an increase in perceived quality. If retailers can convince shoppers that the product is of sufficient quality, the shopper may buy the product even if the price is high or has been increased.

An additional factor is the shopper's degree of *price knowledge*. If the shopper has a limited knowledge of competitors' prices no points of comparison (benchmarks) exist. In this case, value evaluation becomes increasingly subjective unless tangible factors such as product composition can be assessed. Under conditions of increasing subjectivity, retailers may use other tactical elements (store ambience, promotion) or the retailer's reputation (image) to convince the customer of the high value of the products on offer.

Shopper Price Comparison

A large amount of research has been carried out to explain the price comparison behaviour of shoppers (Kerin, Jain and Howard 1992; Marmorstein, Grewal and Fiske 1992; Wakefield and Inman 1993; Urbany, Dickson and Kalapurakal 1996). *Price search*, or the degree to which shoppers compare alternative prices for a comparable item, is the major part of price comparison activity. Price search can be *inter-store* or *intra-store*, meaning that shoppers may compare prices between stores or between individual products (within a category) in the same store, respectively. A number of factors affect the degree of price search – economic factors (personal disposable income), search costs, temporal factors, shopping purpose and the shopper's psychological state.

Decreases in *personal disposable income* may trigger an increased motivation to search for the lowest price for reasons of economy. This must be balanced with the costs of such a price search, as the shopper may make a mental cost/benefit analysis balancing the money to be saved by finding a lower price against the costs (time and money) involved in finding that lower price. Time is also important, as it is a cost in the price search cost/benefit analysis. Shoppers with a limited amount of time may either defer purchase if they are unsure about the price on offer, or may simply curtail any price search and buy the product most conveniently available.

The *purpose* of the shopping trip may also affect the degree of price search. Shopping trips undertaken for essential purchases may see differing degrees of price search to those undertaken for more leisure-related reasons. The shopping task is a key aspect of shopping purpose and may also affect price search behaviour. The products to be purchased may either be well known or new to the shopper. In the first case, greater product knowledge may decrease price search as the shopper is confident that price knowledge is high. In the second case, price knowledge may be low, so price search may increase.

The shopper's *psychological state* may also affect the degree of price search. Behavioural studies indicate that individuals are predisposed to information (price) search behaviour. A factor affecting this predisposition is involvement or the degree of importance attached to the purchase by the shopper (see Chapter 3 on Shopper Behaviour). Increases in involvement tend to magnify any predisposition to price search behaviour. To explain this further, suppose that of two shoppers one has a high predisposition to price search, the other low. As involvement increases, both shoppers will tend to adopt a higher degree of price search activity although the difference between the two is unlikely to change dramatically.

Looking in more detail, an additional factor can be introduced to account for the motivation to price search. *Perceived price dispersion* (PPD) is based on a shopper's judgement of the degree of price variance among the available purchase options. The shopper will then weigh the expected gains from price search against the costs involved. As PPD increases, so does the expected financial gain, so price search will increase as long as search costs are not prohibitive. Research shows that in many cases an increase in PPD does in fact lead to a higher degree of price search (Bucklin 1969; Urbany 1986). When added to personal disposable income, two simple relationships involving the degree of price search can be identified. The degree of price search increases as personal disposable income decreases and/or perceived price dispersion increases.

More recent research by Urbany, Dickson and Kalapurakal (1996) provides a more complete explanation of the determinants of price search behaviour. PPD is an important factor by virtue of the cost/benefit analysis undertaken by shoppers. Other factors added to the model are shopper knowledge, habit and social returns. The findings show that more knowledgeable shoppers search more as they tend to be more efficient, see more value in price information and recognize that prices change, so information needs to be *updated* regularly. *Habit* incorporates the ideas about shopping purpose and the shopper psychological state. Shoppers who are predisposed to price searching will do so extensively while shoppers who price search may develop a comparison routine that becomes a matter of habit. *Social returns* relate to the individual benefits associated with price knowledge, such as those derived from market mavenism or the 'tendency to collect marketplace information with the intent of sharing it with others' (Urbany, Dickson and Kalapurakal 1996). Market mavenism has been linked to a number of elements of shopping behaviour, one of which is increased information (price) search. Essentially, market mavenism gives the individual a sense of importance or respect as a valuable source of price information. This sense of importance or respect is a benefit in kind that justifies further price search activity by affecting the cost/benefit calculation.

An interesting viewpoint is put forward by Kaufmann, Smith and Ortmeyer (1994) relating to *source credibility*, the source being the price-setter – i.e. the retailer. A belief among shoppers that retailers are rational (high source credibility) leads to an assumption that the prices set by those retailers must reflect the intrinsic value of the products in question. This retailer's price is then seen as the market price so perceived price dispersion will decrease and further price searching will be limited to sale spotting.

Consideration of the purchase situation also identifies the nature of the product and price level as factors affecting shopper price searching. Shoppers need to be able to compare product *quality* as well as price in order to make their judgement of value. As products become increasingly heterogeneous, so comparability becomes more difficult. In this case, search costs rise owing to increases in time and effort (possibly money also) for little appreciable gain in search benefits, causing a fall in the degree of price searching. Increasing homogeneity leads to increasing comparability, reduced search costs – and, so, increased price search. The absolute price of the product type also affects price searching owing to an increase in the perceived risk – i.e. a small percentage variation in price is a significant amount of money. Search benefits increase and, providing that search costs do not increase proportionately, price search also increases.

Tying all the various factors discussed above together gives a clearer picture of the factors behind a shopper's price search behaviour (see Figure 9.1). Increases in personal disposal income, time constraints, perceived search effort, perceived retailer rationality and product homogeneity usually reduce the degree of price search, while increases in absolute price, social returns, shopper knowledge and perceived price dispersion usually increase the degree of price search.

Price search is encouraged when:	*Price search is discouraged when:*
• Absolute price increases	• Absolute price decreases
• Social returns increase	• Social returns decrease
• Shopper knowledge increases	• Shopper knowledge decreases
• Perceived price dispersion increases	• Perceived price dispersion decreases
• Personal disposable income decreases	• Personal disposable income increases
• Time constraints decrease	• Time constraints increase
• Perceived search effort decreases	• Perceived search effort increases
• Perceived retailer rationality decreases	• Perceived retailer rationality increases
• Product homogeneity decreases	• Product homogeneity increases

Figure 9.1 Factors affecting price search behaviour

An additional factor is the *scope* of the price search – i.e. between stores or within the same store. Cost/benefit analysis can also be used to explain this, as if shoppers perceive the costs of inter-store price comparison to exceed the benefits of such a search, the degree of price search will fall. It is apparent that it is more difficult to compare prices between stores than it is to compare prices within the same store. It is true that the perceived benefits of inter-store price search may be higher, but costs tend to be the deciding factor. For this reason, inter-store price searching tends to be more limited than intra-store searching. It should be noted, however, that the factors discussed above will also affect the degree of both inter-store and intra-store price search. Research on inter-store price comparisons (e.g. Nystrom 1970) shows that a lack of information and/or cognitive limitations may have an effect. A lack of information is due in part to the cost of inter-store price search (time and effort mainly), while cognitive limitations mean that some shoppers do not have the mental skills to handle what is an increasingly complex comparative process. This being the case, inter-store comparisons are often made on the basis of a very limited sample. Shoppers may select a small number of products, undertake a price comparison then extrapolate the results to gain the inter-store comparison. In this case, a shopper's view of the overall prices charged in two stores may be based on only a handful of comparable products sold in each.

Retailers' Financial Considerations

Retailers, like any other business, seek to *maximize profit*. It has already been noted that price, along with buying price, costs and sales volume, has an important impact on profit. Retailers must, therefore, take great care in setting prices to ensure that a maximum sustainable profit is achieved. The task is made harder by the selling space limitations imposed on store-based retailers – i.e. the price of a product must reflect the profits it will make and how much store space it will occupy. A widely used method to achieve an accurate measure of profitability is *direct product profitability* (DPP).

Direct Product Profitability (DPP) is the 'detailed measure of an individual product's profit contribution ... the calculations involve adjusting the gross margin of a product to reflect allowances, payment discounts or any other form of income, and then subtracting any costs directly attributable to that product as it passes through the retail system' (Pinnock 1986). Put in more simple terms, DPP measures the true profitability of a given product by allowing for *hidden costs and income*. Take this on a stage further to account for the space occupied by the product, and *DPP per unit of selling area* can be calculated. This is perhaps a more useful measure as it can show the retailer how best to use the available selling space. Figure 9.2 contains the basic and more detailed DPP formulae.

To give an example of a DPP calculation, suppose that a retailer has two different products in its assortment, products *A* and *B*. The retailer has selling space for only one of these two products, so needs to know which to keep and which to delete. Data are collected on each product and used to

DPP = Adjusted Gross Margin[1] (AGM) – Direct Product Costs[2] (DPC)

DPP per square foot of selling space =

$$\frac{\text{Adjusted Gross Margin}^{1}\text{ (AGM)} - \text{Direct Product Costs}^{2}\text{ (DPC)}}{\text{Selling space requirements}}$$

Figure 9.2 Direct product profitability formulae
Notes:
1 Adjusted gross margin is the total gross margin + allowances for gains such as volume discounts.
2 Direct product costs typically include warehousing, transport, store and headquarters' costs.

calculate DPP and DPP per square foot of selling space. On the basis of the DPP calculation, product *A* is retained and product *B* is deleted (see Table 9.2). It is interesting to note that product *A* would be selected by retailers with selling-space constraints as the DPP per sq. ft is more than double that of product *B*. If, however, space was not an issue for the retailer it is likely that product *B* would be selected as the normal DPP is slightly higher.

Table 9.2 Direct Product Profitability

Factor	Product *A*		Product *B*	
	(%)	Cash	(%)	Cash
Gross margin	25.0	2.75	28.0	3.08
Additional income	1.5	0.16	1.8	0.20
Adjusted gross margin	26.5	2.91	29.8	3.28
Direct product costs	11.0	1.21	13.5	1.48
Direct product profitability	15.5	1.70	16.3	1.80
Selling space requirements	1.10		2.55	
Direct product profitability per unit area	14.1	1.55	6.4	0.71

Competitor Issues

The importance of competitors in a retailer's pricing decision relates to the *comparative nature* of price evaluation. Shoppers judge value (and hence price) by comparing a given purchase alternative against some benchmark that is often based on competitors' prices and products. As an example, a purchaser of a new car will compare the price of that car with the price of the realistic alternatives. Relative product quality of all alternatives will be assessed and set against the price charged for each. Value perceptions will then be formed. Retailers must be aware, therefore, that shoppers often assess their prices against those of the competition. The extent and nature of this comparison relates to the shopper factors discussed earlier (see Table 9.1), the specific products and the competitors themselves.

The products offered within a retailer's assortment can be classified by considering shopper knowledge. In most retail situations, shoppers are familiar with only a limited number of products in the total assortment. 'Familiar', in this case, means that shoppers have an idea of a normal price range or a perception of acceptable value based on an understanding of the product's composition (features, constituents, etc.). The former are known as *known-value items* or KVIs, the latter as *competitor comparison products* or CCPs (see Chapter 8 on The Retail Assortment for further details). CCPs are used as a benchmark or point of comparison between stores while KVIs are often used to estimate the overall store price level. The setting of a competitive price for CCPs and KVIs may have quite limited profit impact but may have a huge impact on the retailer's price image with respect to its competition. KVIs and CCPs can be identified by shopper-based marketing research.

Having identified the key products for price comparison, retailers must identify the *competitors* with whom they will be compared. The degree of assortment overlap dictates the extent of competition with other similar retailers (see Chapter 8 on The Retail Assortment). This overlap may be actual or perceived, based on fact or judgement, respectively. It has already been noted that *perceived assortment overlap* is important, as detailed comparative analysis by shoppers can be impractical, especially in the case of large or complex assortments (see Chapter 8 on The Retail Assortment). Both actual and perceived assortment overlap are, therefore, important as they indicate to the shopper which stores need to be compared and analysed for inclusion into their *store choice set* (the small number of stores from which the shopper finally selects). Determining all those stores that have significant assortment overlap (actual or perceived) will indicate all those competitors' prices that must be considered by the retailer, as they may be considered by the shopper.

Pricing Objectives

Knowledge of the key factors affecting the pricing decision can now be considered alongside the retailer's overall strategy to produce pricing objectives. These objectives then provide the basis for *pricing strategy selection* as well as the tactical approach. Objectives may be internal or external (to the retailer) in nature, offensive or defensive, and may be short- or long-term in outlook. A number of typical objectives can be identified that may be used individually or in combination (see Table 9.3).

Table 9.3 Common Types of Pricing Objective

Objective	Description
Long-term profit maximization	Often seen as the overall objective of all retailers
Short-term profit maximization	A response to short-term demand for funds
Market penetration	Sacrifice short-term profits for increases in market share and, hence, longer-term profitability
Market defence	Countering competitive pricing actions in the short or longer term
Market stabilization	Seeking to price at a market level to avoid price wars
Quality-led value positioning	Making price less important than quality in the shopper's determination of value
Price-led value positioning	Making price more important than quality in the shopper's determination of value
Integrity	Building shopper perceptions of a fair pricing approach
Start-up	Market-entry pricing strategies
Rundown	Market-exit pricing strategies

Source: Adapted and expanded from McGoldrick (1990).

Profit maximization, both short and long term, is an objective used by virtually every retailer. Increasingly, retailers are using *maximum sustainable profit* (short or long term) rather than the absolute maximum. The difference is that sustainable profit implies *continuity*, and embraces the concept that an ever more sophisticated shopper is more likely to realize when excess profits are being made. 'Market-based' objectives relate to the degree of competition, and cover aggressive, neutral or defensive intentions. *Aggressive intentions* (market penetration) involve gaining market share, usually by actual price reductions or promotional pricing. *Neutral intentions* (market stabilization) see price competition eliminated in favour of other tactical elements such as the assortment, design, service, etc. *Defensive intentions* (market defence) seek to counter competitors' actions in order to avoid any loss of market share. Value positioning objectives focus on the shopper, making either *price* (price-led value positioning) or *quality* (quality-led value positioning) the key determinant of the shopper's value evaluation (recall that value is measured by considering the quality gained for the price to be paid). Integrity also focuses on the shopper with the intention of building a reputation for fair pricing. The two final objectives relate to market entry (start-up) or exit (rundown). Start-up shares similarities with market penetration as market share is being built, while rundown seeks to liquidate stock in the most profitable way.

Pricing Strategies

Once pricing objectives have been identified, a strategy can be selected to achieve those objectives. In general, a pricing strategy may set prices below, at or above the market level. The factors mentioned earlier (shoppers, competitors, the retailer itself) will affect pricing strategy selection. Four generic approaches can be considered as well as two specific strategies. The four generic approaches utilize the price/quality relationship and are referred to as *premium*, *economy*, *penetration* and *skimming*. The two specific approaches are a modern development of the generic approaches, namely *every day low pricing* (EDLP) and *high/low pricing* (HLP).

Four Generic Strategies

The basis of the four generic strategies is value evaluation or the trade off between *price* and *perceived quality*. Price may be seen as high or low, as may perceived quality, giving the strategies shown in Figure 9.3. It should be noted that retailers should consider what aspects of quality are important (product quality, brand name, store image, etc.) as 'quality' itself is a very broad and often misused term. It is also true that actual quality is not the issue, *perceived* quality is. If a retailer can convince the shopper that the products sold are of high quality this is to that retailer's benefit even if the products are not, in actuality, of greater quality.

Figure 9.3 shows expected value as a straight line through all points where price and perceived quality are equivalent. Expected value has two extremes, a high price for a high perceived quality (*premium pricing*)

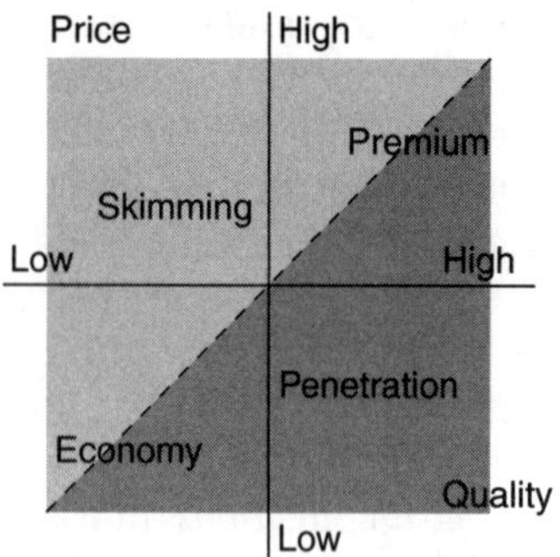

Figure 9.3 Four generic pricing strategies

and a low price for a comparably low perceived quality (*economy pricing*). In both cases, the price would be seen as fair or the market price. Prices can also be seen as offering value in excess of that expected (penetration) owing to the price being below the expected level for the perceived quality gained. A skimming price sees lower than expected value, as the perceived quality does not match the price. Examples of the usage of these generic strategies would be discounters (economy), outlet shops (penetration) and luxury or fashion goods retailers (premium or skimming).

Every Day Low Pricing

Every day low pricing (EDLP) is a strategy that sets a stable price at a point somewhere between competitors' regular prices and promotional (sale) prices. The approach is, therefore, all about setting a low, rather than the lowest, price on any given day. The strength of EDLP is that the price is kept constant throughout the year, so, if an average is taken for a significant time period (say, one year), the approach will typically give the lowest average price. Given that a low price is set, EDLP can either be an economy or a penetration pricing approach. In the first case, EDLP would be no different to a discount retailer approach where low prices are charged for correspondingly low-quality products. In this situation, EDLP would not offer any new benefits to shoppers with existing discount stores to choose from. The second case begins to explain the worth of EDLP as a superior value-for-money approach. If shoppers perceive that assortment quality is in excess of the price charged, purchase intentions are likely to increase. In addition, if shoppers know that the prices will remain the same over time, price comparison analysis may be scaled down once the shopper is convinced that EDLP provides the best value for money. In this sense, successful EDLP relies on the shoppers' perception of penetration pricing.

From the retailer's point of view, EDLP offers a more manageable system based on much more predictable sales forecasts and financial performance. The large fluctuations in demand experienced by retailers using frequent sale tactics are not experienced by EDLP retailers. Low prices do mean that margins suffer, although, when averaged over the full year trading margins can be more healthy than retailers that sell a lot of items at promotional prices. Overall profitability could be affected, as a company switching to EDLP may see a reduction in average profit margins. This reduction is countered by the benefits gained from a more efficient system. Greater accuracy in sales forecasting allows for improved stock management that in turn allows high *demand conversion* – i.e. stockouts can be minimized, giving potential purchasers every chance to purchase.

Marketing costs may also reduce as the costs associated with regular promotional events (e.g. sales) are reduced. It is also true that a consistent message can be delivered throughout the year, allowing reductions in the communications budget. Price wars may also be averted, as it is unlikely that many retailers will be able to successfully undercut the EDLP retailer over the longer term. Some researchers also point to an improved customer service owing to the more focused and consistent retail marketing approach. It should be said, however, that service gains vary from retailer to retailer.

On the negative side, EDLP has been found to be hard to maintain. Successful EDLP requires products to be sold at low prices throughout the year. Furthermore, it is often the case that a proportion of those products will need to be major brands (also KVIs and CCPs). This has to be true if shoppers are to be able to compare prices with non-EDLP competitors and make judgements about the value of shopping with the EDLP retailer. Small or specialized retailers will, therefore, usually find it difficult to make an EDLP approach work in the long term. An additional problem concerns shoppers' value judgements. In some cases, shoppers perceive low-price products to be of low quality, so would see EDLP as an economy approach. In this case, EDLP would have no benefits over a discounter's economy approach.

High/Low Pricing

High/low pricing (HLP) is a mixed approach that sets prices at levels both above and below EDLP. A regular price is set at a higher level than competitors' EDLP levels, but frequent promotional (sale) prices are set that undercut EDLP. This method has traditionally been favoured by retailers, with department store 'January' sales and seasonal clearances common events. The approach works successfully if the sale periods are kept to a minimum. In these circumstances, shoppers pay higher prices for the bulk of the year, then can gain greatly reduced prices on sale stock. Margins are usually good and shoppers' value perceptions are not affected as it has been found that shoppers judge sale items on the pre-sale price. HLP, when used correctly, is a combination of premium prices (sometimes skimming) throughout the year with a short period of penetration pricing. The danger with the HLP approach is the temptation to increase sale periods in order to increase sales volume. In this case, shoppers begin to believe that the non-sale prices are inflated and believe that waiting for the sales (that will inevitably come) is the best option. A greater proportion of items are sold at sale prices, hence margins suffer.

From the retailer's perspective, HLP can offer a number of benefits. First, the same assortment can appeal to a large proportion of shoppers. Shoppers buying at the full price may be those that see the product as being more important than the price – i.e. are *less price sensitive.* As time goes on, more price-conscious shoppers may be encouraged into the store as the first sale begins. As the prices are increasingly reduced so bargain hunters will start to become interested in the assortment. Excitement and interest can also be generated by sales or promotional prices.

An additional benefit is that shoppers' value perceptions can remain unharmed by HLP provided the sales are not too frequent. Continuous low prices (e.g. EDLP) can send the wrong message to shoppers and can damage their perception of a retailer (e.g. the assortment is of low quality). HLP can convey the message of service and quality, as shoppers use the pre-sale price in their judgements if sales are limited in duration. The use of pre-sale prices to judge quality also means that the low prices charged during sales will be seen as exceptional value (penetration price), so sale stock should be sold quickly, thus freeing up store space and working capital for new products.

On the negative side, a number of benefits associated with the EDLP approach may be lost – i.e. reduced price wars, reduced communications expenditure, more forecastable sales and increased efficiency (see the section on EDLP for further details).

Tactical Pricing

Tactical pricing is the day-to-day setting of prices for specific products and, as such, is the implementation of the pricing strategy. A number of tactical approaches can be considered that relate to differential pricing and price points. *Differential pricing* involves a number of different prices being set at the same time or over a period of time for the same product(s). Different prices may be set for the same products, on offer at the same time, owing to differences in store location and, hence, trade area (geographic pricing), promotional activity (promotional pricing) or as a result of competitors' prices (competitor pricing). A *price point* is the specific price charged and is, therefore, the point of comparison between alternative purchases. Price points may be set to trigger responses in the mind of the shopper (psychological pricing), assist in purchase selection from a category (category pricing) and aid multiple unit purchases (unit pricing).

Geographical Pricing

A large body of research exists to suggest that the price for a given product may vary between regions (for further details see Greenhut and Ohta 1975). The reasons for this price variance may relate to relative location, market factors, the macro environment or retailer price policies. *Relative location* may affect the delivered cost of the product, as the costs of transportation usually increased as proximity to centres of production or distribution decreases. Retailers wishing to make a set profit margin per product across all stores would, therefore, need to set higher prices for more remote stores. Prices may also vary owing to *market factors* such as 'fair' price levels (market prices) or competitive pressures. In the first case, prices may simply be accepted as being higher in a given region, so retailers wishing to sell at the market price, or some percentage above/below, would set higher prices than for other regions. In the second, levels of local competition may differ, leading to varying price pressures. In many cases, more competition tends to force down prices, so rural areas with few stores may see higher prices than more saturated urban or near-urban areas.

Macro-environmental factors such as the standard of living, currency variations, government policies and legislation may also cause regional price differences. A higher standard of living could again raise market prices, as could currency variations. Government policies and legislation could affect the way that retailers operate (store aspects, packaging, price controls) which may cause prices to change. *Retailer price policies* could encompass geographic price variations by virtue of the relative importance of certain markets or trade areas. Many companies make greater efforts to satisfy their home market and may set lower prices to achieve this aim. Less important markets may receive different, usually higher, prices.

Promotional Pricing

Promotional pricing either involves an actual price change for a given product or category, or an effective price change owing to the quantity or composition of the purchase. The key promotional pricing methods are detailed in Table 9.4.

Table 9.4 Promotional Pricing Approaches

Approach	Description
Bundling	Several products of different types sold together at one total price
Multiple-unit	Several units of the same product sold at one total price
Sale	Discounted price for a certain time or on a given amount of stock
Introductory offer	Discounted price for the launch of a new product
Special event	Price changes for featured items
Seasonal	Price variations on the basis of the time of year
Leader line	Key items, competitively priced
Matching	Price promise guarantees
Oddball	All products sold at the same price

Bundling and *multiple-unit* pricing increase both the volume and overall price of the purchase. Bundling pricing puts different products together and sells them for a total package price, while multiple-unit pricing puts a number of packs of the same product together for one overall price. Shopper value evaluation is more difficult in both cases, although more so for bundling where two different products have to be evaluated separately then collectively. The goal of both approaches is to increase purchase volume, and bundling can also be used to stimulate sales for a given product. Consider two examples, suppose in the first case that two 100g jars of coffee were sold for a combined price of £4.49 against a typical price of £2.49 per 100g jar. A shopper would see a price saving of £0.49 overall and may purchase for this reason. Suppose, that the retailer now sold a chocolate bar (usual price £0.39) with a 100g jar of the same coffee (at the usual price of £2.49), the shopper may buy the bundle, as the chocolate bar is effectively free.

Sale and introductory offer pricing involve discounting for a given period of time or for a given quantity of stock. In the case of sale pricing, retailers may wish to sell off old stock or set prices that will encourage shoppers to visit the store. The former allows retailers to release tied up storage space and help cash flow, while the latter may result in additional purchases of non-sale items as shoppers, drawn in for the sale items, are tempted to buy more than was intended (for further details on the retail sale, see Chapter 10 on Retail Promotion). *Leader line* pricing is related to sale pricing, although the price cuts are not usually so extensive and may be offered for a longer period. The prices on a small number of items, usually those that will have a high price impact, are reduced in order to convey a lower price image to shoppers. It has already been noted that shoppers may base inter-store price comparisons on a small number of products owing to the difficulties involved in comparing every product. This being the case, leader line pricing, if the correct products are discounted, can affect these inter-store price perceptions.

Special event and *seasonal* pricing approaches set prices according to specific happenings or times of the year. Prices may be increased or decreased for a variable amount of time – e.g. for an in-store demonstration or tasting session (special event), or for a holiday period such as Christmas, New Year or Easter (seasonal). Both methods are based on the concept that certain events will stimulate demand for certain products, as will certain times of the year. Times of high demand may see prices rise to stimulate profit margin or fall to stimulate volume.

Matching offers seek to provide a guarantee that the shopper cannot get a cheaper price for the same product in any competitor's store. The usual offer is to refund the difference between the two prices or multiples of that difference. The tactic has become increasingly common as retailers become aware that the more sophisticated shopper is becoming more value-conscious. An additional reason for matching offer popularity is that not all customers actually claim on the guarantee even if low prices do exist elsewhere. It is probable that the majority of shoppers are reassured by the guarantee and perceive that a rational retailer (perceived retailer rationality) would not offer such a guarantee unless they were sure that nobody could beat them on price. In this case, the degree of price search will decrease, hence shoppers would not be aware of lower prices even if they did exist.

Oddball pricing in its simplest form is the 'everything for one price' approach. Stores have a range of products that are all sold at the same price (e.g. £1.00). Shoppers believe that some products must represent excellent value as the quality far exceeds the set price level. In truth, such a belief can relate to only a limited number of products, otherwise the retailer would make very little, if any, profit. More usual forms of oddball pricing could better be described as 'multiple-oddball pricing'. In this case, a number of set price levels exist in the store, with products on sale at each.

Competitive Pricing

Competitive pricing is the setting of specific prices relative to competitors' prices. It has already been noted (see Chapter 8 on The Retail Assortment) that retailers pay particular attention to competitor comparison products (CCPs) and known-value items (KVIs). Both types of product account for only a small proportion of the total assortment but are used by shoppers to evaluate price differentials amongst competing retailers. The setting of a competitive price for CCPs and KVIs may have quite limited profit impact but may have a huge impact on the retailer's price image. In addition, shoppers may abandon further price comparisons as the perceived benefits from such a search are seen as minimal. Price matching plans (see above) are also competitive pricing tactics, where an additional price differential guarantee is given.

Psychological Pricing

Psychological pricing is the practice of setting prices that influence the customer on either a conscious or subconscious level. In general terms, the practice involves either whole-number price endings (£150) or 'just-below' price endings (£7.99 or £25.95). The practice itself has been in existence for at least 100 years, with one US study undertaken in 1948 showing that 64 per cent of a sample of prices ended in odd digits – i.e. the 'just under' approach (Rudolph 1954). More recent studies put this figure at more like 80 per cent. The main body of research in this area concerns price endings or the actual combination of right-most digits used – e.g. £7.98 versus £7.99 versus £8.00. Prices set below a whole figure (£7.99) tend to indicate a discounted price whereas whole number figures (£150) tend to indicate that price is less important than quality for value evaluation. Schindler and Kibarian (1996) found that, for certain types of product, a price ending in .99 outsold the higher price ending in .00 by 8 per cent, although only the purchase volume was affected rather than the purchase decision itself. A number of explanations have been put forward to explain the effect of price endings, namely shopper 'incidental' learning and familiarity, number processing and anti-theft policies.

Incidental learning (Hawkins and Hoch 1992) is the process by which shoppers learn, over time, to associate a particular price ending with a given retailing context. As an example, a .99 ending price is usually seen as being a sale or discounted price (Berman and Evans 1992) owing to the extensive prior use of such price endings for special offers or sales. Over time, therefore, shoppers learn to make the association between .99 and a discount. The increasing use of discounted prices as a retail marketing tactic has strengthened the association and developed it to the point that shoppers are surprised not to see a .99 price ending for certain categories of product. In this case, familiarity with .99 endings encourages their use, which in turn increases familiarity still further.

The *number-processing* explanation (Schindler and Kibarian 1996; Gendall, Holdershaw and Garland 1997; Schindler and Kirby 1997, Stiving and Winer 1997) is based on the notion that shoppers process prices by looking at the most significant (*left-most*) digit first. The reasoning behind this is that left-most digits give the best indication of the order of magnitude. Add to this possible limitations in number processing ability (Brenner and Brenner 1982) and shoppers tend to estimate prices based on the left-most digits. This being the case, a price 'just below' the whole number will be underestimated by shoppers as it will be assumed to be an order of magnitude lower. As an example, suppose a shopper sees two prices, one at £9.99 the other at £10.00. Shoppers perceive the prices to be in the £9 range and £10 ranges, respectively, although the actual difference is only £0.01.

The *anti-theft* policy (e.g. Harper 1966; Hogl 1988) is widely believed to have been developed in the early 1900s by Macys in New York, USA. Prices at the 99 cent level were introduced to force salespeople to issue change, and thereby make it difficult for them to pocket the shopper's payment without recording a sale (Kreul 1982). Shoppers liked the prices owing to the novelty aspect, and sales increased.

Looking in more detail at psychological pricing, a number of interesting factors emerge. Gendall, Holdershaw and Garland (1997) found that .95 price endings did not affect sales to any greater extent than .99 endings. Nagle (1987) reported a similar finding for other odd-ending prices. Two probable reasons for this result are incidental learning (familiarity) and number processing. Shoppers expect to see .99 endings, so are more comfortable with them as they are easily understandable. Left-most digit processing would indicate that the right-most digits are largely unimportant as they give the least help in assessing price magnitude. This being the case, retailers can make an extra £0.04 per product with no discernible affect on demand if .99 endings are used in place of .95 endings.

An interesting finding (Sullivan 2000a) concerns the use of .98 ending prices. Comparison of shoppers' perceptions for prices with .99, .98, .96 and .95 endings reinforced the finding that no significant demand differences exist between .99 and .95 ending prices. A similar finding resulted for .98 and .96 ending prices, although respondents were less confident in their value evaluation than for the odd-ending prices. A range of actual products of a similar nature with .95, .96, .98 and .99 ending prices were then evaluated. Quality levels, as determined by product features, were different enough to allow perceived quality to be accurately measured by respondents. Results showed that products with .99 and .95 ending prices were seen as offering better value than .96 and .98 ending prices. This finding was repeated even when the prices of each product were swapped so that higher-quality products had .98 or .96 endings. This research highlights the pronounced effects of price endings.

Category Pricing

Category pricing involves the setting of specific and relative prices for a number of similar products. Research shows the simple price-setting methods, such as a set profit margin-based approach, fail to provide the best pricing structure (Vilcassim and Chintagunta 1995). One reason behind this finding relates to shoppers' evaluation of value on a price/quality analysis. If a category of products has a range of prices that are difficult to compare, judgements of value may be more difficult to make. Evidence shows that relative pricing can make the judgement of relative perceived quality easier, thus leading to an easier value evaluation. In this situation, it would be reasonable to expect that shoppers would find the purchase decision easier to make, a factor that can be seen to influence store choice. To give an example (Sullivan 2000b), two sets of category prices were tested on shoppers to gauge reactions to approximately even or uneven relationships. Findings show that the even relationships gave shoppers more confidence in their price/quality judgement and shortened the time spent on purchase evaluation. Uneven relationships caused some confusion among shoppers, resulting in reduced levels of confidence in price/quality judgements and an extended purchase evaluation. This finding is linked to the concept of the *ladder of perceived quality* (see Chapter 8 on The Retail Assortment), where definite perceived quality intervals were found to be beneficial in shopper choice behaviour.

Unit Pricing

Unit pricing is the process of offering a pack price as well as a price per unit. To give an example, a 3kg pack of product *A* will have a pack price associated with it (say £9.99) as well as a price per kg (£3.33). This process is mandatory in a number of retail sectors but can still be used to show price integrity by making the price totally transparent in that shoppers have all the required data to evaluate the purchase. In general, unit prices decrease as pack size increases, except when promotional pricing on smaller sizes or human error is present. Unit pricing may also be used in combination with some promotional pricing methods to allow shoppers to assess the particular offer on an actual price-per-unit basis.

Conclusions

The last three decades has seen UK retailers using price as a key retail marketing tool. The freedom to vary prices at will, an increasingly sophisticated shopper and greater levels of competition are some of the reasons for this increased activity. Retailers must be aware of the fundamental importance of pricing given its impact on financial performance, perceived assortment quality and competitor comparison. The majority of retailers do not manufacture their own products, so the retail price decision typically concerns the addition of a *mark-up* to the purchase price. The setting of this mark-up is a deceptively simple task that involves analysis (shopper, competitor, financial), objective-setting, strategy selection and tactics development.

Shopper analysis deals with issues such as price sensitivity, price comparison behaviour and value evaluation. It is important for the retailer to realize that certain shoppers and certain types of purchase will have higher or lower levels of associated *price sensitivity*. The success of lowering a price for a given product to stimulate demand is, therefore, dependent on the level of price sensitivity. High sensitivity causes a potentially large demand effect, low sensitivity quite the opposite. Price comparison behaviour and value evaluation are, to a certain extent, linked. Shoppers assess value by considering price and perceived product quality, as well as alternative purchases that would satisfy the same need. All retailers need to convince shoppers that they are offering high value even if this is at the top (high price, high quality) or bottom (low price, low quality) of the market. The value evaluation process may, or may not, involve a number of price comparisons either within a given store or between competing stores. Price comparison tends to be more extensive as risk increases (high price, high involvement, heterogeneous products) and the belief in a market price decreases (low perceived retailer rationality, high perceived price dispersion). Put more simply, when the benefits of price search outweigh the costs, price searching is more extensive.

The retailer must recognize that the selling price effectively places the limit on potential profit. For retailers to make the maximum sustainable profit prices need to be set to reflect shopper value evaluations, costs, space considerations and operational issues. An effective measurement to achieve this is *Direct Product Profitability* (DPP), or the measurement of a product's actual profit accounting for hidden profits and costs. Extend the DPP measurement to DPP per unit of selling area, and price-setting can be far more accurate.

When it comes to the actual *pricing decision*, retailers can consider a number of objectives and strategies. Objectives may be based on the market (aggressive, neutral, defensive), on value positioning (price- or quality-led), on the retailer's image (integrity) or may be operational (start-up or rundown). Selection of the right combination of objectives is important as it directly impacts on the selection of a pricing strategy. Retailers may utilize any of the *generic pricing strategies* (premium, economy, penetration and skimming) but tend to either offer low prices throughout the year (every day low pricing, EDLP) or use a combination of higher prices and sale prices (high/low pricing). EDLP is seen as a superior value-for-money approach that gives the shopper less incentive to price search and the retailer a more manageable system and reduced marketing costs. Successful EDLP requires a relatively high sales volume and strong shopper perceptions of penetration pricing (low price/high quality) rather than economy pricing (low price/low quality). High/low pricing is seen as a mixed value approach with less price-conscious shoppers buying at the high prices and price-conscious shoppers buying during the sales. High perceived quality can be maintained as shoppers expect sales and do not draw negative impressions of sale items provided sales are of limited frequency and duration. If, however, sales are extended, shoppers reconsider their assessment of non-sale prices, seeing them as inflated.

Retailer pricing tactics concern the setting of specific prices based on *differential pricing* or *price points*. Differential pricing is the practice of setting different prices for different regions (geographical pricing), time periods (promotional pricing) or in response to competitors (competitor pricing). The tactics demonstrate that a retailer appreciates minor changes need to be made to standard prices in order to fit prevailing shopper characteristics, maintain financial performance and manage the competition. Price-point tactics involve the setting of the actual price and may be used to influence the shopper (psychological pricing), assist in purchase selection (category pricing) and encourage multiple-unit purchases. Perhaps the most interesting is psychological pricing, where shoppers may be influenced by the left-most or right-most digit in the actual price. Shoppers may equate .99 with price consciousness, .00 with quality, may favour .99 or .95 endings and may be suspicious of .98 or .96 endings. Whether the reasons for this are due to psychological processes (number processing) or experience matters less than the impact. Retailers can make higher profits using the correct price-point ending.

Retail pricing is, therefore, a process of analysis and decision aimed at setting and fine-tuning price points. Striking a balance between shoppers' value evaluation and price comparison and the retailer's financial considerations is the key. Simply increasing a price from £6.96 to £6.99 may in fact increase, rather than decrease, demand. This doesn't sound logical, but it's certainly profitable!

References and Further Reading

Berman, B. and Evans, J.R. (1992) *Retail Management: A Strategic Approach*, Macmillan, New York.

Brenner, G.A. and Brenner, R. (1982) Memory and Markets, or Why are you Paying $2.99 for a Widget?, *Journal of Business*, 55, 147–58.

Bucklin, L (1969) Consumer Search, Role Enactment, and Market Efficiency, *Journal of Business*, 42, 416–38.

Gendall, P., Holdershaw, J. and Garland, R. (1997) The Effect of Odd Pricing on Demand, *European Journal of Marketing*, 31, 11/12, 799–813.

Gilbert, D. (1999) *Retailing Marketing Management*, Prentice-Hall, Harlow.

Greenhut, M.L. and Ohta, H. (1975) *Theory of Spatial Pricing and Market Areas*, Duke University Press, Durham, MD.

Harper, D.V. (1966) *Price Policy and Procedure*, Harcourt, Brace & World, New York.

Hawkins, S.A. and Hoch, S.J. (1992) Low Involvement Learning: Memory Without Evaluation, *Journal of Consumer Research*, 19, 212–25.

Hogl, S. (1988) The Effects of Simulated Price Changes on Consumers in a Retail Environment – Price Thresholds and Price Policy, Esomar Congress Proceedings, Lisbon.

Kaufmann, P.J., Smith, N.C. and Ortmeyer, G.K. (1994) Deception in Retailer High–Low Pricing: A 'Rule of Reason' Approach, *Journal of Retailing*, 70, 2, 115–39.

Kerin, R.A., Jain, A, and Howard, D.J. (1992) Store Shopping Experience and Consumer Price-Quality-Value Perceptions, *Journal of Retailing*, 68, 4, 376–98.

Kruel, L.M. (1982) Magic Numbers: Psychological Aspects of Menu Pricing, *Cornell Hotel and Restaurant Administration Quarterly*, 23, 70–5.

Marmorstein, H., Grewal, D. and Fishe, R.P.H. (1992) The Value of Time Spent in Price Comparison Shopping: Survey and Experimental Evidence, *Journal of Consumer Research*, 19, 52–61.

McGoldrick, P.J. (1990) *Retail Marketing*, McGraw-Hill, London.

Nagle, T.T. (1987) *The Strategy and Tactics of Pricing*, Prentice-Hall, Englewood Cliffs, NJ.

Nystrom, H. (1970) *Retail Pricing: An Integrated Economic and Psychological Approach*, Economic Research Unit, Stockholm School of Economics.

Pinnock, A.K. (1986) *Direct Product Profitability: An Introduction for the Grocery Trade*, Institute of Grocery Distribution, Watford.

Rudolph, H.J. (1954) Pricing for Today's Market, *Printers Ink*, 247 (28 May), 22–4.

Schindler, R.M. and Kibarian, T.M. (1996) Increased Consumer Sales Response Through Use of 99-Ending Prices, *Journal of Retailing*, 72, 2, 187–200.

Schindler, R.M. and Kirby, P.N. (1997) Patterns of Rightmost Digits Used in Advertised Prices: Implications for Nine-Ending Effects, *Journal of Consumer Research*, 24, 192–201.

Stiving, M. and Winer, R.S. (1997) An Empirical Analysis of Price Endings with Scanner Data, *Journal of Consumer Research*, 24, 57–67.

Sullivan, M.N. (2000a) Odd and Even Ending Pricing, Unpublished Working Paper, Coventry University.

Sullivan, M.N. (2000b) Price Intervals in Category Pricing, Unpublished Working Paper, Coventry University.

Urbany, J.E. (1986) An Experimental Examination of the Economics of Information, *Journal of Consumer Research*, 13, 257–71.

Urbany, J.E., Dickson, P.R. and Kalapurakal, R. (1996) Price Search in the Retail Grocery Market, *Journal of Marketing*, 60, 91–104.

Vilcassim, N. and Chintagunta, P.K. (1995) Investigating Retailer Product Category Pricing from Household Scanner Panel Data, *Journal of Retailing*, 71, 2, 103–29.

Wakefield, K.L. and Inman, J.J. (1993) Who are the Price Vigilantes? An Investigation of Differentiating Characteristics Influencing Price Information, *Journal of Retailing*, 69, 2, 216–33.

Retail Promotion

CHAPTER 10

This chapter:

- Explains why a retailer must communicate with its customers
- Defines the key communication objectives
- Examines the communication message from retailer to shopper
- Delineates key communication methods and media

Retail Promotion

Introduction

A retailer, like any other company, needs to *communicate with its customers* (shoppers). The purpose of such communication is to ensure that existing (and new) shoppers are aware of the retailer, hold positive attitudes about it, have extensive and appropriate knowledge of its offering, and of course spend money in the store. These purposes can be assigned to three broad groups of communication objectives, namely informing, persuading and reinforcing. *Informing* involves giving information to build awareness that a product, service or retailer exists and explain what a retailer is offering (assortment, prices, store image, etc.). *Persuading* concerns creating a favourable attitude, providing a stimulus to favour one retailer over another, or one point of view against another. *Reinforcing* relates to the dispelling of doubts about an action already taken, building support/loyalty to a point of view, purchase or retailer, and ensuring a good climate for future sales. Achieving these communication objectives requires knowledge of the communication process, the participants, the content of the communication, the delivery method and a number of other factors that will be discussed below (for a more detailed coverage of the communication process see Adcock *et al.* 1998).

The basic communication process involves a message being sent from the *sender* (the *retailer*) to the *receiver* (the *shopper*). The message may contain any sensory stimuli, although visual (images) and aural (sounds) stimuli are the most common, and is designed to achieve one or more of the broad purposes mentioned above. Communication is, however, more than just a message being passed from the sender to the receiver. Effective communication requires the receiver to have *understood* the message in the way that the sender intended. This means that the sender of a message has to have a *response* to know whether communication has taken place. This response, usually referred to as *feedback*, allows the sender to develop the message in such a way that the receiver will understand it. In this sense, communication is a *two-way process* (see Figure 10.1)

The transfer of a message between sender and receiver involves three basic stages, *encode*, *deliver* and *decode*. Each of these stages is an opportunity for the original message to be altered, as the message may be encoded in a different way, may be distorted in delivery or may be decoded incorrectly. It is vital, therefore, for the retailer to have a clear understanding of the communication process as well as detailed knowledge of the receivers (*target shoppers*), the message delivery method (*promotional method and media*) and any environmental factors that may affect message delivery (*noise*).

Target shopper knowledge concerns individual differences (physiological, psychological and sociological) and specific behavioural factors. Individual differences are important as differences in characteristics such as intelligence, education, culture, experience and background can affect the way that messages are decoded. Messages with complicated language will, for example, be decoded in different ways by people with differing language knowledge and abilities (for further details on individual differences see Chapter 3 on Shopper Behaviour). Specific behavioural factors relate to message reception behaviour – or, put more simply, the media that a given individual is exposed to, e.g. television, radio, in-store display features, etc.

The method of message delivery refers to the *communication method* and the *media*. The communication method is the mechanism by which a given message is delivered, while the media is the actual delivery system. To give an example, advertising is a communication method that may use media such as television, radio or billboards. Media break down into personal, where there is an element of personal contact, and non-personal, where no personal contact exists. *Personal media* include internal company communications, personal selling, personalized marketing (e.g. telesales) and trade fairs and exhibitions. *Non-personal media* include television and cinema, print media, radio, outdoor media, point-of-sale (POS) displays and packaging. Communications methods include advertising, publicity, sales promotion, personal selling, direct marketing and sponsorship.

Noise is a broad term that covers any extraneous factor that can affect the transfer of a message (Adcock *et al.* 1998) by distorting its content or making the message difficult to receive. To give an examples from the retail

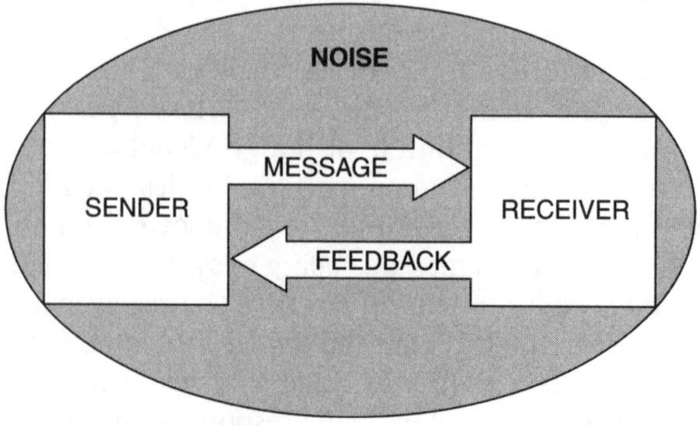

Figure 10.1 The communication process

Retail Locations

Store Interiors

Store Interiors

Retail Assortment

Currys
TING PRICES!
RY WEEK
AND THAT'S A FACT
NEVER BEATEN ON PRICE
CUTTING PRICES! EVERY WEEK

adams
1/2 price
Even more lines added!

Window Display

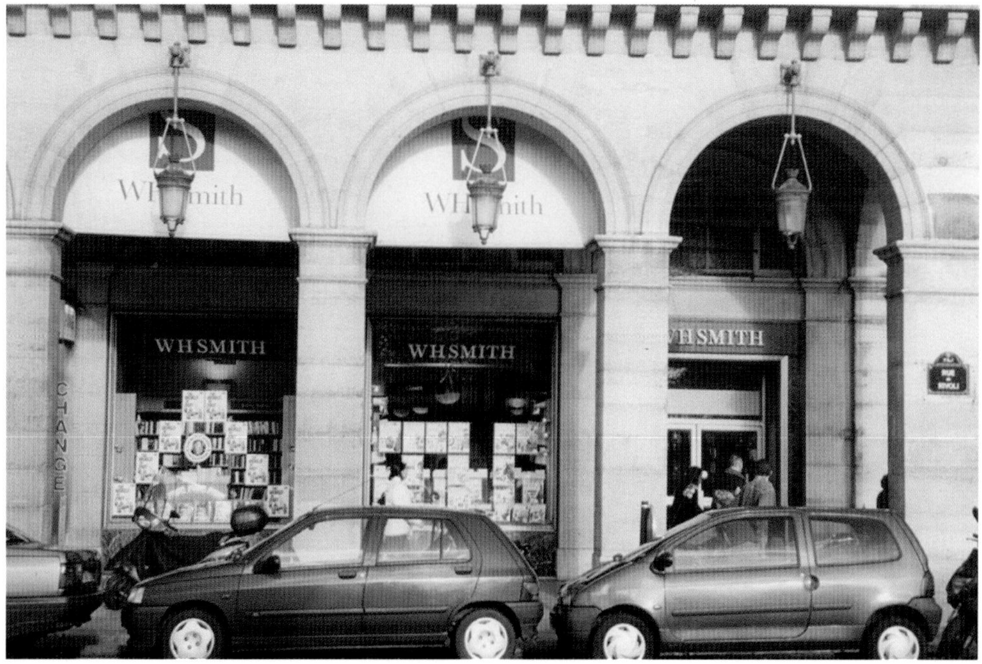

Retail Fascia Approaches 1

Retail Fascia Approaches 2

context, suppose that a retailer wished to communicate a price reduction message to shoppers and had chosen to use a sticker placed on the product itself. This POS method would involve a simple message that should be easily understood (decoded) by the shopper. On a given day, the store may be very busy, causing some shoppers to have an obscured view of the product itself. This may mean that the price reduction message is never received owing to noise – other shoppers, in this case. Now consider a nearby competitor advertising the same product at a lower price than the store in question. When shoppers see the price reduction message it may be distorted if they have seen the competitor's message – i.e. it will not be seen as a particularly special offer. Noise is again the cause of this distortion.

The Retail Context

As has already been noted, retailers are seeking to communicate with shoppers to achieve a number of objectives. These objectives will typically include increasing store traffic by encouraging new shoppers to visit the store, increasing expenditure for all shoppers or specific groups, increasing sales of a given product or category and developing the store image or corporate brand. Communication aimed at achieving these objectives may take place within the store or within the trade area/market.

A number of factors influence a retailer's promotional efforts, namely location issues, merchandising policies, competition, target shoppers, media availability and manufacturer support (Burnett 1988; Fulop 1989). *Location issues* concern store age, specific location and trade area size while *merchandising policies* and *target shoppers* are interlinked and refer to the most effective ways of getting the promotional message across. *Competition* will affect the nature and scale of a retailer's promotional efforts owing the necessity of gaining shoppers' attention. If a competitor has allocated a large budget to its promotional campaign, the retailer will need to match the expenditure or increase effectiveness if shoppers are to listen to their message rather than the competitor's. *Media availability* relates to access to the delivery mechanism for the promotional message and *manufacturer support* concerns issues such as co-operative promotion.

Co-operative Promotion

A retailer will typically sell a range of products from a range of different manufacturers. Each manufacturer would obviously like to see its own products promoted to ensure that shopper attitudes remain positive and sales are increased. Retailers would find it impossible, and certainly not desirable, to promote every product in the assortment as their stores would become increasingly confusing for shoppers and the retailer's own retail tactics would be affected. It is the case, therefore, that retailers usually select only a small number of *manufacturer-led promotions* at any given time. As with any transaction, if buyer power is high (retailers, in this case), suppliers usually end up with a poorer deal. Manufacturer-led retail promotions follow this pattern, with the poorer deal being the provision of support for the retailer. Such situations are referred to as co-operative promotion or, more specifically, *vertical co-operative promotion*. 'Vertical', in this sense, refers to the manufacturer/retailer supply chain. *Horizontal co-operative promotions* are undertaken by collections of retailers seeking, usually, to promote a shopping centre, district or location. In this case, retailers are combining to increase traffic to their area and increase sales potential for all.

The advantages of co-operative promotion are a higher promotional budget that may allow more intensive campaigns or more expensive media to be used. Vertical co-operative promotions may also see benefits for the retailer as knock-on effects from manufacturer-led activities reflect on the retailer. It could be the case, for example, that a manufacturer's local press campaign, promoting a special offer on certain products on sale in a given retailer's stores, may also provide valuable exposure for that retailer. Disadvantages tend to be more pronounced for vertical co-operative promotions, where retailers must take care to select the products that fit with current tactics and their overall image, as well as ensuring that promotions are not too frequent, and so lose impact.

The Retail Promotional Mix

The *retail promotional mix* contains all the communications methods open to the retailer, and can be divided into two groups. Communications that take place within the store are known as *store-based promotions*, while those that take place outside the store in the market are known as *market-based promotions* (see Table 10.1). Store-based promotional methods include point-of-sale (POS) display, personal selling, in-store sales promotion, in-store advertising and the sale. Market-based promotional methods include sales promotion, advertising, direct marketing, sponsorship and public relations (PR). Window display is another market-based method, although one that is the closest to in-store promotion. The relative importance of these elements for a retail pharmacy was measured by Abratt and Anley (1994) who found that 65 per cent of promotional spending was accounted for by personal selling, 10 per cent sales promotion, 22 per cent advertising and 3 per cent PR. This research gives an indication of relative importance, although it should be noted that display was not considered.

Table 10.1 The Retail Promotional Mix

Promotional method	Characteristics
Store-based	
• POS Display	• Presentation of products to shoppers
• Personal selling	• Interaction with store personnel
• In-store sales promotion	• In-store inducements to purchase
• In-store advertising	• In-store messages to shoppers
• The retail sale	• Promotional prices for a specified period
Market-based	
• Sales promotion	• Inducements to purchase
• Advertising	• Messages to shoppers
• Direct marketing	• Direct contact with shoppers
• Sponsorship	• Link to related event, individual or company
• Public relations	• Information management via 'news' sources
• Exterior design	• Communication with passers-by (window display)

In an attempt to explain the composition of the promotions mix, Davies (1991) linked *retail strategy* and *promotional strategy*. Retail strategy was simplified to be either price- or image-led, while promotional strategy was equally simplified and was dominated either by advertising or PR. Davies also indicated the importance of promotions, identifying either primary or secondary emphasis. The matrix that can be produced from such a treatment (see Figure 10.2) identifies four generic approaches to retail promotion. *Price-led retailers* with a focus on advertising will tend to use informative press adverts, as well as TV and radio to convey low prices. Similar retailers with a focus on PR, however, would favour in-store promotion and store design features. *Image-led retailers* with a advertising focus would concentrate on tactical adverts and sponsorship, while those with a PR focus would seek editorial coverage and word-of-mouth communication.

Sales Promotion

Sales promotion consists of a broad set of activities designed to induce some immediate response or provide a novel way to transmit the communications message (Hasty and Reardon 1997). The Advertising Standards Authority's (ASA) Code of Sales Promotion defines sales promotion as 'those marketing techniques, which are used, usually on a temporary basis, to make goods and services more attractive to the consumer by providing some additional benefit whether in cash or in kind'.

Two main types of sales promotion exist – known as single-event and continuity. *Single-event* sales promotion involves single purchase or trial, and is typically of a limited time duration. *Continuity* sales promotion involves multiple purchases or trials, and may be of a longer time duration.

Eight major sales promotion methods exist that can be grouped under three headings, money-based, interest-based and value-based. *Money-based* methods involve an effective reduction in the purchase price either by an actual price reduction or a volume discount. The price change may be immediate or delayed, meaning at the moment of purchase or some time later, respectively. *Interest-based* methods seek to generate positive

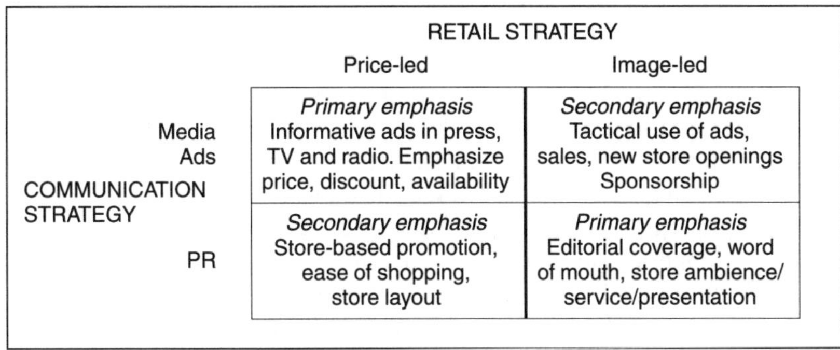

Figure 10.2 Retail promotion/strategy matrix

shopper attitudes towards a purchase, category or entire assortment by presenting the items in an eye-catching way. *Value-based* methods raise the attractiveness of the purchase by giving the shopper increased value for money without an effective lowering of the price. In effect, the shopper is getting more for the same price.

The objectives of sales promotion are numerous, although the most important are generating sales, increasing store traffic, building and reinforcing loyalty, increasing customer knowledge and encouraging trial, building and reinforcing store image and data collection. The ability of sales promotion to increase sales is supported by Kahn and Schmittlein (1992), who show that purchases made on the basis of sales promotion are seldom planned in nature, and so will typically represent an increase in a given shopper's expenditure.

Money-Based Sales Promotion

Money-based sales promotion methods in most common use are coupons, frequent-buyer programmes and rebates. *Coupons* give the shopper the opportunity to gain money off future purchases or gain volume discounts (e.g. 'buy one get one free'). *Frequent-buyer programmes* include loyalty cards, expenditure-based discounts and benefits in kind (e.g. air miles) that aim to reward loyal shoppers for their expenditure (loyalty programmes will be discussed in more detail in Chapter 12 on Customer Loyalty and Related Issues). *Rebates* give shoppers money-off purchases after a certain period of time. Shoppers may be encouraged to buy the item now then receive a cash rebate some time in the future. The length of time before the rebate can be claimed (redemption period), the effort required to claim the rebate (redemption effort) and the value of the rebate all affect the proportion of eligible shoppers that actually claim a given rebate (redemption rate). As the redemption period increases, so the redemption rate falls as shoppers simply forget about the rebate. The redemption rate also falls as the redemption effort increases or the redemption value decreases on the basis of a simple cost/benefit calculation.

Money-based sales promotion must be used carefully as shopper price perceptions can be affected. In much the same way as price reductions can affect shopper value perceptions, price-reducing sales promotion can trigger reductions in perceived quality if the time duration of the promotion is too long. Such a change in shopper value perceptions is known as *equitable price re-evaluation* (see The Retail Sale later in this chapter). Rebates may limit equitable price re-evaluation as actual price reduction does not take place at the same time as purchase. Shoppers have been found to make a distinction between the rebate and the buying price, and tend not to see the method as having much to do with the purchase price. Frequent-buyer programmes also tend not to damage shoppers' price perceptions as they are a special form of rebate. Shoppers gain benefits linked to their level of expenditure, and usually have to wait a certain time before those benefits are converted into cash or a cash equivalent. Considering all these methods, immediate redemption money-based methods (e.g. coupons) risk affecting shopper price perceptions if used over a long period of time, so single-event sales promotion is recommended. Delayed redemption methods (frequent-buyer programmes, rebates) can avoid significant changes in shopper price perceptions if the redemption period is suitably long. For this reason, such methods can utilize continuity or single-event sale promotion. In the case of frequent-buyer programmes, shoppers will normally value such promotions only if they are continuity events. The reason is that shoppers often see only the cumulative redemption value as significant, as the value gained in any given week or month is comparatively small.

Interest-Based Sales Promotion

Interest-based sales promotion methods typically comprise demonstrations and sampling, and special events. *Special events* could be seasonal (a department store showing its new range of clothes) or related to a current event (sports such as the Olympics), while *demonstrations* and *sampling* tend to relate to specific products or categories but could also be linked to a special event. *Competitions* are often classified as interest-based sales promotion, although different types of competition may also be considered as money- or value-based. Competitions give the shopper something for nothing and can provide an air of excitement. In reality, therefore, competitions are usually a combination of methods as they are designed to create interest and may offer money- and/or value-based prizes. In terms of duration, it is unlikely that an interest-based method could be successfully used on a continuity basis, as shoppers will soon become bored with the same special event, demonstration or sampling. A programme of activities could be considered to extend the lifetime of such methods, although it may still be the case that shoppers become bored with the concept as a whole. In general, therefore, interest-based methods tend to fit best with single-event sales promotion.

Value-Based Sales Promotion

Value-based sales promotion methods of most importance are advertising specialities and premiums. *Advertising specialities* are products offered to shoppers on a 'no-purchase-required' basis – i.e. shoppers, usually on presentation of a leaflet or voucher, can get a free item when they visit a given store. A *premium* is a complementary or unrelated product that is offered as an inducement to purchase – e.g. a free mug after the purchase of five jars of coffee. A self-liquidating premium involves an additional payment for the product, although the quality of the product usually compensates for the extra expenditure. These methods can usually be used on a single-event or continuity basis dependent on the nature of a given value-based approach, although single-event is more common.

Looking at premiums in more detail, Low and Lichtenstein (1993) considered perceived value effects between the product itself and the free gift (premium). In a situation where the perceived value of the product itself is significantly higher than the perceived value of the premium, shoppers see the incentive to buy as rather limited. The incentive to buy increases as the perceived value of the premium increases, although only up to the point where the product itself and the premium have comparable perceived values. Beyond this point, shoppers become suspicious of the premium as the 'free' item is apparently more valuable than the product itself. In rational situations, the premium and the product would reverse roles, so shopper confusion (and suspicion) increases. As an example, consider the following premiums: a free pair of socks with every £10 tie or a free pair of trousers with every £10 tie. Which is the more believable?

Point-of-Sale Display

Display may relate to the *interior* or *exterior* of the store. A number of display issues are covered elsewhere in this text (see Chapter 7 on Store Design), namely style, architecture, layout, product display and atmospherics. The packaging of individual products is also an issue, although this tends to have a limited overall effect in most retail situations. The most important factor that remains to be covered is window display, or the designing of an area visible to passers-by.

Window Display

Window display has traditionally been a major form of promotion for many store-based retailers. Increasing sales and store traffic are the main objectives attached to window display, although reinforcing store image and encouraging trial are also appropriate. In fact, a number of these objectives are inter-related, as sales increases may be achieved partly by an increase in store traffic and encouraging trial. A greater number of shoppers gives the retailer more opportunities to make sales, and trial is an important part of the process by which shoppers become regular purchasers of a given item. An increase in store traffic can be achieved if the display gains the attention of passers-by and provides a sound reason why a store visit would be desirable. Trial may be encouraged by developing interest in a specific category or by informing shoppers about a store-based promotion currently in operation. Store image may be reinforced in much the same way as product packaging. Both convey an image to the customer that, if correctly designed, can act to reinforce customer perceptions.

The main features of window display are visual appeal, relevance and interest value. The *visual appeal* of a display directly affects the ability of that display to gain shoppers' attention. *Relevance* can be expressed as the degree to which the display fits the current mindset of the shopper. Highly relevant displays tend to gain shoppers' attention, as individuals tend to notice (perceive) stimuli that relate to a current need. Shoppers will largely ignore irrelevant displays, as they have no important information to offer. *Interest value* is related to relevance, although should more accurately be described as a means of persuasion. Shoppers may have noticed a display because it was visually appealing and related to a current need – i.e. was relevant. Convincing the shopper that a store visit would be worthwhile is linked to building interest value – i.e. will this store's offering satisfy the need in question?

A number of the display and atmospheric factors discussed elsewhere in this text (see Chapter 7 on Store Design) can be used to maximize visual appeal, stress relevance and build interest value. A number of the in-store display methods may be considered, such as the majority of those suggested by Rosenbloom (1981). The fact that window displays are typically enclosed means that those atmospheric elements (peripheral stimuli that can be sensed by the individual) that require physical contact in order to be perceived cannot be used. Smell, touch and taste may be impossible to detect through a pane of glass, for example. Visual atmospheric elements such as colour, lighting level and the appearance of objects (size and shape) may be used, as may sounds if a suitable speaker system is available.

Window Display Methods

Display methods that can be considered are themed, lifestyle, project and classification dominance. *Themed* displays are the most common, involving a connection with an event, activity, season or other feature. The nature of the display relates to the theme itself – e.g. a skiing display in a sports shop window may feature artificial snow, skis, boots and other features and products commonly associated with a ski holiday. *Lifestyle* displays seek to present products that fit with the way the shopper lives – e.g. a clothing store may show people wearing the clothes that fit the shopper's self-image. *Project* displays bring a number of products together to show a solution rather than just a number of constituent parts – e.g. a PC retailer may show a PC, modem, printer, fax and scanner together to demonstrate the complete home office. A *classification dominance* display is designed to present the shopper with a large amount of choice in a given area and is used by retailers using choice as an important part of their retail approach.

Themed displays can be visually appealing as shoppers can see a particular scene, rather than just a collection of products. Choosing the right theme can increase relevance as it should fit the moment and, so, the needs of many shoppers. Interest value can be gained by showing the products on offer in the environment within which they will be used. Lifestyle displays share many of the same characteristics as themed displays, so are visually appealing (scene), relevant (if the fit is good with the shopper's lifestyle) and can generate interest value (products fit lifestyle). Themed and lifestyle displays are typically types of project display, as the solution to an event or lifestyle is presented rather than individual products. Project displays are, therefore, also visually appealing, relevant and can generate interest value. Classification dominance displays can certainly be visually appealing and may be relevant if the particular category on display fits with a shopper's current needs. Similarly, interest value may be generated if choice is an important consideration for that shopper. In general, though, such displays tend to be less successful in terms of visual appeal, relevance and interest value.

Window Display Atmospherics

It has been noted already that the absence of direct physical contact means that atmospheric elements such as smell, touch and taste are usually not appropriate for use in window displays. Visual factors usually have the most impact, although sounds may be used if passers-by can hear them. *Visual factors* cover colour, lighting levels and the size and shape of objects. *Sounds* typically relate to music, background noise or conversations.

Colour can be used to provide a contrast with the surroundings, give perspective and depth, and stimulate the shopper. Window displays, as with any stimulus, have an increased chance of being noticed as the degree of contrast with the surroundings increases (Hering 1868; Anstis 1974; Steinman and Levinson 1990). Colours that clash with the surroundings or stand out in any other way should gain the attention of passers-by. Perspective and depth add to the visual appeal of the display, and are particularly useful in displays seeking to present a scene (themed, lifestyle and project). Warm colours (reds, yellows, oranges, etc.) can be used to trigger a more aroused (excited) mood state that effectively encourages shoppers to make a store visit decision rather than be neutral. Lighting may be used in much the same way as colour, although the ability to excite is limited. High- or low-intensity lighting may contrast with the surroundings and may help to convey perspective and depth. The shape of the objects used in a display can gain attention by virtue of contrast, as can their relative size. Perspective and depth can also be conveyed, although the ability to excite shoppers is limited.

Music is the most commonly used sound in window display. Like visual factors, music can be used to provide a contrast with the surroundings and stimulate the shopper, although it has no effect on perspective and depth. Contrast has the same effect as that noted for visual factors and may be achieved by varying the volume, tempo, pitch or popularity of the music. The ability to stimulate shoppers is based on the ability of music to potentially evoke certain moods in shoppers. Loud music is seen as more animated while soft music is said to be more peaceful. Fast-tempo music is more happy than slow while high-pitch music is seen as more exciting.

Successful Window Displays

A number of *criteria for successful window displays* can be considered. Edwards and Shackley (1992) suggest that successful window displays fit the retailer's image, link to product benefits, are interesting, have a central theme and make good use of colour, lighting, props, perspective and depth. Size and contrast are also important features, as the average window display is not seen by approximately 70 per cent of passers-by and 20 per cent of shoppers visiting the store in question. The benefits of a successful display are increased sales overall and increased sales of underperforming or new products. Sales increase still further when the window display in linked to a store-based promotion, as shoppers are given a greater incentive to visit the store – i.e. interest value increases. A final feature of successful displays is the possibility of *after-effects*. The research showed that positive store perceptions gained from window displays can last for longer than the display itself.

Advertising

Advertising has a very wide scope, covering a range of activities from television commercials to signs placed in a shop window. Advertising in the retail sector may be market- or store-based, including advertisements in many media and messages inside the store, respectively. The objectives of advertising are much the same as for retail communication in general, although market-based advertising is increasingly being used to build/reinforce the retailer's image and brand name. Store-based advertising overlaps with display and usually covers in-store signage. More modern store-based advertising utilizes multi-media technology to present pictures and/or sounds to shoppers. The stores owned by sports good manufacturer Nike contain this new technology, with numerous TV screens placed around the store showing advertisements.

A number of factors must be considered when designing retail advertising campaigns. The first consideration is the characteristics of the subject – i.e. the store itself or aspects of that store's retail offering (e.g. the assortment). Related to this are the key benefits offered to the shopper that may relate to products or the store experience. The retailer's knowledge of the target shoppers can now be used to develop the advertising message and select the most appropriate media.

Market-Based Advertising

Market-based advertising undertaken by a retailer is very similar to that undertaken by any other commercial organization. For this reason, this section will focus on specific retailer advertising activities only (further details on advertising can be found in Adcock *et al.* 1998). Shoppers receive the advertising message outside the store environment and, as such, are beyond the control of that retailer when the message is decoded. This means that retailers share many of the business world's problems with ensuring the effectiveness of advertising campaigns – or, to quote Lord Leverhulme and John Wannamaker, 'I know that half of what I spend on advertising is wasted, but the trouble is I don't know which half'. This hasn't put retailers off, however, as an increasing number of the highest-spending advertisers in the UK are retail companies such as Gap, J Sainsbury and the Dixon's Stores Group.

Market-based advertising by retailers can either be informational or image-related. *Informational* advertising is designed to provide shoppers with information about the retailer, the retailer's offering or promotional activities such as price reductions (sales). *Image-related* advertising contains little information but seeks to maintain a raft of intangible associations with the retailer, the retailer's brand or products offered within the store. Historically, a large proportion of retailers' market-based advertising was accounted for by informational messages covering a description of the retailer and its offering and promotional activities in particular. More recent times have seen the increasing usage of image-related messages owing to the increasing appreciation of the importance of the perceived store shopping experience (see Chapter 7 on Store Design) and the development of more sophisticated retailer brand approaches (see Chapter 8 on The Retail Assortment).

Note: Market-based advertising undertaken by a retailer shares exactly the same principles as that undertaken by any company. For further reading in this area, please refer to a suitable Marketing Communications text.

Store-Based Advertising

Store-based advertising includes all the methods by which a message can be communicated to a shopper while in the (controlled) store environment. The message may again be informational or image-related, although tends to be the former in most cases. Traditional methods include signage, announcements, packaging and display and printed information (e.g. leaflets). *Signage* covers any printed material of a sufficient size to be read from a distance and covers the range from simple announcements (assortment location, special offers, etc.) to more poster-based messages (analogous to posters seen by the side of roads, for example). *Announcements* cover any message relayed to shoppers 'verbally', typically via a public address system, and tend to relate to special offers or other sales promotional efforts. *Packaging and display* are covered elsewhere in this text (e.g. Chapter 7 on Store Design) and typically relate to more image-related messages. *Printed information* may include leaflets that are presented in the selling areas. Examples of traditional methods are given in Table 10.2.

Table 10.2 Examples of Store-Based Advertising

Method	Examples
Traditional	
Signage	From special-offer signs (price or volume reductions) to lifestyle posters (e.g. demonstrating outfits in a clothing store)
Announcements	Special offers, information on demonstrations or special events, customer information (services or assortment)
Packaging and display	Product packaging (style and content), presentation of products (abundance, category dominance, etc.)
Printed information	Assortment information, product advice (e.g. DIY stores 'how to do' leaflets), special offers (coupons)
Modern	
TV and video	Product demonstration videos (e.g. sports good stores, DIY stores), lifestyle ads (fashion stores), information provision
Interactive	Information points or 'kiosks' (e.g. loyalty card kiosks to obtain special offers, redeem benefits or gain information)

More modern methods include in-store TV and video, and interactive information systems (see Table 10.2). These methods provide for a greater diversity in message content and delivery, as well as more *interactive* (two-way) and *personalized* communication. TV and video is commonly used in stores where image-related messages are required – e.g. fashion stores. Market-based commercials can be transplanted into the store environment to achieve many of the same objectives. TV and video may be used to present an image, demonstrate products in use or simply bring certain products or special offers to the shopper's attention. A good example is Nike, which utilizes a large number of TV screens in its own-branded stores to demonstrate products being used by sports personalities. The future of store-based advertising may rest with more interactive methods that use information technology (IT) and multi-media as a means of communication. *Information kiosks* offer simple data base enquiries to the customer as well as communicating certain sales promotion efforts of products to the shopper. More recently, such kiosks have been combined with loyalty card schemes to provide a *personalized information kiosk*. Shoppers insert their card into the machine and receive personalized offers, or can redeem their accumulated benefits. Examples in the UK include stores such as Boots plc and J. Sainsbury, where shoppers may convert accumulated benefits into vouchers or may obtain certain special coupons.

Direct Marketing

Direct marketing, or the use of direct media to reach a target, is increasingly being used by retailers in an attempt to build closer relationships with shoppers. The approach shares many similarities with more traditional advertising in that a given message is delivered to shoppers via a variety of media. Differences emerge in the actual media used, the precise targeting of the shoppers and the opportunities for personalizing the message. Direct media typically include *mail* (electronic and postal) and the *telephone*, and typically allow one-to-one contact with shoppers unlike mass-media advertising (TV advertisements, for example). The ability to communicate on a one-to-one basis also gives the opportunity for unique messages for individual shoppers.

The reasons for the increased use of direct marketing are numerous, although the most important are summarized in Table 10.3.

Table 10.3 Reasons for the Increased Use of Direct Marketing by Retailers

Reason	Explanation
Better targeting	Geodemographic data and profiling possible
Personal communication	Shoppers treated as individuals, unique message for each
Flexibility	Easy to change message content or delivery
Controlled timing	Each message delivered to individual at right time
Cost effectiveness	Due to the reasons mentioned above
Data availability	Data collection systems being used (e.g. EPOS)
Processing technology	Ability to quickly and effectively process shopper data

Better targeting refers to the ability of direct marketing to more accurately identify potential shopper targets. As an example, a retailer may have data on shoppers that includes a postcode. This postcode can enable quite a detailed forecast of the shopper's profile to be produced based on various geodemographic data base systems (e.g. Mosaic, produced by Experian). This more detailed knowledge of the shopper's possible profile allows the right retail offering to be communicated in a personalized way. This *personalization* is important, as shoppers are more likely to read a promotional message if it is relevant to them and is presented in the right way. *Flexibility* means that the promotional approach can be altered quickly while control exists in the *timing* of message delivery. *Cost effectiveness* is high, as few wasted messages are produced owing to more accurate targeting and more effective messages. A final point that has had a big impact on the increased use of direct marketing is the availability of *shopper data* and the ability to process it quickly and effectively. Retailers can choose to buy shopper information from one of the many market research companies or may utilize in-store methods of data collection such as electronic point-of-sale (EPOS). Once available, advances in *computer hardware/processing technology* mean that a large amount of data can be analysed in a relatively short time.

To give an example, a large high street retailer may traditionally have used advertising to reach its shoppers (undertake market-based promotion). This approach would not guarantee particularly effective communications as shoppers would have to be watching the right TV programme, listening to the right radio show or reading the right newspaper or magazine. Research could be carried out to ensure that the best choice of TV, radio or print media was used, but the degree of accuracy would not be that high. The same retailer, having installed an EPOS system, now has accurate in-store data on sales. Add to this a store or loyalty card and a given transaction can be associated with a given shopper – i.e. the card is swiped, the details read and 'attached' to the transaction. This information can then be used to build personalized messages to that shopper using the contact details associated with the card, such as postal address, telephone number or e-mail address. Over time, quite an accurate *profile* of each shopper can be built.

Note: The use of direct marketing by retailers shares many similarities with other companies of any sort. For further reading please refer to a specialist Direct Marketing text (for example Tapp, 2000).

Public Relations

The Institute of Public Relations (IPR) defines public relations (PR) as 'the deliberate, planned, and sustained effort to establish and maintain mutual understanding between an organisation and its publics'. PR can either be used to *generate favourable publicity* or *lessen the negative effects of unfavourable publicity*. PR is usually used alongside the retailer's other promotional activities and can achieve any of the three broad communication objectives – i.e. it can *inform*, *persuade* and *reinforce*.

PR has a number of advantages over other promotional methods. *Credibility* can be high as the message is delivered to the receiver by an independent source that is not being paid by the company in question.

The fact that no direct payments are made also means that promotional costs are low. *Reach*, or the number of people receiving the message, is high as more attention tends to be paid to editorial or news sections than advertisements, for example. Increased attention to the message also means that a greater amount of *information* can be included in the message. Finally, PR can be undertaken quickly and can be highly *flexible*. PR also has two main disadvantages both relating to control. It has already been noted that an independent source delivers the message to the receiver and this fact leads to the possibility of *message distortion*. A newspaper may, for example, report a given news story in quite a different way to that intended by the retailer. It is also the case that the retailer cannot control the *timing* or *frequency* of the publicity.

There are four major areas that can be relevant in achieving good public relations, namely media relations, editorial and broadcast material, controlled communications, and face-to-face events. *Media relations* involve creating and managing relevant news stories. *Editorial and broadcast material* covers press conferences, news releases, personal interviews, feature writing and press visits and briefings. *Controlled communications* cover the area of publicity material for company use and includes annual reports, educational material, leaflets and audio-visual presentations. *Face-to-face events* include other ways of reaching the chosen audience direct, such as conferences, exhibitions, special events and demonstrations.

The use of PR by retailers is increasing for a number of reasons. The key reason concerns the increasing sophistication of shoppers. Advertising messages can no longer guarantee a wide audience of converts as shoppers' attitudes are increasingly critical of the source. A reduction in source credibility means that the message is seen to come from an organization that has a reason to present a distorted version of the facts. Add to this noise generated by the increasing competition between large retailers for advertising share of voice and advertising is not seen to be a form of communication that is not totally effective. The competition between retailers intensifies the need for effective communication in order to communicate and reinforce differentiation and positioning in general. If advertising cannot guarantee success, other communications options must be considered. PR, as has been noted, does not have nearly the same source credibility problems as advertising, so appears on the face of it to be more suitable.

Moss, Warnaby and Thame (1996) consider PR to fulfil four broad roles for the retailer. *Propaganda* informs but the truth is not necessarily essential, while *dissemination of information* involves informing truthfully. *Scientific persuasion* involves an attempt to change attitudes via a reasoned argument and *mutual understanding*, finally, attempts to build a consensus. Usage of PR in a sample of retail companies showed propaganda to be the most commonly used method, with only limited usage of dissemination of information and scientific persuasion. Mutual understanding was not used by any of the retailers.

Current usage of PR covers four main areas – recovery strategies, relationship strategies, product and store promotion and store image building. *Recovery strategies* involve the actions taken after adverse publicity – e.g. a product quality scare or a survey showing a retailer to be more expensive than competitors. *Relationship strategies* are concerned with building shopper loyalty by building positive shopper perceptions – e.g. perceived retailer rationality (see Chapter 9 on Retail Pricing). *Product and store promotion* seeks to place relevant stories or news items about favourable aspects of the store or the store's assortment; independent surveys of product quality are an example of this feature. Store *image building* relates to the retailer's overall image and may concern issues such as ethics, honesty, fair operations, etc. The current trend of UK supermarket retailers taking on large companies seeking to maintain an artificially high price (in the retailer's view) is an example of this and is often known as a 'Robin Hood' campaign (see Chapter 9).

Personal Selling

Personal selling is an important promotional method for all retailers, typically accounting for a large percentage of the overall promotional budget. The main reason behind this importance is that shoppers' perceptions of the performance of sales staff tend to determine their satisfaction with the retailer and purchase experience. This is particularly true for high-involvement retail situations such as jewellery and furniture.

Three basic types of personal selling exist, namely transaction processing, routine selling and creative selling. *Transaction processing* is the lowest level of personal selling, with sales staff limited to simple duties such as the checkout. Low-involvement retail situations tend to adopt this approach as little personal selling is required. *Routine selling* offers a higher level of personal selling with sales staff designated to provided customer support such as giving advice on the assortment. Involvement will be higher than transaction processing and stores such as DIY/hardware tend to adopt this approach. Personal selling that is highly in-depth is known as *creative selling*. In this approach, usually adopted by high-involvement retailers, sales staff provide in-depth customer support that may be unique to each encounter. A good example would be an interior design store where sales staff may produce a design tailored to the specific needs of the customer.

Successful personal selling can build customer satisfaction, as shoppers often build bonds with employees (sales staff) rather than the company. Good personal selling can build positive attitudes – or, more importantly, can avoid negative attitudes and the associated word-of-mouth communication. The benefits shoppers gain from personal selling can either be functional (sound product advice, for example) or social (a productive or enjoyable encounter). In this sense, personal selling is closely linked to the area of *customer service* and *relationship management* (for further details see Chapters 11, 12 and 13).

The Retail Sale

The *retail sale* has been an integral part of the retail environment for a great deal of time and is seen as a promotional method in its own right. A sale involves retailers selling off slow-moving or seasonal items to make way for more profitable or attractive items and help cash flow. The concept of lowering price to stimulate purchasing is based on the simple economic theory that states that as the price of a non-luxury item is lowered so demand for that item increases. Historically, retailers used sale tactics quite sparingly and for a limited time duration. This caused sales to have a marked effect on shoppers with great interest generated in large department store sales, particularly those held at the end of the Christmas period. Shoppers were known to queue outside the store with the aim of taking advantage of the reduced prices on offer. Indeed, in the UK it was not uncommon for shoppers to sleep outside the store in order to keep their place in the queue. Stern (1962) referred to such behaviour as 'planned impulse purchasing'. The whole concept of the sale is an integral part of the high/low pricing strategy (see Chapter 9 on Retail Pricing) where prices were maintained at a 'high' level throughout the year only to be reduced for a short time during sale periods.

A number of shopper perceptions of sales were identified by Betts and McGoldrick (1996), namely excitement and atmosphere, competition, risk, camaraderie, guilt relief, fear of missing out and the emotional and financial benefits of getting a bargain. The concept of *excitement and atmosphere* has already been mentioned and relates to the nature of the sale as an *occasion*. The fact that sales were traditionally rare caused shoppers to see them as a not-to-be-missed event. The experience also had social overtones, with *competition* between shoppers for the best deal. Many have argued, with varying degrees of justification, that sale behaviour is more animal in nature and, as such, reflects the more basic elements of the human psyche. So competition with other shoppers (survival of the fittest) and the desire to beat the retailer gave sales a certain, almost primitive attraction. The *risk* attached to sale purchasing (lower certainty, stock-outs, etc.) also adds to the excitement and competitive nature of the sale.

Camaraderie suggests that sales see shoppers forming a bond owing to shared interest. Modern theories of group, rather than individual, survival would go some way towards explaining this effect as individuals may be motivated by a common cause rather than an individual one. *Guilt relief* is based on the perception that buying an item at a reduced price is a way of saving money and is, therefore, perfectly respectable and not frivolous in any way. This is certainly true if and only if the shopper actually needed the item in question, and had deferred purchase in order to take advantage of a future sale price. In many cases this is not true, but shoppers feel happy with this line of reasoning anyway and tend to ignore this distinction. The *fear of missing out* is a related issue, caused by a perception that the item may not be on sale again and that competition from other bargain hunters for the item will be significant. Shoppers are almost justifying the purchase by saying that if everybody else wants it, so should they.

Finally, shoppers gain both *emotional* and *financial* benefits from sale purchasing. Acquisition utility (Thaler 1985) implies that shoppers see the pre-sale price, take this as an indicator of quality, and so view the transaction favourably, believing that the money saved is in the order of the difference between the pre-sale and sale prices. As has already been noted, sale shoppers see such expenditure as a money-saving exercise and tend to ignore the actual price paid. A number of emotional factors have been already been mentioned, to which can be added the satisfaction felt by shoppers who have got a bargain. Feelings such as smartness, resourcefulness and pride all contribute to the transaction utility (Thaler 1985) associated with a bargain purchase.

Looking in more detail at shopper sale behaviour, two broad situations can be considered. The first concerns shoppers *trading-up* by taking the opportunity to buy high-quality items at affordable prices. This is probably the most frequently observed sale behaviour with shoppers being given the chance to buy items that would normally be outside their price range. Much of the excitement associated with traditional sales is generated by this opportunity to meet aspirations that are usually far out of reach. The second broad situation concerns *trading-down*, where shoppers buy poorer-quality items at very low prices. The rationale behind such purchase behaviour is that as the price is so low even a limited-quality product still represents excellent value for money. Trading-down is often seen for seconds, damaged stock or end-of-line items. Betts and McGoldrick (1996) identify a number of more specific behavioural tendencies, detailed in Table 10.4.

Table 10.4 Behavioural Tendencies of Sale Shoppers

Behavioural tendency	Characteristics
Deferred purchasing	Future sale anticipated, current purchase postponed until the sale arrives
Tactical delay	Further cuts in sale price anticipated, purchase delayed until lowest price reached
Anticipated needs	Sale items purchased with a view to satisfying a need sometime in the future
Stockpiling	Increasing purchase quantity while prices are low to bring forward potentially higher-price future purchases
Planned impulse purchasing	The deliberate planning of sale purchasing with little consideration of specific purchases to be made
Risk taking	Risky purchases justified by the hunt for a bargain that may turn out to be misguided
Refund security	The return of non-sale price items to be replaced by similar items at sale prices

Source: Adapted from Stern, H., The significance of impulse buying today, *Journal of Marketing*, Vol. 26, No. 2, pp. 59–62, with permission.

Deferred purchasing is commonly seen during the run-up to traditional sale periods. Non-seasonal items such as suits or household products may be required well before the sale period but purchase may be postponed until the sale arrives so that a more economic purchase can be made. *Tactical delay* is based on shopper knowledge over further cuts to already discounted sale prices. Shoppers may visit a sale on its first day, see an item that they would like to buy but wait for a few days in the hope that the price will be further reduced in order to stimulate demand. This stance is a balance between the potential economic gains and the risk of stock-out. Anticipated needs and stockpiling are similar, owing to the action of purchasing a sale item that is not actually needed immediately. *Anticipated needs* concerns a purchase that will fulfil some need in the future while *stockpiling* involves increasing the purchase quantity of an item so that future purchases at the normal price may be reduced. Purchasing Christmas cards in the January sales is an example for former, buying several bottles of perfume at the sale price is an example of the latter.

Planned impulse purchasing and risk taking are also linked, as both involve behaviour of a quite irrational nature. *Planned impulse behaviour* (Stern 1962) sees the shopper planning to make purchases at the sales with little thought of the specific purchases to be made. *Risk taking* follows on from this as purchases may be made with little evaluation or consideration. Many shoppers can point to a box or bag standing in a cupboard somewhere that contains a sale item that has never been used. This can be seen as a common outcome of a planned impulse purchase that involved a high degree of risk.

The final behavioural tendency implies that shoppers are becoming more sophisticated when it comes to sales. *Refund security* is the practice of buying an item at a non-sale price knowing that a refund can be gained should a sale occur sometime in the near future. A large portion of the risk associated with a full-price purchase is removed, although this assumes that sales are a regular and predictable event. In recent times, this has indeed been the case; sales have become a much more common event.

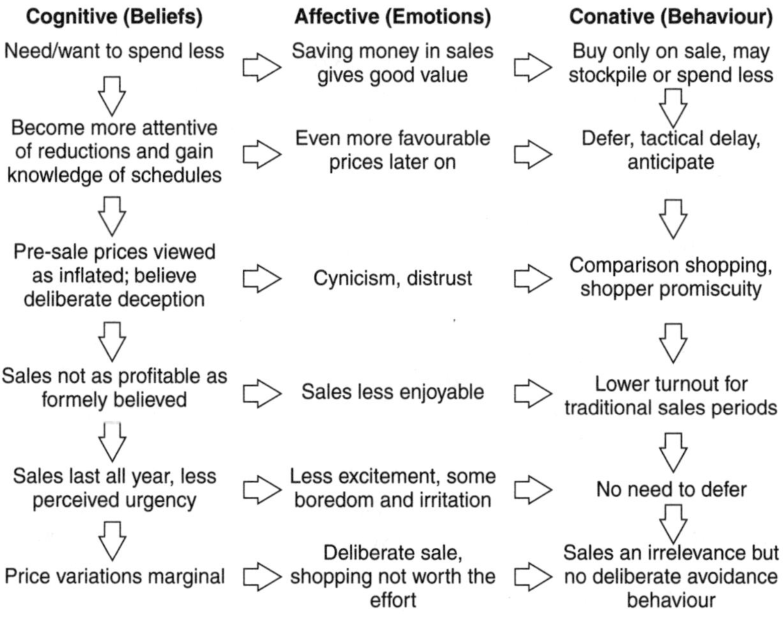

Figure 10.3 The development of a sales attitude problem

As mentioned above, recent times have seen an increase in the duration and frequency of sales. Shoppers have become more realistic about sales as a result, with a certain amount of sale fatigue developing. *Sale fatigue* occurs as shoppers become increasingly less excited about sales, build negative perceptions about them and reconsider their assessment of perceived retailer rationality (the degree to which retailers are seen as credible – see Chapter 9 on Retail Pricing). As sale fatigue grows, so do the negative perceptions about the prices that frequent sale retailers adopt (high/low pricing). This leads to the process of equitable price re-evaluation, where shoppers see sale prices for a significant proportion of the year and begin to assume that sale prices are in fact market prices. To explain: sale prices for a limited period are understood by shoppers to be special events. As the sale becomes a more regular event so sale prices are increasingly seen as a fair price. If retailers can afford to sell at the reduced sale prices for long periods, surely those prices must represent acceptable value for money rather than exceptional value for money? Sales fatigue has lead to an increase in every day low pricing (EDLP) among retailers (see Chapter 9 on Retail Pricing) and the beginnings of an attitude problem towards sales among shoppers (see Figure 10.3).

Conclusions

Communication with shoppers is essential if traffic is to be stimulated, product and category sales encouraged and store image maintained. Retailers, unlike many other companies, can communicate with shoppers in the store environment as well as the market. This communication follows the simple process of *sender – encode – receiver – decode*, where a message of some description passes between the two parties. Retailers, like all those engaged in communication activities must ensure that the right message is sent in the right way to the right shoppers. Success in this area is based upon an in-depth knowledge of the recipients (shoppers).

The retailer's *market-based promotional mix* is much the same as any other company with a number of methods at their disposal (advertising, sales promotion, direct marketing, sponsorship and public relations). Modern times have seen an increase in the importance of advertising, although recent advances in information technology (IT) and data collection have brought direct marketing methods much more to the fore. Public relations is also increasingly popular, assisting retailers in their recovery strategies, relationship management, product and store promotion, and image building. This more 'trusted' source of information is seen as more effective than 'obviously biased' advertising.

It is in the area of *store-based promotions* that retailers differ from many other companies. Retailers have the opportunity to closely control the environment in which messages are sent and received, giving them a much higher chance of message exposure and, potentially, understanding. Store-based promotions include in-store sales promotion, advertising, personal selling, the sale and point-of-sale (POS) display. Display is covered in detail in Chapter 7 on Store Design, while window display and the sale can be seen as promotional activities that span the store and market boundary. Sales promotion offers money savings, interest or value enhancement as a means of encouraging sales, and must be used with care if impact is to be maintained. Advertising covers the traditional methods of signage, announcements, literature and packaging, although more modern approaches based on TV/video and interactive technology are becoming increasingly important. Personal selling typically accounts for a large proportion of a retailer's promotional budget owing to the huge impact sales staff can have on the shopper's shopping experience. It has been shown that in some retail situations (particularly high involvement) the quality of the shopper's interaction with the sales staff has the biggest effect on that shopper's perception of the store.

Probably the most infamous promotional method used by retailers is the *sale*. Historically, sales were a big event that attracted queues of shoppers looking for a bargain. Shoppers adopted quite atypical shopping behaviour that has been referred to as *planned impulse behaviour*. This behavioural change occurred because sales were something special and were relatively infrequent. Modern times have seen retailers extending the duration and frequency of sales to the point where shoppers no longer see them as a special event. Indeed, shoppers now expect frequent sales and have changed their sales behaviour, adopting a more rational approach. This sales fatigue has rendered the sale quite ineffective and has led to an increasing usage of the every day low prices (EDLP) rather than the high/low (sale) (HLS) approach.

So if the sale is taking a less prominent role in the promotional mix what methods are being used in its place? Market-based methods such as mass-media advertising have certainly become more prominent, as have a mix of store-based methods. It is probably true to say that, despite the decline of sales, retailers are using an increasingly broad set of promotional tools to achieve their objectives.

References and Further Reading

Abratt, R. and Anley, J.M. (1994) The Promotions Mix Practices of Retail Pharmacies: Towards an Appropriation Model, *International Journal of Advertising*, 13, 367–77.

Adcock, D., Bradfield, R., Halborg, A. and Ross, C. (1998) *Marketing – Principles and Practice*, Pitman, London.

Anstis, H.F. (1974) A Chart Demonstrating Variations in Acuity with Retinal Position, *Vision Research*, 14, 589–92.

Betts, E.J. and McGoldrick, P.J. (1996) Consumer Behaviour and the 'Retail Sales' – Modelling the Development of an 'Attitude Problem', *European Journal of Marketing*, 30, 8, 40–58.

Burnett, J.J. (1988) *Promotion Management: A Strategic Approach*, West Publishing, St Paul, MN.

Davies, G. (1991) Retailer Advertising Strategies, *International Journal of Advertising*, 10, 189–203.

Edwards, S. and Shackley, M. (1992) Measuring the Effectiveness of Retail Window Display as an Element of the Marketing Mix, *International Journal of Advertising*, 11, 193–202.

Fulop, C. (1989) The Role of Advertising in the Retail Marketing Mix, *International Journal of Advertising*, 7, 99–117.

Hasty, R. and Reardon, J. (1997) *Retail Management*, McGraw-Hill, New York.

Hering, E. (1868) *The Theory of Binocular Vision*, Plenum, New York.

Kahn, B.E. and Schmittlein, D.C. (1992) The Relationship Between Purchases Made on Promotion and Shopping Trip Behaviour, *Journal of Retailing*, 68, 3, 294–316.

Low, G.S. and Lichtenstein, D.R. (1993) The Effect of Double Deals on Consumer Attitudes, *Journal of Retailing*, 69, 4, 453–67.

Moss, D., Warnaby, G. and Thame, L. (1996) Tactical Publicity or Strategic Relationship Management? An Exploratory Investigation of the Role of Public Relations in the UK Retail Sector, *European Journal of Marketing*, 30, 12, 69–84.

Rosenbloom, B. (1981) *Retail Marketing*, Random House, New York.

Steinman, R.M. and Levinson, J.Z. (1990) The Role of Eye Movement in the Detection of Contrast and Spatial Detail, in E. Kowler (ed.), *Eye Movements and Their Role in Visual and Cognitive Processes*, Elsevier, 115–60.

Stern, H. (1962) The Significance of Impulse Buying Today, *Journal of Marketing*, 26, 2, 59–62.

Tapp, A. (2000) *Principles of Direct and Database Marketing*, FT Prentice-Hall, London.

Thaler, R. (1985) Mental Accounting and Consumer Choice, *Marketing Science*, 4, 3, 199–214.

Sullivan, M. & Adcock, D. (2002)
"Retail Marketing". Thomson.

P. 15.
The establishment of retailing on new sites has a 4-fold impact upon the local area:

1. The physical role in respect to its siting, eg. if the development is in a derelict area or on a greenfield site.
2. The economic effect that retail has on a locality, both as an employer + generator of rateable income.
3. It becomes the focus for consumer spending in the area.
4. The social role that shopping + shop visiting have, affecting many patterns of local interaction.

P21.
The role of retailers is to make an acceptable + affordable combination of goods + services available to given customers at the right time + in the right place.

Pg. 27.
Macro environment = consists of larger societal forces that affect the whole market eg. political, economic, demographic, social, cultural, ethical + technological. Greatest recent change is the development of electronic/internet retail, + the opportunities + threats posed by this.

<u>Micro</u> environment = consists of the forces close to the company that affect its ability to serve its customers eg. trends in the product/market chosen by a company, its publics, suppliers, + competitors, etc. For a retailer this will include issues such as how big a group should be to benefit from economies of scale + critical competitive mass while remaining responsive to the needs of the customers.

Pg. 50
The <u>SOR</u> model = Stimulus - Organism - Response.

Pg. 51.
The buyer decision process = need recognition, investigation, and action.

Pg. 52.
The buyer decision process:

Need recognition → Information search → Evaluation of alternatives → Decision → Post purchase behaviour.

Customer Service as Satisfaction and as Competitive Advantage in Retailing

CHAPTER 11

This chapter:

- Shows how service is an integral part of the total retail offering
- Defines customer satisfaction
- Examines key issues in provision of service staff

Customer Service as Satisfaction and as Competitive Advantage in Retailing

Introduction

Retailers resell 'goods' and 'service products' in relatively small quantities. With goods this will typically involve the transfer of ownership of a tangible item, for service products such as a packaged holiday or an insurance policy, there will usually be some physical evidence to reinforce the product sold. The retailer of either goods or services might operate from a high street shop but could easily use a mail-order catalogue, a direct-response coupon in a magazine or interact with customers via a tele-sales centre or an Internet site. However the core product is only part of the service offered by the retailer, as there are many occasions when customers want to know more about the item before confirming the purchase. This is one area where a retailer can *augment a product* by providing additional service to the prospective buyer.

Service is an integral part of every 'total offering' and the role good-quality service plays in ensuring satisfaction is crucial for retailers. While this is true for all categories of goods it is particularly important with the so-called '*shopping goods*', those high-involvement items where customers will spend a considerable amount of time and effort in gathering relevant information and making comparisons. Another area where service can enhance an offering is with *intangible products*, such as holidays or airplane tickets. There is often a need to increase the credence qualities of the offering and this can be achieved if retail staff are able to answer queries in an informed and appropriate manner. It is at these 'moments of truth' that good retailers prosper and poor ones fail. The successful retailers are usually those that have well-trained staff able to offer information and advice as part of the service to customers. In fact retailing offers the perfect situation for what is sometimes called '*mass customization*', the *personalization* of a standard product by adding *individual extras*.

Customer satisfaction is derived from the comparison (by the buyer) of the value/benefits received (or perceived to have been received) with the sacrifices (including costs) made to obtain those benefits. Many authors have suggested that people's shopping motives are functions of many variables that are not necessarily purchase related. It is maintained that an understanding of the shopping motives requires the consideration of satisfactions that shopping activities provide, as well as the utility obtained from the merchandise that might be purchased'. When considering satisfaction it is not enough to look at the utility but also the *satisfaction* from shopping as a possible leisure activity. Shopping should be fun, because when a customer is enjoying their shopping experience then it is much easier for them to say 'yes' to a purchase. In this case, service can play an even greater role – for example, in a restaurant or a pub where the service provided is a major part of the offering. The appearance, attitude and assistance given directly by store staff, or indirectly by retail employees in remote locations (e.g. mail-order company telephonists) could be a critical issue in many transactions. It could also be important in any retail location where giving helpful service might not lead to an immediate sale but, by raising the image, could make it *more likely for the future.*

The role of service in achieving a *sustainable competitive advantage* for a particular outlet can be seen very clearly when that retailer offers the same basic (core) product as their competitors. Items as diverse as branded computers or audio and many FMCG food products are often available in several directly competing outlets. Perhaps the role of (personal) service can be best discussed by comparing similar products available from a mail-order supplier (or a Web site) with the same item available from a local retail outlet. However there is more to service than personal contact, and all dimensions of service provision and issues of service quality must be considered. Of course it is not service alone that creates competitive advantage, in fact there are obvious examples where purchasing from a well-staffed friendly location might not be the preferred option if that retailer does not have the appropriate minimum requirements in other areas (e.g. ABTA bonding for a travel agent, or manufacturers approval for a car repair garage). Therefore the contribution of service to competitive advantage cannot be viewed in isolation.

For the purposes of this chapter, retailers should be seen as the original *independent service providers* who act to facilitate customers' purchases. Perhaps the study of successful franchise retailers can highlight some of the key benefits derived from a committed staff. The operational independence and high level of motivation to succeed apparent in such operations suggests that there are conditions that lead to a different internal culture for some organizations. By contrast, some employees in traditional retail outlets feel restricted, forced to shape their activities according to the constraints of their employer's business, and they are very often poorly paid with few career prospects – typically in a dead-end job! These maybe extreme stereotypes but there is some truth in them.

Providing service staff is an expense for a retailer. The history of retailing shows that one of the great changes in retailing occurred in the 1950s and 1960s with the move to *self-service* retailing in many sectors. This led to major reductions in staffing, and much of the cost saving was passed onto customers in the form of lower prices. In order to encourage customers to select items from the shelves significant changes were made in display and merchandising methods. It also made retailers realize that they had to make the most effective use of their in-store selling space. As Corstjens and Corstjens (1999) state 'retailers realise that their shelfspace, nourished by their store traffic, is a resource. In the past they gave it away; then they thought of selling it to manufacturers... . More sophisticated retailers will exploit the resource for their own use.' But display alone may not be enough, and that is why it is necessary to review the role of service staff and consider how they can augment the activities of a retailer. In fact some customers do not like searching for the items they want, especially in a large store, and they also resent the delays and congestion at the checkouts. These customers would prefer to be served by a salesperson, or at least be able to find a helpful member of staff to assist them whenever they have a problem. Good self-service retailers such as Tesco greet customers at the entrance to the store and ensure that all staff, whatever their prime role, are prepared to help shoppers to locate and choose products and are able to provide other useful information if asked.

Issues that will be covered relate to the choice of the appropriate service activities, and the determination of the right level of service provision – and, most importantly, how to empower retail employees to adopt a *marketing orientation* that is aimed at creating satisfied customers. But first it is necessary to study some of the general aspects of services and service provision from the growing literature in the area of services marketing.

What Are Services?

Zeithaml and Bitner (2000) suggest 'put in the most simple terms, *services are deeds, processes, and performances'* (emphasis in the original). These authors then draw a distinction between *services* and *customer service*. It is the latter that is relevant to this book and can be defined as the service provided in support of a company's core product. But although customer service is usually supplied free of charge, and should not be confused with services provided for sale, many of the key characteristics are common to both. There are four main distinguishing features of both *services* and *customer service* that must be considered by any retail organization:

- *First* services are *intangible*, they cannot be seen or evaluated before receipt. Therefore service levels are often uncertain and the benefits unknown.
- *Second* the production of a service in *inseparable from the consumption*. Customers are inextricably involved and can affect the outcome of any service encounter (moment of truth for the supplier).
- *Third* services are *perishable*: they exist in real time. It is difficult to synchronize supply and demand, resulting in customer frustration at times of high demand and wasted resources when demand is low.

- *Fourth* service delivery is *variable*. Every service encounter is a new event, and for the customer it is the people who are delivering that service who are usually thought of as 'the supply company'. There is no certainty that the service delivered will be consistent over time, as it depends on so many uncontrollable factors.

These features lead onto some very real dilemmas for retail organizations such as those listed in the questions below. There are no certain ways of answering these, and other similar questions, but in the best retail organizations the relevant issues are continually reviewed:

- How can a retailer decide which are the *most appropriate customer service* activities when services are so intangible?
- How can a retailer *project the advantages and benefits* of its customer service levels to its customers? After all customer service is intangible.
- How can a retailer *select, train and motivate customer service* employees when service delivery is inseparable from consumption?
- How can a retailer *accommodate fluctuating demand* when service provision is perishable?
- How can a retailer ensure a *consistent level of customer service*, compatible with its chosen *quality position*, when service delivery is so variable?

Zeithaml and Bitner (2000) describe four specific 'provider gaps' that separate the actual provision of a service from the expectations of customers. They suggest each should be tackled and so they developed a four-stage programme with each stage targeted at closing one of the gaps:

1. *Listen to customer requirements*. This relates to the gap where retailers do not know what customers expect.
2. *Design appropriate services and set monitoring standards*. A gap will occur if the retailer selects the wrong service activities and measures.
3. *Deliver/perform the service properly*. Obviously this is aimed at the 'performance' gap.
4. *Ensure the performance matches the promises made to customers*. Customers form their expectations based on the promises made to them by the retailer.

In theory this is a simple sequence that should lead to the satisfaction of customers through meeting the expectations they have. In practice, many problems occur. For instance, not all customers are identical, therefore there are variations in the level of service expected or desired by different groups. And there are inevitable cost constraints that make some provision seem uneconomic. As shown above, services are *inseparable* and *variable*, they do not always take place as planned. A further problem comes because customers are also variable – what someone expects prior to a purchase might be affected or even altered during or after the actual buying occasion. Yet the customer is always right. Stew

Leonards, the world's largest dairy store is said to have two rules engraved by its entrance:

1. *First* the customer is always right.
2. *Second* if the customer is ever wrong, reread rule 1.

In some ways these rules sum up the problems faced by retailers with respect to customer service.

What Do Customers Want?

This is the first stage of Zeithaml and Bitner's programme. Obviously *marketing research* plays a big part in finding out what customers expect. If the objectives of the research are well defined then the results should help establish what the buyers want in all aspects of a retail offering, including customer service. But as Adcock (2000) suggests, it is very difficult to decide how much research should be conducted – too little and the organization ends up 'flying by the seat of its pants', too much and it is choked with data and this makes decision taking difficult. Langley (1995) calls this 'paralysis by analysis'.

Marketing consultant Paul Fifield (1998) suggests that 'Marketing strategy doesn't need market research but desperately needs some answers. Good and practical marketing strategy has to be based upon reasonably well-understood customer needs, wants and motivations'. There are many books available on research methods; and many techniques – e.g. *customer panels* are very relevant to retailing. However there is a risk in getting too involved with the actual process when it is really crucial to keep in mind that the purpose of all data collection and analysis is to provide *information* so that *better decisions* can be taken.

Customer service levels ought to be planned and measured against the expectations of shoppers. But while most retailers have an intuitive sense of what is required, research studies will give a clearer picture. However if a customer is asked 'What do you want?' and they know that customer service is to be given at no extra cost, then they are likely to ask for a lot more than is probably reasonable. Certainly the research should differentiate between the *desired* service level, which is the most a customer could expect, and the *acceptable* service level which is considered adequate and sufficient. Between the two there will be a *zone of tolerance* that describes the variation that customers are willing to accept (Figure 11.1). This is an important concept as there are few absolute levels with regard to customer service. Service levels are often established with reference to *benchmark standards* that reflect the comparable services that are being provided by competing retail outlets.

Research should be aimed at establishing details regarding the *minimum acceptable level* and the specific components of service that every customer expects, as well as the additional services that could be desired. Exceeding customers' expectations could make them extremely happy and will probably surprise them, but it is not necessarily good marketing. This is because customers make their purchase choice based on their expectations and might not chose a supplier

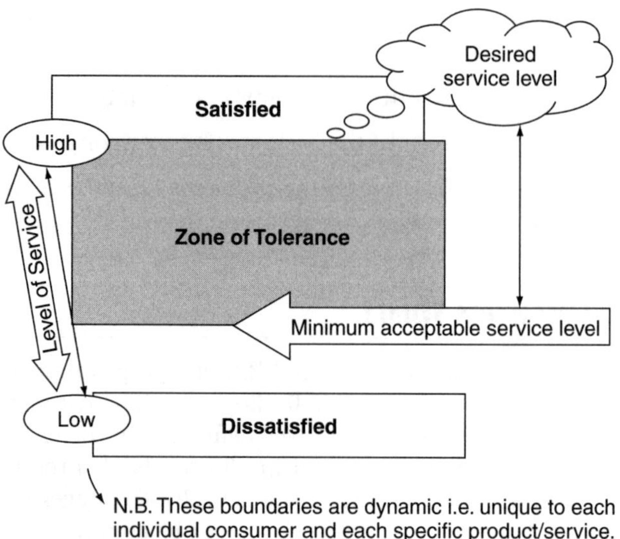

Figure 11.1 Zones of tolerance
Source: Parasuraman and Berry (1993).

who actually delivered more than promised because of ignorance of the total offering.

Zeithaml and Bitner (2000) suggest that the tolerance zone can expand and contract depending upon different customers and different situations. In particular they suggest that:

- Different customers possess *different zones of tolerance*
- The zones of tolerance vary for *different service activities*
- Zones of tolerance vary for *first-time and recovery services.*

These are, perhaps, obvious issues but it is surprising how often they are forgotten when researching what specific services each group of customers' expects. Service recovery is important in its own right, and will be discussed in Chapter 12.

Johnson-Hillery, King and Tuan (1997) went further in a study of the satisfaction levels of elderly consumers. In the USA, as in many other Western countries, there is a dramatic shift in age demographics with a rise in the older age groups. This group has significant buying power and for some categories of product provides a very attractive segment. Johnson-Hillery and her co-authors drew together research into the specific needs of elderly consumers and found that:

- The elderly consumer is more likely to mention *service* as a reason to shop at a particular store
- Elderly consumers are especially sensitive to the *treatment* they receive from retail sales personnel
- Retailers should *improve the services that are offered* to elderly consumers.

However the study did show that retail sales staff, those who actually deliver the service, perceived the expectations of elderly customers to be even greater than is actually the case. This could be because these elderly consumers have moderated their expectations in the light of poor experience. There is often a great deal of difficulty in establishing such facts. In fact the study was at pains to point out that the 'retail sales personnel generally are not the individuals making merchandise [and service] decisions for retailers'. Thus the suggestion is that the problem of inappropriate service provision lies with the store management. In fact retail sales staff are a very good source of information regarding the needs of all consumers, and yet many research programmes ignore these *internal employees* and fail to probe them for their knowledge.

Anthony Rucci, executive Vice-President of the Sears group, is convinced that the concept of an '*employee–customer profit chain*' has been crucial to the understanding of what is important to customers (Rucci, Kirn and Quinn 1998). It means the company has a realistic understanding of how both employees and customers actually think and behave, and Rucci considers that this has enabled his firm to gain a competitive advantage through high levels of customer service. This is more than market research studies, it requires the setting up of regular *two-way dialogues* with both shoppers and sales staff so that the retailer can listen to customers as well as stimulate discussions by suggesting new initiatives. *Shoppers' panels* and *focus group* studies are both ideal qualitative techniques suitable for such exchanges.

Another aspect that must be considered is that research is often focused on the *past*. Customers relate to events within their own experience and find it difficult to anticipate the future. It is often left to innovative retailers to introduce new service initiatives such as the current trend to 'personal shoppers' who accompany customers around major department stores. The point is that marketplaces are *dynamic*, always changing, and as Popcorn (1991) stated 'if your customers reach the future before you, they'll leave you behind'. Since customer service can be a significant source of competitive advantage, it is vital for retailers to continually monitor the *changing expectations* of their customers and to review the provisions offered. It is always possible for retailers to anticipate future requirements and to create relevant new services. In doing this 'innovative' retailers can actually *lead customer expectations*, provided that they remember that service levels are only one element of value received by consumers.

Creating superior value for customers requires a detailed understanding of the entire value chain, and an appreciation of the many different elements in every total offering that a customer might receive. It is possible that when some extra new service is set against the possibility of lower prices that there will be some segments who would prefer the 'no-frills' offering. It is the retailers who are able to both anticipate and meet the future expectations of their customers who will be successful. In this they have to think ahead on behalf of their customers, but this is possible only if there is a good *two-way communication* between the retailer and the shoppers as well as with those of the sales staff who serve the customers.

Designing Appropriate Services and Setting Monitoring Standards

Levitt (1976) once wrote about the 'industrialisation of services'. By this he meant that organizations should seek to standardize the activities of their service workers in an attempt to reduce the variability in delivery. In some aspects of customer service this is appropriate, but in other areas it is necessary to establish a culture of customer care and to encourage and empower employees to respond. Ritzer (1993) suggested that we are seeing a 'McDonaldization of society'. But even this famous 'fast-food' retailer can get its service strategy wrong, especially as customer expectations change over time. As Donkin reported in a 'confession' in 1994:

> Customers ... told McDonald's they were loud, brash, American, successful, complacent, uncaring, insensitive, disciplinarian, insincere, suspicious and arrogant ... We thought we knew about service. Get the order into the customer's hands in 60 seconds – that was service. Not according to our customers. They wanted warmth, helpfulness, time to think, friendliness and advice ... we had failed to see that our customers were now veterans in the quick-service market ... What was revolutionary in the seventies was ghastly in the caring nineties.

The lesson is that in order to develop appropriate services it is necessary to listen to customers and monitor their changing needs.

When designing services it is important to remember that the customers' role is inseparable at the time of delivery so any service design should allow for different levels of *consumer participation*. Hubbert (1995) suggested that there are three levels of participation across different services. These range from:

- *Low.* Customer presence required only during service delivery, as in the example of a fast-food restaurant.
- *Moderate*. Some *customer input* is required for the service delivery. This could be a full-service restaurant.
- *High*. The customer *co-creates the service*. Perhaps a good example is that of a personal shopper accompanying the customer around a department store.

For the low-involvement services it is those activities that can be standardized that are most appropriate, thus leading to a *standards-based* approach to the training of employees and the controlling of such services. However such an approach does not lead to a customized product, nor does it reflect the variability of individual shoppers. The top hotel chain in America is Marriott, and this organization is determined to succeed by offering the highest level of customer service in all its locations across the world. They have developed a *'culture-based'* approach to service. The culture among the hotel staff is aimed at doing whatever is necessary to satisfy a customer. In addition Marriott offer a service to visitors that involves a planning co-ordinator contacting a guest before their visit to find out if there are any extra activities that could be pre-booked, or any additional requirement that could be met. Of course many top-class hotels have a concierge or some other member of staff always available and willing to make theatre bookings, or summon a taxi, or recommend a good night club. These service actions all *customize* a visit, as no two guests have identical requirements. They occur only if the culture is right.

Marriott claim they 'never forget a guest', by which they aim always to be able to know the preferences of their customers in advance of any stay. Of course, this is facilitated by a very efficient and comprehensive data base that supplies the information on the many customers of the group. For smaller local retailers the data base is often in the head of the proprietor, for instance a local butcher serving one of the authors knows exactly which cuts of meat are preferred, keeping them available for the days when he knows they will be required.

For many retail organizations, the decisions about modifying existing customer services and creating new services will be taken in the light of current experience and ongoing knowledge of regular customers. It is more appropriate to consider the *evolution* of services from an existing provision rather than a major *revolutionary* change in the offering. However it is instructive to consider the issue from the perspective of a new provider, and there are a number of challenges facing a retailer when designing a new package of customer services. Lynn Shostack (1984) suggests four basic issues that are important in the development of new services:

- ► *First* they must be *objective*, not subjective
- ► *Secondly* they must be *precise*, not vague
- ► *Thirdly* they must be *fact-driven*, not opinion-driven
- ► *Lastly* they must be *methodological*, not philosophical.

Zeithaml and Bitner (2000) explain these by saying:

> Often new services are introduced on the basis of managers' and employees' subjective opinions about what the services should be and whether they will succeed, rather than on objective designs incorporating data about customer perceptions, market needs, and feasibility. A new service-design process may be imprecise in defining the nature of the service because the people involved believe either that intangible process cannot be defined precisely or that 'everyone knows what we mean'. Neither of these explanations or defences for imprecision is justified (emphasis is in the original).

Another action that cannot be justified is to simply purchase a *customer relationship management* (CRM) package from a consultant. The current vogue for CRM is something that requires to be carefully considered, because customer service provision should be specifically designed to fit the needs and strategic position of an individual retailer.

The New 'Service' Development Process

The process of new service development should be very similar to the '*stage-gate*' process (Cooper 1990) utilized for many new product developments. The 'gates' provide an opportunity to evaluate a particular stage in the development and then to make the appropriate GO/NO GO decisions regarding the continuation of the process onto the next stage. Typically it starts with a *strategy review* that identifies gaps in current provisions and establishes marketing objectives and cost parameters for the development. Then the first stage is *idea generation*, which is then followed by more detailed assessments of proposals. These are discussed more fully, along with Cooper's (1993) stage-gate process, in Adcock (2000). That text also differentiates between the small 'tweaks' made to improve an offering and ensure it is relevant for future competitive positioning, and the more radical 'twists and twirls' which represent a more fundamental change to what is being offered.

As with any new product it will take more than market research to answer the really key question which is: Will the new service actually appeal to customers and enhance the performance of our organization? The only way to test this in practice is to introduce the new initiative. The timing of any new service is critical. There will be *windows of opportunity* when success is more likely – if it is launched before the market is ready or in an effort to play 'catch-up' after most competitors then there could be problems. Sometimes it is appropriate to carry out a *test marketing launch* on a small scale as a form of experimentation, and monitor the results with a view to rolling out the new activity if it seems successful. As in all retail initiatives, it is important to remember that the objective is to trade *effectively* and *profitably*.

Do Customers Really Want It?

One particular issue regarding the retail service mix and taken from the research on elderly consumers (Johnson-Hillery, King and Tuan 1997) concerned layout and display rather than actual service delivery. But the two aspects of a retail marketing mix are intimately intertwined. Customer service is really just those actions that are necessary to ensure that the outcomes from the interactions between an organization, its systems and processes, the service employees and the customers are as *satisfying* and *effective* as possible:

> Elderly consumers expressed concern that retailers had too much merchandise on the racks which in turn made the aisles hard to move through and the items hard to find. The concern did not appear to be one of decreased mobility but rather one of inconvenience. Although it is important for retailers to have adequately stocked shelves, too much merchandise on the floor may actually be detrimental to sales... . Retail sales personnel in the focus group interviews also reported that crowding was a concern for younger consumers with children because push chairs could not fit through the aisles in clothing departments... . Currently there is a trend in retailing to hold a minimal amount of stock, if any, in a storage area separate from the selling space. This is understandable from a retailer's

> perspective because retail selling space is at a premium. Therefore, areas once utilised for back-stock are now being used for selling. However, to best serve customers of all ages and to maximise selling per square foot, managers may need to address the philosophy that 'less is more'. Jamming too much merchandise on racks, which makes the aisles hard to move through and merchandise difficult to find, maybe doing more to decrease sales than improve them.

This warning leads directly to the need for proper evaluation of the 'total retail offering' based on relevant monitoring standards. Obviously this is another area for on-going research. Most retailers collect a great deal of data regarding 'who are their regular customers', 'where and when they shop' and 'what they buy'. The increasing use of *transactional data* collected at the *point of sale* via loyalty cards and bar codes means there is no shortage of data. This can often be fused with additional information from other sources, perhaps covering factors such as 'the attitudes and preferences of customers'. All of this sort of data can be important, but it often fails to explore other critical issues such as 'where a retail encounter fits into the customer's life', 'what difficulties are experienced' and 'which services are the ones that really energize that customer'. *Qualitative studies* which go further than just simply checking against pre-determined standards and describing activities are an essential part of any monitoring system. They don't replace the continuous quantitative research, but certainly complement and enrich it.

Customization Through Customer Service

Many of the major developments in postwar shopping have come about because of advances in mass marketing and mass merchandising. Retailing has come a long way from the local 'mom and pop' family stores that dominated before the 1950s, offering a personal service to each and every shopper. While there have certainly been many economies of scale, the multiple chain stores have had to sacrifice many elements of the specific and individual approach to customers. The best compromise has been to *segment markets* and to try to discover *niches* where standardization of merchandise is possible.

The difficulty with segmentation is that those within the same segment are not exactly alike – they may have similar basic needs, but they often desire something different in the way they obtain the basic product. The large DIY 'shed' retailers such as B&Q offer excellent prices for standard packets of screws, but if you want 12 screws and there are only 10 in the packet you feel frustrated having to buy 8 extra. When it comes to more complex items such as DIY central heating items, then some customers know exactly what they want, while others require a well-informed member of staff to advise on what is needed to do the job. In fact, B&Q does claim to offer help and advice to any customer, as well as providing free information sheets on DIY projects in their stores.

What happens at B&Q is good personal service, at least it is when a knowledgeable service employee can be found in one of their huge warehouses. However, it is possible to go much further in customizing an offering without sacrificing the economies of mass merchandising. If you want a particular shade of paint for home decorating, then take in a colour reference and choose from the many hundreds that can be made up in the store. Using a standard white base, colour dyes can be added and mixed to create an exact match to your requirements. In this case the customer is not receiving a simple add-on service, but they are part of something more personal. This is increasingly being called *mass customization*; another example could be the creation of your perfect pizza by adding toppings to a standard base in a grocery store.

Some writers have suggested that mass customization is an oxymoron, suggesting that it can't be done, or at least it can't be done at the same cost. Of course a customized offering could command a higher price, or it could be just more desirable so that producing a personalized offering wins the sale in the highly competitive world of retail. Hart (1994) suggests that 'There is nothing simple about mass customisation', he then goes on to try to define it. He offers two definitions:

> first the visionary definition: mass customisation is the ability to provide your customers with anything they want profitably, any time they want it, anywhere they want it, and any way they want it. This is quite a goal – a goal that will, in all honesty, rarely be achieved by an organisation ... . This leads to a second, practical definition: the use of flexible processes and organisational structures to produce varied and often individually customised products and services at the low cost of a standardised, mass production system.

Hart was writing with respect to manufacturing and other companies, but the concept of mass customization is particularly appropriate to retail stores and customer service activity. By applying a little creativity it is possible to offer greater choice, better support for the merchandise, and also to turn the shopping experience from a chore into a pleasure. Hart suggested four key areas that should be examined in order for an organization to decide its strategy regarding mass customization:

- Customer sensitivity
- Process amenability
- Competitive environment
- Organizational readiness.

A study of these areas will soon show what is possible, and in many retail stores there are opportunities to pursue this type of approach. In fact, a retail organization must be very clear about its objectives. The choice is to offer superior customer service in order to gain a comparative advantage over competing stores in the same market, or alternatively to offer mass customization in order to attract a wider range of customers and endeavour to satisfy each one individually.

The benefits of customization can certainly make a difference for traditional retailers as they try to compete against the new .com e-tailers. Waskom (2000) suggested that 'there will always be a place for brick-&-mortar stores ... the most successful retailers will ... turn their stores into exciting, experience laden destinations, converting their customers from mere shoppers into visitors who spend'. The use of customer services and the development of individually customized offerings can be a major element in this area.

Delivering and Performing the Service Properly

The service encounter provides the most critical opportunity for a retailer to customize the delivery to an individual customer. There will be several degrees of levels of customer involvement, as suggested in the earlier discussion of research by Hubbert (1995). It might be more appropriate to consider these along a continuum rather than three distinct levels (Figure 11.2).

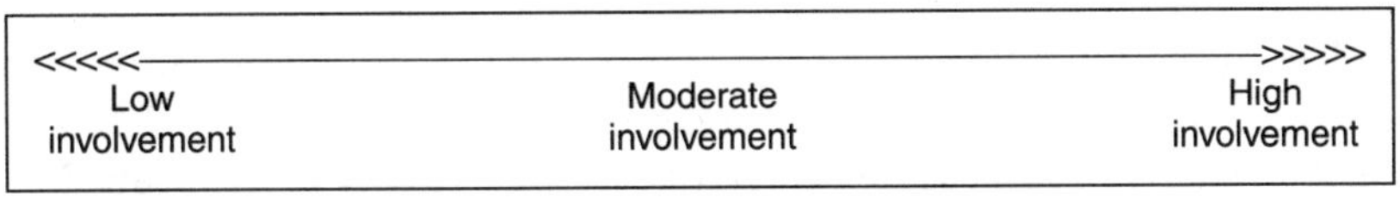

<<<<<—		—>>>>>
Low involvement	Moderate involvement	High involvement

Figure 11.2 Continuum of involvement

Whatever the level of involvement, the actual customer service encounter is the 'moment of truth' when the customer really judges the retailer provider. Jan Carlzon of Scandinavian Airways (SAS) introduced the term 'moments of truth'. He suggested (1987) that each of SAS's 10 million customers came into contact with approximately five SAS employees, leading to 50 million contacts, but few lasting any more than 15 seconds at a time. He went on to say that 'SAS is thus *created* 50 million times a year, 15 seconds at a time. These *moments of truth* are when SAS must prove itself to its customers and ultimately determine whether SAS will succeed as a company' (emphasis in the original).

For retailers the moments of truth are represented by customer service encounters, and these are often longer than the 15 seconds of SAS. But they are equally critical. Evert Gummesson (1991) described the service staff as 'part-time marketers', employees whose job is to interact with customers but who are not directly part of the marketing department, nor responsible to the Marketing Director. But these employees are the service received by shoppers; they are the organization in the eyes of the consumers, and therefore they are marketers. However they may not be directly rewarded for their influence on the retailer's image or its long-term marketing success, although many retail staff do receive commission based on short-term sales targets achieved.

Zeithaml and Bitner (2000) suggest that there is 'concrete evidence that satisfied employees make for satisfied customers, and satisfied customer can, in turn, reinforce the employees' sense of satisfaction in their job'. Another way of looking at it comes from adapting the words of Helen D'Antonio: '[Customer service] and dancing have a lot in common.

In both, if the partners prove compatible, the union is pleasurable. However, if plagued by blunders, the pairing quickly becomes awkward.'

Therefore it should never be forgotten that good service is both the training and motivating of employees and the creation of an environment that encourages positive contributions from customers with regards the service encounter.

Delivering 'Good' Service

The obvious sequence in delivering customer service is that a retailer should:

- *Recruit* the right people
- *Develop* those employees to deliver a quality service
- Provide the necessary *support systems, processes* and *environment*
- *Reward* and *retain* the best staff.

To suggest that the best way to deliver good customer services is to employ the right people might sound self-evident. It is, *but it still has to be made to happen*. In recruiting the right people it is necessary to draw up a job description that gives prominence to the *critical customer service activities*. This can then be developed into a set of ideal specifications for such staff. However there is often a problem that arises because of the tension between the very important role for service personnel and the low pay, based on tight financial controls, that is often applied to them. Somehow a balance has to be struck between the needs of efficiency and cost control and the benefits of effectiveness in delivering service. It is not an easy balance but it does make the retention of good service staff, once they have been recruited, even more critical.

There are five major aspects of service quality. These are derived from SERVQUAL, a multidimensional scale, developed some 20 years ago, to measure customers' perceptions. It was based on empirical studies and the emerging categories were then reduced to five key groupings:

- *Reliability* – the ability to perform dependably and accurately
- *Responsiveness* – willingness to assist customers promptly
- *Assurance* – knowledge and credibility of service staff
- *Empathy* – care, courtesy and attention as perceived
- *Tangible aspects of a service* – appearance and physical cues.

Sasser, Olsen and Wyckoff (1978) went further suggesting that although customers will first assess the more obvious advantages from any service, they may also want additional *secondary benefits*. Two of the most common are:

- The need for *security* (safety of the customer and his/her property)
- The reassurance that the service activity will be *completed*.

The training given to staff should be relevant to all of the above aspects of a quality service. Each of these elements will require individual attention with regards delivery, and each should be monitored on a regular basis. Some will require skills to be learned, whilst others are more dependent on the attitudes of the staff member, and most depend on the pressure and workload experienced by an individual service employee. The latter point and the tangible issues require specific attention from senior retail management. This must include decisions on the number of customer service employees as well as such aspects as the staff uniforms, the actual point-of-sale (POS) leaflets and forms used, and the physical environment within which the service is performed.

e-service – The Challenge Facing .com e-tailers

If the service is performed in a physical location this will include the comfort and cleanliness of the store and other atmospherics, all of which help to make shopping a pleasure rather than something to be endured as discussed in Chapter 7. However it must be remembered that a service encounter occurs every time a customer interacts with a service provider. Shostack (1984) suggested there are three types of encounters that can be experienced:

1 *Face-to-face* encounters

2 *Telephone* encounters

3 *Remote* encounters.

Remote encounters take place without any direct human contact such as an Automatic Bank Teller Machine (ATM) or an Internet connection. Providing online customer service is proving difficult for many companies because of the lack of actual contact. It is often the limitations of the processes, and especially the systems used, that is the problem, in particular when there is a lack of two-way communication between supplier and customer. Only a few .com e-tailers are really taking the issue seriously at present and the current customer experience seems to be that e-mails are fired off into the ether and they never seem to get a helpful reply. Perhaps there is a kind of 'black hole' out there in the cyberspace!

So how can a .com e-tailer fulfil its service promises from the other end of a modem? Good suppliers will be aware of the need for responsiveness and assurance with regards customers. Tele-sales companies solved this in the past by moving into real-time solutions and talking to customers. Web-based retailers need to do the same. New ways of using the Web are continually being developed and by the time this book is published there will be many more creative solutions than at present. Customers are likely to make contact by e-mail, fax or telephone and all contact addresses should be easily accessible to customers. Companies must make it easier for customers to make contact, and they must then make that contact (the 'e-moment of truth') effective.

To do this the retailers must become more responsive to customers. There is now new sophisticated software being developed to filter e-mails so that customer service requests are not crowded out by other traffic. *Real-time voice systems* are also becoming available so there should be no excuse for any delay in replying quickly. It is now possible to use available dial-up contacts, and that should avoid the frustration of either supplier or customer going offline during a service encounter. Other developments in technology allow service staff to synchronize browsers and then walk customers through a site by feeding them Web pages relevant to their individual needs.

The developments will keep coming. As long as the need for good customer service remains the ultimate objective and the technology is chosen because it helps achieve that goal, then things will improve for committed .com e-tailers. But we are living through a real technological revolution and it is very tempting to follow the advances in technology rather than utilizing them to improve service. If a company allows the technology to dominate, and forgets that the purpose of a retailer is to deliver a product to, and satisfy the needs of a customer, then there will be problems for that supplier.

The 'Retailer's Dilemma': Better Service or Lower Costs?

Retailers compete by offering combinations of goods and services that they judge will meet both the primary and the appropriate secondary needs of customers 'better' than competitors. Customer service can be seen as one of the *augmented features* of a total retail offering.

The necessity for good staff training and motivation to provide a good service are obvious areas where attention can be focused. Marketing can play a part here, both by ways of improving *internal communications* with customer service staff, and by providing *feedback* from the marketplace on how customers react to particular initiatives. However, Levitt (1976) suggested that: 'No matter how well trained or motivated, people make mistakes, forget, commit indiscretions, at times get hard to handle.' The fact is that much service delivery depends on *people* – or, more often, specifically on a single *person* who has the responsibility for delivering the service. This is true in a McDonald's fast-food outlet, as well as for a very knowledgeable owner/manager of a shop selling complex high-tech electronic equipment.

With regards the employees working in a retail store there is often a real problem. Schlessinger and Hesketh (1991) found that over 90 per cent of all jobs in restaurants, hotels, grocery, department stores, and other retail outlets in the USA could be classified as 'truly dead-end jobs'. They suggest that 'for the most part these jobs are poorly paid, lead nowhere, and provide little if anything in the way of health, pension, or other benefits'. They also found that during some periods the average real wages in these sectors actually fell. There is no reason to suppose that the situation is any different in the UK and Europe. Drucker highlights this in his article 'The New Productivity Challenge' (1991), where he suggests the 'most pressing social challenge developed countries face is to raise the productivity of service workers'. He further throws doubt on whether 'capital' can replace people, as he concludes that in service work the people are the 'tools' of production. So the motivation and training of staff are crucial in service delivery, and retailers must undertake a *cost/benefit analysis* to contrast the competitive benefits of desired service levels with the cost of effective provision.

Ensuring That the Promises Made to Customers Are Met

The monitoring of services must use comparisons with the performance standards set, but it is essential that the actual evaluation should be based on the *value judgement of the customer*. Decisions regarding the mix of services should already have been taken and any promises made to customers should be consistent with the planned level of provision. But when evaluating service delivery, whether they are face-to-face or remote encounters, it is the *perception of the customer as to what was received* that is crucial. This should be evaluated against what the customer expected in terms of quality and satisfaction, and the apparent competitive benefit to the retailer.

It is against this background that regular on-going *monitoring schemes* should be developed. There are many techniques available that can be used to judge the different qualities of the services offered. Usually a combination of surveys and observational methods are used. Some, such as the use of 'mystery shoppers' – where a researcher masquerades as a genuine shopper and evaluates a retail assistant – are sometimes criticized by research professionals. There are anxieties regarding the ethics of such methods and the objectivity of the results, but there is no doubt that useful feedback can be obtained.

The advantage of surveys is that this type of research looks at service activity from the customer point of view. Some surveys are continuous, formal and structured perhaps using shoppers' panels as the sample respondents, but a lot of useful data are also available from customer complaints or informal contacts with actual shoppers. Talking to customers asking if they require any additional assistance can produce some information, but all too often it receives the standard reply of 'no thank you'. Researchers have to get beyond the polite, non-involved response and explore the deeper feelings of customers. For this, the use of *focus groups* and *in-depth interviews* is very effective. Such techniques are well covered in most standard texts on Marketing Research.

Conclusions

Customer service is both a *competitive advantage* and an *organizational cost*. It requires a serious strategic approach in order to decide what should be provided. The ideal test is to ensure that every service provided adds value to the retail operation and enhances the volume/value of business in a competitive marketplace to an extent that more than covers the cost of provision. Unfortunately this is impossible to judge in practice and so service provision becomes a qualitative decision. Nevertheless it is important that the level and standard of customer service provided is *consistent with*, and *reinforces* the rest of the retail marketing mix.

There is a simple four-step sequence that should be followed with regards customer service:

- Listen to *customer requirements*
- Design *appropriate services* and set *monitoring standards*
- *Deliver/perform* the service properly
- Ensure the performance *matches the promises* made to customers.

While simple to follow, the actual decisions required are extremely hard to make. An explicit customer service strategy should be unique to the retailer developing and implementing it. There is no prescriptive solution and there is little point in offering a 'me-too' copy of a competitor's service. In fact the variability of service delivery, and the inseparability of service production from the individual customer, means that straight copies are not really possible. What could be common is the message from customers as to what services they would expect to receive. The first step in the process is to listen to customers, and continue to do this as changes do occur all the time. Also to realize there is a *zone of tolerance* regarding the minimum acceptable level and the desired level of service.

The actual designing of services is definitely specific to each organization. However, as with any new 'product' it is crucial that a provider checks that the service is actually required and in fact will energize the customer by offering a real benefit. The role of services in the customization of products must not be underestimated. When every offering is a commodity then price alone dictates the purchase, but levels of service are a key weapon for retailers in *de-commoditizing their merchandise*. This could be crucial for traditional stores threatened by the growth in e-commerce.

Having decided on the services to be offered there is no excuse for not performing them properly. This involves planning and the provision of appropriate resources as well as ensuring that all processes are compatible with the desired services. *Investment in staff*, and their motivation and training, is vital. It should be apparent that it is also less costly to retain good customer service staff than to continually recruit and train new ones. This has implications for human resource policies within a retail organization. The extension of performance is the monitoring of that performance and the rewarding of good employees. Proper standards are required and due attention should be given to the issues of service quality which have received much attention since the 1990s.

Customer service is an issue for all retailers. While it is more apparent in face-to-face encounters (moments of truth) in traditional stores, the issue of service is just as important for .com e-tailers. This area is in a period of rapid development, and many initiatives have been proposed to overcome the inherent problems of remote encounters. It is beyond the scope of this text to explore the different solutions to the problems of e-service, but the basic principles can be reiterated – in fact, they apply to all methods of retailing. As long as the customer service decisions are taken in order to *enhance the shopping experience of customers* and they provide *real added benefits* to those customers, then that is fine. If at any stage off-the-peg solutions or clever technology starts to dominate rather than serve, then that is when problems will occur.

References and Further Reading

Adcock, D.G. (2000) *Marketing Strategies for Competitive Advantage*, Wiley, Chichester.

Borrus, A. (2000) How Marriott Never Forget a Guest, *Business Week*, February 21, 74.

Carlzon, J. (1987) *Moments of Truth*, Ballinger, Cambridge, MA.

Cooper, R.G. (1990) The Stage-Gate System: A New Tool for Managing New Products, *Business Horizons*, May/June.

Corstjens, J. and M. Corstjens (1999) *Store* Wars, The Battle for Mind*space* and Shelf*space*, Wiley, Chichester.

D'Antonio, H. (2000) Winning at Customer Service Takes Time and Money, *Information Week*, 20 March.

Donkin, R. (1994) No Relish for the Cheese & Pickle Sandwich, *Financial Times*, 28 October.

Drucker, P.F. (1991) The New Productivity Challenge, *Harvard Business Review*, November–December

Fifield, P. (1998) *Marketing Strategy*, 2nd edn, Butterworth-Heinemann, Oxford.

Gilmore, J.H. and Pine, B.J. (1997) The Four Faces of Mass Customisation, *Harvard Business Review*, January–February.

Gummesson, E. (1991) Marketing Orientation Revisited: The Crucial Role of the Part-Time Marketer, *European Journal of Marketing*, 25, 2, 60–75.

Hart, C.W.L. (1994) Mass Customization: Conceptual Underpinnings, Opportunities and Limits, *International Journal of Service Industry Management*, 6, 2, 36–45.

Hubbert, A.R. (1995) Unpublished doctoral dissertation; reprinted in Bitner, M.J., Faranda, W.T., Hubbert, A.R. and Zeithaml, V. (1997) Customer Contributions and Roles in Service Delivery, *International Journal of Service Industry Management*, 8, 3, 193–205.

Johnson-Hillery, J., King, J. and Tuan, W.-J. (1997) The Difference between Elderly Consumers' Satisfaction Levels and Retail Sales Personnel's Perceptions, *International Journal of Retail and Distribution Management*, 25, 4, 126–37.

Langley, A. (1995) Between Paralysis by Analysis and Extinction by Instinct, *Sloan Management Review*, Spring.

Levitt, T. (1976) The Industrialization of Services, *Harvard Business Review*, September–October.

Parasuraman, A., Zeitaml, V.A. and Berry, L.L. (1987) SERVQUAL, A Scale for Measuring Consumers Perceptions of Service Quality, *Journal of Retailing*, 64, 1.

Popcorn, F. (1991) *Popcorn Report: Targeting Your Life*, Random House, London.

Ritzer, G. (1993) *The McDonaldization of Society: An Investigation into Social Life*, Pine Forge Press, Newbury Park, CA.

Rucci, A.J., Kirn, S.P. and Quinn, R.T. (1998) The Employee–Customer Profit Chain at Sears, *Harvard Business Review*, January–February.

Sasser, W.E., Olsen, R.P. and Wyckoff, D.D. (1978) *Management of Service Operations*, Allyn & Bacon, Boston.

Schlessinger, L.A. and Hesketh, J.L. (1991) The Service-Driven Service-Company, *Harvard Business Review*, September–October.

Shostack, G.L. (1984) Service Design in the Operating Environment, in W.R. George and C. Marshall (eds), *Developing New Services*, American Marketing Association, Chicago, 27–43.

Waskom, K. (2000) Destination Retail is on its Way, *Marketing News*, Chicago, March 13, 15.

Zeithaml, V. and Bitner, M.J. (2000) *Services Marketing*, 2nd edn, McGraw-Hill, New York.

Customer Loyalty and Related Issues

CHAPTER 12

This chapter:

- Explains the importance of creating and retaining customers
- Defines customer loyalty
- Reviews the importance of relationship marketing in the retail context

Customer Loyalty and Related Issues

Introduction

Does the 80 per cent/20 per cent rule apply in retail? Alfredo Pareto formulated his famous rule of the critical few–the less critical many from his experience in manufacturing industries. But irrespective of the actual percentages – and there is no evidence supporting a precise 80 per cent figure – every retail store will have a number of *key shoppers* (the critical few) who are more important to its trading success than the great mass of its other customers (the less critical many).

No organization can afford to ignore their high-spending shoppers, in fact every retailer should identify and seek to understand these key customers, and then devise strategies for retaining them. Drucker (1968) once said the purpose of a business is to create and *retain* customers, but most organizations have limited budgets so it is sensible to invest more heavily in specific key customers, and thus target resources to those areas where the return is greatest. Of course the retailer must never forget the need to satisfy all its customers – too many dissatisfied shoppers, and the store is in real trouble – but there is a difference between this and proactive retention.

Customer loyalty is increasingly being seen as vital to the success of any retail organization, because it is recognized that attracting new customers is a lot more expensive than holding on to existing ones.

But are the major spenders the loyal customers of so many marketing programmes? The answer is 'not necessarily so'. There is a lot of confusion about loyalty and even more about the links between satisfaction and loyalty, and between loyalty and the 'lifetime value' of an individual customer. These issues need to be explored so that retailers can invest resources into developing and retaining the customers that they want, build strong relationships with the most valuable shoppers, and avoid confusing 'frequency of visit' loyalty with 'share of customer spend' loyalty.

Hooley, Saunders and Piercy (1998) suggest that

> to confuse retention and loyalty can be dangerous. Retention may be achieved through a 'bribe' – discounts for repeat purchase, and so on. Achieving high customer loyalty is likely to be far more difficult and requires greater long-term investment. The practical difference is great. The 'customer loyalty' card schemes at Tesco and Sainsbury are more about customer retention than loyalty and satisfaction, and it is likely that their effects will last only until there is a better offer available.

Maybe the decision by Safeway to discontinue its ABC card scheme in 2000 was taken because they believed it was not doing enough to encourage loyalty.

A comment by Goldscher (1998), writing for the US candy industry, suggested that

> it wasn't so long ago that customers were fiercely loyal. Today they are frighteningly disloyal .... Every store owner wishes to believe in a 'Customer for life' concept, yet in reality it is nothing more than a delusion. The fact is no customer is for life. Customers are for a measurable period of time. Customers today are selective, driven by sales, advertising and friends .... Realistically the goal should be to capture the customer under certain circumstances for a period of time ... to gain as much of the customer's attention as possible. (emphasis in the original)

With this in mind all retail marketers need to consider the relationships that do exist between a retailer and its customers, and design programmes which can *optimize the contact for the future* .

O'Malley (1998) was very blunt when considering the other side of buyer–seller relationships, stating 'but customers aren't stupid – if they feel that the relationship exists simply to make another sale, then they will seek to dissolve it'.

This chapter will consider the topic of *relationship marketing* in a retail context, and will then develop a framework for studying both shopper retention and loyalty. It will also explore the explosion of *customer relationship management* (CRM), and consider the successful personal shopper programmes whereby sales consultants working for major fashion stores actually make selections for their 'high-spending' clients. In particular, it will ask if any of the current types of 'loyalty' schemes actually achieve their goal, as well as exploring the issues of customer privacy and whether the building of data bases really help retailers to know customers better.

Relationship Marketing

The 1990s witnessed a dramatic increase in, and study of, *relationship marketing*. Initially this was fuelled by activities within B2B marketing, especially the work of the IMP (International Marketing and Purchasing) group, as well as people working in services marketing. It has now become a major focus in many marketing situations. The concept is very simple, and is encapsulated in O'Malley's definition (O'Malley, Paterson and Evans 1997):

> Relationship marketing involves the identification, specification, initiation, maintenance, and (where appropriate) dissolution of long term relationships with key customers and other parties, through mutual exchanges, fulfilment of promises and adherence to the relationship norms in order to satisfy the objectives and enhance the experience of the parties involved (emphasis in the original).

An alternative, simpler, and much-quoted definition from Morgan and Hunt (1994) is that '*Relationship marketing* refers to all marketing activities directed towards establishing, developing and maintaining successful relational exchanges' (emphasis in the original). The one omission from this latter definition is the idea of *ending a relationship* when it is not delivering benefits to both parties. However, the difficult question of what is, and what is not, relationship marketing was referred to by one of its early proponents, Evert Gummesson (1997), when he wrote 'Much of what has been written about RM is theoryless, a stack of fragmented philosophies, observations and claims which do not converge.' This frustration is understandable, but it should not detract from the importance of a close, and on-going relationship between supplier and customer built upon the mutual benefits possible to the parties. Nor should the fact be ignored that every contact between a retailer and a customer is another input into a *developing relationship* – either good or bad – between the parties. Grönroos (1996) states that marketing is 'the management of a firm's market relationships', and the relationship with customers is obviously the most critical.

There is, however, a world of difference between managing *single exchanges* (episodes/transactions) and the building of *long-term, positive interactions* linking two parties in the hope (or expectation) that purchases will inevitably take place because of the strength of the relationship. In the first, a retailer could be offering an assortment of products – say, some local postcards and a selection of cheap mementos – in a small seaside gift shop. The sales are mainly to tourists, but there is really little chance of a long series of purchase transactions although there is a possibility of persuading a customer to buy more than one item when they visit the shop. The emphasis here will be on the *merchandising* and *promotional* stimuli so that the single short-term transaction is maximized. At the other end of the scale is a grocery hypermarket, which would want its customers to come every week. But, of course, it is not so simple, relationship marketing should not be seen solely as the opposite of transaction marketing. For instance, the supplier of shop fixtures and fittings to an independent retailer might be involved in only a single transaction. However if the new retail shop is to be set up properly a deep interactive relationship has to develop, even if there is unlikely to be a further transaction for many years. By contrast, a series of regular low-value purchases of, say, a chocolate bar from a local convenience store is hardly going to involve the two parties in a deep meaningful relationship. That is probably out of all proportion to the benefits, neither party will feel much commitment to any strong relationship: it is enough for customer to know the store is there and open long hours when required.

Blois (1998) argues that

> The current enthusiasm for 'relationship marketing' brings with it a number of problems. In particular, unless a counter intuitive definition of a 'relationship' is used, it is impossible for firms not to have relationships ... what is important is that a firm should determine, given its particular circumstances, what types of relationships are appropriate with each of its customers (emphasis in the original).

Gummesson (1999) now suggests the term 'Total Relationship Marketing' (TRM) to define marketing 'directed to long-term win–win relationships with individual customers, where value is jointly created between the parties involved'. Both authors would accept that there is a range of relationship levels, and, of course, deep mutual relationships can be developed between committed parties. These are the real aim of relationship marketing programmes, but there are costs involved with the building of such relationships so investments are required before any real benefit is achieved.

Example

Gummesson (1999) cites the following example:

Hanna Andersson is a mail-order children's clothing business in Portland Oregon. One way they can build loyalty and reward customers is their Hannadown program. Quoting from the catalogue he tells of the personal message to customers: 'When your kids outgrow their Hanna clothes, send them back to me in good used condition, and I'll reserve you a credit for 20 per cent of the purchase price. That's a real head start for on your next order! Meanwhile we'll donate your clothes to kids in need, where they'll become favorites all over again'.

This is a really good programme offering both a financial benefit (money off next purchase) and an emotional one (donate to kids in need) for customers while the mail-order company gains repeat business and builds a data base of these customers.

Gordon (1994) suggested that 'Retailers are ready for *relationship marketing*. [They] are following the lead of catalogers and other mail-order marketers by adopting the relationship marketing strategies being used by these competitors' (emphasis in the original). Gordon was, of course, correct in understanding that the direct-mail activities of the mail-order houses, in both the USA and in Europe, had always been aimed at enhancing the relationship with customers in the hope of stimulating additional sales (see the Example above). But he was writing against the background of what he called the 'Field of Dreams' in US retailing. As he wrote:

> In the 1970's and 1980's when it came to store expansion, retailers believed that 'if we build it, they will come'. Building

> [of new retail outlets] was undertaken to the point of saturation, even though sales did not keep pace. Store space more than doubled in twenty years (from 8 sq. foot per capita to more than 18 sq. foot in the late 1980s). Retail sales in constant dollars fell from $190 per sq. foot to $160 per sq. foot. And shopping trips to [retail] malls fell from 12 hours per month to four (emphasis in the original).

These statistics provided sobering thoughts for the US retail industry, but there was also evidence of greater success for those stores who could identify and concentrate efforts on the small number of regular customers, both to retain them and stop them switching to alternative suppliers, and to encourage future transactions.

Example

Grönroos (1996) gives the following example of a Chinese rice merchant which was told to him while teaching in Bangkok:

In a village in ancient China there was a young rice merchant, Ming Hua. He was one of six rice merchants in that village. He was sitting in his store waiting for customers, but business was not good.

One day Ming Hua realised that he had to think more about the villagers and their needs and desires, and not only distribute rice to those who came into his store. He understood that he had to provide the villagers with more value and not only with the same as the other merchants offered them. He decided to develop a record of his customers' eating habits and ordering periods and to start to deliver rice to them.

To begin with Ming Hua started to walk around the village and knock on the doors of his customers' houses asking how many members were there in the household, how many bowls of rice they cooked on any given day and how big the rice jar of the household was. Then he offered every customer free home delivery and to replenish the rice jar of the household automatically at regular intervals.

For example, in one household of four persons, on average every person would consume two bowls of rice a day, and therefore the household would need eight bowls of rice every day. From his records Ming Hua could see that the rice jar of that particular household contained rice for 60 bowls or approximately one bag of rice, and that a full jar would last for 15 days. Consequently, he offered to deliver a bag of rice every 15 days to this house.

By establishing these records and developing these new services, Ming Hua managed to create more and deeper relationships with the villagers, first with his old customers, then with other villagers. Eventually he got more business to take care of and, therefore, had to employ more people, one to take care of the bookkeeping, one to sell over the counter in the store, and two to take care of deliveries. Ming Hua spent his time visiting villagers and handling the contacts with suppliers, a limited number of rice farmers whom he knew well. Meanwhile his business prospered.

This old story from China is a simple example of relationship marketing in practice. Of course it was more successful because the competitors did not respond, but there are three important lessons of relevance to any relationship marketer.

- *First* seek direct contact with customers
- *Second* get to know these customers well, their activities cycles, and anything that might help build a relationship with them
- *Third* develop a customer-orientated service system.

In some ways the first and second activities will be part of any good retail marketing programme. *Direct contact,*whether in store or over the Internet, has long been recognized as a positive incentive leading to a purchase. Of course this must be set against the low-cost self-service operations in most supermarkets and other similar outlets. This low level of personal contact is perhaps the reason for the difficulties these companies face when trying to create effective 'loyalty card' schemes. Getting to know customers and their activity cycles is also crucial if the marketing offer is to be relevant to the needs of all customers, but it can offer particular advantages if utilized effectively. The successful use of *personal sales consultants* in some major fashion stores, whereby the consultant establishes a personal relationship with high-spending, but time-poor, clients is now being copied elsewhere. The client leaves it to the trusted consultant to make selections. Sara Lauchlan, a consultant at the fashionable London store, The Cross, calls the practice 'body-bagging'. She claimed in a *Sunday Times* interview (2001), 'We fill a suitcase with clothes and send it to our customers anywhere in the world. They rely on us to know their size, and taste. Things rarely come back.' This is the extension into the third activity. This is where creative actions aimed at true relationship building can make a real difference.

It is not as easy as this, however, as Fournier says (Fournier, Dobscha and Mick 1998): 'Ironically, the very things that marketers are doing to build relationships with customers are often the things that are destroying those relationships.' He contrasts the suppliers' thirst for information, such as 'sales clerks hounding customers for information every time they buy a battery' and 'juggling the flood of invitations to participate in frequent buyer reward programs' and many other irritations. As he suggests, 'customers cope', they tolerate the intense pressure but don't delight in it. Perhaps retailers should remember that a good exchange, and in particular a good relationship, can be achieved only if there is commitment by *both* parties, as well as the reward of mutual added value to *both* supplier and customer. Remember the quote from O'Malley, Paterson and Evans (1997) given in the Introduction to this chapter, which stated that if a customer feels exploited by a supplier they can just walk away and shop elsewhere. It is perhaps easier to describe how *not* to build relationships than how to build them.

Building Relationships and Customer Relationship Marketing

Retailing is obviously a service-driven industry, and, of course, one of the objectives of marketing is to ensure satisfaction for customers. All readers of this book should already understand the role of service in creating high levels of satisfaction. The reason why a retailer might be interested in relationship marketing is based on two premises:

1 The quality of a relationship can enhance the *level of satisfaction* perceived by a customer

2 The greater the level of satisfaction then the longer a specific relationship will last, and there will be a *positive increase in the return* (in financial terms) from that relationship.

There is nothing wrong in trying to increase the levels of satisfaction, but retailers should be very careful when assuming that such an increase will necessarily lead to longer relationships, or that such relationships will automatically be the more profitable.

The first consideration should be the goal of *increased satisfaction*. Ravald and Grönroos (1996) argue that increasing the *value* of an exchange as perceived by customers is crucial to increasing satisfaction; more recently there has been much written on the subject of *value-based* marketing. In marketing terms value is the difference between the *benefits* received and the *sacrifices* made as perceived, and evaluated, by the customer. In considering this simple equation the benefits of a good relationship can be added to the other benefits received in a purchase. If they are seen as greater than the cost of entering that relationship then total *customer value* is increased. A good relationship will deliver increased benefits, but it will also involve costs for both the retailer and the customer.

Good relationships are really established during the interactions between a customer and a supplier. In retail terms this is most often the visit to the store, or virtual shopping location, but can also be during other contacts such as a telephone call to the retail organisation. It is crucial to recognize the role of each individual shopper, not only as a purchaser but as a definer of value so that benefits are created *with* the customer not *for* them. Therefore a retail salesperson taking the opportunity to cross-sell to a shopper they have just met is usually not creating customer value but is, rather, exploiting an opportunity presented by a customer contact.

Customer value can be created only when there is a fuller understanding of a particular customer or group of customers. It is wrong to assume that you know what the customer wants, and this is why organizations trying to develop relationships try to build data bases of existing and potential customers, the assumption being that the more that is known about a customer, the greater will be the opportunity to find ways of increasing value. Customer value can be created in a variety of ways. It could be that the benefits from the product can be improved by adding more features or making it more reliable. Retailers can easily try to *increase the value* of any service they offer – maybe home delivery or by ensuring that all salespeople are sufficiently trained and knowledgeable. Another value creator could be image, such as that reflected by the highly prized carrier bags from London department store Harrods. Value can also be increased through a reduction in the costs of any interaction;

this can be measured as financial cost but could just as easily be a function of time, convenience and effort. By using well-chosen locations, or offering a 'no-quibble' returns policy customers will benefit, but as stated above it is crucial that the activities offered do really reflect the things that are important to the chosen target group of shoppers.

Example

Kotler and Armstrong (2001) use the example of McDonald's to explore how value is created by activities both at the retail premises and elsewhere in the delivery network. They say:

'People do not swarm to the world's 24,500 McDonald's restaurants only because they love the chain's hamburgers. In fact, according to one national survey, consumers rank McDonald's behind Burger King and Wendy's in taste preference. Still, McDonald's commands over a 16 per cent share of the nation's fast food business, and over 40 per cent of the burger segment. Consumers flock to McDonald's *system*, not just its food products. Throughout the world, McDonald's finely tuned system delivers a high standard of what the company calls QSCV – quality, service, cleanliness, and *value*' (emphasis in the original).

Of course the key question is: 'How does a retailer find out what is important in terms of customer value, and what is not required'. The obvious answer is to undertake continuous market research. The focus in *customer relationship management (CRM)* has been on building an effective data base with details of previous purchasers and then utilize this to find ways of delivering *value*. With some organizations the data base has become an end in itself, and all too often the data are driven by what is available, such as details of age and sex. It is too rarely understood that the purpose of a data base is to try to enhance *value*. Of course, there is a role for data-gathering and information-processing. IT systems can help in this respect. However the recent increase in consultancy companies offering CRM programmes is not necessarily helpful. It is not a short-cut to building strong relationships. In fact Dr Paul Fifield, formerly senior examiner at the Chartered Institute of Marketing and a consultant himself, has likened the adoption of CRM to the hopes of gullible patients buying old patent cure-all remedies such as snake-oil. He is very critical of what he describes as 'well-intentioned meddling with the customer data-base', and in some cases that is all a CRM programme offers. IT solutions are appropriate only when it is necessary to manage large quantities of data, and these solutions must be both customer-focused and need-driven. Problems often arise when the activities of the data gatherers goes too far so that the customers feel they are being asked for irrelevant and unnecessary information – or, more seriously, if they perceive an invasion of their privacy.

Relationships develop because the parties involved wish to *co-operate* with each other. This could be because both share a set of beliefs, a common ideology such as Body Shop where both the organization and the majority of its customers value the ideals regarding natural resources and an abhorrence of unnecessary animal cruelty. Relationships can also come about because of the recognition of particular, calculated advantages (often financial) that could accrue by the commitment to a specific partner, and the fact that such benefits are not otherwise available. Maybe this could be a credit arrangement with a local supplier whereby the customer gains by not requiring cash for every visit, and the retailer gets regular sales. These two categories of relationships are not exclusive, both types of benefits could be present at the same time. The requirement for every long-term relationship, however, is that the two parties *commit themselves to each other*, usually forgoing alternative offerings, and that they each trust the other to continue to provide the mutually beneficial added value required.

In the earlier example of Grönroos' rice trader, if one of the regular customers found a special offer at another merchant and bought a sack of rice at a discount price, what effect might that type of 'opportunistic' behaviour have on the relationship with the regular supplier? Alternatively if one week the merchant miscalculated and was unable to deliver the regular order to a customer who was just coming to the end of the previous supply (a failure of a Just-in-Time or JIT delivery). How might the customer view such a failure? Morgan and Hunt (1994) have explored the requirements of both commitment and trust as mediating factors in the development of strong relationships and found each to be important, as well as the fact that trust is crucial for commitment to fully develop. Retailers wishing to build strong partnerships must interpret these issues, and they usually require:

- Mutual benefits
- Two-way communication
- Shared information
- Adaptability
- Respect for the other party.

Too, Souchon and Thirkell (2000) tested the Morgan and Hunt theory in a retail setting, albeit with a small sample of 34 clothing stores in New Zealand. They found positive correlations between the perception of customers as to the relationship efforts of a store and the measures of both trust and commitment. Interestingly they found that this perception was higher in smaller stores. They concluded that 'This may suggest that, in the eyes of clothing store customers, relationship marketing activities are the responsibility of, and undertaken by, individual staff members as opposed to being a store wide directive from store management'. While not proven outside of this small-scale research it is certainly something that retailers should consider, and maybe direct activities to seek to retain those staff who excel at building relationships with customers. Reynolds and Beatty (1999) explain this in terms of the fact that in smaller stores there is more opportunity for a given customer to interact with the *same* salesperson over repeated sales encounters. If the loyalty is focused on the salesperson rather than the store, then the risk is that when the salesperson changes the customer will also move on.

Customer Retention in a Retail Context

Reichheld (1996) said: 'It's not how satisfied you keep your customers; It's how many satisfied customers you keep'. In this one-liner he was able to encapsulate the dilemma facing retailers. Most retailers rely on a large number of shoppers visiting their stores every week. Depending on the category of merchandise stocked, these visits could range from once a week to, maybe, only once a year for regular customers. It is also important that activities do not deter the infrequent shopper, although the more regular purchasers will be the focus of relationship strategies.

There is a paradox that can impinge on all retailers if they are not aware of it. The problem comes because over a single sales episode it is probable that a casual, irregular shopper could offer a higher profit margin than a regular customer because of the presence of the relationship costs associated with the latter purchaser. These costs could be long-term discounts, or free credit, or some other repeat buying incentive. However, over the buying lifetime it will be the regular customer who is the most valuable. The innovative US retailer Stew Leonard says that whenever he sees a 'sulking' customer he also sees the possible loss of $50 000. That is because the average spend in his supermarket is $100 per week. Multiply that by the 10 years (500 weeks) that he reckons to retain a customer and we have $50 000. It will be even more if an unhappy customer tells a number of friends, and they also change stores.

When deciding upon activities that can lead to high levels of customer retention and repeat purchasing, there is a significant difference between those that are possible within a *remote* interaction, and those suitable in the *personal-contact* environment of a physical store. The difference comes about because the remote contacts, such as the Internet or a telephone contact (also used to support mail-order retail), require a shopper to log on – or give their name/account number at the start of a transaction. The technology is such that a full data base record of the customer, their buying habits, previous transactions and other relevant information can immediately be available to the retailer. This can be used to adapt any future offer to meet the specific, individual needs of that customer. In a personal contact, in-store location such recognition depends upon the salesperson. On all too many occasions the customer identification does not occur until the end of a transaction when some opportunities for customizing and enhancing a new offer have already been lost. This is why the role of a salesperson is a critical factor in a small-store context, and cannot easily be replicated in a larger outlet. However there are still opportunities to build repeat business even at this late stage, as promotional offers regarding future purchases can be awarded at the conclusion of a purchase. The ASDA supermarket prints customized coupons for their shoppers at the checkout as one attempt to stimulate customers to return again.

Of course, the fact that a customer has already revisited the store is a form of retention, even if there is no recognition of the past transactions until the end of the current purchase event. As has already been said, the first retail marketing task is to get a customer to *visit*, or in the drive for retention to *revisit* the outlet or site, the second is to persuade them to make a *purchase* while in the store. The fact that a shopper actually revisits a store does not necessarily mean that a deep meaningful relationship exists, nor does it mean that the customer is exclusively loyal to that particular retailer. It could just be that there are some good, calculated financial reasons why a repeat visit takes place. Most likely this will be to do with the perception of the store when compared to any available competing offers in the same category. Thus retention could be based on any of the factors within the retail marketing mix such as location of store, its image/reputation, the design and the atmosphere of the outlet, the range, assortment and quality offered, the competitive pricing of products, specific promotions, or the level of service given. Thus modifying the conclusions of Chapter 1, retention is possible if a retailer continues to make an *acceptable* and *affordable* combination of goods and services *available* to given customers at the *right* time and in the *right* place. Retailers should be aware that some retention created in this way leads to a form of *spurious* loyalty (Dick and Basu 1994) based only on current deals or special offers. This type of retention is at best short term, lasting just until a better offer is available elsewhere.

Retail marketing should ensure that as much as possible is done to ensure retention by enhancing the marketing effort by specific activities that increase the reasons a customer might be enticed to return. Activities designed to affect *patronage behaviour* can include special shopping nights for account-card holders, appropriate, carefully selected promotional offers communicated via direct mail to previous purchasers, special terms or products reserved for particular customers and many other creative deals. This type of activity is designed to reward a customer for *past patronage* by offering positive inducements to buy again in the future. This is retention through the *marketing offering*. Such schemes are best called 'customer reward programmes', and any resulting retention or repeat purchase behaviour should not be confused with real exclusive loyalty.

From the customers' point of view, the attractiveness of a scheme will be judged on four dimensions.

1 The *cash value* of the reward as a percentage of the required spending. For instance the supermarket group J Sainsbury has REWARD cards that offer a nominal 1 per cent, although this is rounded down due to points being awarded for every *full* pound spent.

2 The *choice and value* of any reward. Is cash sufficient? J Sainsbury give £2.50 for each 500 reward points, but also negotiate other deals worth double this if the reward voucher is used in a number of non-competing retail outlets such as restaurants and clothing stores. However the value of rewards earned does not increase with the length of the relationship nor additional spending by customers over time, but it is reset to a zero base every time a reward is claimed.

3 The perceived likelihood of *achieving a reward*. In the Sainsbury case a spend of £250+ is needed for each voucher, say about one month's total grocery shopping for a family; in some other schemes it can take much longer to 'earn' the benefits.

4 Finally the *ease of use* of the scheme. Modern technology using swipe cards has made retail schemes much easier than the collection of tokens which was a feature of many earlier schemes. However, there are many older people who still remember their family Co-operative store 'dividend number' which was learned by heart a generation ago, as this had to be quoted in order to benefit from one of the original reward schemes run by the various Co-op shops in the past.

Some customers are retained just because they are not concerned enough, or too lazy, to change suppliers. This suggests that there is a 'zone of tolerance' with some customers who remain as regular customers although not particularly satisfied. Gould (1995) writes: 'My Bank has successfully retained me despite its worst efforts to alienate me, however I would not count myself a loyal customer.' Jones and Sasser (1995) go further in describing the category of 'Hostages', who remain loyal (are retained) because of the fact that there are just no possible alternative suppliers. They suggest that this group may be *trapped*, but are likely to take every opportunity to complain and ask for special service and the resulting effect on the morale of employees, and the negative impact on unit costs, can be dramatic. Perhaps this type of buyer is not required. There is nothing wrong in retailers devising a strategy that actually deters those customers who are not wanted, provided this can be achieved without offending those who are to be welcomed.

Retention is also present when a customer feels a deep emotional relationship with a retail supplier. This is the focus of the best loyalty schemes offered by retailers. O'Brien and Jones (1995) suggest that

> Some of the best examples of building customer loyalty can be found in traditional small businesses. For many years, successful neighborhood merchants and restauranteurs have understood intuitively the broader strategic purpose behind an effective rewards program. Such business people make it a point to get to know their best customers personally and often reward them with special services and attention – notifying them when sought after merchandise arrives, for example, or giving them a free drink or special dessert. They know that delivering increased value to profitable customers turns them into loyal customers; and that loyal customers become even more profitable over time.

The problem is that as companies increase in both size and complexity this personal contact is lost, and along with it the ability to decide which rewards are really valued by key customers. Gould talks about 'exceeding customer expectations' but not exceeding them on *every* dimension. He suggests the critical areas of greatest importance to customers are usually to be found in the areas of *value*, *service* and *dealing with complaints*. The warning from O'Brien and Jones is that not all customers are the same, both in the things they value and in their importance to the supplier's business. The usual practice of large companies is to offer equivalent rewards to all customers in the hope of retaining them. As O'Brien and Jones say: 'Offering average value to everyone wastes resources in *over-satisfying* less profitable customers while *under-satisfying* the more valuable ones' (emphasis in the original). Such programmes rarely achieve their objectives.

The best schemes offer *differential benefits* to both retailer and buyer that rise over time. Therefore the rewards to an individual customer should increase as the level of patronage and the length of the relationship extends. Over the same time the value and importance of that customer to the retailer, and the retailer's profit, should also be developing. Of course these increased benefits will of themselves build a barrier to either party leaving the relationship. This type of long-term relationship is often described in terms of loyalty, but if it is based solely on financial benefits it will not offer the many extra dimensions that can be enjoyed when a more complete emotional loyalty develops.

What is Loyalty?

Loyalty has been described as the 'Holy Grail' of retailing. However it is important that retailers understand that loyalty cannot be bought – *committed loyalty* has a high degree of mutual respect, and that has to be earned. It is when attempting to define loyalty that some difficulties with the concept become apparent. 'Used loosely, as it usually is, the term *'loyalty'* conjures up various notions of affection, fidelity or commitment' (McGoldrick and Andre 1997, emphasis in the original). In particular there is an ongoing debate as to whether loyalty is best viewed in a direct *behavioural* context as repeat purchase, or an *attitudinal* context so that it leads to favourable opinions and cognition. These are not exclusive positions, and it should be apparent that loyalty could be seen as a composite of both. Dick and Basu (1994) put the two together in a matrix which can be compared to the work of Jones and Sasser (1995) as shown in Chapter 4 (Figure 4.1). Both matrices are shown in Figure 12.1.

Jones and Sasser (1995)

	LOYAL	DISLOYAL
SATISFIED	Advocates	Mercenaries
DISSATISFIED	Hostages	Terrorists

Dick and Basu (1994)

		Repeat patronage HIGH	Repeat patronage LOW
Relative attitude	HIGH	Loyalty	Latent loyalty
Relative attitude	LOW	Spurious loyalty	No loyalty

Figure 12.1 Loyalty matrixes
Sources: Jones and Sasser (1995); Dick and Basu (1994).

Primary measures of behaviour, such as recency and frequency of store visit, and 'level of spend' per visit, are increasingly being used to measure loyalty. *Repeat purchase intervals* and *spend* are probably the most quantifiable and measurable dimensions of behaviour, but such criteria cannot offer any insight into the underlying reasons that affect store choice, store visit or purchase decisions. They cannot take into account the *psychological factors* driving the behaviour, nor do they give any indication as to the *level of satisfaction* felt by a customer. Apparently loyal behaviour, such as regular repeat purchase, might indicate deep emotional feelings towards a particular supplier, but, alternatively it could be the result of a convenient habit. The measures already discussed do not give any indication about the importance of a particular retailer in the total purchases of an individual customer in a product category. In the past Marks & Spencer, the UK's favourite supplier of underwear, would have expected that a very large proportion of a customer's purchases in this category would be the St Michael brand. In the USA this is described as 'share of closet', or as adapted by restaurant chain, Taco Bell, 'share of stomach'. This is a measure of the importance to a particular customer and is a measure of loyalty that goes beyond the usual primary ones above. Therefore behavioural measures by themselves are insufficient as an indication of loyalty.

Example: The Double Jeopardy Effect

An interesting phenomenon that has been researched by Professor Ehrenberg of the London Business School is called 'double jeopardy'.

This research indicates that retailers with smaller market shares suffer in two ways cumulating in double jeopardy. In a retail context this could be:

- First a retailer with a smaller market share will obviously have fewer customers.
- Second (the double jeopardy) those customers often chose to visit less often (less loyalty).
- And it is also possible that they spend less per visit.

This is not always the case with some strongly focused niche operators but might well be. Compare a major grocery supermarket, say Tesco, and a local convenience store. It might be that a regular weekly visit is made to Tesco resulting in an average spend of £50–£100. The occasional visit to the convenience outlet to buy some forgotten product will be only a few pounds at most.

Dowling and Uncles (1997) produced the representation of the double jeopardy effect shown in Figure 12.2.

Strong, emotional loyalty is a positive attitude that is likely to result from a feeling of attachment to or affection for the people, products or services of a specific retailer. Of course, such feelings could lead to strong repeat purchase behaviour, but there could, in some circumstances, be

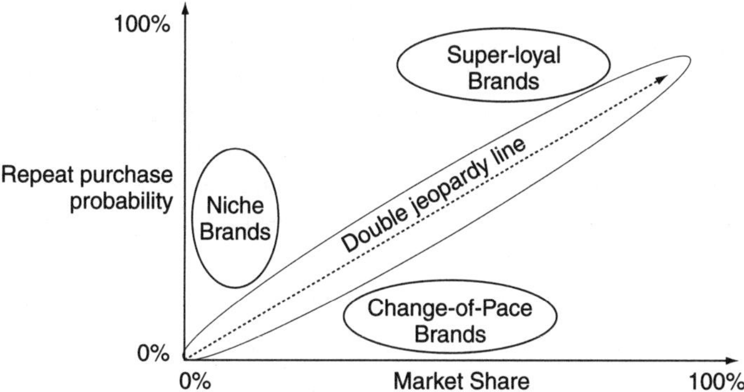

Figure 12.2 Double jeopardy and brand loyalty
Source: Dowling and Uncles (1997: 75).

understandable reasons why this is not always realized. Perhaps a customer feels a strong attachment for a store offering designer clothes, but the regular price of such garments might be well above what can be afforded. However at the annual sale there could be a few bargains available, and that might be an opportunity to actually purchase an item. There could, therefore, be strong emotional loyalty but very little benefit to the store from any regular purchasing by the customer. Nevertheless the customer could demonstrate loyalty by the pleasure taken in wearing the clothes and by word-of-mouth recommendations directed at other potential customers who might purchase more regularly. Such endorsements are extremely important, but of course they are even more valuable if the referral comes from a customer who is buying on a more regular basis. Adapting a comment by Day (1969), we would suggest that 'in order to be truly loyal, the consumer must hold a favourable attitude towards the brand [store], in addition to repeatedly purchasing [from] it'.

There is some evidence from many industries that indicate that *exclusive* loyalty rarely exists. Dowling and Uncles (1997) suggest that customers are likely to have a repertoire of two or three brands (suppliers) within any category from which they regularly buy – i.e. *polygamous loyalty*. When considering loyalty schemes it is necessary to decide whether the objectives are to build a bigger share of a consumer's *total purchases* or to develop a stronger *emotional bonding* with a customer that could also lead onto other advantages.

Customer Loyalty Schemes: Do They Really Work?

There is a regrettable tendency in some marketing today to follow the initiatives of competitors rather than thinking out suitable, creative and effective strategies for your own organization – 'If you see a good idea – copy it!' However as some UK supermarkets have found, loyalty card schemes are not always the answer to their problems. Certainly Tesco still have their Club Card, but that was the first scheme launched, J Sainsbury retain their Reward scheme, but Asda experimented and did not follow, and Safeway actually ended their ABC card in 2000 to concentrate on other marketing initiatives. There is no doubt that the Tesco Club Card is successful, and it does help create a great deal of valuable customer information as well as providing a basis for targeted offers. But such benefits do not come without *costs* and every organization has to evaluate the returns from such schemes. According to Dowling and Uncles (1997) the assumptions made by companies undertaking loyalty programmes are:

1 Suppliers who are able to form 'close' relationships with their customers tend to have '*better*' (more loyal) *customers*.

2 These 'loyal' customers are more *profitable* to a supplier (greater spend, lower servicing costs, less price-sensitive favourable recommendations).

3 It costs more to entice a new customer to do business with a company, than to get an *existing one to buy again*.

Thus gaining and maintaining loyalty is a real source of *sustainable competitive advantage*. Further the *two-way flow* of information made possible within a close relationship will help to ensure that future offers are relevant to customers and hence those customers are more likely to be retained. These assumptions are then combined with some widely held beliefs about loyalty. However, retailers should carefully evaluate such beliefs before designing any programmes. They will need to assess whether there are any customers who really want a close, involving relationship with them. Then, even if close involvement exists, it is arguable if many customers will actually be exclusively loyal to a single retailer. It is also crucial to decide whether the hard-core loyals are more profitable because they are also heavy and frequent buyers, and if it is possible to create and reinforce that loyalty. There is no doubt that through the use of data bases and other IT, marketers can establish *customized communication* with customers, but does this really increase the bonds?

The study of research in a number of markets, not just retail, by Dowling and Uncles (1997) suggests that the beliefs held by suppliers about their customers are at best too general, and at worst actually wrong in many markets. It is important that retailers understand issues such as how involved a customer might wish to get before embarking on a generic loyalty scheme. If there is scope for strong emotional links to be developed then one type of programme might be appropriate, especially if it focuses on developing an emotional closeness. In other cases a simple scheme rewarding past purchases, creating value in an appropriate manner and encouraging future buying is probably the best.

As O'Malley (1998) says 'loyalty' programmes are developed for a variety of reasons, including:

- To *reward* loyal customers
- To generate *information*
- To manipulate consumer *behaviour*
- As a *defensive measure* to combat competing schemes.

Some of these objectives are more difficult to achieve than others. For instance, there is a great deal of evidence to suggest that loyalty schemes do very little to change behaviour. However they often give additional value to specific customers, thus rewarding them for past patronage. Data-gathering is also problematic, both because of the nature of the sample in the scheme, and the cost/type of data available as an output. Many schemes actually produce *too much* data – so much so that it is impossible to use it as a basis of useful marketing information. So, while the opportunities for data collection are obviously present, and some of the data are very relevant for future decision making, the scope of the data produced must be focused on the *marketing needs* of the organization and not on the collection of data for their own sake. It has been reported that Tesco spent over £10 million in initial data-gathering for their loyalty scheme, and then a great deal of management time assessing what was actually useful. The company is now able to use some of the data to identify changes in individual purchasing behaviour, and thus to target customized offers to individual club card members. However the question has still to be asked if these results are actually cost-effective. Also for a smaller company the investment necessary may simply be too high to even contemplate.

There is no doubt that some retailers do view schemes as a defensive promotion, this is probably the reason for J Sainsbury continuing with their REWARD scheme. Most organizations that operate loyalty schemes do so as one part of the marketing effort – that is, in addition to, not instead of, all other marketing activity. There are some indications that customers can become loyal not to the supplier but to the *loyalty scheme itself*, so that if the scheme changes then previous behaviour regarding the supplier will not necessarily continue. In many markets customers shop around for the best deal, and if that happens to involve a loyalty scheme then its value to the customer will be assessed and will be included in any evaluation. But in trying to decide if loyalty schemes really work it is first necessary to be very clear as to the objectives of any specific scheme.

Conclusions

Loyal customers arc important to most retailers, although there are some (e.g. a tourist gift shop) which still must rely on stimulus–response styles of marketing. This is because of the nature of their offering and the fact that their customers are unlikely to return to buy. Building relationships and customer loyalty is a *strategic decision* for a retailer. If it is decided that it is appropriate then it should be seen as a perpetual striving for even better relationships and even greater loyalty. *Spurious loyalty*, based on the bribery of an unmatchable promotional deal, should not be confused with deeper commitment towards a supplier. But 'loyalty' is an elusive target, and building and sustaining loyalty an imprecise art. Many of the schemes set up in the 1990s had the goal of establishing a higher level of customer retention in profitable segments by providing increased levels of satisfaction and value to certain customers.

The best schemes recognize that every customer differs, both in the things that they perceive as valuable and in the stage of relationship development they have reached. It is necessary to accommodate this, and to offer benefits that change and increase as the relationship develops. Understanding the dimensions and the evolution of loyalty can help to make the creation of suitable schemes a bit easier. Every loyalty initiative should be considered as just one part of an overall targeted marketing programme. It must therefore be consistent with other activities, and it can both support and be supported by them.

There are no clearly defined prescriptions for developing and increasing loyalty, and in fact there can be a number of different objectives for any loyalty programme. These range from rewarding past patronage, retention of key customers for the future, and enabling a retailer to compete in the most effective way. It is crucial that the objectives of any marketing activity are considered first, before adopting a specific scheme or buying into an expensive programme, such as CRM, which might not be suitable for the retailer or their chosen area of business.

References and Further Reading

Blois, K. (1998) Don't All Firms Have Relationships?, *Journal of Business & Industrial Marketing*, 13, 3, 256–70.

Day, G.S. (1969) A Two Dimensional Concept of Brand Loyalty, *Journal of Advertising Research*, 9, September, 29–35.

Dick, A.S. and Basu, K. (1994) Customer Loyalty, Towards an Integrated Framework, *Journal of the Academy of Marketing*, 22, 2, 99–113.

Dowling, G.R. and Uncles, M. (1997) Do Customer Loyalty Programmes Really Work? *Sloan Management Review*, Summer, 71–82.

Drucker, P. (1968) *The Practice of Management*, Pan Books, London.

Ehrenberg, A.S.C. and Barwise, T.P. (1990) Double Jeopardy Revisited, *Journal of Marketing*, July.

Fifield, P. (1999) Snake Oil <Viewpoint 4 @ www.fifield.co.uk.>.

Fournier, S., Dobscha, S. and Mick, D.G. (1998) Preventing the Premature Death of Relationship Marketing, *Harvard Business Review*, January–February.

Goldscher, S. (1998) Count the Ways to Loyalty, *Candy Industry*, Northbrook Ill, September.

Gordon, H. (1994) Retailers are Ready for Relationship Marketing, *Direct Marketing*, 56, 9, 38–43.

Gould, G. (1995), Why it is Customer Loyalty that Counts (and How to Measure It), *Managing Services Quality*, 5, 1, 15–19.

Grönroos, C. (1996) Relationship Marketing: Strategic and Tactical Implications, *Management Decisions*, 34, 3, 5–14.

Gummesson, E. (1997) Relationship Marketing as a Paradigm Shift, *Management Decisions*, 35, 4, 267–72.

Gummesson, E. (1999) *Total Relationship Marketing*, Butterworth-Heinemann, Oxford.

Hooley, G., Saunders, J. and Piercy, N. (1998) *Marketing Strategy and Competitive Positioning*, Prentice-Hall London.

Jones, T.O. and Sasser, W.E. (1995) Why Satisfied Customers Defect, *Harvard Business Review*, November–December, 88–99.

Kotler, P. and Armstrong, G. (2001) *Principles of Marketing*, 9th edn, Prentice-Hall International Inc., Englewood Cliffs, NJ.

Kirwan-Taylor, H. (2001) Soft Sell, *Sunday Times STYLE*, 25 February.

McGoldrick, P.J. and Andre, E. (1997) Consumer Misbehaviour: Promiscuity or Loyalty in Grocery Shopping, *Journal of Retailing and Consumer Service*, 4, 2, 73–81.

Morgan, R.M and Hunt, S.B. (1994) The Commitment – Trust Theory of Relationship Marketing, *Journal of Marketing*, 58, 3, 20–38.

O'Brien, L. and Jones, C. (1995) Do Rewards Really Create Loyalty?, *Harvard Business Review*, May–June, 75–82.

O'Malley, L., Paterson, M. and Evans, M. (1997) Intimacy or Intrusion?: The Privacy Debate in Relationship Marketing in Consumer Markets, *European Journal of Marketing Management*, *13 (6)*.

O'Malley, L. (1998) Can Loyalty Schemes Really Build Loyalty?, *Marketing Intelligence & Planning*, 16, 1, 47–55.

Ravald, A. and Grönroos C (1996) The Value Concept and Relationship Marketing, *European Journal of Marketing*, 30, 2, 19–30.

Reichheld, F. (1996) *The Loyalty Effect*, Harvard Business School Press, Boston, MA.

Reynolds, K.E. and Beatty, S.E. (1999) Customer Benefits and Company Consequences of Customer–Salesperson Relationships in Retailing, *Journal of Retailing*, 75, 1, 11–31.

Too, L., Souchon, A. and Thirkell, P. (2000) Relationship Marketing and Customer Loyalty in a Retail Setting, *The Research Paper Series*, Aston University, RP 0015.

Customer Care and Handling Complaints

CHAPTER 13

This chapter:

- Reviews ways of dealing with customer dissatisfaction
- Defines a complaints' handling procedure
- Shows how communication from customers may be encouraged

Customer Care and Handling Complaints

Introduction

There should be no doubting the fact that a retailer cannot survive in business without customers. The well-documented problems of many Internet *retailers* are the result of not gaining customers fast enough at the start of their trading. However the reason why Marks & Spencer have closed their European stores, and C&A its UK outlets, is because neither store was able to make a profit in these areas. The most obvious cause was that not enough customers were visiting these stores in spite of many years of trading in the locations. These problems can be put down to *changing tastes* and the *dynamics* of the retail marketplace. Chapter 12 looked at building a customer base and, if possible, increasing the loyalty of customers. This is a crucial role of marketing and the focus of most attention. But shopping is a very personal activity; every individual has their own requirements, and every shopping experience relies on some form of *interaction* between the shopper and the retail supplier. There are many millions of such encounters every year and, as Jan Carlzon (1987) suggests, these 'moments of truth' determine the success or failure of a supplier.

With so many encounters, and the fact that in a service environment the interaction between customer and retailer could be variable dependent upon both customers' requirements and retail staff actions, it should not be surprising that sometimes things go wrong and customers are not satisfied. In this event, the customer has three choices:

- *First* they could forget the problems and *forgive the store*, so carrying on as though no problem occurred. This is very unlikely.
- *Second* they could just decide *never to visit that store again*, taking their custom elsewhere but not making a formal complaint regarding the

problems. This happens, and on many more occasions than is recognized by some retailers.

- ► *Third* the customer can *complain* to the store and hope to get some compensation for the problem, while postponing any decision regarding future shopping until the complaint has been heard.

If the second choice is the one made by a customer, then the store has lost him or her. If customer management is based on the 'leaky bucket' theory, then it will be the role of marketing to continually top up the 'bucket' of customers by creating new shoppers to replace those being lost through the 'holes in the bucket'. This is a difficult task, made much worse if customer defections are due to poor merchandise, poor service, or other fundamental problems with the store. It is generally believed that a dissatisfied customer will tell at least another 12 people, maybe more, about a bad experience. This 'word-of-mouth' communication is very powerful, and therefore a dissatisfied shopper could influence many others to abandon a particular store.

In the first two of the above choices the customer does not communicate with the retailer regarding the problems. Studies suggest that nine out every 10 customers do not complain to the supplier about problems. Stores therefore have no direct data that could indicate that there is any type of problem. They might have other data, store-visit data, store-purchase data, or image and attitude data from various market research studies. Stores sometimes place too great an emphasis on shoppers' panels, and even mystery shopper research to identify where things might be going wrong – but, as with all research, there are many benefits but some real blind spots. Such data rarely have the *sensitivity* to detect a small problem. However if the problems are left without any corrective action they could well grow into major problems, threatening the whole future of the store.

The real need is to encourage a *dialogue* with all shoppers, not just those in the sample selected by the research agency, and to try to make it easy for everyone to communicate with a store about both the good and the bad aspects of the operation. In practice, many more such communications will come from dissatisfied customers than from satisfied ones. Of course there is a risk that any information gathered in an unstructured and random way will be heavily biased, and could be received in quantities that make the processing of such communications difficult. It is not market research but there will be issues highlighted by such informal contacts that could form the basis for future market research, so that a more balanced view can be formed about a specific matter. The quantity of data should not deter such an initiative, in fact the more customers who can be encouraged to enter into a dialogue, the stronger the relationship that will develop between them and the store.

Some of the issues discovered will be general ones, and very soon a pattern will emerge indicating areas of concern. These will usually require more detailed study and appropriate corrective action. Other issues will be specific to a particular customer and a particular shopping experience. Such complaints will be received even if no procedures are in place to encourage communications from customers. Every service organization understands that mistakes will occur from time to time. It is inevitable where variable, personal interactions are involved. It is also possible in other retailing formats, for instance an Internet order might fail to be delivered owing to some problem of the support staff or back-up systems. Whatever the specific cause, the effect on the customer will be acute. Complaints must be handled both to 'recover' the customer's goodwill, and future custom, and to correct any underlying problem before it can recur.

This chapter will consider both the benefits of encouraging communication from customers, and the specific role of handling complaints and taking the necessary corrective action in a retail setting.

Learning from Losing a Customer

Frederick Reichheld (1996) suggested that:

> On average corporations lose half their customers every five years. This fact shocks most people. It shocks the CEOs, most of whom have little insight into the causes of the customer exodus, let alone the cures because they do not measure customer defections, make little effort to prevent them, and fail to use defections as a guide to improvements.

The statistic of 50 per cent loss every five years might seem dramatic, but it is based on only 10 per cent per year, a relatively small figure. Nevertheless over an extended period the impact can easily be recognized. The task of good retail marketing is to identify the 'defecting' lost customers and find out why they no longer shop at a particular store. There is a great deal of valuable information available from these customers and they are often only too happy to tell why they have changed suppliers. If a retailer has both the willingness to *listen* and the ability to *react*, then it will be able to modify its operations, make appropriate changes and establish a marketing mix for the store that is more acceptable for the future. Such changes must be made in the full understanding of the continuing needs of existing customers, it would be foolish to change solely to satisfy those who have defected. However, it is usually possible to make a few small but significant changes to satisfy the defectors, and yet not alienate those who remain loyal.

In some cases the data base held by a retailer will include the names and addresses of customers, both current and lapsed, and this can be used to develop a research population for the study of customer defections. However in many instances the data do not exist and other ways have to be found in order to communicate with lost customers, and to learn from their experiences. But it is more than the lack of a suitable data base that precludes some retailers investigating defections, Reichheld (1996) suggests seven principal reasons:

1 Many companies aren't really alarmed by customer defections – or they are alarmed *too late*.

2 It is unpleasant to study *failure* too closely, and in some companies trying to analyse failure can even be hazardous to careers.

3 Customer defection is often hard to *define*.

4 Sometimes '*customer*' itself is a hard thing to define, at least the kind of customer worth holding on to.

5 It is extremely hard to uncover the real *root causes* of a customer defection and extract the appropriate lessons.

6 Getting the right people in an organization to *learn lessons* and then *act on them* is a challenge.

7 It is difficult to conceptualize and set up the mechanisms that turn the analysis of customer defections into an *on-going strategic process*.

Many of these reasons are *cultural*, they imply that retailers might not wish to learn from the experiences of dissatisfied customers, but in an open organization, committed to learning and possessing a market orientation, these restrictions should not apply. There is a 'blame culture' in some organizations – if things are going wrong, it must be somebody's fault – but marketers should strive inside their company to achieve a different attitude. Unless this is achieved marketers will be seen as a protagonist by other retail managers, and the co-operation that is so necessary to achieving marketing objectives will not exist.

In fact, marketing should not automatically assume that it is the only function that can bring information into a company regarding customer problems. As Reichheld (1996) points out, in the US credit card bank MBNA every executive has to take a turn to listen in on calls to the customer service department, even taking some calls themselves. The lessons are far-reaching, as no manager is able to isolate themselves from the role of learning from dissatisfied customers. Nevertheless marketing does have an important role in ensuring that this learning actually takes place. As with most areas of business, *prevention* is far better than cure. If problems can be identified before they become too large, then actions can be taken while there is still time to avoid worse problems and maybe lose more customers for good.

It is very beneficial to establish close co-operation between complaints/ customer service departments and marketing. In some cases, the two departments can be directly linked, and the communications with dissatisfied shoppers that can result are of importance to all the future decisions regarding the marketing mix. It can be a good practice to include an allocation for *customer compensation payments* within the marketing budget. This is not because compensation is a payment for past mistakes but because it can be seen as a promotional investment in regaining a customer for the future. The difference in the attitude to such payments makes the investment a positive rather than a negative issue.

Communicating with Unhappy Customers

All efforts to communicate with 'lost' or dissatisfied customers about the reasons for defecting should be centred on the marketing department. If there is no data base then efforts should be made to construct one, or to identify a sample of the population from whom relevant data can be obtained. Alternatively there could be a number of initiatives that are designed to encourage those customers to communicate directly back to the company. At the simplest is the use of regular *in-store surveys*, or maybe putting *customer comment cards* in a prominent place with an in-store or a free-post return. If these are accompanied by a short letter from the managing director, and seem to be routed back to him, a reasonable response can be achieved. Otherwise a *free-phone telephone hot-line* or an *interactive Web site* could be used. Of course there are 'great' Web sites and the rest, if a site is to be used it must be designed to invite comments and not be predominantly promotional with a small insignificant icon for comments. The more inviting the site, or more user-friendly the process, then the greater thc chance of a response from a larger number of customers, and this should be translated into better learning regarding shopper expectations and frustrations. It has been suggested by researchers that more than 90 per cent of unhappy customers actually do not complain.

It is, however, as well to avoid what is the downside of some phone-based communication systems. You perhaps know how the automatic answering system works – dial the number (it could even be a premium-rate number) then a recorded message tells that all customer service operatives are busy, but your call is very important and therefore please don't hang up, you will be answered shortly. Karr (Karr and Blohowiak 1997) also describes this 'mind-numbing' experience, but his sequence focuses on the options available. For instance: 'push one if you want to hold forever; push two if you'd like us to transfer you to another busy extension; push three to speak to someone who has totally no idea what you're talking about.' However the sequence goes, the result is invariably annoyance so that when you finally get through to a live service representative there is an emotional need to yell to relieve the frustration rather than describing the original problem and asking for help in resolving it. Robert Townsend (1971) in his classic, and irreverent text *'Up the Organisation'* gave the good advice

> call yourself up – when away on a business trip or vacation, pretend you're a customer. Telephone some part of your organisation and ask for help. You'll run into some real horror stories. Don't blow up and ask for name, rank, and serial number – you're trying to correct not punish ... but you'll see what indignities have been built into your organisation's defences.

It is easy to make fun of the situations that exist, and to believe that no similar problems would occur if the organization were well run, but unhappily these examples are far from isolated events.

When a customer is in contact with an organization it will usually be because they are in need of help to correct a problem, and/or they genuinely care about the organization. When it was stated above that any communications process must be *user-friendly*, this is to ensure that:

1 The situation is not made worse because of a *complex complaints procedure*

2 The customer is encouraged to communicate, even with regard to small issues because they know that their comments will be taken *seriously* and treated as *important*.

To help achieve these objectives a retailer should ensure that any 'careline' phone number is publicized as widely as possible, and is not confused with the general store number. When voice-activated answering is used, and it can be very effective in achieving real time savings, then the customer service option should route directly to a trained service person and not to another automatic option. In this respect there is a real advantage in providing excess capacity in this area, even to the extent of routing as a priority to nominated managers should the actual service staff be inundated with calls. This has the benefit of reducing waiting times and allows the customer an opportunity to give the specific and personal facts, as well as receiving an immediate promise of action and a commitment to respond within an agreed time scale. Remember the emphasis should be on *retaining* the customer (or *recovering* them) first, and correcting the problem second.

If a Web site is also used then a facility for e-mail to a named person is effective. The person does not have to be real, just the use of a name makes it more personal as long as there is a 'real' someone standing in for the name all the time, and the e-mail receives immediate attention with a personal rather than automatic reply. It is perhaps possible to integrate all the means of communications – having made it easy for the customer to take the initiative and contact a store, it is then up to the retailer to ensure that action follows without any undue delay. As Josa Young (2000) wrote: 'Ultimately good, polite service pays off. Now that much business is done on the relatively impersonal Internet, real people on the other end of the phone are more important than ever'.

It is crucial for all retailers to remember that they actually make *promises* to their shoppers in the form of the retail marketing mix. This is the most basic issue in retail marketing. Any perceived failure to meet the promises will lead to dissatisfaction. No matter how efficient a retailer is, there are going to be times when mistakes are made that lead to a failure to keep the initial promises. But the processes actually established by a store that enables its customers to communicate regarding those failures must also be considered as part of its promise. The promise to ensure satisfaction may not be initially and explicitly given, but it is likely to be implicit in every action taken to achieve a sale.

There are a number of ground rules for good practice in communicating with dissatisfied customers:

- *Acknowledge* the issues
- *Concentrate* on the facts
- *Promise* action
- Don't take things *personally*.

If someone breaks a promise to you, a product you bought fails to work properly for instance, the response is *anger*. This can be quite mild or very intense, or anywhere on the continuum between. Anger is a powerful emotion and the best way to contain it is to concentrate on the facts and the actions to correct the situation. Before this can be accomplished the complainer has to feel you are taking things seriously and listening to them. This is more than hearing them, and yet it is not simply a question of taking all the blame onto the store. It is better to say 'I appreciate the problems this failure has caused, let's see how we can put it right' rather than 'I am sorry we made a mistake'. *Acknowledging the issues* is the first step in gaining the trust of the complainer, but the acknowledgement must be achieved in a positive way that allows a way forward. When trust is established, or at the very least some level of understanding regarding the overall problem, then it is time to move into the actual facts. Unless a free-phone link is being used it is appropriate to ask to phone back immediately and actually do so as this also shows a caring attitude. Also a personal phone contact should be used, where possible, to respond to both letter and e-mailed complaints.

'The customer is *always* right', so the facts as they are described by the customer are to be considered as the starting point, even if there are inconsistencies at first. To move into this phase of the communications it is possible to ask, 'how can I help you unless you give me all the details?'. This will enable the interaction to move past the initial anger into a more constructive communication. Customer service staff should ask appropriate questions and clarify the actual words used by the complainer in order to avoid later misunderstandings. These must be taken down carefully and confirmed with the customer, this will continue to develop trust and ensure an on-going dialogue. It is then necessary to make a further promise to sort things out and to make good on the failure. Acknowledging a problem but failing to promise prompt action will just lead to a build-up in the frustration of the complainer. Action means:

- Clearly communicating *what's going to happen* and *when*
- Ensuring that the customer *perceives* the actions as *appropriate*
- Then *following things up* to meet the promises made regarding the matter.

Actions are very different from apologies, actions are all about recovering a customer, and will probably involve more than the basic compensation. Remember customers are both intelligent and intuitive. Treat them as adults because they know when you are trying to appease them and when you're actually offering them real and substantial help. They may still be angry, and may take it out on the customer service people who are the store as far as the customer views the situation, but, if handled well by trained staff, there should be some real benefits beginning to emerge. In fact studies in several countries have shown that those customers who actually do complain and then have their complaint dealt with quickly and fairly, tend to be better disposed towards a store than customers who have never had a problem. A stronger relationship is thus developed.

The final rule for all those involved in customer service must be to treat the problem *objectively*, and not to get involved personally. It does not matter what you think about a complainant, nor how much abuse you have received as a proxy for your store, treat all issues in an objective way, definitely efficient, and do not take the problems of your organization in a personal way. This is easy to say outside of the actual organization, but if it becomes personal then the situation will be even more complex and may never get resolved. Of course, there are times when a customer service supervisor suspects the customer is not right, or is trying to claim without good reason. Such incidents are, thankfully, very rare but when they do get noticed they require special attention.

Handling complaints is not the same as encouraging communications from customers. The initial communication is the first step, and if planned in a customer conscious way will establish the foundation for the necessary action. Further communication will inevitably follow and this should go all the way through to the resolution of the problem. Within this, it is far better to customize the contacts and to avoid using any impersonal standard letters. The emphasis must be on *two-way interactions,* and all activity should be seen as part of the marketing mix for the specific customer involved.

How to Handle Complaints

Josa Young (2000) has written that

> more customers do battle with shops in January than at any other time of the year. There are all those faulty Christmas presents to return and rash sales promises to regret... . However for a nation of shopkeepers, the British have very low standards of customer care, and lag far behind those in the US who will take back unwanted products without a murmur.

Perhaps this quote puts the problems of handling complaints into some perspective. On the one hand there are the *unwanted purchases*, perfectly suitable but just not required, on the other there are the items of merchandise that are *required but not working properly*. Both can trigger a visit to a shop with a view to getting something done. In the first case the customer is the supplicant, they made an inappropriate purchase and want to remedy to situation. Whether or not a store wishes to help in this respect and thus show goodwill towards the shopper is a matter of policy. It goes a long way beyond the statutory rights of customers, and is more a marketing initiative than anything else. If such a policy is to be adopted then the systems must be put in place to implement it efficiently.

The second type of post-purchase activity is when an item is 'not of the necessary quality' and thereby requires a remedy from the store, and compensation for the dissatisfied shopper. This is the area where serious complaints and real anger are to be found.

Returns Policies

Stores that allow customers to bring back unwanted purchases for refund or exchange do not need to offer any compensation. Marks & Spencer instituted their returns policy in the 1960s. It is now rightly admired and much copied. It relies on clever psychology regarding customer behaviour in that the shopper will take more items home, and will return only a small proportion, if they feel that they are not committed to keeping them.

Shoppers in this situation gladly accept the inconvenience of revisiting a store to get a refund because they recognize the returns policy as a real customer benefit, and do not build in any negative values for the trouble involved. Within the mail-order sector returns are an expensive but necessary issue. David Jones, former MD of Grattan, told a group of managers that the problem with selling from the picture in a catalogue was that it was easy to make a dress or some other item look like 'a million dollars'. The reality was not apparent until the item had been delivered to the customer. To counteract this inconsistency, and to create reassurance in the minds of home-shoppers 'no-quibble' returns is the norm in the industry. Obviously the online Internet retailers need to follow this lead, although this nascent style of shopping has a long way to go before it eliminates all the fears of customers, and starts to build a reputation for keeping promises.

Customer Complaints

As had already been said in this chapter, even the best retailer will receive complaints from time to time. The key determinant of the future impact is the way a retailer actually deals with them. While it is estimated that over 90 per cent of unhappy customers do not complain, when complaints are actually received there is sufficient evidence to support the intuitive assumption that the faster and more effectively the complaint is handled, the greater the chance of that customer returning to shop again at the store.

The first step in the effective handling of complaints is to *encourage* those complaints. This both reduces the number of non-complainers who might defect and be lost without trace, and ensures that the complaints are actually received, perhaps with the customer feeling reassured that the store wants to hear about every problem. The next step is to concentrate on putting things right for the unhappy customer. This action should not have to wait for any internal investigation as to the cause of the problem, but there should be a desire to *reimburse* the customer, satisfying them as regards the problem, and to do so without any *undue delay*. Obviously the underlying causes must be investigated but that is an internal matter that is of little importance to the customer until his or her poor experience has been rectified. The order of actions is therefore

1 *Encourage*

2 *Handle*

3 *Investigate.*

Hart, Hesketh and Sasser (1990) suggest that with respect to the second step – the actual handling of complaints – there are four key issues to consider. The first is the need to act fast, the others are:

- Think *Value* not *Costs*
- Aim to *Recover* not *Replace*
- Ensure the right staff are properly *trained* and *empowered.*

Think Value

This is the $3000 pizza. The value of a customer to a retailer is the *lifetime value over a series of potential future purchases*. No store can afford to be complacent in this respect, and comparing the future value of a customer, as a real marketing 'asset', to the costs of a customer service programme can put the matter into a dramatic perspective. Accountants can report on the cost of such a programme; it is unfortunate that they cannot easily evaluate the benefits. It is usually left to the retail marketer to argue about the costs of not handling complaints properly. For this, it could be important to calculate the average lifetime spend per customer, to forecast the percentage of customers likely to complain and the probability that a dissatisfied shopper will influence at least 12 others. It is not 'rocket science', but the argument relies on qualitative assumptions and thus can be open to much scrutiny in stores where a cost culture is paramount.

There are those within every organization who draw attention to the bogus complainers, those who 'try it on' in order to see if they can get something for nothing. Of course, they exist. But there are not as many of them as some retailers believe. The dilemma is whether a full investigation should take place before compensating a customer, or recompense be made first to ensure a fast resolution of the matter. It is impossible to be dogmatic, both courses of action involve costs. If time is taken to investigate first, then it is likely that greater levels of compensation will be necessary owing to the delays involved. Also the customer could feel a lack of trust from the store, which will reduce the value of any subsequent resolution of the problem. If the bogus complainers receive a pay out that is a direct, costly and dangerous precedent. The best advice that can be given is to trust customers, risk a few unwarranted payments and compile a data base of complainers so serial complainers can be identified. In fact some companies operate a joint data base to try to identify those few fraudsters. It is easy to say to someone who has complained several times before 'you must be a very unlucky person, Mr(s) *X*, as we see you had a problem last year... . To ensure we can really find out the problem we will conduct a full investigation this time and will let you know in due course'. This approach really works, it is based on the premise that few customers suffer twice and if the second complaint is genuine then extra recompense is not really very costly.

Recover not Replace

This maxim relies on the desire of a retailer to retain its customers. To think about the problem from the customer's perspective has always been crucial to successful marketing. It will be obvious that if a product fails to work and has to be returned for replacement, there are a number of additional costs faced by the dissatisfied shopper. These include the time and trouble involved in contacting the store and returning the goods; the inability to use the product immediately after purchase; and the disappointment caused by the product not working.

If the only compensation is a replacement item then there is no attempt to defray these extra costs; the result will be that the customer still feels let down by the store. It does not recover the shopper's goodwill towards the store, and does not compensate the shopper for something that was not their fault. Really effective compensation acknowledges the additional costs and frustration experienced by the customer, and does something to offset it. Such additional compensation does not have to involve a full audit of the additional costs, it might be enough to give a £5 voucher in a grocery supermarket, or a free bottle of wine in a restaurant, or some other appropriate gesture. Such extras are not costly to a retailer, they buy at trade prices so that reduces the cost involved without diminishing the value to the customer. A grocery voucher has the resultant benefit that the customer has to return to the store to spend it, thus helping to build future trading and full customer recovery.

What is required is a change in the thinking of a retailer that then becomes part of the culture of the store. Every member of staff should be able to deal with returned goods and procedures should be in place to facilitate this. Young (2000) suggests that in too many shops the staff seem to follow the 3 Rs: 'anything from *reluctant* and *resistant*, right through to *rude*'. The only 'R' that really matters is *recovery*, and that is a very different concept. It is not normally the fault of the retail staff, they are usually doing their job in the way they have been trained. Sometimes it is made even worse by using bonus payments on sales actually made, but losing them if returns occur. What is needed is a culture supported by systems that acknowledge the principle of customer recovery, and suitable budgets and training that stretch right across every member of staff who might interact with a dissatisfied customer. This requires some marketing activity to be directed internally towards the employees of the store in order to champion the benefits of recovery, and to attempt to create an appropriate environment in which it can operate effectively.

Training and Empowering Staff

As is obvious from the above, complaints will not be handled effectively, nor customers recovered, unless the right systems are in place and all staff are focused on recovery and customer satisfaction. In fact most retail staff do really want to help solve customers' problems, even when, as Karr suggests (Karr and Blohowiak 1997), 'some customers are whining lunatics!' The problem is that sometimes things get off to a really bad start, the angry customer affects the hard-pressed sales assistant and then it's downhill all the way. This inevitably leads to a 'Lose–Lose' situation where the customer is lost, and probably tells many others about the poor experience, and the staff member feels stressed by the incident. The ideal is a 'Win–Win' situation where the customer is satisfied, and regained for the future, and the employee feels a real sense of achievement.

Most customer care training programmes include some study of *conflict resolution techniques*, and it is crucial that every employee is trained in this respect before going onto the sales floor. But this is not enough, the right systems are necessary to empower the staff in recovery. It could be that a senior member of staff is always on call for problem situations, but in some ways this diminishes the role of the other staff members. It is far better to have a regime in place whereby any faulty item is immediately exchanged or refunded, with no quibbles, and a standard up-front compensation is offered. This meets the terms of the Sale of Goods Acts, adhering to the legal minimum, required, but goes further in attempting to recover immediately. A statement that the matter will be investigated fully as well as a promise of further communications can support it. The further communication could then be used to encourage the customer to return with a further personalized incentive of 20 per cent of purchases at the next visit, or some other inviting offer.

There must be systems in place to deal with those customers who fail to offer proof of purchase, receipts, or seem to want something other than a standard replacement, but these are details that can be worked out. But as details they are *marketing* details, based on a premise of trusting customers, and not *operational* details that are dictated by suspicion and costs.

Perhaps the most difficult area is when the complaint is not in respect of faulty merchandise but refers to poor *service levels*. Such problems must be given serious consideration, but the systems for tackling them will be different, and the empowerment will not necessarily pass to all employees. However, it is still a cultural concern, the aim is not to punish unhelpful employees but rather to help them to improve the levels of service offered as a positive step for the future. Bringing this development into regular training programmes, is an obvious solution. Many stores utilize a half-hour early morning time for staff training on one day every week. Sometimes such sessions are wasted, being used for a few internal briefing notices, in other organizations they are part of a continuous learning culture focused on a goal of enhanced customer satisfaction. In the latter cases the marketing managers should get involved, participating in the training and bringing information from the marketplace into the discussions. The best training involves full consideration of relevant issues, it should not be one-way lecturing. The marketing contribution is to represent the views and expectations of customers, disseminate information regarding the market and stimulate the search for a shared understanding that could suggest future actions. Training is not something to be left to the store managers alone, but requires a much wider involvement if the benefits are to be achieved.

Conclusions

Retailing is about *customer satisfaction*. In this respect many activities aimed at stimulating shoppers to buy dominate retail marketing. The emphasis in most marketing programmes is on constructing valuable offerings and creating the right environment for a purchase to occur. But even in the best-run stores problems will occur, and customers will have reasons to complain. Because of this there are two important issues to be addressed:

- *First* how can a retailer learn from those unhappy, 'lost', customers and thereby discover problems, and correct them so that they do not recur?

- *Second* how can the retailer recompense the few dissatisfied customers and try to ensure the relationship with these customers continues? The objective is to regain the *trust* of the shopper so that they feel positive about the retailer, rather than angry, frustrated and even vindictive.

The most fundamental need is to establish some *contact* with these unhappy customers. If communications can take place then it should be possible to learn about the problems as well as giving an opportunity to recover the situation. There are many ways open to a retailer to communicate with customers, and in many cases the retailer will actually have a data base containing their names and addresses. Even if this is not available, it is still possible to identify unhappy customers. Perhaps the best source is the customer care/complaints department. All complainers should be identified, as they can then be targeted as sources of information regarding the failures of the store.

If initiatives are introduced to make communication with the store – including complaining – easier, then the level of learning is increased and the number of dissatisfied shoppers who defect without any form of future contact is reduced. Such initiatives involve all forms of communication tools including the telephone and the Internet. The important issue is that all contact methods must be as user-friendly as it is possible to be.

Once contact is established, then action can be taken to rectify matters. As far as the customer is concerned the priority must be to build on the contact by properly acknowledging the problem and immediately taking action to recover the customer. It is an entirely separate thing to carry out an internal investigation to correct the problem, a complaining customer will want a solution without any delay. The investigation should not delay compensation for a customer.

In order to stand a chance of recovering the customer, and their future business, it is necessary to do more than act fast. It is also not enough to just replace any faulty item. What is necessary is a culture of putting everything right for the customer and recognizing that the problem will cause that customer a lot more trouble than the cost of the merchandise. That is why the concept of thinking about the *value* of a customer not the *cost* of replacement is crucial.

If the culture is right and the attitude is customer-focused, then there is every chance that customers will not only be compensated but they will become even stronger advocates of the store than those who have never had a problem. To help stimulate this climate of 'customer consciousness', marketing can play a part. The use of internal marketing techniques that utilize marketing skills to communicate with employees can be seen alongside the role of a marketer as the advocate for customers in all decisions taken within a retail organization. By offering information gleaned from unhappy customers to colleagues inside the organization it is possible to find solutions to improve the situation for the future. Such dialogue should not be aimed at finding scapegoats, or blaming the miscreant, but rather in learning from mistakes and putting policies and systems in place so that the whole retail organization can signal its commitment to achieving greater customer satisfaction in the future.

References and Further Reading

Carlzon, J. (1987) *The moments of truth*, Ballinger, Cambridge MA.

Cook, S. (2000) *Customer Care: How to Create an Effective Customer Focus*, Kogan Page, London.

Hart, C.W., Hesketh, J.L. and Sasser, W.E. (1990) The Profitable Art of Service Recovery, *Harvard Business Review*, July–August.

Karr, R. and Blohowiak, D. (1997) *The Complete Idiot's Guide to Great Customer Service*, Alpha Books, New York.

Reichheld, F.F. (1996) Learning from Customer Defections, *Harvard Business Review*, March–April, 56–69.

Tack, A. (1994) *Profitable Customer Care*, Butterworth-Heinemann, Oxford.

Townsend, R. (1971) *Up the Organisation*, Michael Joseph, London.

Young, J. (2000) I Want my Money Back, *Times* Weekend, 15 January, 4.

Retail Demand Management

CHAPTER 14

This chapter:

- Defines the key factors in the perceived store shopping experience
- Explains retail demand management
- Reviews the management input–output system
- Defines disequilibrium management

Retail Demand Management

Introduction

A retailer, like any other business, seeks to maximize sustainable profit – i.e. strives to obtain the maximum return from its operations while maintaining long-term shopper loyalty. In reality, profit maximization for a retailer means a well designed store continuously full of shoppers purchasing the right products at the right prices. If this is achieved, shoppers' *perceived store shopping experience* (or PSSE, see Chapter 7 on Store Design) should be high. This will not be achieved if the location is incorrect (the store will not be full), the promotion ineffective (shoppers may not be encouraged to visit), the customer service poor (shoppers may not revisit) or indeed if any element of the retail tactical mix fails. Assuming that the retailer has optimized its tactical mix, the retail system still has to be managed – i.e. shoppers need to be able to enter the store at their chosen time, pass through the selling space at their own pace and exit the store in a similarly efficient manner. Problems with any of these three phases may lead to shopper dissatisfaction which, if not quickly dealt with, may lead in turn to an emptier store. The management of these three phases is known as *retail demand management*.

Retail demand management can be viewed as the management of an *input–output system*. Shoppers enter the store (input to the system), spend time shopping (time spent in the system) then leave the store (output from the system). Continuously maintaining this system at its maximum realistic capacity while optimizing the retail tactical mix should lead to optimal performance (profit maximization). In an ideal world, shoppers would arrive at the store at a set rate throughout the store's opening hours. Demand would then be constant and predictable, allowing the retail system to be easily optimized. The store could be designed to accommodate a known number of shoppers with an appropriate selling space arrangement and the exit facilities (payment systems and doors) capable of handling the traffic load. Unfortunately, retailers do not operate in this ideal world. In reality, demand is relatively predictable but rarely constant and it may be called *irregular* (Kotler 1973). Recalling the survey undertaken by East *et al.* (1994, see Chapter 3 on Shopper Behaviour), suppose you were to take visits to your local grocery store on a Monday at 11 a.m. and on a Saturday at the same time. It would be quite a surprise if there were not a significantly larger number of shoppers in the store on the Saturday. Retailers can, through prior research or past experience, estimate levels of demand to a greater or lesser extent. A system then needs to be developed to handle all levels of shopper demand.

The starting point for retailers is to understand how the input–output (retail) system works. To achieve this, a simple model can be developed that utilizes elements of *queuing theory*. Input and output levels are compared over a given period of time to indicate if the volume of shoppers in the store is increasing, stable or decreasing. Based on this result, *retail demand management policies* can be introduced with the aim of keeping the volume of shoppers at an optimum level. These policies essentially relate to modifying the input or output rates although the time spent in the store can also be considered. This process is called *disequilibrium management* (Shemwell and Cronin 1994).

An Input–Output Retail Demand Management Model

The input–output model mentioned above can be developed to account for a number of key factors (see Figure 14.1).

The *input rate*, or the number of shoppers entering the store in a given time period, can be seen to be dependent on accessibility and shopping patterns. The *output rate*, or the number of shoppers exiting the store in the same time period, is affected by constraints relating to the system itself, physical factors and store personnel (staffing). Table 14.1 gives a simple illustration.

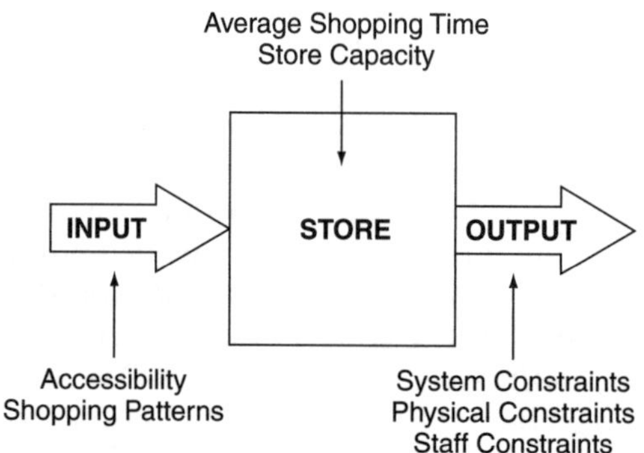

Figure 14.1 An input–output retail demand management model

Table 14.1 Input–Output Example

Suppose that a small store has a maximum capacity of 40 shoppers. The input rate to the store is 10 shoppers (per 10-minute period) and the output rate 5 (per 10-minute period). The average time spent in the store by shoppers is 10 minutes. The store would reach its maximum capacity after 70 minutes.

Time (min)	Shoppers in	Shoppers out	Shoppers in the store
10	10	0	10
20	10	5	15
30	10	5	20
40	10	5	25
50	10	5	30
60	10	5	35
70	10	5	40

Input Factors

The number of shoppers visiting a store is, of course, caused by a wide range of factors and may be affected by all areas of the retail tactical mix. Focusing on demand management means that we must only consider two factors – namely, *accessibility* and *shopping patterns*.

Accessibility

Accessibility has already been discussed in detail earlier in this text in connection with retail location and infrastructure (see Chapter 5 on Retail Location) and has been defined as 'the ease with which potential shoppers can get to the retail area'. Clearly, the easier it is for a shopper to get to the store the more likely they will be to do just that. Issues of relevance include pedestrian flow and entry routes, public transport services, the road network, parking and visibility (for more detailed coverage of these issues refer to Chapter 5 on Retail Location). The old retail adage of *location; location; location* is relevant in this respect. Traditionally stores actually located near to where customers congregated, this then changed with the advent of out-of-town shopping to those areas where accessibility was best. One of the arguments in support of Sunday opening was that traffic congestion would be lower. However, as anyone who has queued on a Bank Holiday to get into a retail park, or maybe an IKEA store on a Sunday, can testify, the converging of many shoppers into a single location can cause acute problems. These frustrate shoppers before they actually enter the store.

Store owners and retail park managers are in continual discussion with local authorities regarding general access, and often there are only limited solutions possible. However with respect to the accessibility from the car parks or public transport there is much a store can do to improve the matter. The provision of well-planned car parks and supplying courtesy buses that bring shoppers to the door, are some of the many initiatives designed to ensure customers enter a store with positive feelings that could transfer through into actual purchase decisions. Store owners must give the question of 'accessibility for all' considerable attention, and many issues regarding able-bodied customers will be obvious from casual observation. Recently legislation regarding access for people with disabilities has focused attention on this large and important minority; the law now determines the minimum acceptable provision, but for all shoppers, able-bodied or those with a disability, it may be advantageous to go beyond these minimum standards.

There is an obvious link between the input and output factors. For instance a *one-way flow* around a car park, or the provision of a *pick-up area for bulky or heavy items*, or even *home delivery* will help the input problems. In fact anything that avoids the output issues affecting the accessibility of a store must be considered.

Of course the provision of home shopping by telephone or the Internet is another way of modifying the accessibility of a store. For those customers shopping in the virtual market via the Internet, it will be the accessibility of the Web site, rather than the physical location, that is crucial. For telephone customers it is the speed and efficiency of the telephone answering that determines this issue.

Shopping Patterns

It has already been noted that shoppers are often habitual in their choice of shopping time owing to personal commitments (work and domestic), shopper perceptions of crowding, financial issues and the level of involvement (see Chapter 3 on Shopping Behaviour). East *et al.* (1994) found that grocery shoppers were highly habitual in their choice of shopping time (89 per cent chose the same day, 67 per cent the same time of day), with Thursday to Sunday being the most popular days. This example illustrates that for low-involvement retail situations, such as grocery, shopping patterns are definite and quite predictable. It is interesting to note that availability can actually affect shopping patterns. The patterns are not fixed for all time. This can be seen when considering the provision of 24-hour opening by some supermarkets which has led to a number of customers shopping at previously unheard-of times. The Internet also never closes, although at some times of high traffic it can go frustratingly slowly, but it is obvious that in a virtual marketplace different, and variable, patterns will develop.

In considering higher-involvement retail situations, it will be found that shopping patterns become less easily defined and much less predictable. This is mainly owing to trips being made on a rather less frequent basis, so habitual behaviour does not have such a good chance of developing (for further details see Chapter 3 on Shopping Behaviour).

The key issue facing stores regarding shopping patterns is how to provide a service at the *right level* and at the *right time*. Banks found that they had to be available on Saturday both to satisfy customers and to match the competition from Building Societies. Although they can also offer their service automatically through 'hole-in-the-wall' cash machines (ATMs), and many offer both a telephone and an Internet service open 24 hours a day, there is still a need to match the demands of some customers for a branch visit within particular opening hours. At times of peak demand it is critical that both the access and the provision in the retail outlet are able to cope with the high numbers of shoppers. The dilemma facing a store is how to achieve a reasonable compromise between opening the premises when demand is low, and the business might not cover the running costs of the store, and not offering sufficient access or capacity when demand is high. This dilemma is greatest with regards opening hours for 'bricks and mortar' stores, as the level of service available when the store is open can be varied much more easily. Obviously there is no such dilemma for virtual stores.

To overcome some problems with shopping patterns it is possible to encourage some shoppers to visit at *off-peak times*. Initiatives such as '12-hour spectacular sales', evening opening for loyalty card holders, extra discounts every Wednesday for pensioners, set price menus for early-bird meals, 'happy hours' with doubles for the regular price between 6 and 7 o'clock and many other promotions have a real effect on shopping patterns. They are more than promotions, they are real attempts to *modify the behaviour of potential customers* to achieve a better match between the provision of a retail service and the demand for that service. Retail marketing does not always give sufficient attention to this aspect of trading, and although a lot of time can be involved in setting up relevant initiatives it is almost always worthwhile, with the rewards coming from increased business with little increase in costs.

Store Factors

Store factors cover the store's actual capacity to cope with shoppers, and to meet their needs in a satisfactory manner. It includes *physical factors* of layout and flow around the store. This can be linked to the average time spent in the store by shoppers – the dilemma in this respect is to balance an extended store visit that gives the opportunity for a greater level of spend with a short visit that might be more acceptable to some customers. Of course, shopping is now viewed as a major leisure activity, enjoyed by many participants, but there is still a balance to be achieved between the need to entertain these shoppers and the harder drive to encourage them to purchase and spend. Additionally within store factors the issue of *stocking levels* can be crucial, as this determines if a product is available for immediate purchase or if it has to be ordered. It includes the question of the damage to trading and satisfaction that might occur owing to a stock-out situation.

Store Capacity

Each physical, 'bricks and mortar' store has a maximum capacity for both practical and legal reasons, whilst online retailers and mail-order organizations do not have the same constraints. The desire for profitability means that in physical locations retailers must get the most from a given maximum capacity. Many retailers measure their trading success by measuring such factors as sales and profit per sq. metre of floor space. Many stores have found ways of increasing the selling area of their store, reducing the stock room, in order to make maximum use of the high-priced asset that is the retail store.

Decisions regarding *physical store capacity* are very long term, this is because the choice of actual store, its size and its suitability to display the chosen merchandise will usually involve a long lease or the purchase/construction of a building. The building will provide a fixed amount of space, and in reality it cannot be changed easily without considerable trouble and expenditure. Even decisions regarding internal layout are relatively long term, yet these factors will affect the atmosphere and the total shopping environment with a direct link to customer behaviour. Every physical store has to balance the display area for merchandise with the space required for customers, including perhaps fitting rooms as well as comfort facilities, and the service areas where transactions can actually take place. It is possible to offer limited areas for merchandise, as in the catalogue retailers Argos and Index, where the merchandise is held in backroom areas to reduce the need for space. Other stores put everything they have out on display – this gives customers a chance to touch and see the items and possibly to indulge in impulse buying, but if it is too crowded it can be counter-productive. Other stores aim for a reasonable compromise. There is no one formula as to the best policy, and stores will often experiment with display layouts while monitoring shopper response by observation and more direct research.

Every extra sq. metre given over to customers will be a reduction in available space for merchandise. If it were possible to increase margins while maintaining the number of shoppers, then such a debate would be irrelevant. In fact some customers might be prepared to pay more to shop in a less crowded outlet, but unless the store is really confident of its competitive position this could prove to be unacceptably risky. Therefore the issues discussed in Chapter 7 on Store Design become vital aspects of the total store capacity. In reality, a *maximum, realistic volume* will be somewhat below the actual maximum for both shoppers and merchandise because unnecessary crowding is very likely to affect the majority of shoppers in a negative way, typically causing them to reduce their level of expenditure.

Observational research techniques are often used to study the flow of customers around a store. Generally consultants can suggest ways of increasing the flow of shoppers, but unless these efficiencies are linked to the marketing objectives they can lead to shorter visits and reduced expenditure. A balance is required – stores might encourage shoppers to travel all around a store (maybe IKEA where all merchandise has to be seen and viewed), and few short cuts are available. The positioning of stairs and escalators will be constrained by building and fire regulations, but it can also be utilized to ensure that shoppers pass through particular departments where additional stimuli to spend are provided. The same idea of traffic flows can be used for online retailers – the Web site and the links that enable a shopper to find their way to chose and buy products is as much an art as it is a science. The right compromise has to be found between a complex routing with opportunities for additional purchases as opposed to a simple direct route to find a single item. The type of merchandise and the context of the retail outlet will help to establish boundaries for such decisions, but the actual layout of any store is more likely to be based on instinct rather than analysis.

Average Shopping Time

Average shopping time is important to retailers from one perspective, as the quicker a shopper can be passed through the retail system the more shoppers that system can accommodate. The opposite view is that shoppers need a certain amount of time to feel confident that the right purchases or purchase considerations have been made, as well as allowing them a chance to make unplanned, impulse purchases. Clearly if the number of shoppers who can be accommodated in a given time period increases so does the potential for increasing sales and profits. This doesn't mean that shoppers can be rushed, as this will probably lead to feelings of dissatisfaction allied to a deterioration in the perceived store shopping experience.

As mentioned above, good store design can reduce shopping time by making the merchandise easier to find and enabling customers to avoid any overcrowded areas. Of course, increased shopper knowledge can decrease shopper time – for instance, regular visits to a local supermarket, or good signing of departments, or the provision of a store map as in IKEA. The benefits of staff training can also be felt in assisting customers find items, unlike the grocery supermarket visited by one author who was told by a staff member that the store is always moving stock around so even staff are confused! It is one thing to assist a customer to find specific items, it is quite another to deliberately plan for a customer to take extra time in store in the hope of extra spending. Both of these are appropriate elements in the overall marketing mix, and they are not incompatible!

Different types of merchandise and different types of retail situation will require different amounts of shopping time. The category of '*shopping good*' has traditionally been used to describe infrequently bought consumer items where customers typically spend quite a lot of time and effort considering the available options and comparing the benefits of each one. These might be clothing or domestic appliances or jewellery or cars. Obviously the shopping time for such products will be very different from that given to purchasing the weekly grocery or the petrol for a car. Typically low-involvement retail purchases such as grocery will show shorter shopping times as compared to high-involvement situations such as jewellery.

Even for the same merchandise it will be probable that different types of shoppers also require different amounts of time. The category of shoppers whose behaviour is described as 'aimless wandering' (Chapter 3) will have a much longer shopping time, especially when compared to categories termed 'routine managers' and 'purposeful organizers'. In addition, different shopping groups may also exhibit different shopping times – e.g. a solitary shopper may require a different time to consider a purchase when compared to a family group. While it is necessary to take account of the type of merchandise when considering average shopping times it is far less feasible to concentrate on one type of shopping behaviour, as all potential shoppers should be encouraged if possible. The exception is the obvious time-waster, more than an 'aimless wanderer' – there are 'window shoppers' who might never buy. They are probably harmless, but if they do interfere with actual purchasers they should be given very little staff time. The real problem is distinguishing this category from any other. If staff receive a high level of commission on sales completed there is a real temptation to pursue any interested shopper even if no sale is likely.

In order to ensure that customers are satisfied with their shopping visit it could help to provide some degree of *entertainment* or *desirable facility* for customers. A crèche for children is an increasingly popular aid to reduce shopping time and frustration for mothers, but more immediate is the provision of informative videos and high levels of service personnel for customers requiring such help. The retail marketing task is to deflect the customer into the retail store and help to decide an appropriate compromise with regards store design, provision of services and customer desires.

Stock Levels and Out-of-Stock Problems

Chapter 8 considered issues regarding the *width* and *depth* of stocking levels. With the variability in demand, a balance has to be struck between too much stock and the reassurance that everything is always available, the cost being poor utilization of selling space, and reasonable stock levels, risking more out-of-stock situations. In practice most stores tend towards the latter position, but they try to provide *re-ordering facilities* to minimize delays in satisfying customers. The overall purpose of a retailer is to provide a service to a shopper that enhances the availability of merchandise. If the retailer cannot provide that service, then that store will lose custom. Hence there is a need to minimize unfortunate instances of stock problems.

The *logistics of supply*, perhaps the use of intermediate warehouses as a stock buffer for a group of outlets within a multiple store and other operational initiatives, are as important to the retail marketing programme as to the store operations. If, however, an out-of-stock occurs why should the customer be penalized, surely it is part of the marketing role to ensure some form of compensation which could ensure that the shopper feels valued as a customer? American retailers use the term 'customer recovery' to describe programmes designed to retain rather than lose customers when a problem occurs. In Asda supermarkets they use 'smiley vouchers' that are given to disappointed shoppers so that if the product is bought on a subsequent visit it will be supplied free of charge. While this is more formalized than some of their competitors, one of the authors was offered a home delivery from Sainsbury of a selection of eight items after finding them out of stock during a shopping trip. It is not only grocery stores who offer such service, although it is not often well publicized because of the costs involved with this type of scheme. The marketing view should be for the retailer to think in terms of the *cost of losing a customer* rather than the cost of an extra service because of a one-off problem. Dominos Pizza talk of the '$3000 pizza', this reflects the fact that the average purchaser of a pizza could spend an average $3000 on subsequent purchases over a period of time. If that customer is lost, then they might be lost for good and that is $3000 of turnover lost. The same thinking applied to out-of-stocks should see every customer as a potential for a stream of spending both now and well into the future. A little extra cost now could really ensure that this potential is not lost.

Output Factors

The final part of the retail experience concerns the output factors, in particular the rate at which customers can *exit a store*. This is determined by both variable and fixed factors. *Fixed factors* give a maximum output rate for a given store and are determined by the physical dimensions of that store – for instance, the number and size of the exits – and the capacity of the routes to those exits give a maximum possible exit rate. This is clearly a fixed factor, constrained by physical limitations that can be changed only by alterations to the fabric of the building. The *variable* output component can be altered to suit the requirements at any specific time. For instance, the number of checkouts in a supermarket is a fixed factor, the number actually staffed and open at any one time is a variable.

The retail system relates to the way that *output is managed* and the nature of the 'superficial' store design elements, such as *payment* and *queuing facilities*. Again there is a fixed element to this such as the total amount of queuing space and the number of payment points. There is also a variable component in the procedures adopted to manage output and the temporary store changes that may accommodate changes in output rate. Of course staffing levels is a key variable, allowing flexibility at times of fluctuating demand, although there is always a minimum below which no store can operate. 'Staffing' in this context refers to the *transaction-processing role* of retail employees. This transactional role can be made more or less efficient by the systems in place, and while this may seem to be a purely operational decision it does impinge directly on the shopping experience and customer satisfaction, so should be evaluated from a marketing perspective.

Physical Constraints

It has already been mentioned that decisions regarding physical store capacity are very long term, this applies equally to the accessing of a store, the internal layout and flows and the means of exiting. Usually any decisions regarding store layout will consider all aspects together although the emphasis on attracting customers in, and ensuring a good shopping experience, sometimes overshadow exit considerations. Customer satisfaction is, however, a post-purchase measure and frustration at the exits can greatly affect this. For instance, the problems of getting out of a store with a bulky purchase can directly affect post-purchase satisfaction.

There is a link between the physical constraints, the systems utilized and the staff involvement in exiting. A retailer that allows collection by car from the rear of the store is probably considering all of these. Sometimes the physical constraints and the systems involved are deliberately restrictive to deter theft – so-called 'shop lifting'. Because of this there is usually a staff and a systems involvement if merchandise and shoppers are to be allowed to use multiple exits. The location and number of exits from any store will have a great deal to do with the overall shape and position of the building and the safety regulations including such issues as emergency exits. However, output includes the payment, wrapping and leaving a store with a purchase, and as such the number and location of payment points is not as fixed as the final exits. There is a trade off between space allowed for queuing and payment and the space for displays. The number of payment points should reflect the *maximum level of expected demand*, even if they are not always staffed.

Payment points can be located near to the physical exits or may be positioned conveniently throughout a store. If the latter arrangement is used, there must be a regime in place that can identify when a customer has paid for an item at an internal cash desk as compared to someone trying to leave without paying. From the marketing perspective, payment tills close to the merchandise and systems that assist shoppers so that they are not inconvenienced with elongated delays nor in managing 'difficult-to-carry' items will all add to satisfaction. This is why the retail marketing team should be involved as an *advocate for customers* whenever the physical layout of a store is being considered.

System Constraints

Even if the physical factors of exiting are tackled in a satisfactory manner, there are key systems considerations. These can affect online retailing as well as traditional stores. At least in stores cash can be tendered and the transaction processed. With the Internet the payment will usually be made using a credit card, with all the attendant worries regarding fraud, and the delivery of the merchandise will not be immediately available for a customer. However in all retailing, the systems in place to enable selection, purchase and finally physical acquisition of an item must be designed to complete a transaction in the least stressful manner. The reason why the systems are not always as consumer-friendly as they might, and should, be is that they are often used to control stock levels, and trigger replenishment orders as well as processing a customer's purchase. The use of *bar codes* (article numbering systems) and the *scanning* of many items is now very sophisticated, and such developments are both operationally efficient and customer-friendly, and certainly have ensured that mistakes in pricing have all but been eliminated. Nevertheless there are still times when the supermarket check out is crowded, so stores like Safeway have introduced a 'Shop & Go' initiative; this system is based on consumer trust and certainly accelerates the processing of groceries. In other areas it is now possible to fill up a car with petrol, paying at the pump with a credit card and avoiding a queue to pay. These and other developments that utilize modern technology are very customer-focused.

It is not just the payment for purchases that can affect output efficiency, the actual *handling of the product* is also vital. In a physical outlet it may be possible to have all chosen purchases passed onto a central collection point by the staff rather than inconvenience customers by insisting they carry items around as they make their selections. Perhaps the ultimate in such systems is the opportunity to indulge in home shopping for groceries and other items via the online Web sites of Tesco, Sainsbury and Iceland. The products are then assembled for the customer and delivered to the home address in an efficient manner. This removes much of the hassle relating to both input and output. The question is whether this is a new systems initiative or just a modern interpretation of traditional home shopping: it is probably a combination of both.

Groceries can be delivered fresh within hours of an order, but this is possible only because the physical store is relatively close. For many Internet purchases the delivery period can be rather frustratingly long. A book ordered from Amazon.com, but actually dispatched from the USA, can take up to eight weeks to arrive. This does not apply to all such purchases but unless the online retailers find solutions to the 'snail-mail' systems used for delivery, they will not appeal to all shoppers. There is evidence that some of the payment systems are being redesigned to reduce fraud, but as yet no real evidence of new thinking regarding the distributive systems for physical products.

Staff Constraints

Some virtual markets are managed without direct contact between customers and staff; however even in these areas there are backroom staff carrying out the routine activities within the systems being utilized. The employees of a retail organization are crucial, whether they directly interact with shoppers or provide back-up. In all service industries, including retail, it is a continual challenge to match the levels of demand with suitable supply provision. For all physical stores, and also many other retail formats, there is a dependence on people to provide the service. It is all too easy for a retailer to forget that it is simply a service, and that alternative providers could supplement it if the service levels were to fall. Services are direct, they are perishable and they cannot be stored. This coupled to the interactive nature of retail means that *staffing levels* are crucial to satisfaction. This is equally true at the payment point as it is within the store. The good news is that staff can be trained to be very flexible, working on the check out tills when demand increases and carrying out other duties when customer numbers are lower. The emphasis on performing only those tasks essential to customers in the rush periods, and perhaps supplementing provision by the use of part-time employees is well established. The objective is to maximize capacity in 'bottleneck' tasks relying on the fact that if one part of the system is at full capacity then other sections of the system are possibly underused. It must be emphasized that all the direct contact staff are 'part-time members of the marketing team' whenever they interact with a customer.

Outcomes of the Input–Output Retail Demand Management Model

The example given in Table 14.1 shows one possible outcome where the input rate is greater than the output rate. Others outcomes can be identified where the input level is equal or less than the output level. Figure 14.2 illustrates these various different outcomes.

The ideal outcome is one where, after a run-in period, the input and output levels are approximately equal. In this case, *store capacity utilization* will be optimal. As the input level starts to exceed the output level the number of shoppers in the store increases. Initially this will result in

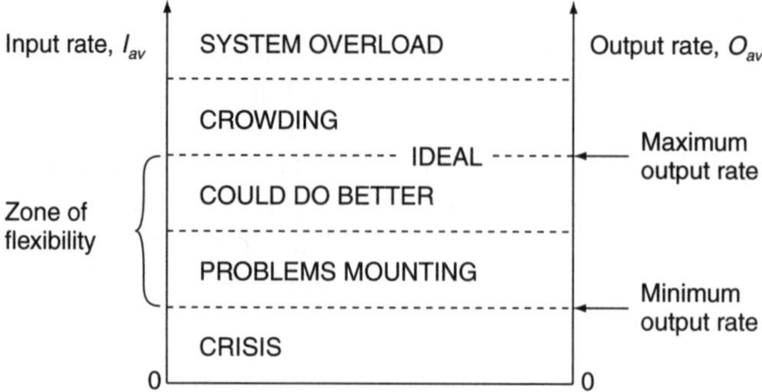

Figure 14.2 Outcomes of the input–output model

crowding, a particularly serious problem for the retailer given the changes in shopper behaviour that its presence can produce (see next section for further details). As crowding increases in severity the point will be reached where the store cannot physically accommodate any more shoppers (system overload). If, however, the management of the store has ensured that the output level exceeds the input level, the store will get progressively more empty. Initially this will result in quite favourable conditions for the shopper and sub-optimal space utilization for the retailer (could do better). If the situation continues, the store will suffer from increasing levels of under-utilization of space, to the point where the store will begin to lose money (problems mounting). Eventually, such low levels of space utilization will place the retailer in a perilous position (crisis).

The retailer does, however, have the ability to vary the output rate within its *zone of flexibility*. Transaction-processing staff levels can be reduced, for example, thus reducing the number of shoppers who can be handled. The retailer's costs will reduce and potentially serious financial problems may be averted. This process has a limit, though, as any given store will have a minimum output level if it is to remain open. Technically, this would be one transaction-processing staff member only. If input levels fall below this minimum output level, the retailer's performance will have reached crisis level.

Crowding

Crowding is the state of psychological stress that results when one's demand for space exceeds the supply (Stokols 1972). It is a subjective experience of an excessively high rate and amount of environmental stimuli leading to the belief that task performance (the shopping process) is being restricted by others or from intrusions by others into one's own personal space. The subjective element of the experience means that perceived crowding is a more accurate term to use as, in Stockdale's words (1978), 'crowding is in the eye of the beholder'. The most common behavioural changes under conditions of crowding are adjustments in shopping time, deviations in shopping plans, reduced levels of social contact, greater conformity to store traffic patterns, reduced levels of exploratory behaviour and the use of buying-process shortcuts. Typical behaviour under conditions of crowding involves reduced shopping time, curtailed shopping plans (low priority items ignored), limited interaction with other shoppers or staff, movement in the same direction and at the same speed as other shoppers, limited information search on potential new decisions, and the use of shortcuts (e.g. brands as a cue for product quality) to speed up the purchase process. These changes in behaviour are known as *behavioural adaptation strategies* (Milgram 1970) and are due to stimulus overload. In effect, the shopper cannot perform the required task (shopping) as too many factors are beyond his or her control. Action is taken to rectify this situation, usually involving *simplification of the task*. In the store environment this translates as a *downsizing of the shopping plan*.

A number of factors influence perceptions of crowding and behaviour under conditions of crowding. Hui and Bateson (1991) suggest that *perceived control*, or the degree to which a shopper is in command of a situation, is an important factor in a shopper's perception of crowding. As perceived control increases, physical and psychological well-being increase, leading to reduced perceptions of crowding. More detail can be added to this approach by considering two factors that affect perceived control, *consumer density* and *consumer choice*. Consumer density is the number of shoppers in a given store area and, as such, is objective. Consumer choice is the degree to which shoppers believe that it is their decision to stay in the store environment, and is largely subjective in nature. An increase in consumer density and/or a decrease in consumer choice will lead to a decrease in perceived control that will, in turn, lead to an increase in the perception of crowding. The specific environment also has an effect on perceived crowding, as each shopper will make a judgement on an appropriate consumer density for a given store. This judgement is part of *manning theory*, and allows stores to be classified on a scale from high to low required consumer density.

The *psychological profile* of the shopper will also affect crowding, owing to the importance of that shopper's perceptions – i.e. perceived crowding is more relevant than actual crowding. Eroglu and Machleit (1990) found that different shopper types, task- and non-task-orientated, had different perceptions of crowding. *Task-orientated* or *utilitarian* shoppers were found, under certain conditions, to perceive greater retail crowding than that perceived by the *non-task-orientated* or *hedonic* shoppers (see Chapter 3).

The implications of crowding for the retailer are quite simple. If shoppers perceive a store to be crowded it is probable that their store experience will suffer, possibly leading to a negative perception of that store. In addition, behavioural adaptation strategies show that it is highly likely that the 'crowded shopper' will spend less time in the store, will concentrate on higher-priority items only and will not seek out information on potential new purchases. This being the case, it is probable that that shopper's expenditure will not be as high as it might have been had the store not been perceived as crowded. This will be particularly evident for purchases with a high service element (e.g. clothing). In such a situation, shoppers require a certain amount of contact with the sales staff prior to purchase, but tend to limit such interaction under conditions of perceived crowding. Under these circumstances, the purchase is likely to be *deferred* to a later date.

Retail Demand Management Tactics

Further analysis of the input–output model discussed earlier (Table 14.1) shows that four broad options are available to the retailer to keep the store at or close to its ideal point (Figure 14.2); manage input rate, change output rate, alter average shopping time and implement recovery measures. *Managing the input rate* relates to shopping patterns and accessibility while *changing the output rate* can be achieved by changes to the staffing level, the system itself and the physical nature of the store. *Altering the average shopping time* primarily relates to store design, but could also cover shopper targeting policies and expectations management. *Recovery measures* seek to moderate the negative effects of short-term crowding on shoppers. If shoppers' waiting time cannot be reduced, for example, measures can be introduced to make that time more bearable.

Demand management problems can be considered to be either *foreseen* or *unforeseen* (Shemwell and Cronin 1994). Marketing research and past experience can allow shopping patterns to be *predicted* to a reasonable degree of accuracy. Complete accuracy is very rare, if not impossible, owing to the influence of uncontrollable factors in the retail and macro environments. A competing store may, for example, have had a fire that forced it to close. The next nearest store may, therefore, experience an increase in demand. These occasions can give retailers the opportunity to obtain new customers and so must be exploited. These points indicate that foreseen demand changes can be *planned for*, unforeseen changes must be *reacted to quickly* and *effectively*.

Demand management problems may also be *manageable* or *unmanageable*. As an example, a small store near to a sporting venue may find huge peaks in demand around the start and end of the game. The demand increase is foreseen but may not be manageable – i.e. the store may simply not be large enough to cope with the increased number of shoppers arriving in a short time period. In this case, the store owner can either increase the size of the store, or accept that the situation cannot be managed.

Putting these two factors together (see Figure 14.3) adds extra detail to the four tactical areas mentioned at the start of this section. It is apparent that if a demand increase is unforeseen input rate management tactics cannot manage it. Such tactics seek to change demand 'in advance', so once shoppers have arrived at the store there is little a retailer can do to change the input rate apart from turn them away. This obviously builds shopper dissatisfaction and may damage the image of the retailer. In this case, the retailer must either change the output rate to increase throughput or must adopt recovery measures, to avoid a negative perceived store shopping experience. If unforeseen demand cannot be managed, the only options for retailers are to use recovery measures, or

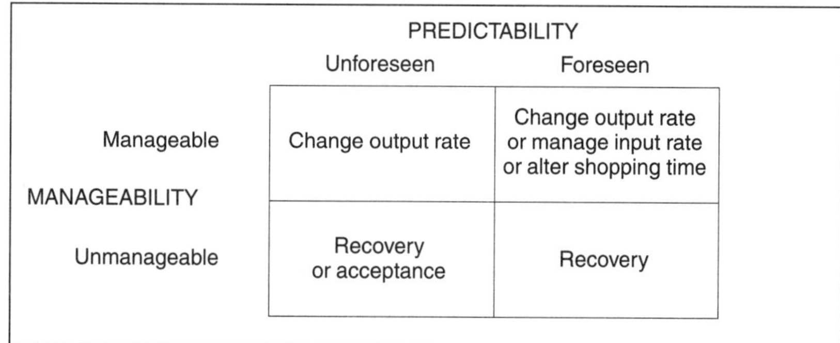

Figure 14.3 The predictability/manageability matrix

accept the situation and take no action. In cases where demand changes are foreseen, the retailer can either manage the input rate, change the output rate or alter the average shopping time. If the situation cannot be managed, the retailer must resort to recovery measures.

Input Rate Management

It has already been noted that input rate is dependent on *accessibility* and *shopping patterns*. Input rate management is, therefore, concerned with these two factors and has the task of either increasing or decreasing input rates. Many accessibility issues such as traffic queues and road access are uncontrollable factors from the retailer's point of view as they cannot easily address such problems. The best they can hope for is to influence the local planners to upgrade facilities to match the periods of greatest demand. It is not feasible to use general access to decrease input rates, especially with respect to car-based shoppers, but of course there is some control possible where public transport is a major feature if agreement is reached with the providers.

In general, input rates need to be increased to counter periods of low demand while rate decreases are associated with avoiding severe crowding or system overload. It is also true that input rates may need to be increased owing to overall poor performance rather than demand fluctuations. It should be noted, however, that this situation will often require more wide-ranging changes in other tactical areas such as pricing, the assortment or indeed promotion and changes in shopping patterns are sometimes only temporary.

To increase input rate where appropriate it might require activities that 'sell' the benefits of shopping at less busy times (e.g. more relaxed, faster, easier, with service being more readily available). This could be supported by incentives for shoppers to visit during *slack periods* (in-store promotions), or direct appeals to groups who are less time-constrained (e.g. elderly, unemployed). It is always possible to change opening hours within legal limits given laws on Sunday trading, and on the hours when retailers can sell products such as alcohol.

To decrease input rate a programme of *de*-marketing is necessary. By making shoppers aware of the busy times and the poorer shopping experience at such times it is possible to deter some customers. However the risk is that many more potential shoppers will form a poorer view of the retailer in the process. Less contentious are initiatives that make *shopping at peak times more expensive* – e.g. parking costs – or difficult – perhaps by restricting supply of shopping trolleys – but these are really negative operational solutions to a marketing problem. Because loyal shoppers are usually the most valuable customers it would be more proactive to introduce initiatives that take care of these loyal or regular shoppers first. For instance Debenhams, the retail department store, holds special events for store card holders on the evening prior to a sale starting. This gives this group a chance to purchase sale merchandise prior to the wider public, and it is also supported by extra discounts available to this group.

Store Capacity and Output Rate Management

Many of the factors involved in the management of the shopping experiences have already been mentioned. The issues of particular relevance will be those related to average shopping time, the physical constraints of a store, the retail systems used and staffing. These all have a direct application to physical stores but in different ways are just as relevant for online virtual retailers. A further consideration must be the question of customer recovery, how to regain the custom from shoppers following an unsatisfactory visit to a store or a Web site (see Chapter 13).

Shopping time can be effectively managed if the *store design* allows for efficient shopping. This is primarily controlled by the layout and often marketing finds that decisions have been taken at an early stage and any modifications to improve the management of the customer experience involve a great deal of internal debate. It is often easier for marketing input, especially in the area of staff training, to be focused on ensuring that all customer service is delivered quickly to minimize a shopper's downtime (waiting to be served). This can be achieved by educating shoppers on store layout, utilizing good signing and arranging merchandise in obvious category groupings, the objective being to facilitate more efficient shopping and a better shopping experience. The example given earlier of the IKEA store maps actually reduce the occurrence of shoppers trying to move against the main customer flow, so with all customers moving in the same direction an efficient system results. For online shopping the time will be spent navigating the Web site, and the use of effective links leads to much the same types of efficiencies.

With regards modifications to the physical constraints, these usually are made to increase the *maximum throughput rate*. They can involve changes to the building or its physical layout, the building or renting of temporary selling space or storage capacity. In the summer months many restaurants and cafes extend their serving areas onto the pavements in front of the premises, which is just one way of extending outside the store's physical limits.

It is rare for physical limits to be altered to match demands in periods where a reduction might be acceptable. However, it is possible to take some selling space out of a store and utilize it in a very different, and maybe less productive, way if it actually offers other benefits to shoppers, enhancing their shopping experience. A restaurant might not offer the same turnover per sq. metre but could provide an area for *relaxation* where a possible purchase can be considered and a store visit prolonged. A *crèche* can certainly allow parents to focus their attention away from their children and onto the merchandise. An *information desk* can provide much-needed help and assistance and so increase the probability of an informed purchase. A *display area* where a craftsperson can be seen working – say, making interesting silver jewellery – can provide a focal point and encourage shoppers to consider other purchases. There are many other creative ideas but each must be evaluated in respect of the costs, including the opportunity costs of lost selling space compared to the benefits of a better shopping experience.

When it comes to managing demand, especially peak level, within a store, it is necessary to have a *customer consciousness* in exploring the flexibility that can be created from the retail systems that are in use. For instance: What is the most efficient and fairest way of organizing customer queuing? Should a number be given to customers so each can be served in turn or a single queue feeding several cash points as in many Banks and Post Offices? Could other additional temporary transaction-processing be used to increase capacity, for instance placing cash tills on customer service desks? In what ways could technology (such as EPOS and EFTPOS) be utilized to increase throughput levels? And is it possible to prioritize exit points at busy times, maybe having exits for those with only small purchases, such as queues for 'less than 10 items', as in many supermarkets?

Of course, there are early warning signs, especially if the number of shoppers entering a store is monitored effectively and this could then be linked formally by a procedure giving warning of potential crowding so that extra staff can be in place before any problems occur – maybe calling staff back from rest breaks, or transferring staff from back-of-store operations to assist during a peak demand period.

Of course this requires the co-operation of staff, and suitable terms of service and relevant training. Such arrangements may seem a long way from the marketing role but are absolutely critical to the success of many retail organizations. Therefore a retail marketer should demonstrate the benefits of:

- *Cross-training* employees to relieve short-run demand surges
- Match staffing levels to *predicted demand levels*
- Training staff to *increase throughput levels.*

These internal staff actions are as beneficial to the achievement of marketing objectives as any persuasive promotional campaign. It must always be remembered that a bad experience could lose a customer *forever*. The cost of customer recovery is usually much greater than the additional costs of coping with irregular peak demand periods.

Recovery essentially means targeting disaffected customers and devising a marketing programme that will retain or retrieve these customers instead of losing them to competitors. The best type of recovery is to *anticipate problems* before they occur and try to deal with some of the major factors such as crowding and queuing so that the worst effects can be eliminated. A number of researchers have suggested strategies to deal with perceived crowding; usually these are based on increasing consumer choice to avoid *bottlenecks*. Retailers could, for example, give shoppers a number of potential store starting points when consumer density is high. Other strategies relate to the provision of information to help customers make informed choices, or tactics that might distract shoppers and so make the problems less uncomfortable, or modifications to the design of the store.

Making information more easily available may allow shoppers to simplify their shopping process by cutting down the time spent on information searching. If this simplification is enough for the shopper to regain sufficient control over the situation, the amount of purchases may not be reduced to such a large extent. It could also allow shoppers to decide on the time they would prefer to visit a store and so coming at peak times is not a major shock. *Distraction* aims to affect a shopper's judgement of crowding. If, for example, music is played in the store shoppers have been found to have a different perception of the environment (see Chapter 7 on Store Design). It can be argued that the effect of the music is to change the shopper's level of perceived control. Store design can also be modified to allow *threshold consumer density* to be increased and shopping to be easier under conditions of perceived crowding (see Chapter 7 on Store Design).

Conclusions

Retail demand management is not the sole preserve of marketing. In fact, in many companies there is very little marketing involvement in such matters but, as can be seen in this chapter, there is much more to reaching marketing objectives than external marketing. Retail marketing is about getting the best results in a service industry where the function of the retailer is to add value in a way that benefits a customer. *Managing* demand, rather than simply *stimulating* it, is a crucial activity.

The shopping experience can be considered within an input–output system that attracts customers into a store, making it easy to enter, ensures that time spent in the store is both rewarding and enjoyable, then after a purchase has (hopefully) taken place, leaving the store without trouble. This can be seen easily with respect to a 'bricks and mortar' store, but applies equally to mail-order and online shopping, even though some elements of the latter actually help to protect customers from the physical frustrations of physical stores. Perhaps the greatest contribution of marketing could be to ensure all employees of a retail organization can appreciate the situation from a customer perspective. Thus the marketer must act as an *advocate of the customer*, reflecting customer need into the store design, the systems utilized and the way the staff are trained and prepared for their job of satisfying those needs. But that is not the whole task, as customer satisfaction is a balance between the benefits expected or received and the perceived cost in acquiring them. If a marketing initiative can manage the expectations of customers to ensure there are few unrealistic expectations, and can also help to reduce the worst effects of any problems that might occur, then there is a greater chance of long-term satisfaction. All the issues discussed in the chapter are focused on such an objective. Many of the activities rely on the marketer as *influencer* and not an *implementer*, but with regard to all communication with customers and customer-focused strategies there is a greater role.

This chapter should be studied with the thought in mind that marketing can make *promises* to customers, but it takes everyone and a whole organization to deliver *satisfaction*.

References and Further Reading

Crandall, R.E. and Markland, R.E. (1996) Demand Management – Today's Challenge for Service Industries, *Production & Operations Management*, 5, 2, 106–20.

East, R., Lomax, W., Willson, G. and Harris, P. (1994) Decision Making and Habit in Shopping Times, *European Journal of Marketing*, 28, 4, 56–71.

Eroglu, S.A. and Machleit, K.A. (1990) An Empirical Study of Retail Crowding: Antecedents and Consequences, *Journal of Retailing*, 66, 2, 301–21.

Hui, M.K. and Bateson, J.E.G. (1991) Perceived Control and the Effects of Crowding and Consumer Choice on the Service Experience, *Journal of Consumer Research*, 18, 2, 174–85.

Kotler, P. (1973) The Major Tasks of Marketing Management, *Journal of Marketing*, 37, 42–9.

Milgram, S. (1970) The Experience of Living in Cities, *Science*, 167, 1464–468.

Sasser, W.E. Jr. (1976) Match Supply and Demand in Service Industries, *Harvard Business Review*, November–December, 133–40.

Shemwell, D.J. Jr. and Cronin, J.J. Jr. (1994) Services Marketing Strategies for Coping with Demand/Supply Imbalances, *Journal of Services Marketing*, 8, 4, 14–24.

Stockdale, J.E. (1978) Crowding: Determinants and Effects, *Advances in Experimental and Social Psychology*, 11, 197–245.

Stokols, D. (1972) On the Distinction Between Density and Crowding: Some Implications for Future Research, *Psychological Review*, 79, 275–77.

Zeithaml, V.A. and Bitner, M.J. (1996) *Services Marketing*, McGraw-Hill, New York.

Strategic Aspects of Retailing

CHAPTER 15

This chapter:

- Shows how marketing is a profitable exchange between supplier and customer
- Defines key factors in retail marketing strategy
- Shows the importance of competitive positioning in the retail marketplace

Strategic Aspects of Retailing

Introduction

Marketing is based upon an incredibly simple yet powerful concept, *the creation of a profitable exchange between a supplier and a customer*. This book has explored many of the dimensions of this concept and has suggested ways in which such an exchange can be achieved in a retail setting. The issues involved start with some wide-ranging decisions on retail location, true to the maxim that retail success comes from the application of *location; location; location*. They then move into the micro retail environment and focus on specific elements in the retail marketing mix such as pricing and customer care.

In Chapter 2 there was an attempt to put retail marketing strategy into context. It was suggested that

> Marketing strategy is ... difficult to pin down. Fifield offers 10 definitions, each from an eminent academic, and each emphasising that person's own specific premise regarding strategy. This leads to confusion, and Fifield seeks to reduce this. Rather than produce his own definition he opts to suggest what marketing strategy does, and on this there is a much greater consensus.

This led to the suggestion that:

> Marketing strategy is the process by which the organisation translates its business objectives and business strategy into market activity.

In Chapter 2, there was no further attempt to define strategy, nor to examine the components of a good strategy as opposed to a poor one. However there was a strong argument to establish that the three key determinants of success or failure in every retail situation and marketing exchange are:

- ▶ The *competitive market environment* in which the activities have to be performed

- The *customers* who are the target of the retail marketing activity
- The *capabilities and competencies* of the retailer to undertake those activities.

The crucial test of a strategy is whether it appears to be *feasible* in a given competitive market when considering the target customers and the capabilities and competencies that the retailer has available.

The word 'strategy' is derived from the Greek word *strategos* (στρατηγος) which means 'general', one who leads an army. As such, strategy can be seen as including every major decision that is made in the battle for success in the very competitive retail marketplace. As with any battle there will be major decisions concerning the *future direction* of the retail business, and other decisions that are more *tactical*, regarding how to manoeuvre into a more favourable position by modifying one or more component of the retail marketing mix. There is no clear dividing line between strategy and tactics – in fact, some relatively small tactical decisions can sometimes have a much more significant strategic effect than anticipated. For instance, a change in the balance of merchandise stocked could remove a loss making line but if it leads to some customers visiting competitor shops to find out whether the item is available in another store, it could affect a lot more than the original product.

The obvious areas of strategic importance relate to the *markets to be served*, the *class* and *range* of merchandise that are to be offered, and the overall position regarding *price*, *quality* and *value*. Each of these involves crucial decisions that are difficult to change in a short time frame. Such positions are not fixed for all time as any study of the development of Tesco from a low-price convenience store to a high-quality major supermarket will show. The decision of Jack Cohen, founder of Tesco, to trade on a 'pile it high sell it cheap' basis created a trading strategy that enabled the company to be very successful over many years. However, when the need to change was identified it became a liability that took several years to replace, and many more years for the perception of the company to alter in the minds of consumers.

When considering the strategic aspects of retailing it is necessary to start with the *overall objectives* of the company – or, for a new store, its founder. From these it will be possible to propose options regarding how these objectives might be achieved. After evaluation of the options, decisions can then be taken regarding *overall direction* of the retail venture and this is when more specific considerations as to markets, products and position will be debated. This type of market based planning provides a logical way of operating and is especially relevant to established retailers. However, for new ventures it can be very different. When Anita Roddick started the Body Shop, she had no overall plan for the company, just a desire to offer a range of 'ethical' products and a feeling that there must be an opportunity in this respect. She had a vision and the objectives were to bring this to life in her own retail operation. If she had foreseen the problems and logically evaluated all the options, it is possible a different outcome would have ensued. In the development of the Body Shop the strategy was developed on a sequential basis, considering problems as they arose and taking decisions from within a limited number of alternatives as a momentum developed and the company became ever more successful. Now that the Body Shop is an established multinational operation, the objectives for the company will also have developed. They are now more likely to involve specific aspects of how to build on the successes already achieved, and how to avoid any threats that could affect these.

So the question as to what is, and what is not, 'strategic' remains poorly defined. Perhaps it is best viewed from within the market planning sequence that follows five questions:

- Where are we *now?*
- Where do we *want to be?*
- How can we *get there?*
- Which way is *best?*
- How can we ensure that we are *on course?*

The strategic decisions tend to be concentrated in the third and fourth steps, in particular the decisions regarding *option choice* – 'which way is best?' This is where the business objectives and business strategy are translated into *market activity*. This market activity is then expressed in terms of the 'Key Marketing Factors in Retailing'. In Chapter 4 these were put in four natural groupings:

1. LOCATION AND PERCEIVED IMAGE
   - Physical/virtual location
   - Retail image, position and reputation
2. INTERNAL ENVIRONMENT AND CORE PRODUCT
   - Internal atmosphere/environment
   - Range/assortment of goods offered
3. IN-STORE STIMULI
   - Relative price/value perception
   - Promotional effectiveness
   - Service levels, both during and after sales
4. RELATIONSHIP ISSUES AND BUILDING LOYALTY
   - Strength of any on-going relationships that might exist.

There could be strategic consequences regarding initiatives within any one of these groupings. However as all these market activities actually merge together into a *holistic offering*, seen and evaluated by potential customers, it is always appropriate to reconsider the wider direction of any retail operation by asking the questions:

- Does our total offering really have a *competitive advantage?*
- Are we still attracting the *right customer groups?*
- Does our operation have sufficient *resources* and *capabilities* to continue successfully in the future?

These questions relate back to the *determinants of success*, Ohmae's (1983) strategic triangle of Competitors – Customers – our Company (Figure 15.1).

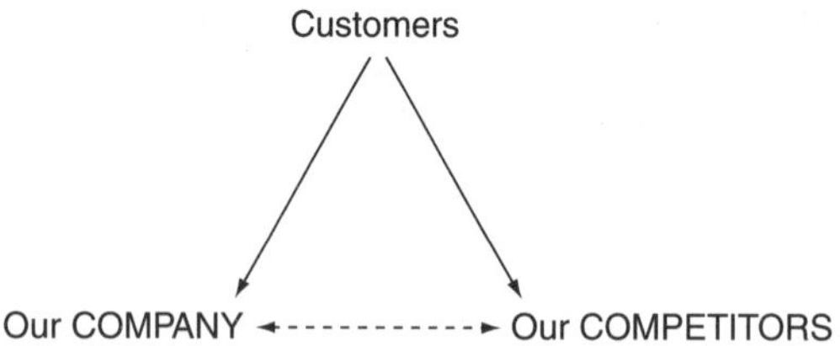

Figure 15.1 Ohmae's strategic triangle
Source: Adcock, Halborg and Ross (2001:70).

Competitive Positioning in a Retail Marketplace

There are many different competitive positions that are possible for either a single retail store, or perhaps a multiple retail group. The structure of the marketplace and the strength of any existing positions will determine the feasibility of any specific one. It could be that the store is already the market leader in its segment, in which case it will be necessary to develop strategies that defend this position from attack. It is very easy to become complacent, believing success will continue but Marks & Spencer now know that this is not an option. In part the problems of Marks & Spencer have been attributed to the success of the Matalan retail operation, but it is clear that Matalan has a very different market position to that occupied by M&S.

The competitive position occupied by a retailer could be described in term of the *market share* of the store (group). This could be as a *leader,* or maybe a *challenger*, or perhaps a *small niche operator*. It is also possible to position the retailer as a high-quality provider, a full-service retailer, a discounter or a category killer, or some other description, perhaps related to the merchandise and how it is offered. There is a great deal of argument over how to define the boundaries of a particular retail market, but in some ways it is unhelpful to be too specific. A 'category killer' such as Toys 'Я' Us might dominate and lead its market, but it could still be in competition with a 'PoundShop' with regard to stocking-filler toys at Christmas. Nevertheless the position of Toys 'Я' Us is very clear, it does dominates the toy market by offering large outlets with extensive choice and competitive prices. It is hard to ignore the store and it is likely that it will attract shoppers even if some might use a visit to the store to benchmark offerings before considering alternatives.

The best starting point when assessing the competitive positioning of a retailer is an initial broad definition of the *market boundaries* such as toy market, grocery food market, fashion market, etc; it is then possible to consider the retailers who compete in this marketplace. In defining a market it is necessary to take heed of the warning given by Moran (1973), when he suggested that:

> In our complex society there are no more product classes; not in any meaningful sense, only as a figment of some file clerk's imagination. There are only use classes – users which are central to some products and peripheral to others – on a vast overlapping

> spectrum. To some degree, in some circumstances almost anything can be a partial substitute for almost anything else.

Moran was writing about new products and why they fail, but he could have easily looked at the reason why some retailers also fail. The idea that Toys 'Я' Us could be in competition with a 'PoundShop', or Marks & Spencer with Matalan must always be considered. The 'overlapping continuum' of Moran is very obvious in any retail arena.

Within every market there will be obvious candidates as:

- ▶ Market leader
- ▶ Challenger
- ▶ Nicher.

Of course, it might be that the same retailer appears in more than one marketplace. For instance Marks & Spencer would like to be considered a UK leader in everyday clothing, but it is also a focused niche retailer of food. Conversely, Tesco is the leader in the grocery food sector, but a niche operator with its clothing range. There are many other examples of retailers using their strength in one area, which is how customers are attracted into the store, then *supplementing the core merchandise offered* with other unrelated but relevant items.

The strategic choices for a market leader will be very different to those for a challenger company. The renowned American academic Michael Porter (1980) suggested that there were only three generic positions that a company could occupy in its market:

- ▶ Cost leadership
- ▶ Differentiation of the offering
- ▶ Focus on a niche market.

He later sub-divided the focus category into *cost focus* and *differentiation focus*. While these categories have been criticized as too simplistic, they still offer an excellent way of reviewing a position. David Sainsbury pointed to the success of his company and the slogan 'Good Food costs less at Sainsbury's' to suggest that a retailer could be both a cost leader and a differentiator. Whilst it is undoubtedly true that every retailer must be efficient (though not necessarily a cost leader) and must differentiate its offering in the eyes of its customers, Porter's argument was that it is very difficult to offer variety whilst driving costs down. Certainly Sainsbury are not a low-cost grocery operator when compared to Kwiksave or Netto, but there is a difference between low-cost and low-price. It is interesting to note that Sainsbury's was once the market leader in UK groceries, it has since lost that position to Tesco – and, more recently, both companies have felt the pressure of renewed competition following the takeover of Asda by Wal-Mart. Asda should be described as a 'challenger' company in the UK grocery food sector.

Every retailer has to consider the *strategic aspects* of their market position. Study of the UK grocery market will show that all retailers are involved in trying to differentiate their offerings while also attempting to be as efficient as possible (cost-conscious). The degree to which each store is successful in achieving its specific differentiated position determines its success in the chosen marketplace. For a leader, it will be appropriate to develop a strategy designed to defend their position. With Tesco, this is achieved by an interaction of several factors, all in the marketing mix, rather than concentrating on a single element of the mix. Tesco have cleverly interwoven quality merchandise with a breadth of range, supported by good service and reasonable prices – and, importantly, is perceived to offer these. It is very difficult for a challenger company to attack on all these fronts.

Marks & Spencer also believe the *quality, service* and *value* are part of its market position but, as recent consumer surveys have shown, there is little perception as to the comparative level of superior service and even less as regards value. In other markets the leader could rely on fewer comparative factors for instance Amazon.com concentrate on price above anything else. Asda tries to combine its 'Price Promise' with a welcoming atmosphere signalled by a 'greeter' at the door with a big 'Can I help you' badge. The point to be considered is that 'cosmetic activities' do very little to change market positions. If Asda really want to be perceived as the friendly supermarket, then they will have to make a more strategic investment in a number of its activities and allow time for shoppers to appreciate them.

If a retailer decides to adopt the position of a nicher, there is the need for it to be seen as the *dominant operator in a focused sector of the market*. It is necessary to try to dominate a specific area of merchandise, maybe TieRack is a good example, or to 'own' a particular segment of consumers in the way Watersons academic bookshops try to gain exclusive positions on many university campuses.

Managing Customers Strategically

The task of attracting the right customers into a store is more than simple segmentation. Of course, all retailers should consider the profile of its *preferred ideal shoppers,* as well as determining any groups that it might wish to deter. This will then enable the store to draw up strategies that might achieve such a result. With the help of Andersen Consulting, Marks & Spencer have introduced a new strategy termed Local Store Cataloguing. The aim is to tailor the range of merchandise in each of its 680 stores to the customer profile for that individual store, (previously the only determinant of the range had been the size of the store). The Marks & Spencer head office had both planned and allocated the assortment and all stores of a similar size received and stocked the same range irrespective of their local conditions. The change seems simple and logical, but it has taken the company a long time to realize that there is a strategic link between customers and the assortment offered. Under the new policy there is no change in the overall image or positioning of a store, but there is a subtle change in the relationship to customer needs.

There are too many retailers who define customers in terms of 'demographic labels', that is the age, sex and income of customers. Shopping behaviour is not driven by such categorizations, it is an *emotional* activity and therefore it is better to define customers by their *motivations* rather than their descriptions. Good retailers develop strategies to appeal to specific *behavioural groups*, and that is the key to meeting customer needs. The type of segmentation that might be appropriate could be individual customer profitability based on store data with respect to spending patterns, balanced by the cost to serve. It could be that some customers are routine purchasers who cost little to serve and purchase regularly. Tesco.com maintains a basic shopping list on behalf of its regular customers that provides a basic order for future purchases. Other shoppers will not have regular standard requirements, and they might also be more demanding in terms of service expected. Retailers must attempt to identify the 'cash cow' shoppers and develop strategies that encourage them whilst deterring those customers who could be described as 'dogs'. (Note the categories of 'cash cows' and 'dogs' actually refer to businesses in the well-known BCG matrix (Boston Consulting Group). However they could easily be applied to customers.)

In general marketing, Doyle (2000) reports on a variety of Pareto's 80:20 rule. Drawing on the work of Cooper and Kaplan (1991), he suggests that 20 per cent of customers can account for over 200 per cent of profits, while 80 per cent are actually responsible for losses that reduce the final profit by more than half. Most retailers are only too happy to serve anyone who visits their store: that is fine provided no costs are involved in attracting that customer, and provided that the cost of serving that customer is lower than the profits obtained. In order to achieve this, it is necessary to strategically evaluate the profitability, and long-term potential of every shopper. Sometimes stores that offer deep price cuts to attract shoppers do not get any additional business and lose money when serving some customers. For instance, Somerfield supermarkets use an array of very attractive promotional offers, many at half price, in order to build store traffic. However, there does not seem to be any evaluation as regards the number of shoppers who purchase only from the current promotional products. Casual observation suggests that this is happening, and that there are many customers who are unlikely to balance the buying of the loss-leader products with full-price, profitable purchases. Perhaps if Somerfield had loyalty card data they might be able to investigate this behaviour.

Managing customers strategically means thinking seriously about all customers; deciding which ones must be the focus of attention; developing strategies to achieve satisfaction for the chosen customers; and then encouraging these customers to return. Garth Halberg summed up the issue when he wrote: 'Marketers can't afford to be democratic. They must invest their efforts and their budgets where they will produce the most return. The most valuable customers deserve special treatment to build and retain their loyalty. The risk of not giving it to them is great. If a marketer treats high profit consumers like everyone else ... they will treat the marketers brand like any other.' The message is clear, and successful retailers develop appropriate ways of responding. This could involve finding ways of creating customer data, such as via the Tesco Club Card, that can be utilized in a strategic way with regard to shoppers.

Competencies and Capabilities

The final, strategic aspect of retailing refers to the ability of a store, or retail organization to *provide the service promised* to its shoppers. It is very easy to promise too much, but the result will inevitably be dissatisfied customers and a reputation for poor service. The twin concepts of *competence* and *capability* refer to two closely related, yet distinct, aspects of retail provision. *Competencies* are the available skills that a retailer can build upon. These can be enshrined in high levels of customer service, or may be some other skills such as the way a retailer utilizes the available technology. *Capabilities* are enshrined in the actual behaviour of an organization, including the ability to stretch its resources to create a more competitive offering.

Hamel and Prahalad (1994) suggest that for every organization there will be some competencies that are critical to success – the core competencies – and these should be identified and developed. They also recommend organizations to try to identify those competencies that they do not currently possess that could be crucial in the years ahead. This is because it might not be possible to acquire such competencies unless a start is made in developing them before they are needed. For instance with the growth of e-tailing the competence with regards to designing and maintaining a Web site might be considered crucial. It might be possible to buy in the skills, but there are good strategic reasons for developing skills inside the retail organization.

The skills and resources, especially the *human resources of retail staff*, must be developed into the capability to provide a service at the required level for the chosen shoppers. Kotler (1997) once wrote: 'Marketing makes promises to customers, but it takes the whole organisation to deliver satisfaction'. A good retail manager will be able to assess the requirements for delivering 'satisfaction' and express these in term of capabilities. While much of the work to train staff and create the required capabilities will rest with the personnel function, it is crucial to marketing success that there is a match between the promises made and the capability to perform. Strategic investments in resources, competencies and capability development should therefore be planned in conjunction with marketing, and marketing initiatives prepared in the knowledge of what is really possible.

Conclusions

This book has concentrated on the specific marketing tasks necessary in order to succeed in a competitive retail marketplace. These are based on a need to attract customers into a store, or other retail site, persuade them to make purchases while in the store, and then encourage them to return for further visits in the future. Each event can bring the store and its customers closer together, so that an extreme result could be a strong relationship based on commitment and loyalty. This does not always occur, and it may be enough for a retailer to get a share of the passing trade sufficient to meet the objectives of the business.

Many of the activities that assist the achievement of a retailer's objectives are purely *tactical*. Nevertheless behind every tactic there will be a strategic direction and a number of key decisions that have a long-term effect on the business. These are also of a strategic nature. Therefore without actually defining what is, and what is not, 'strategic', it is important that every decision is considered for its longer-term implications. This will apply to any attempt to position a retailer within a given market. It will also be determined by the competitive position actually occupied by that retailer. It will apply to attempts to attract or deter shoppers from the store, and be determined by the shoppers who actually visit an existing outlet. In fact, as Marks & Spencer have found, there are many risks inherent in trying to appeal to new segments of shoppers, without giving due attention as to how changes might impinge upon traditional customers. Many retailers have to appeal to a wide number of customers, it is always easier to be a highly focused niche operator than a more general supplier. The 'wheel of retailing' continues to turn, affecting all markets, and requiring *decisions as to the future*, rather than analysis of the past.

To meet the needs of customers, and fully satisfy those who are particularly important, it is necessary to ensure that the retailer pays due consideration to the competencies and capabilities that underpin its offerings. These are critical to marketing success, although often not under the control of the marketing manager. There tends to be a strong focus on the current requirements in this respect, so one role of a retail marketer might be to predict the requirements into the future. It will then be possible to assess what new competencies might be required, and if this is done these new skills and resources can be acquired in good time to meet the future needs of the business.

References and Further Reading

Adcock, D.G. (2000) *Marketing Strategies for Competitive Advantage*, Wiley, New York.

Cooper, R. and Kaplan, R.S. (1991) *The Design of Cost Management Systems*, Prentice Hall, Englewood Cliffs, NJ.

Doyle, P. (2000) *Value Based Marketing*, Wiley, New York.

Fifield, P. (1992) *Marketing Strategy*, Butterworth-Heinemann, Oxford.

Hallberg, G. (1993) *All Consumers are Not Created Equal: The Differential Strategy for Brand Loyalty and Profits*, Wiley, New York.

Hamel, G. and Prahalad, C.K. (1994) *Competing for the Future*, Harvard Business Press, Boston, MA.

Hooley, G.J., Saunders, J.A. and Piercy, N.F. (1998) *Marketing Strategy and Competitive Positioning*, 2nd edn, Prentice-Hall, Englewood Cliffs, NJ.

Kotler, P. (1997) *Marketing Management: Analysis, Planning, Implementation and Control*, Prentice Hall, Englewood Cliffs, NJ.

Moran, W.R. (1973) Why New Products Fail, *Journal of Advertising Research*, April.

Ohmae, K. (1983) *The Mind of the Strategist*, Penguin Books, London.

Porter, M.E. (1980) *Competitive Advantage*, The Free Press, New York.

Online Retail Marketing

CHAPTER 16

This chapter:

- Explains the growth of modern online retailing
- Compares online and offline retail strategies

Online Retail Marketing

Introduction

Electronic commerce (e-commerce) refers to transactions that are made totally over the Internet. Typically, the buyer will visit the seller's Web site, will search through an online assortment of products and will then place the order online using a suitable means of payment. Broadening out this definition, it is possible to identify four different types of e-commerce, namely *business to business*, *consumer to consumer*, *consumer to business* and *business to consumer*. The term 'Internet retailing' is applicable to all four of these types as business to business can relate to store-based wholesalers, consumer to consumer to the original concept of a marketplace, business to consumer to traditional retailing, and consumer to business to a sort of auction. The most widely talked-about type of Internet retailing (or online retailing) is business to consumer although this typically accounts for only a small part of total online retailing sales. The major part of online retailing, typically accounting for over three-quarters of turnover, is business to business transactions. The majority of business to business transactions are accounted for by traditional *buyer–supplier* relationships that are not, strictly speaking, related to store-based wholesale. Consumer to consumer is certainly a 'primitive' form of retailing, indeed it can be said to be a distant ancestor of the modern retail system, but this is not the focus of this text. Consumer to business is a concept that, while having parallels with an auction, has more in common with co-operative buying than it does retail. This being the case, business to consumer will be the focus of this section.

Online Retailing Today

Online retailing is considerably more advanced in the USA than in Europe or the rest of the world. The reason for this is that the USA is a step ahead of the rest of the world with a high level of Internet usage *per capita* and a comparatively large number of online households. It is for this reason that the USA can be used as a guideline for the likely development of online retailing in Europe and beyond. This is not to say that the rest of the world will develop in the same way as the USA, as a number of situational factors make the two different in some respects. These factors will be discussed in due course.

Online sales in the USA, according to the Boston Consulting Group (BCG), were worth $20 billion in 1999, or approximately 2 per cent of total retail sales. Put into perspective, catalogue sales in the USA for the same period amounted to around 10 per cent of retail sales. Clearly, then, online retailing is still relatively undeveloped. In comparison, online sales in all of Europe amounted to $3.6 billion in 1999. Just over two-thirds of all online retail sales in the USA are accounted for by the top four areas: computer hardware and software, travel, financial services and collectibles. Financial services account for the highest penetration, taking approximately 15 per cent of all financial services business, followed by computer hardware and software at 9 per cent, books at 5 per cent, music/video at 2 per cent and travel at 2 per cent. In comparison, the highest share in Europe is accounted for by financial services at approximately 5.5 per cent, followed by computer hardware and software at 3.5 per cent, books at 2 per cent, music/video at 1 per cent and travel at 1 per cent. Examples of the growing penetration of online travel retailers in the UK are the discount airlines EasyJet and Go that claim to be selling 60 per cent and 50 per cent of their tickets online, respectively.

A number of different types of online retailer exist, ranging from individual companies selling a limited assortment to companies that are more akin to an offline retailer selling a wide assortment of products on a 'one-stop-shop' basis. Current thinking suggests that the wide-assortment online retailer will follow in the steps of its offline counterpart and begin to grow in prominence. This is not to say that more specialized online retailers will not exist, more that the bulk of sales will increasingly move to the larger operators. As with anything to do with the Internet, this forecast is an educated guess rather than a solid prediction.

The large online retailers mentioned above are known as 'Portals', and share many similarities with traditional offline retailers. A major selling point is their ability to bring a wide range of products from a wide range of suppliers to the immediate attention of a wide range of shoppers. In the online world this is achieved virtually, in the offline world physically. Offline retailers grew on the back of this proposition; there is evidence to suggest that their online counterparts will do the same. *Vertical portals* tend to concentrate on a specific retail area, while *horizontal portals* cover a wider area and are the true 'one-stop-shop' of the Internet. An example of a successful portal in the UK is Microsoft's MSN, that was the most-visited site at the end of 1999.

The rapid development of online retailing in the USA and Europe is reflected in the sales forecasts currently being made. Forecasts by Forrester Research for the USA show online retailing increasing its share of total retail sales to 4 per cent in 2004 and between 15 and 20 per cent by 2010. In Europe, BCG forecast online sales to almost treble in value terms to $9 billion by the end of 2000. Growth is expected to be triggered by a continued increase in Internet usage, an increasingly online-literate shopper and a realization by companies that online retailing can offer easy access to the global marketplace.

Factors Affecting the Development of Online Retailing

In assessing the prospects for the development of online retailing, a number of positive and negative factors can be identified. On the positive side, online retailing is convenient, flexible, offers significant operational and financial benefits for the retailer, can reach a large number of shoppers, and can be tailored to individual shopper requirements. In addition, Internet usage is on the increase and technological advances will make access faster and more convenient. On the negative side, delivery can be a problem, hidden costs for the retailer can be high, social contact is largely absent, physical contact with products is impossible, browsing and impulse purchasing are harder to encourage, payment can be an issue, instant gratification is not the norm, and the ability of the retailer to influence shoppers may be more limited.

The convenience and flexibility of online retailing is based on the ability of the shopper to have access to a wide assortment of products at the 'click of a mouse'. Online retailers are not constrained by store size, so can offer as many products as can be efficiently handled. Assortments can be changed quickly, particularly if the online retailer is not the manufacturer. The operational benefits for the online retailer relate to the absence of physical store constraints mentioned above, as well as the costs of such an operation. In addition, intermediaries may be cut out of the supply chain, thus reducing channel costs. Using the example of Amazon.com, probably the best-known online retailer, the company carries very limited stock and directs orders straight to the biggest book wholesaler in the USA. Stock levels are low, so working capital is limited and the assortment is huge so shoppers have access to a much wider selection of books than could easily be displayed in an offline book store.

Other operational benefits include the ability to reach a wide number of potential shoppers (technically every online shopper in the world) thus ensuring significant *scale advantages* over an offline retailer. Data can also be gained on virtually every aspect of the transaction such as search time, most-frequently visited sites and previous purchases. This being the case, the online retailer can, in theory, develop a tailored marketing approach to every single one of its shoppers. Such '1–2–1' marketing is the ultimate in segmentation and targeted marketing, and is a much less attainable dream for offline retailers.

Internet usage is increasing across the board, owing to a reduction in the cost of getting online and an increase in the acceptance of the medium. Shoppers are now able to buy the required hardware and software at a more reasonable price and can choose from an increasing array of Internet service providers (ISPs) offering cut-price access deals. Call charges are certainly higher in Europe than the USA but many ISPs are now lowering call charges in an attempt to penetrate the market. Increasing acceptance of the Internet is a function of greater understanding and easy access at work or at school. As more children use the Internet at an earlier age so the number of likely future Internet shoppers increases. The online experience will also improve, as access becomes faster with the use of faster-line speed connections (ISDN) and more convenient with the launch of mobile phone access to the Internet.

The negative factors attached to online retailing relate primarily to practicalities, both for the retailer and the shopper. A major problem for Internet retailers is *delivery* and *logistics*. The business requires a high-capacity delivery and logistics system capable of handling a large number of small packages. As the volume of online purchasing increases, so does the pressure on distribution systems. Just as the shops are crowded around Christmas time, so the distribution systems servicing online retailing have been swamped, particularly in the USA. Add to this the costs of delivery that must be absorbed by the retailer or passed on to the shopper, and hidden costs begin to appear. One of the strengths of offline retailing is that shoppers handle their own distribution by choosing the goods and paying for them at the checkout. Delivery is also taken care of by the customer and at the customer's own expense. Other hidden costs for the online retailer are incurred in the process of running and servicing a Web site to ensure that the Web is reliable to the accepted 'five nines', or 99.999 per cent goal.

An additional issue for the retailer relates to the ability to *influence the shopper*. The lack of physical contact with the store environment limits the extent to which the retailer can design that environment to increase the shopper's propensity to buy. Much of this text has been concerned with the tactics used by traditional offline retailers (assortment, pricing, promotion, service, store design, etc.) to influence shoppers. Online retailers have advantages in assortment size and pricing transparency, but do not currently have the technology to match in-store tactics such as point-of-sale (PoS) promotion, personal service and store design issues such as display and atmospherics. It has been shown in this text that a shopper's shopping experience is strongly influenced by such in-store tactics, so it is probable that online retailers suffer in this respect. The relative inability of online retailers to encourage both *browsing* and *impulse purchasing* is an additional weakness in this area.

Shopper-related negative points concern the ability to replicate the positive aspects of the offline shopping experience. Chapter 3 on Shopping Behaviour highlighted a type of shopper who shopped for much more hedonic than utilitarian reasons – i.e. was process- rather than outcome-orientated. Online retailing cannot currently offer the same *social aspects* as offline, nor can the *physical contact* with the environment be offered. Many shopping activities require social contact such as personal assistance from store personnel or interaction with other shoppers from within the shopping unit or from other shopping units. Physical contact is also an important part of many shopping situations such as fresh groceries (fruit and vegetables) and jewellery. An additional problem with online retailing is its inability to offer the shopper immediate gratification. In offline retailing, the shopper can usually take the purchase home with them, thus gaining the benefits of the purchase immediately. These benefits may be tangible (immediate use of the product) or intangible (emotional), and cannot be gained to the same extent in a system where the product is not actually touched or immediately available.

A more fundamental issue for online shoppers concerns *payment*, where it is probably true that one of the main features of the Net also gives rise to a perceived weakness. The free and easy access to the Net is a positive point for online shoppers in terms of access, but causes some to doubt the security of online payment. In addition, the usage of credit cards, the most common payment method, is less extensive in Europe than it is in the USA. These two factors may build a significant barrier to online sales.

The Future of Online Retailing

A number of positive and negative factors affecting the growth of online retailing were outlined in the previous section. Before covering these factors in more detail, it is useful to draw a parallel with a distant relative of online retailing, *catalogue shopping*. Catalogue shopping is arguably the grandparent of online retailing as the two concepts fall into the distance retailing category and both offer the benefits of the convenience of a wide assortment of products, at affordable prices, from the comfort of the shopper's own home. Sears launched the first catalogue in 1888 in the USA and sales grew at an average growth rate of at least 25 per cent per annum for the next five years. Delivery was certainly an issue, but convenience and novelty were more important factors. The novelty soon wore off, however, and the growth in catalogue shopping slowed to the current day where sales in the USA are steady at approximately 10 per cent of total retail sales. Is it likely that online retailing will follow this pattern?

Most online retailing experts discount any significant parallels with catalogue shopping. The benefits to the retailer and shopper are too great, they argue, for online shopping to peak at such a low level of retail penetration. Looking at the positive points presented above this is certainly the case with retailers able to make their offering available in a personalized way to a wide body of shoppers throughout the world. Add to this the ability of the Internet to solve many of the constraints experienced by European offline retailers and the momentum from the supply side is apparent. The main constraints are currently property prices, site availability, planning restrictions, advertising regulations (bans exist in Denmark on advertising to children, in France on advertising in English and in Germany on comparative advertising) and restrictions on opening hours. The continued development of secure payment systems (smart cards or digital cash) will alleviate security concerns, while the linking of Web sites to call centres should improve customer service.

On the strength of this analysis it would appear that online retailing has a solid future. A number of negative points still have to be addressed, however, such as cost implications and the shopping experience. The former may recede as online retailing grows in scale, Internet technology develops and distribution systems adapt. The latter is a much more difficult question to answer. The search for an answer begins with a detailed discussion of online retail marketing.

Online Retail Marketing

Earlier chapters in this text have covered the key areas of retail marketing tactics. To recap, the main considerations for retailers are the location of the store, the products to be offered (assortment), the prices that are charged for those products, the promotion of those products both inside and outside the store, customer service and relationship management, and store design. It is clear that online retailing is quite different to its offline counterpart, hence tactical differences are likely to emerge.

Online Location

Online retailers have few concerns over location, as physical accessibility is not an issue for shoppers. As long as the retailer can maintain a reliable Internet link, location can be anywhere in the world that can offer the appropriate workforce. It could be argued that being linked from the most frequently visited Web sites is an important locational issue although this is really more of a promotional factor. What is certainly true, is that online retailers have to maintain a much smaller portfolio of sites and can limit their physical locations to a minimum. The implications for *operational cost* are significant, with offline retailers suffering a large disadvantage.

The Online Assortment

The main features of online retailers' assortment decision concern the types of products that can be sold, the ability to offer a wide range of products and categories and the availability of a high level of choice.

What kinds of goods and service will sell over the Internet? A useful starting point is the distinction between high- and low-touch products. *High-touch* products are those that a shopper would prefer to have physical contact with before purchase (clothes, shoes, fresh groceries, etc.) while *low-touch* products are those that can be assessed by shoppers without physical contact (books, PCs, travel, CDs, etc.). It has already been noted that the Internet cannot give the physical contact associated with offline retailing, so it would be assumed that only low-touch products would be appropriate. Evidence from current sales shows that financial services, travel, books, CDs, computer hardware and software and music/video have the highest online sales. All these products or service can be classified as low-touch products – i.e. customers are happy to assess quality without any physical contact.

The above analysis would point to a limited range of products being sold online. This finding is not clear cut, however, as clothing is a major part of catalogue retailing and shopper perceptions of high- and low-touch products will vary. The catalogue experience shows that high-touch products (clothes) can be purchased with no actual physical contact. A fact that highlights the differences between shoppers in terms of their perceptions of what constitutes a high- or low-touch product. It is probable that a continuum of products will exist from largely high-touch to largely low-touch, and that online retailers will be able to extend their sales out of largely low-touch product areas. Technological change, particularly developments in virtual reality, may facilitate this move into higher-touch product areas if *virtual contact* can replicate actual physical contact. As an example, if online clothing retailers could offer a 'virtual fitting service', more shoppers may be persuaded to shop online.

An additional point concerns the *physical characteristics* of the product itself. Small purchases can be delivered to the shopper quite easily, while very bulky items require significantly more involved delivery. This being the case, it would be expected that bulky items would be harder to sell online. The distribution and logistics problems mentioned earlier in this chapter would also be exacerbated by a move to transporting increasingly bulky items. It is also the case that delivery costs would increase that would either have to be absorbed by the online retailer, thus increasing costs relative to their offline competitors, or be passed on to the shopper. The *nature of the product itself* is also important. Products requiring specialist handling (e.g. perishable or fragile items) may also present a problem for the online retailer.

Whatever the types of product sold online, online retailers have the ability to offer a large assortment of products and a high level of choice. The main reason for this ability is the absence of any physical space constraints, aside from those associated with logistics and distribution. Offline retailers have store selling space as a scare resource, online retailers have no such limitation. Online book retailers such as Amazon.com, for example, can offer a full catalogue of products and are constrained only by product availability. This constraint is addressed by a direct-order link to America's largest book wholesaler, alleviating many of the logistics problems.

Offering a larger assortment of products does raise a number of potential problems over and above those mentioned above. As the *depth of the assortment* (the number varieties of a given product) increases, so does shopper choice. It has already been noted that too much choice can lead to shopper confusion, as there are simply too many options to consider. This perceptual overload can often lead to purchase deferment or an unsatisfactory purchase experience. In both cases, the shopper's perception of the online retailer may be affected. Online retailers must, therefore, be aware that the benefits of choice often follow an inverted U-shape curve, similar to that noted for atmospheric elements in store design (see Chapter 7). Up to a point more choice leads to greater shopper satisfaction. As choice increases past the optimum level so shopper dissatisfaction increases.

An additional problem with larger assortments relates to *increasing assortment width* – i.e. a greater number of different types of product or product categories offered. Assortment overlap between different retailers, both actual and perceived, has been found to affect the nature of competition. As overlap increases between stores, so the level of competition also increases. It is possible, therefore, that the level of competition may increase as online retailers become more like horizontal portals. This increase in competition is fuelled by the decreased costs (time and money) associated with shopping around online.

Online Pricing

The fundamental factor affecting pricing for online retailers is *price search behaviour*. To recap, a shopper's level of price searching (between stores or within one given store) is essentially a cost/benefit analysis. Costs are those associated with searching for price information, and benefits are the financial and emotional benefits of making purchases at more attractive prices.

Online retailing allows a large number of different suppliers' prices to be checked much more easily than for an offline situation, indeed software is available now that will go some way towards carrying out this task automatically. The typical costs associated with offline price-searching – transport time, cost and effort – are greatly reduced in an online situation, as all the information is available at the 'click of a mouse'. Access speed and online fees can equate to search costs but the overall cost burden (both financial and personal) is significantly reduced. The online price searching cost/benefit analysis now gives *extra incentive for searching* so shoppers' price knowledge will increase. Add to this the time constraints being increasingly experienced by shoppers (especially working parents) and increased price-searching becomes even more likely. The reason for this is that time pressures tend to increase the costs of price-searching, as the time required to make such a search is seen as a scarce resource. Reduce the time requirements and price-searching becomes more of a realistic option.

The impact on pricing of increased price search and price knowledge will be an increased pressure on either price uniformity or the provision of higher perceived quality products. Most analysts believe that price uniformity is more likely, so it is probable that online markets may become more commodity-like in nature. This being the case, a move towards a market price should increase the usage of every day low pricing (EDLP).

Online Promotion

Online retailers have opportunities to communicate with shoppers within the market (market-based) and the store (store-based) in much the same way as their offline counterparts. No major difference will exist in market-based promotion, as the same methods will be available to both. Advertising can be equally as productive, as can sales promotion, public relations and sponsorship. Opportunities for *direct marketing* could be said to be greater, owing to the nature of the contact between shopper and retailer. Online retailers can gain a lot of information about the shopper's shopping habits automatically and can, therefore, develop highly personalized approaches. Setting up the store so that the shopper can access products in the most desirable order is an example of this.

The ability to use store-based promotions will be different, as the online retailer is not in physical contact with the shopper. Online shoppers can only see or hear, they cannot touch, taste or smell when in the virtual store. This limits the ways in which the message can be delivered but does not necessarily mean that messages will not be successfully received and decoded. In fact, it can be argued that store-based advertising, for example, could be more effective, particularly in the area of interactive communication. Point-of-sale (PoS) display will be affected by the absence of physical contact, although advances in 'virtual store design' may alleviate this problem. The one area where a major problem does exist is personal selling. The absence of physical contact dilutes the service encounter, causing problems for retail situations where service is important – i.e. high-involvement products. Such situations often require creative selling approaches that are very difficult to replicate online. Consider the example of an interior design company mentioned earlier in this text. The production of a tailored design requires considerable interaction between the shopper and the salesperson. This is not possible in an effective way online. In addition, the shopper must feel that the 'designer' has fully appreciated his or her needs. This is again difficult to ensure without personal contact. For this reason it is reasonable to suggest that those retail situations requiring higher levels of personal selling (creative selling and some types of routine selling) will not translate well onto the Internet.

Online Customer Service

Customer service offers two benefits to shoppers. *Functional benefits* relate to time, effort and specialist advice, while *social benefits* concern issues such as friendship and intimacy. Functional benefits can be adequately delivered by the online retailer, social benefits cannot. The absence of direct physical contact means that online retailers cannot offer the same quality of encounter as the traditional retailer, and so social benefits are limited. In contrast, functional benefits offered by online retailers can be enhanced, especially those relating to efficiency. The relative importance of social and functional benefits depends on the individual shopper and the service situation. Some shoppers require both functional and social benefits, others do not. Situations requiring higher levels of service (high-involvement products mainly) require both types of benefit. The greater the benefits gained by the shopper in the service encounter, the greater the potential satisfaction and the more likelihood of repeat patronage.

Looking in more detail at customer service shows that customer satisfaction can be made or lost in three key areas – the shopping system, the buying system and the consuming system. The *shopping system* covers all actions taken by the shopper prior to purchase, including product and price search, and contact with sales staff. The *buying system* includes all actions relating to a shopper's purchase, such as queuing and product availability. The *consuming system* takes place outside the store and covers the actual use of the product(s) concerned.

It is within the *shopping system* that online retailers are incapable of offering the same level of service as offline retailers. The inability to offer personal contact has been shown to be an important weakness for higher service situations such as those characterized by creative selling approaches. In these situations, online retailers cannot hope to match offline retailers. The weakness becomes less important for lower-service situations such routine selling and transaction processing.

In contrast, online retailers have a number of advantages when it comes to the *buying system*. The purchase experience can be made as convenient as possible by providing excellent service in terms of waiting time and payment-processing. High-demand periods can be more easily accommodated, thus eliminating the need for the queues often seen in traditional stores. Many shoppers find poor service in the buying system to be irritating and some will see it as a reason to switch to a different store. Unlike the shopping system, all types of service situation (transaction, routine selling and creative selling) are affected by poor buying system service.

When comparing offline and online retail, few differences exist in the ability to offer service appropriate for the *consuming system*. Both types of retailer can offer after-sales support, although the online retailer cannot achieve the personal contact offered by their offline competitors. For certain products and retail situations this may be a problem, but only for those high-service situations characterized by creative selling. Even in these cases, a significant proportion of after-sales service is given on a remote basis over the telephone or by correspondence hence the problem is unlikely to be a major one.

It is difficult to generalize about the relative importance of service encounters in the shopping, buying and consuming systems, as different shoppers and retail situations will exhibit a different relative importance. What can be said is that in situations where shopping system service dominates, online retailers will be at a serious disadvantage provided social benefits are sought by shoppers. Situations where the buying system dominates are likely to have reduced service in most cases, so the differences between online and offline become less important. In the situations where the consuming system is key, the differences between online and offline are minimal.

Online 'Store' Design

The online retailer's 'store' is effectively their Web site. As such, the store is remote in nature, as the shopper has no physical contact with the shopping environment. This means that conventional aspects of store design cannot be directly translated to online retailing, although a number of the concepts can be applied. The extent of online store design is dictated by the nature of the technology used. Low-technology online retail stores tend to be a *catalogue* with search and ordering facilities while higher-technology stores may include *virtual stores* of varying degrees of design sophistication.

Low-technology stores are the first generation of online retailers that essentially offer an easy-to-use catalogue service on the Internet. The design of the store follows much the same principles as the design of a catalogue with an index/contents to allow the customer to search through the assortment (search engine) and an ordering facility. The 'layout' of such a store relates to the *ease of navigation* around the site and has little in common with offline retailing. Display also has little in common with offline retailing, as the assortment will tend to be displayed on an item-by-item basis rather than a category-by-category basis. Even if this is not the case, the physical presentation of products to the shopper is much more simplified in such an online retailing situation.

Atmospheric elements can be utilized in low-technology online stores, although only visual and aural factors can be considered as odours, tastes and textures cannot be transmitted to the shopper. Foreground and background colours and lighting levels can be changed to produce psychological responses, as can sounds and music. The nature of the environment would suggest that online retail atmospherics share many common features with marketing communications and advertising in particular. Research in this area would suggest that colours and sounds can enhance message delivery in certain cases. First, the colour or sound has to fit the environment (congruency), so outdoor products may benefit from colours such as blue, green and yellow, and sounds relating to the countryside (wind, animal noises, etc.). Secondly, moods could be affected by the use of warm or cool colours, or music of a certain tempo, volume or style. Atmospherics may not, however, have such an impact as in offline stores although the ability to control and isolate may be increased making the effect of online atmospherics easier to predict (full coverage of atmospherics can be found in Chapter 7 on Store Design).

The use of more advanced technology (e.g. virtual reality) may allow online stores to be designed in a much more sophisticated way. Simulating an offline retail store environment could negate many of the drawbacks of low-technology online stores and produce much more than an easy-to-use catalogue. Such high-technology stores could utilize a variety of layouts in much the same way as offline stores, although the ability to start at, or jump to, any point in the virtual store would be considerably more convenient for the shopper. Clearly, this has benefits for the shopper in terms of reducing shopping time or increasing shopping efficiency, but may mean that online retailers find it hard to achieve the same level of *assortment exposure* as their offline competitors.

High-technology online stores can also utilize offline retail display techniques effectively, indeed the presentation of products to the shopper can be enhanced when physical constraints are eliminated – i.e. a product can be studied from all angles rather than just the display angle. Atmospherics can now be used in a much more widespread way, borrowing many of the techniques used by offline retailers. It is still likely that only visual and aural elements would be practical, given current technology and cost considerations.

Conclusions

Online retailing is on the increase but still accounts for only a relatively small proportion of total Internet business. Points in its favour are convenience and flexibility, operational and financial benefits for the retailer, wide customer reach and the ability to personalize the offering. Negative points include logistics, its remote nature, the absence of instant gratification and the level of control open to the retailer. Will online retailing grow? Yes – but by how much?

Parallels can be drawn with catalogue (mail-order) sales, where growth was rapid in the early stages but soon plateaued at a relatively low penetration level. Catalogues failed to significantly encroach on traditional retailing areas, and did not manage to convert a sufficient number of shoppers. In effect, the benefits of convenience were not sufficient to outweigh the key costs of *delayed gratification* and the *lack of physical contact*. When considering the future of online retailing it should be noted that the benefits are increased (when compared to catalogue shopping) and the costs are reduced by speeding up delivery and simulating contact. Are these advances enough to allow online retailing to go beyond catalogue shopping? To try to answer this question, it is necessary to look at the key elements of online retail marketing. Can a sufficient number of shoppers be persuaded to adopt? Location, pricing and most parts of the promotional mix present no problems while assortment and design are potential obstacles. The key problem area is likely to be that of *personal selling* and *service.*

Location presents few problems for the online retailer as all potential customers (i.e. those that have Internet access) can be reached from any location. Indeed, the online retailer has significant advantages over its offline counterpart in this area. Pricing will become more transparent as reduced price-searching costs (particularly time) will lead to an increased incentive to search. Add to this the ease of searching via software tools and shoppers will be much more price-aware. A consequence of increased search is an increased awareness of an equitable price that in turn will tend to pull prices downwards and act to stimulate demand. Whether online retailers will make profits is a different matter. Promotion also presents few problems although the absence of physical contact limits the scope of store-based methods. This problem will not necessarily obstruct the development of online retailing but it may give offline retailers an advantage in the short term before technological advances allow the gap to be closed.

The absence of *physical contact* will tend to limit the assortment that can be sold online. High-touch products will be difficult to sell online to the majority of shoppers, as will perishable or bulky items. On the positive side, the online retailer can offer a vastly expanded assortment owing to the absence of physical constraints (store size), although this can be seen as a negative if too much choice is given, leading to shopper confusion or the degree of assortment overlap means that the level of competition increases. The absence of physical contact also places limitations on the online perceived store shopping experience for many shoppers and retail situations. Negative points concern display and atmospherics, where the absence of physical contact limits display and atmospherics to visual and aural elements only. Layout can certainly be improved, with shoppers given multiple entry and exit points to the store or even a store personalized to their own requirements. It is true, though, that many shoppers enjoy physical contact with the store and would not have the same experience with online stores. In addition, the online retailer has a much more limited ability to influence the shopper 'inside' the store.

Certain retail situations and certain shoppers demand *customer service*. The most effective service encounter usually involves direct physical contact and will give the shopper a combination of function and social benefits. Physical contact is not possible for pure online retailing, so service encounters cannot be optimized. This weakness is important for high-service situations (such as those involving creative selling) but becomes less important for medium- and low-service situations (routine selling and transaction-based, respectively). In addition, the weakness is also most noticeable for shopping system service, may have a broadly neutral effect on buying system service and has little effect on consuming system service. For these reasons, it is likely that online retailing will find it hard to penetrate high-service situations, or those where the shopping system is particularly important (e.g. jewellery, design services).

So what is the future for online retailing and online retail marketing? In the short term, all areas are possible except for higher-touch product categories and higher-service situations. Online retail marketing will need to evolve, possibly drawing from advertising and direct marketing more than from more traditional retail marketing areas.

Index